Christianity, Politics and the
Afterlives of War in Uganda

New Directions in the Anthropology of Christianity

Series editors: Naomi Haynes, Jon Bialecki, Hillary Kaell, and James S. Bielo

Emphasizing ethnographic depth and theoretical innovation, *New Directions in the Anthropology of Christianity* showcases the work of a fresh generation of researchers, as well as outstanding senior scholars, to provide researchers at all levels with rich sources of comparison and new analytical frameworks. The series publishes monographs and edited volumes on a range of topics on Christianity around the world, focusing on a few key themes: Politics and Christian nationalism; Economic development and humanitarianism; Engagement with religious others; Gender and sexuality; and Environment.

Prioritizing the comparative study of Christianity, the series strengthens a global network of scholars with overlapping interests, while providing a unique vantage point on the growing subfield of anthropology of Christianity.

Mediating Catholicism,
Edited by Eric Hoenes del Pinal Marc Loustau and Kristin Norget

Pentecostal Insight in a Segregated US City
Frederick Klaits with LaShekia Chatman and Michael Richbart

Forthcoming in this series:

Areruya and Indigenous Prophetism in Northern Amazonia,
Virgínia Amaral

Christianity, Politics and the Afterlives of War in Uganda

There Is Confusion

Henni Alava

BLOOMSBURY ACADEMIC
LONDON • NEW YORK • OXFORD • NEW DELHI • SYDNEY

BLOOMSBURY ACADEMIC
Bloomsbury Publishing Plc
50 Bedford Square, London, WC1B 3DP, UK
1385 Broadway, New York, NY 10018, USA
29 Earlsfort Terrace, Dublin 2, Ireland

BLOOMSBURY, BLOOMSBURY ACADEMIC and the Diana logo are trademarks of Bloomsbury Publishing Plc

First published in Great Britain 2022
This paperback edition published 2023

Copyright © Henni Alava, 2022, 2023

Henni Alava has asserted her right under the Copyright, Designs and Patents Act, 1988, to be identified as Author of this work.

This work is published open access subject to a Creative Commons Attribution-NonCommercial-NoDerivatives 4.0 International licence (CC BY-NC-ND 4.0, https://creativecommons.org/licenses/by-nc-nd/4.0/). You may re-use, distribute, and reproduce this work in any medium for non-commercial purposes, provided you give attribution to the copyright holder and the publisher and provide a link to the Creative Commons licence.

For legal purposes the Acknowledgements on pp. ix–xiii constitute an extension of this copyright page.

Series design: Toby Way
Cover image: Catholic liturgical dancers at the 2013 commemoration of the martyrs of Wi-Polo, Paimol. Photo by Henni Alava.

All rights reserved. No part of this publication may be reproduced or transmitted in any form or by any means, electronic or mechanical, including photocopying, recording, or any information storage or retrieval system, without prior permission in writing from the publishers.

Bloomsbury Publishing Plc does not have any control over, or responsibility for, any third-party websites referred to or in this book. All internet addresses given in this book were correct at the time of going to press. The author and publisher regret any inconvenience caused if addresses have changed or sites have ceased to exist, but can accept no responsibility for any such changes.

A catalogue record for this book is available from the British Library.

Library of Congress Cataloging-in-Publication Data
Names: Alava, Henni, author.
Title: Christianity, politics and the afterlives of war in Uganda: there is confusion / Henni Alava.
Other titles: New directions in the anthropology of Christianity.
Description: New York : Bloomsbury Academic, 2022. | Series: New directions in the anthropology of Christianity | Includes bibliographical references and index. |
Identifiers: LCCN 2021054792 (print) | LCCN 2021054793 (ebook) | ISBN 9781350175808 (hardback) | ISBN 9781350175839 (pdf) | ISBN 9781350175822 (epub)
Subjects: LCSH: Lord's Resistance Army. | Christianity and politics–Uganda. | Peace-building–Uganda–Religious aspects–Christianity. | Civil war–Uganda–Religious aspects–Christianity. | Uganda–Politics and government–1979–
Classification: LCC BR115.P7 A386 2022 (print) | LCC BR115.P7 (ebook) | DDC 261.7096761–dc23/eng/20211109
LC record available at https://lccn.loc.gov/2021054792
LC ebook record available at https://lccn.loc.gov/2021054793

ISBN:	HB:	978-1-3501-7580-8
	PB:	978-1-3503-0198-6
	ePDF:	978-1-3501-7583-9
	eBook:	978-1-3501-7582-2

Series: New Directions in the Anthropology of Christianity

Typeset by Integra Software Services Pvt. Ltd.

To find out more about our authors and books visit www.bloomsbury.com and sign up for our newsletters

For Mikko, Eemil, Wilho and Hilja

Contents

List of illustrations	viii
Acknowledgements	ix
Acronyms	xiv
Glossary	xvi
Maps	xviii
Introduction: Towards a political anthropology of Christianity	1
1 The gun and the word: Missionary-colonial history in Kitgum	33
2 Church, state, war	59
3 Learning to listen to silence and confusion: Fieldwork in the aftermath of war	93
4 To stand atop an anthill: Performing the state in Kitgum	117
5 The underside of the anthill: Crafting subdued citizens	139
6 'My peace I give you': Utopian narratives of inclusion and boundaries of exclusion	159
7 Confusion in the church	185
Conclusion: The value of embeddedness and confusion	207
Notes	218
References	228
Index	258

Illustrations

1. Members of the Janani Luwum choir pass a Legio Maria procession while walking for a home visit with a member.   14
2. Stonework floor of the church of St Mary of Lourdes, Kitgum.   18
3. Choir practice at Town Parish.   19
4. Illustration in *CMS Gleaner* article about their work in Acholi (Wright 1919: 135). Reproduced with permission from the Church Mission Society archives.   38
5. Painting on the wall of the Catholic St Joseph's hospital.   42
6. Painting of the martyrs of Paimol on the wall of a parish office at Kitgum Mission.   51
7. Group photo after a baptism service to which an Anglican reverend invited my family at his home village.   109
8. Posters for politicians lined walls and trees in the run-up to the 2016 elections.   148
9. Archbishop Odama and two Comboni missionary bishops at the commemoration of the Paimol martyrs.   160
10. Choir members and children during Sunday service at Town Parish.   177
11. Poster for the Gulu Provincial Peace Week.   182
12. The visiting archbishop of the Church of Uganda leads prayers for peace in the diocese of Kitgum.   208

Acknowledgements

The path of writing that led up to this book has included many twists and turns, steep hills and some serious dead-ends, but also, thankfully, many moments of joy. It's tricky to pinpoint what all the rough patches have ultimately been about, but easy to see what carried me through them, and cleared the path for inspiration: the care, compassion, kindness and encouragement accorded to me by other people.

Writing this book would literally not have been possible without the people who have taken care of my family and me during the times we have been in Uganda: Grace, Juliet, Maureen, Francis, Bosco and Opira. During my longest period of fieldwork in 2012–13, I worked closely with Chiara Lakareber, who helped identify the right people to talk to, negotiated access, translated, and joined me in countless hours of mulling over stories we heard and pondering which ones to follow. Chiara took me and my family into the warmth of hers – for this, my thank you also to Agnes and Lumumba. During later fieldwork, Rom Lawrence stepped in to help, and it has been exciting to see him grow into a medical professional, and a friend, over the years. Warm thanks also to Monica Acan, Pauline Okwanga and Francis Orach for help and good company, and to Janet Amito, for inspiring research collaboration in Entebbe.

I owe a heartfelt thanks to the many people in Kitgum who have shared with me stories and insights of their lives and their churches. A particular thank you to *ladit* Philip Odwong and *mego* Agnes, and their family, for allowing me to share parts of their story in these pages. Most of the people in this book appear behind pseudonyms. I hope that the way I tell their stories does them justice. I especially thank the Town Parish choir for allowing me to sing with them and for considering me a member. *Apwoyo matek, ki Rubanga/Lubanga okony wu ducu.*

For enabling my research, I thank the staff at the parishes of St Mary of Lourdes and of Saint Janani Luwum in Kitgum; at the offices of the Roman Catholic Archdiocese of Gulu and the Church of Uganda's Dioceses of Kitgum and Gulu; at the Catechist Training Center/University of the Sacred Heart; at the Comboni Animation Centre in Gulu; and at the Paimol Martyrs Shrine – particularly its caretaker, Fr. Joseph Okumu. For help with archival sources, my warm thanks to Fr. Ramon Vargas and Fr. Paul Donohue of the Comboni

Missionaries of the Sacred Heart, and to Ken Osborne at the Church Mission Society.

A truly humbling array of people has supported the process of writing this book. It goes without saying that each of the mistakes and weaknesses that remains in it is my own, but without each of these wonderful scholars' guidance, there would have been many more. Naomi Haynes kindly guided me through the art of writing a book proposal, and at the other end of the track, Jon Bialecki provided a generous master class in writing transitions, giving me the perfect nudge of confidence needed to persevere the final stretch. Lalle Pursglove, Stuart Hay and Lily McMahon at Bloomsbury and Suriya Rajasekar at Integra Software Services have been supportive and patient, enabling the process to be smooth, even when my own circumstances were not.

Elina Oinas once told me that when researchers are experiencing a crisis about their writing, the problem is often that they are not writing. Many times, recalling this insight has helped me drag myself back to my desk, and to labour through some seemingly insurmountable obstacle. Even more crucially, when I have been unable to drag myself anywhere at all, Elina has reminded me that by doing less, I would not only be engaging in the feminist political act of prioritizing care over productivity, but might even end up rediscovering the joy of my work in the process. I value these lessons, and her friendship, enormously.

Mika Vähäkangas has provided support over the years in every way an aspiring scholar could have hoped for, while Lotte Meinert, Barbara Bompani and Mats Utas; and later Jay J. Carney and two anonymous reviewers at Bloomsbury have all provided essential and encouraging critiques on earlier versions of this work. Marie-Louise Karttunen has gently trimmed down my excessive wordiness, helped me to find my voice, and repeatedly nudged me from self-doubt to confidence in a process that has flowered into friendship.

Tiina Kontinen signed me on as a post-doc soon after my defence, and I am deeply grateful for all the time, trust and funding that she has invested in my work. For critiques, support and collegiality at the University of Jyväskylä and Tiina's CS-LEARN and GROW projects, my thanks to the projects' co-leader Katariina Holma, as well as Karembe Ahimbisibwe, Twine Bananuka, Laura Del Castillo Munera, Haji Chang'a, Lenka Hanovská, Hanna-Maija Huhtala, Anna Itkonen, Veli-Mikko Kauppi, Minna-Kerttu Kekki, Rehema Kilonzo, Marianne Lampi, Benta Matunga, Alice Ndidde, Ajali Nguyahambi, Anja Onali and Henrik Rydenfelt.

I am forever grateful to *ladit* Ron Atkinson, for friendship, and for meticulously commenting on so many of this book's chapters; and to Sverker Finnström, for support at critical times during the last fifteen years. I have had the joy of working with Catrine Shroff and Jimmy Spire Ssentongo on projects on the side of this one, and thank them for every step of them. For different kinds of support, feedback and friendship in and between times spent in Uganda, I thank Anna Baral, Denise Dunovant, Alessandro Gusman, Helle Harnisch, Julian Hopwood, Ben Jones, Emmanuel Katongole, Martha Lagace, Rev. Patrick Lumumba, Fr. Jino Mwaka, Lino Owor Ogora, Fabius Okumu-Alya, Opira Otto, Holly Porter, Nanna Schneidermann, Mareike Schomerus, Philip Schulz, Rebecca Tapscott, Kristof Titeca, Karin van Bemmel, Cecilie Lanken Verma, Letha Victor, Todd Whitmore and Lars Williams.

In Development Studies at the University of Helsinki, I particularly thank Jeremy Gould, Eeva Henriksson, Minna Hakkarainen, Päivi Hasu, Marjaana Jauhola, Juhani Koponen, Mira Käkönen, Pertti Multanen, Anja Nygren, Henri Onodera, Liina-Maija Quist, Eija Ranta, Wolfgang Zeller, and all those who made this community an academic home. In a shared writing group and office, Agnese Bankovska, Sonal Makhija, Jenni Mölkänen, Liina-Maija Quist, Tuomas Tammisto and Heikki Wilenius have provided precious peer support and friendship.

I am grateful to Lotta Gammelin, Elina Hankela, Johanna Sarlio-Nieminen, Heta Tarkkala and Katja Uusihakala for academic friendships. For discussions that have, at various points along the way, helped me find my footing in academia, I thank Nicole Beardsworth, Morten Bøås, Aron Engberg, Maia Green, Sarah Green, Timo Kaartinen, Timo Kallinen, Karen Lauterbach, Hirokasu Miyazaki, Danai Mupotsa, Hans Olsson, Damaris Parsitau, Kopano Ratele, Suvi Rautio, Joel Robbins, Anders Sjögren, Annika Teppo, Rijk van Dijk, Adriaan van Klinken, Elina Vuola, Tea Virtanen and Auli Vähäkangas. As I finalize this book, I thank Venla Oikkonen, Maria Temmes and Mari Korpela, for welcoming me to join them for my next steps.

I completed this book while working in the Academy of Finland-funded GROW (grant number 285815) and CS-LEARN (grant number 316098) research consortiums, which were hosted by the Development, Education and International Cooperation master's programme at the University of Jyväskylä. The original PhD research at the University of Helsinki was supported by the Finnish Graduate School in Development Studies (DEVESTU), Emil Aaltonen Foundation and the Eino Jutikkala Fund of the Finnish Academy of Science and Letters. Additional fieldwork funding was provided by the Nordic Africa Institute, Oskar Öflund Foundation, the Finnish Concordia Fund, the Church Research Institute of the Evangelical Lutheran Church of Finland, Lund Missionssälskapet,

Elina Oinas's Academy of Finland-funded 'Youth and political engagements in Africa' research project, the 'Gender, Culture and Society' doctoral programme at the University of Helsinki, and the Justice and Security Research Programme at the London School of Economics. I am also grateful to the Donner Institute for Research in Religious and Cultural History for supporting my work.

Parts of this book's analysis has previously appeared elsewhere, and I acknowledge and thank for the publishers' and my co-authors' permission to use them. The history of Kitgum Mission, outlined in Chapter 1, was previously published in an article co-authored with Catrine Shroff: 'Unravelling Church Land: Transformations in the Relations between Church, State and Community in Uganda' (*Development and Change*. 2017. 50(5): 1288–1309). A small part of Chapter 2 appears in an article co-authored with Jimmy Spire Ssentongo: 'Religious (De)politicization in Uganda's 2016 Elections' (*Journal of Eastern African Studies*. 2017. 10 [4]: 677–92), and sections of Chapters 1 and 3 in 'The Lord's Resistance Army and the Arms That Brought the Lord: Amplifying Polyphonic Silences in Northern Uganda' (*The Journal of the Finnish Anthropological Society* 2020. 44[1]: 9–29). Sections of Chapters 3 and 4 have been published in the chapter 'The Everyday and Spectacle of Subdued Citizenship in Uganda', in *Practices of Citizenship in East Africa: Perspectives from Philosophical Pragmatism*, edited by Katariina Holma and Tiina Kontinen (Routledge 2020). Finally, earlier versions of chapters have been published in Finnish: Chapter 3 as 'Hiljaisuuden ja hämmennyksen etnografiaa Pohjois-Ugandassa', in the collection *Peilin edessä. Refleksiivisyys ja etnografinen tieto* [In Front of the Mirror. Reflexivity and Ethnographic Knowledge], edited by Katja Uusihakala and Jeremy Gould (Gaudeamus 2016), and Chapter 4 as 'Poliitikot seisovat muurahaiskekojen päällä: valtionrakennusperformansseja Ugandassa' in the volume *Valtion antropologiaa* [Anthropology of the State], edited by Tuomas Tammisto and Heikki Wilenius (Suomalaisen Kirjallisuuden Seura, 2021). For the maps appearing in this book, I warmly thank Tuomas Tammisto.

Lotta Gammelin, Inkeri Kylänpää, Päivi Linervo, Laura Pentti, Sara Pykäläinen, and Laura Riuttanen: thank you for being there all these years. All my friends in Puotila: thank you for caring in ways that make our village feel like home.

My parents, Päivi and Hannu Palmu, and my siblings Maria, Kaisu and Miika. It was in your hands that all care for me began. Considering how we have been sprawled across the world for almost all of my life, I find it remarkable that we continue to stick together. For that I am incredibly grateful, and pray it never changes. My father-in-law Pekka Alava has been an irreplaceable part of my family's life. I don't know how we would have managed without you. Kiitos ukki.

Mikko, the love of my life, and the best parenting partner I could imagine: your care is what has sustained me most of all, through days both joyful and hard. Thank you for your kindness, your patience, your humour, your commitment, and your love. Eemil, Wilho and Hilja: in Acholi, a child is always given a name that carries meaning. As I often remind you, each of your second names could have been given to each three of you: you are our beloved, our joy and our most precious gifts. I am so thankful for each of you, and hope you know that the most important paths in my life are the ones I walk with you.

Acronyms

CMS	Church Missionary Society. Missionary organization of the (Anglican) Church of England, renamed Church Mission Society in 1995.
CC	Concerned Christians. Group formed by Anglicans critical of the leadership of the Church of Uganda's Kitgum Diocese.
CoU	Church of Uganda. Member of the global Anglican Communion.
DP	Democratic Party. Currently a small opposition party that has close historical ties with the Catholic Church in Uganda.
FDC	Forum for Democratic Change. Leading opposition party in Uganda during the early 2000s.
HSMF	Holy Spirit Mobile Forces. Rebel movement led by Alice (Auma) Lakwena.
LC1	Local Council/Local Councillor. Lowest level of the council system established by the NRM throughout Uganda.
LC5	Local Council 5. Highest level of the LC system in Uganda, referring to the district council. In common parlance, 'LC5' refers to the council's chairperson.
LRA	Lord's Resistance Army. Rebel movement led by Joseph Kony.
NRA	National Resistance Army. The rebel group headed by Yoweri Museveni which, after 1986, became the national army. Political arm referred to as the NRM; military arm renamed the UPDF in 1995.
NRM	National Resistance Movement. The political arm of the NRA, party of president Yoweri Museveni.
PC	Pentecostal-Charismatic.

RDC	Resident District Commissioner. Appointed by the president as his representative at the district level.
UNLA	Uganda National Liberation Army, national army during President Milton Obote's second regime.
UPC	Uganda People's Congress. Currently a small opposition party with close historical ties to the Church of Uganda. Party of the former president, Milton Obote.
UPDA	Uganda People's Defence Army, rebel group formed by former UNLA soldiers to oppose Yoweri Museveni's NRA.
UPDF	Uganda People's Defence Forces. Uganda's national army, see NRA.

Glossary

Acholi	A geographical area, a people and a language. In 2020, Acholi comprises the districts of Amuru, Nwoya, Gulu, Omoro, Lamwo, Kitgum, Pader and Agago. The language is a member of the Luo group, and the latest census counts 1.47 million Acholi in Uganda, 4.4 of the population (UBOS 2016b).
Anglican	Concept used in this book to refer to the Church of Uganda (CoU) and its members. The CoU is a member of the global Anglican Communion (see 'Protestant')
abila	Shrine.
adungu	String instrument, originally from the DRC, widely used to accompany hymns at Protestant churches in Acholi.
ajwaka (pl. *ajwaki*)	Healer.
anyobanyoba	'Confusion', literally stirring or mixing.
apokapoka	Division.
bwola	Royal dance, commonly performed at public events, including Catholic celebrations.
Catholic	Concept used in this book, as in Uganda, to refer to the Roman Catholic Church, and to its members.
cen	The vengeful spirit of the victim of a violent death.
Comboni missionaries	Term used in this book to refer jointly to the priests and brothers of the Comboni Missionaries of the Heart of Jesus and the Comboni Missionary Sisters. Prior to the 1970s, the orders were known as Verona missionaries.
cung i wibye	Literally 'to stand on an anthill', translates and refers to politics, particularly the combative and boastful politics related to campaigning.
eklisia	Catholic church.
jago	Subchief
jok / Jok (pl. *jogi*)	power or deity.
kanica	Protestant church.
ladit (pl. *ludiro*)	Respectful title for an elderly man.
lakite	'Somehow'.
lakwena	Messenger.
Lubanga	'God' in the Acholi Protestant Bible.
mego	Literally 'mother', respectful title for an elderly woman.

Mican	The area surrounding the old Anglican mission station and current headquarters of the Diocese of Kitgum of the Church of Uganda.
Mission	When capitalized, refers to the Catholic parish of St Mary of Lourdes and to the neighbourhood around the Catholic mission station just outside of Kitgum Town.
muno	'White', foreigner. Derived from the word for 'enmity' (Crazzolara 1955).
Protestant	Concept used in Uganda to refer to the Church of Uganda and its members.
Rubanga	'God' in the Acholi Catholic Bible.
rwot (pl. *rwodi*)	Chief.
rwot kalam	'Chief of the pen', chief appointed by colonial government.
rwot moo	Anointed, hereditary chief.
Town Parish	A parish of the Church of Uganda in the centre of Kitgum Town, officially known as the Parish of Saint Janani Luwum.
Verona missionaries	Former name of the Comboni missionaries.

Maps

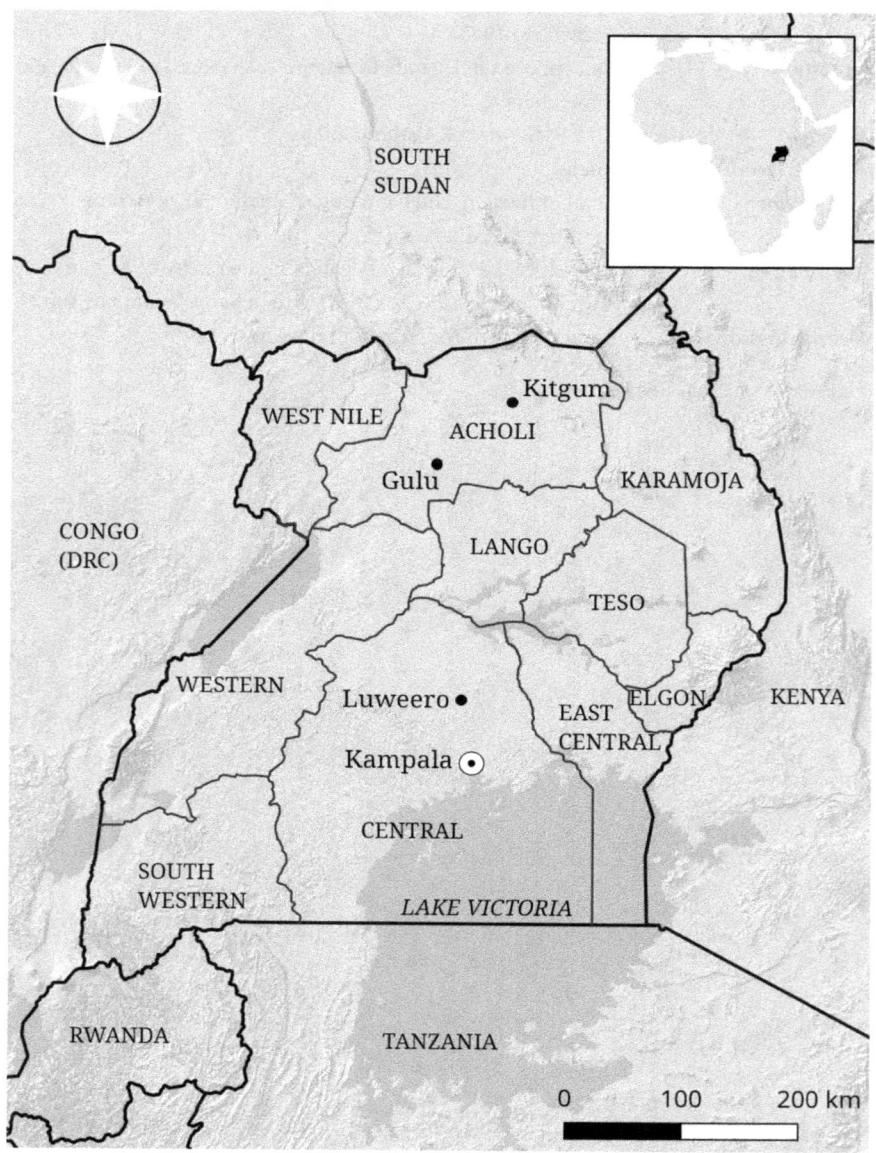

Map 1. Subregions of Uganda. Prepared by Tuomas Tammisto.

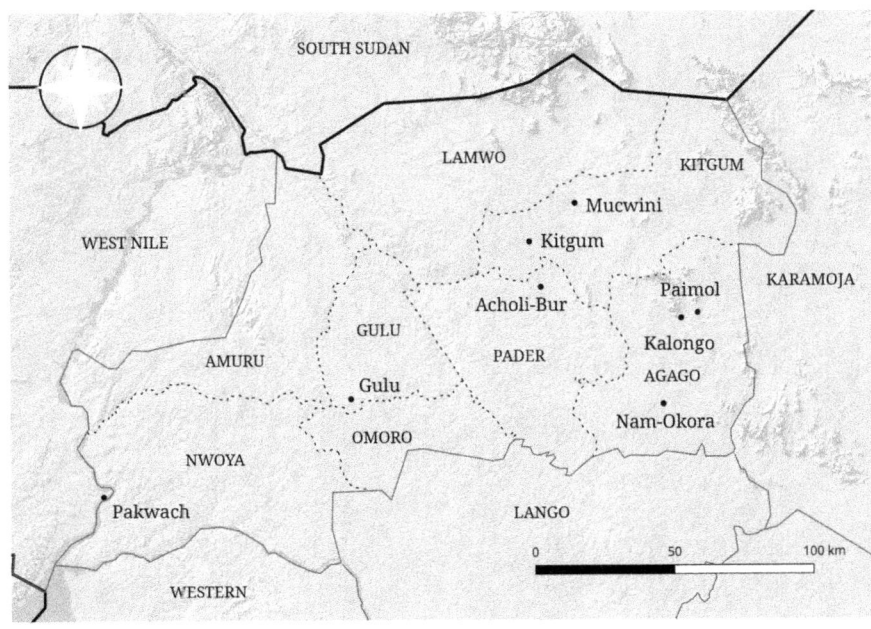

Map 2. Acholi. Prepared by Tuomas Tammisto.

Introduction
Towards a political anthropology of Christianity

- How would you translate church politics into Acholi?
- Anyobanyoba i eklisia. *Confusion in the church.*

Throughout the northern Ugandan war and its aftermath, the Catholic and Anglican Churches[1] have sought to mould political imaginaries in the Acholi region[2] by promoting Christian narratives of peace. These narratives seek to entrench or expand the boundaries of community: to define who belongs to 'us' – whether that be the 'us' of Acholi, Uganda, Christendom or humanity – and on what terms. In the midst of war and its afterlives, how such boundaries are made and unmade is crucial, and churches, to which the majority of the region's population belong, have been well placed to deliberate them. Yet the story of how and why these narratives of peace emerged, why they at times blossomed and at other times failed is far more complex than the somewhat-romantic opening sentences of this book suggest. The story this book tells is also infinitely more complex than the story most commonly told of northern Uganda. In condensed media accounts in particular, Christianity, and more specifically, the Ten Commandments, and the Holy Spirit, are typically mentioned as exotically toxic ingredients of the notoriously brutal Lord's Resistance Movement/Army (LRA), with which the Ugandan government waged war from 1986 to 2006, with devastating consequences for the people stuck in the war's midst. To counter the simplicity of claims that religion simply foments war, or nurtures peace, in northern Uganda or anywhere in the world; that is, to complicate both idealizing and demonizing accounts of the social and political role of religion, this book hinges on the Acholi saying, *anyobanyoba tye;* 'there is confusion'.

Since their introduction by Italian and British mission organizations in the early 1900s, the two mainline churches have played notable roles in the Acholi region's social development and political dynamics. To this day, their local institutional presence surpasses that of any other formal institution besides the state and the military. Church provision of services and public leadership became particularly pronounced during the northern Ugandan war, when many other actors simply packed up and left or fell into disarray. Yet, beyond the visible markers of chapels, schools and hospitals, and clerics' public statements, what meaning do churches and the Christianity they profess actually have? And how can one assess it? It is easy enough to distinguish between the institutions of church and state: a census is published by the state, a catechism by the church; a salary can come from an archdiocese or from a ministry; a piece of land may be controlled by a local parish or by the local government. But where in fact does 'Christianity' end and 'politics' begin?

This book is a response to the conundrum. Tacking between ethnographic fieldwork centred on a Catholic and an Anglican parish in Kitgum town in northern Uganda, and a wide variety of theoretical readings illuminating politics examined from these vantage points, it can best be described as a political anthropology of Christianity. Its main contention is that, to understand the political role of churches and the influence of Christianity on politics, it is necessary to re-think the 'and' in 'Christianity and politics'. The means I offer for this task is the notion of 'embeddedness'. Christianity – and churches as its institutionalized forms – is not separate from the social reality it has sought and seeks to transform. Rather, churches are socially, politically, materially and cosmologically embedded, meaning that the narratives that they promote, both in public and in their members' lives, are likewise embedded. Taking this idea of embedded churches and embedded political narratives as its starting point, the task of the book is to show how churches' narratives of peace have emerged, been enacted and reached their limits, amid the afterlives of war in Acholi, and to what effect.

With this goal in mind, the book addresses three core issues. First, it introduces the notion of embedded political narratives in a bid to show what an anthropology of Christianity can contribute to both political and theological analysis, and as a tool for complicating simplistic analyses of religion's 'impact' on society, in any context. Second, its focus on the largest religious communities in the Acholi region adds both to the existing literature on politics and Christianity in Uganda, and to that on war and its aftermath in Acholi. Third, it develops the notion of 'confusion' as a contribution both to anthropological debates about suffering and 'the good', and to pressing debates in anthropology, conflict studies and social science more generally, on the ethics of research.

In so far as the notion of 'confusion' functions in the book as an analytical tool, it serves to elucidate how individuals and communities, not only in Acholi, but far beyond its borders, grapple with, and nurture hope despite, overwhelming circumstances of loss, violence and pain. Yet, grounded as the book is in research conducted in the aftermath of one of the most devastating wars and subsequent humanitarian crises of the turn of the twenty-first century, and in fieldwork encounters that often left me grappling for what was the right, good and manageable thing for me to do as a scholar, I also offer 'confusion' as a way of thinking about ethics and epistemology as profoundly entwined. From this view, research ethics cannot be contained in institutionalized processes of ethical 'clearance'. Indeed, although calls are regularly made for qualitative social science to be more exact and bold, I call for the opposite. In academia, there is far too much certainty and boldness, far too little space for caution and pause, and far too little humility to acknowledge vulnerability, inadequacy and the profundity of confusion as essential, inescapable facts of our human existence.

The analysis I present is informed by discussions reflected in the snippet quoted in the epigraph, which I jotted down during a conversation with *ladit* (a title of respect for older men) Philip Odwong, a retired teacher and long-time cornerstone of the lay structures of the Catholic Church in Kitgum. Over the years, as new layers have been added to my understanding, I have come to realize how profoundly the story of *ladit* Odwong's life is entwined with local, national and even global interconnections of Christianity and politics, as well as the processes of their entwinement in Acholi, from the time of colonialism, through the war and up until the present. His story thus provides a striking illustration; one I will return to unfurl in increasing detail in coming chapters; of the dynamics, tensions and puzzles that this book seeks to unravel.

Born in 1941, *ladit* Odwong grew up beside the Catholic Mission of Saint Mary of Lourdes, where his family had settled soon after the arrival of Christian missionaries in Kitgum, moving there from a nearby village. Philip was enrolled in the local Catholic school, where he received his education in reading, writing, mathematics – and politics. The latter was enlivened by football matches between Catholic and Anglican schools, during which the children mirrored the two competing churches' mutual enmity by singing disparaging songs about their opponents' religion, sometimes riling things up to the point of stone-throwing. A regular churchgoer, Philip epitomized Catholic ideals, becoming a teacher in a Catholic school and marrying his young bride Agnes in church. In the decades that followed, the family grew to fill the expanding homestead that Philip's father had built on the outskirts of the mission. While Agnes focused on caring for the family, Philip volunteered countless hours in the service of his church, as choir trainer, parish pastoral council member and diocesan adviser for church schools.

Like many educated Catholics of his generation, Philip also grew into a staunch member of the Catholic-leaning Democratic Party (DP), mobilizing the Catholic laity to support the party throughout the regimes of Milton Obote and Idi Amin. In practice, this also meant agitating against the Anglican Church of Uganda (CoU) – the country's de facto state church during the colonial era and much of the time there-after – and Milton Obote's Uganda People's Congress (UPC), with which it was aligned. Under Idi Amin's reign, which targeted the Acholi region with a brutality surpassing many neighbouring regions, Philip's DP alignment almost cost him his life. When Amin's soldiers came to arrest him at the Muslim school where he had just been posted as a teacher, Philip and his wife, who had been hospitalized so as to avoid miscarriage during a high-risk pregnancy, narrowly escaped, walking nearly one hundred miles on foot to reach safety. Miraculously, the baby survived, and at birth, was given the name Oyella Irene; Oyella being the Acholi word for 'trouble'; a name given to one whose pregnancy or birth, or the circumstances surrounding it, is particularly difficult.

When the rebel group led by Uganda's incumbent president, Yoweri Museveni, grabbed power in 1986, and millenarian rebel movements broke out to resist him throughout Acholi, Philip's family, like all others, was struck hard by the war. Throughout the next two decades, when rebel violence and government counter-insurgency operations engulfed Acholi, the family was at most times unable to live in the home Philip's father had established some hundreds of meters away from the fence of the Catholic Mission. At times, enabled by Philip's salary as a teacher, they took residence in the centre of Kitgum town, where little apartments were crammed full of people desperately seeking some safety from the war. At other times, they joined the thousands of others who sought refuge at the Mission's Catechumenate Center, where soldiers provided a modicum of security from rebel attacks, while the mission, enabled by benefactors overseas, provided basic supplies. During the day, those whose homes were near would visit their land to farm so as to supplement emergency food rations, though doing so incurred risks. One could be gunned down or beaten by government soldiers under accusation of being a rebel or of feeding the rebels by farming; or one could be abducted by the rebels, or killed, under accusation of supporting the government. Luckily, when Philip's wife and children were captured, Agnes was immediately released in exchange for cash, and the children were set free after carrying the rebels' loot for some hours, unlike the thousands of children who were abducted during the war and ended up forcefully recruited or dead.

Beneath the confusion of war, political contestation continued at the local level and schools became hotbeds of contestation between Catholics and Anglicans. In 1991, due to one such conflict, and as I detail further in Chapter 2, National Resistance Army (NRA)[3] soldiers arrested Philip together with a group of other Acholi elders and politicians. After months of detention and torture in a place unknown to their families, the group was taken to Luzira Maximum Security Prison in Kampala, and ultimately released by the High Court of Uganda. Thereafter *ladit* Odwong withdrew from active party politics.

Yet withdrawing from party politics did not save Philip from the vagaries of war that, over the fifteen years to come, were to leave countless people in Acholi and the greater Northern Uganda dead, injured or profoundly shaken. In 1993, while driving from Kitgum to lead the Gulu Archdiocesan choir's preparations for Pope John Paul II's pastoral visit to northern Uganda, a group of unidentified soldiers speaking a language other than Acholi shot multiple rounds of ammunition into the vehicle in which Philip was travelling. The passengers in the car ducked, the priest at the steering wheel hit the gas, and miraculously, they made it through with just surface wounds from the breaking windows. Upon reaching their destination, Philip caught his breath, led the choir practice, and together with the other travellers returned to Kitgum. In the official narrative about war in Acholi, LRA rebels were to blame for ambushes on vehicles driving along the region's roads. Yet in Philip Odwong's (2019) memoir, numerous details are provided; including that the soldiers did not speak Acholi; that suggest it was government soldiers and not the rebels who staged the attack on their vehicle; a manoeuver documented, rumoured and debated in countless incidents over the years of war.

The Pope's visit to northern Uganda took place a decade before serious concerted international attention for the region's plight picked up. Yet while the war took place in the shadows of global politics, within its shadows local political debates simmered, not only between the two mainline churches, but also within them. In a bitter contest over land between the Catholic mission and its neighbours (a contest that has still not been fully resolved) *ladit* Odwong refused to publically take sides, opting rather to work behind the scenes to advocate for a peaceful resolution that respected the rights of those he perceived to be wronged. During Museveni's era, Odwong's political home, the DP party, gradually descended into relative national inconsequentiality. Meanwhile, some of Odwong's Catholic DP collaborators shifted sides, just as did countless devoutly Anglican UPC cadres, and stepped into politics under the new dispensation of Museveni's National Resistance Movement (NRM).

Where in *ladit* Odwong's life, and my story of his life, does Christianity end and politics begin? How political were the songs he and other elders sang to me during my fieldwork – songs they had sung to rattle their Catholic/Anglican opponents in football matches arranged between the competing missions in the 1950s – and to what measure were they religious? Or had they just been boyish fun and games? How much did *ladit* Odwong's lifelong participation in daily devotions at Kitgum Mission, and his listening to priests' sermons influence his political thinking, and how? Would the fact that he was known for his political activism have impacted on who chose to join the diocesan choir Philip trained to greet the Pope, or influence the way in which the choir's songs were interpreted by their audiences? And where was the line between Christianity and politics in the dispute over church land at Kitgum mission?

Such are the questions that have driven me along the path that led to this book. In some sense, the questions lead to rather futile conceptual exercises: long-waged battles over the definitions of 'politics' or 'religion'. Yet in a region, a country, and a world where religion and politics have fused, clashed, and coexisted to form patterns of both violence and peace, such questions are pressing. They also tie together the minutiae of everyday life with phenomena at the national or even global level – layers often kept separate in analyses of 'religion' and 'politics' in Uganda and beyond: the morning prayers of adherents, the songs of choir members, the land holdings of parishes, the religious allegiances of political parties and the political allegiances of religious leaders, the cosmological underpinnings of rebel movements, the religious justifications of nation-building, the ways in which people seek out the good and cultivate hope in the midst of untellable suffering, and the cheers of young footballers – all connect, creating patterns of intricate complexity.

Over hours of conversations on verandas, under trees, in sitting rooms and kitchens and in the shade of churches, I heard from *ladit* Odwong, and from other Catholic and Anglican elders, men, women and young people, their stories of churches, of politics, of life. These discussions expanded my understanding of all that was captured by the term *anyobanyoba* – confusion. It was a term *ladit* Odwong taught me when I asked him to translate 'church politics' into Acholi. His answer, '*anyobanyoba i Eklisia*' (confusion in the Church), is the thread that ties this book together.

'There Is Confusion': War and its afterlives in Acholi

For twenty years after President Museveni's NRA came to power in 1986, waves of violent conflict between his government and those opposing him wrought destruction in Uganda.[4] Rebellions erupted in many parts of the country, but the worst and most enduring violence centred on the Acholi region, spilling into neighbouring areas and, ultimately, neighbouring countries.[5] The rebel group that outlasted the others came to be known as the Lord's Resistance Movement/Army, more commonly referred to as 'the rebels' or the LRA, led by Joseph Kony. Initial support for the rebels, which drew on the perception that Museveni was out to destroy the Acholi, eventually shrivelled under the onslaught of violence and accusations of disloyalty the LRA directed at Acholi citizens. But the government also failed to win the population's support. Up to two million people in northern Uganda were forcibly displaced into settlements that were described by the government as 'protected villages' and labelled concentration camps by Acholi opposition politicians. Driven into the camps both by fear of rebel violence and pressure from the government's violent anti-insurgency campaigns, civilians were essentially stuck between the battle lines and subjected to appalling and congested conditions. Relief aid provided by humanitarian actors alleviated civilian suffering but also enabled the government's violent policy of forced displacement to continue (Branch 2011; Dolan 2009; Finnström 2008).

In the early 2000s, after years of neglecting what was going on in Acholi while praising Uganda's compliance with the donors' development agenda, the international community's gaze began to turn to the horrors of the war in the country's north. NGO media stories and awareness-raising campaigns drew particular attention to the plight of the children abducted into the rebel ranks, telling horror tales of people seeking shelter from abduction who walked long distances every evening to sleep in the comparative safety of towns. Emphasizing specific aspects and downplaying others, the war came to be portrayed as a prime example of the millenarian irrationality and savagery of African conflicts, with the LRA leader Joseph Kony being presented as a madman, especially by the much later campaigns of the American NGO Invisible Children (Dolan 2009; Nibbe 2010; Taub 2012; Titeca and Costeur 2015).

Local civil society actors, prominently the Acholi Religious Leaders Peace Initiative (ARLPI) consisting of Roman Catholic and Anglican clerics as well as representatives of the smaller Muslim and Orthodox communities, had worked hard to draw international attention to the protracted crisis. Civil society actors also took part in attempts to mediate the conflict, and debated and critiqued the policies of the various international actors involved in humanitarian and legal interventions in the region. They particularly sought to nuance the simplistic narratives the Ugandan government constructed of the conflict which downplayed the role of the government and shifted all the blame for the war onto the shoulders of the LRA and the Acholi people (Apuuli 2011; Finnström 2008). Given the donor community's desire to retain Uganda as a partner in advancing a neoliberal development agenda and fighting the 'war against terrorism', the government's view of the war had largely been left unchallenged, with the official narrative taking the upper hand. With the failure in 2008 of the last set of peace talks, which had instigated a hiatus in the enormous cost to civilian lives caused by the government forces' lengthy military campaign and the rebels' concomitantly fierce retaliation, the LRA was finally driven out of northern Uganda by military force (Allen 2010; Atkinson 2010; Schomerus 2012, 2021).

Strands of the conflict persist to this day. In 2021, one of the LRA's top leaders, Dominic Ongwen, who himself was abducted into the LRA at a young age, was convicted for crimes against humanity and war crimes by the International Criminal Court (ICC) in Hague (on the ICC case see Allen 2006; Baines 2009; Branch 2011; on Dominic Ongwen's case see Macdonald and Porter 2016; Titeca 2019). Meanwhile, Kony and a small core of his troops continue to evade capture in the border triangle between the Central African Republic, South Sudan and the Democratic Republic of Congo. The politicized ethnic tensions that fed into and were exacerbated by the war are also current in Uganda's day-to-day politics. Socio-economic development in the whole of the greater northern Uganda, including Acholi, continues to lag behind the rest of the country, and a strong sense of marginalization, rooted in the colonial era, prevails (Alava 2020). Thousands of former rebels and abductees have returned to more or less civilian life, as they and their families struggle to find ways to co-inhabit the communities that years of war tore apart (Amony 2015; Dunovant 2016; Finnegan 2010; Mergelsberg 2012; Porter 2016; Victor and Porter 2017; Whyte, Meinert, and Obika 2015). Among the Acholi, debates are still unresolved – and often hard even to address – about the reasons, justifications, and repercussions of the war, and many of the spiritual and cosmological concerns that have figured in important ways in and around the conflict remain unsettled.[6] Although the war is no longer fought on northern Ugandan soil with guns and tanks, its complex afterlives linger. The notion through which this phenomenon is conceptualized in Kitgum, and in this book, is *anyobanyoba*: confusion.

One of the people to speak to me of *anyobanyoba* was *mego* (term of respect for elderly women) Atenyo. She lived near the Anglican Mican (the Acholianized name for 'Mission'), a site given to the Church Missionary Society (CMS) in the early 1910s for the establishment of an Anglican mission station: a joint allocation by the British colonial government and the Lemo clan, whose grazing land the area had previously been (Alava and Shroff 2019). A dispute about the boundaries of that land, combined with a bitter conflict between the leaders and a group of members of the Diocese of Kitgum (see Chapter 6), had led *mego* Atenyo to leave the church of her upbringing to pray with a Pentecostal church nearby. It was the issue of land that brought my research assistant Chiara and I to sit in the shade of the mango tree in *mego* Atenyo's yard, yet our mention of politics when describing my study made her sharply angry. Churches and politics were a mess, and their mixing was even worse, she told us, adding that it had resulted in a close family member's death during the rule of Idi Amin. There was too much confusion. And the same was true for all life, particularly these days. Citing examples from her own family, including children who came to sit with us in the yard, she fumed that young people were wasting their lives using drugs, or killing themselves by going to study only to become infected with AIDS. *Mego* Atenyo placed the blame for this wretched state of affairs on the displacement camps into which most of the Acholi population had been forced for years, even decades, during the northern Ugandan war: 'That's where our people went mad, and up to now, people have gone astray,' she claimed.

'*Anyobanyoba tye*' or 'there is confusion', as the phrase is most commonly translated into English, is an oft-recurring sentiment and statement in Kitgum. The themes I followed in my ethnographic endeavours – the internal politics of the parishes I studied, church land ownership, formal state and district politics and their impact on parish members' lives, and what I was beginning to think of as the politics of imagining a Christian, Acholi or Ugandan community – were all unclear, hazy and constantly evolving. Over the course of months, I became increasingly familiar with phrases like, 'I'm not quite sure'; 'It's hard to know exactly'; 'Things there are a bit confused'; '*Anyobanyoba tye*'. Over the years, 'confusion' also became an essential part of the analytical lens through which I have sought to understand the afterlives of war, and the relationship between Christianity and politics.

The first lexicon of the Acholi language, collated by the Italian Verona missionary[7] Crazzolara, translates *nyòbò* (using the orthography developed by Crazzolara, later replaced by a simpler one) as 'to knead, mix together different materials', as in to 'squash porridge', while *li nyòbo-nyòbo*, an adverb, refers to something mixed or massed together (Crazzolara 1955, 336). A more recent dictionary includes the word, spelt *anyuba nyuba*, and translates it simply as confusion (Odonga 2005, 14), as did my research participants when I asked about the word's English equivalent. English thesauruses define confusion as 'uncertainty about what is happening, intended, or required'; 'the state of being bewildered or unclear in one's mind'; 'a situation of panic or disorder'; and as 'a disorderly jumble' (Oxford Dictionary of English 2020). These definitions highlight a sense of powerlessness and vulnerability, an inability to grasp or control what is going on, as central to confusion. This is certainly what I experienced in myself and in my surroundings in Kitgum, but my informants pointed out that *anyobanyoba* did not necessarily refer so much to an experienced inner or societal state, but to something purposefully created by those who somehow benefitted from things being 'confused'. It is here that the word's equivalent in my maternal Finnish provides a key for understanding what *anyobanyoba* conveys.

In Finnish, *anyobanyoba* translates as *hämmennys*, which, like the Acholi *anyobanyoba*, refers both to the act of stirring (e.g. a pot of porridge) – of confus*ing* – and the state of being confus*ed*. Although in English 'confusion' *can* be taken to denote the act of con-fusion, of fusing together, the term is intuitively associated primarily with a state of being, rather than an act. In contrast, *anyobanyoba* and its Finnish translation, *hämmennys*, instinctively capture the notion's double meaning – the sense of confusion, and the act of confusing – much better than their English equivalent. Thus, confusion can be read as powerlessness and disorientation, on the one hand, and purposeful creation and manipulation of that disorientation, on the other. In the sense that 'confusion' relates to a state of mixed up affairs within a community, the term can also be used as a translation for a certain kind of politics, as indicated by the Catholic elder whose interview I quote in the epigraph: church politics = confusion in the church. All these aspects of confusion are prevalent in the afterlives of war. To analyse Christianity and politics in such a context, this book thus analyses how Christianity – as embedded institutions, communities, practices and narratives – is both implicated in confusion and provides the means through which it is addressed.

Embedded narratives as windows onto Christianity and politics

This book adds to a rich literature on the historic and contemporary roles played by Christianity in African societies. Previous studies have explored the relationships of church and state (Hansen 1984; Phiri 2001; Sabar 2001; Ward 2005); the impact of religion on people's interest in politics and electoral behaviour (Manglos and Weinreb 2013; McClendon and Riedl 2019; Takyi et al. 2010); the role of Christianity in democratization (Dowd 2015; Gifford 1995; Kassimir 1998; Okuku 2003); in conflict (Carney 2013; Longman 2009; Smith et al. 2012); and in the politics of gender and sexuality (Bompani 2017; Chitando and Van Klinken 2016; Hodgson 2005; Musisi 2002; Prevost 2010; Valois 2014). How these dynamics have changed following the rise of Pentecostal-Charismatic (PC) Christianity has been traced by many scholars (Bompani 2016; Freston 2004; Haynes 2018; Marshall 2009; Maxwell 2000; Meyer 2011), whereas recent studies of mainline churches in Africa are comparatively rare, despite the fact that they continue to be hugely influential across the continent (see Csordas 2017; Engelke 2010; Kollman 2010; Maxwell 2000; Premawardhana 2020a; B. A. Williams 2018).

In response to the gaps and challenges of often state-centric political analyses, scholars across disciplines have explored the political nature of African Christianity in itself (Bompani and Frahm-Arp 2010; Bongmba 2016a; Comaroff and Comaroff 1991; Ellis and ter Haar 2004; Englund 2011; Kastfelt 2004; Katongole 2011; Van Klinken 2019). Yet rather than following such studies' suggestion of stepping *beyond* an arena of formal politics, it seems that anthropologists of Christianity have largely vacated it – or left it vacant altogether. Echoing Ruth Marshall's (2014) call, I suggest anthropologists of Christianity should extend their analyses of Christianity into its impacts on formal political processes, taking it beyond the disciplinary boundaries and theoretical concerns of anthropology alone.[8] Why?

Although the anthropology of Christianity has contributed importantly to anthropological theory (Coleman 2017) and to theology (Lauterbach and Vähäkangas 2019; Lemons 2018; Scharen and Vigen 2011), I have heard many scholars of Christianity in Africa observe that the sub-discipline is irrelevant to what they are doing. Even more bluntly, a political scientist once told me during warm-up chat at a workshop on Ugandan politics that religion is a non-issue in the country's contemporary politics. After listening to my presentation of an analysis of the role of religion in the 2016 elections, a collaborative work with Jimmy Spire Ssentongo (2016), the scholar came to tell me we had proven him wrong.

If anthropologists of religion fail to speak of politics, including formal politics, those *specializing* in politics will have every reason to brush anthropological knowledge of religion aside as irrelevant for understanding the contemporary world. Multidisciplinary collaborations have been vital for elaborating this book's central concepts (see particularly Alava and Shroff 2019; Alava and

Ssentongo 2016; Alava et al. 2020); but I believe they are important more generally. Theologian Elias Bongmba, in his analysis of the value of social sciences for African political theology, puts this squarely, 'Scholars would do well to avoid marginalizing discipline-oriented research that does not come from their own discipline, as the need for an interdisciplinary dialogue and approach to understanding religion and the religious experience in Africa remains an important intellectual priority' (2019, 201). To develop political anthropologies of Christianity that contribute to broader debates about religion and politics in Africa and beyond, anthropologists of Christianity should engage more with politics, and with Christianity's multiplicities.

This book advances two conceptualizations for doing so: first, churches are considered as socially, politically, materially, and cosmologically embedded institutions and communities; second, a focus is placed on analysing the political narratives for which churches provide resources and arenas.

To theorize narratives, I draw primarily from the work of political psychologist Molly Andrews and literary scholar Hanna Meretoja. Following Andrews (2014), I understand political narratives as stories that are not necessarily explicitly about activity commonly categorized as 'politics'. Rather, as Andrews argues:

> [I]n constructing the stories about what is and isn't working, and how this compares to a notion of 'how it should be' we are invariably deciding what aspects of social/political/economic/cultural life are and are not relevant to the current problem and its solution – in other words, the lifeblood of politics. Thus, political narratives engage the imagination, not only in constructing stories about the past and the present, but in helping to articulate a vision of an alternative world.
>
> (Andrews 2014, 86–7)

Whereas Andrews's focus is on emancipatory narratives of political change, I draw from Hanna Meretoja's (2014) analysis of the demise and subsequent return of storytelling and grand narratives in novels of the post-Second World War era to temper the inbuilt optimism of Andrews's work. Meretoja recounts how the fragmentation of any notion of sense, and the crisis of humanism exemplified in the trenches and death camps of the Second World War, led novelists in post-war Europe to adopt anti-narrative forms. Subsequently, social theorists of the time drew from these novels an increasing belief in the radical 'incapacity of the subject to constitute meaningful order into reality' (Meretoja 2014, 15). In this vein, narrative representations of reality were critiqued for their tendency to force order upon a fragmented and senseless phenomenon, with the sharpest critique being aimed at myth-like narratives that function to naturalize particular social orders (ibid., 17).

Flag bearers of the hermeneutic revival that followed, such as Paul Ricoeur and Charles Taylor, saw narrative activity as a creative and selective practice of reinterpretation, rather than a violent imposition of narrative order upon experience (Gubrium and Holstein 2008, 244). In this view, narratives are seen as always embedded within certain cultural, social and historical contexts, and hence, within relations of power which individuals may either reconfigure or perpetuate through their own narrative interpretations (Meretoja 2014, 7). An important extension of this idea to the political arena can be found in Michael Warner's theorizing on publics and counter-publics, which highlights that all narrative activity is obliged to situate itself in relation to the pre-existing narrative framings of the public(s) it wishes to address (2002, 77). The predecessors and context of narratives thus set limits for their ability to create, reinterpret or transform.

In this book, I comply with Andrews's assertion that political narratives have the power to articulate visions of alternative worlds, but employ Meretoja's work to cast doubt on the success of political narration, and to insist on the embeddedness of narratives in relations of power – but not only in power. An ethnographic exploration shows how narratives are woven and spoken into the world by institutions, communities and people in situ. However powerful a vision of peace might appear on paper, the vision's effect in the world is both enabled and constrained by the social, political and material realities with which the institutions and individuals voicing it are entwined. What is perhaps most important in Andrews's approach to narratives is that it does not exclude stories that lack the form of explicit political speech; thus, I have been able to think not only with formal narratives spoken from the pulpit, but also with snippets and bits emerging in everyday encounters, such as the times spent chatting while waiting for choir practice to start.

Singing with Saint Mary and Saint Janani: fieldwork in context

On a Sunday in early 2013, a feeling of happy elation prevailed among members of the Janani Luwum choir – more commonly referred to as Town Parish choir – after the English-language service. As a variation from the Anglican hymns which formed 95 per cent of the choir's repertoire, this Sunday we had sung something different. At the request of the choir master, I had shared a South African song I had learned years before, in a kid's church choir in rural Finland.

I had picked this particular one not only because the stanzas were easy to improvise, but because the songs' lyrics – amateurishly translated into English from Finnish for us to sing beside the original ones – resonated with themes I had been learning about from choir members over previous months: 'Forget all the walls, forget all the chains, oh, somehow I know freedom is near. And I know, when I struggle, I will see a new tomorrow!'

It was on the wings of happy post-performance chatter that we left Town Parish church to visit the home of an elderly choir member – one of our booming basses – whose health problems had kept him away from practice for weeks. As we walked, one of the men mentioned they had cheered for me during the previous night's Finland–Spain football match; the others were also chatting about everyday matters. There was nothing striking about this group of choir members: men, women, some from blue-collar jobs, others jobless, some young, some old, just walking along under the midday sun. The conversation paused when we encountered a procession of about fifty people, many wearing white caftans, one with what looked like a bishop's hat and holding incense, all of them

Figure 1. Members of the Janani Luwum choir pass a Legio Maria procession while walking for a home visit with a member. Photo by author.

singing. 'The Leso Maria' (as the Legio Maria is called in Acholi, see Schwartz 2005), choristers whispered.

As we walked on, the choir members debated whether fears about the Catholic-originating African Initiated Church's strange rituals and engagements with spirits were baseless, and how similar the rumours were to those about the Chosen Evangelical Revival (CER). This was an outgrowth of the East African Revival which swept across Kitgum from the 1950s onwards, influencing practices and emphases within the church, but also breaking out as a distinctive, semi-attached group of its own. 'Are CER the ones who pray naked?' one choir member asked, to which another answered, 'No, that was the Garden of Eden' (a small group that had popped up and apparently been chased out of a nearby town some months earlier). Everyone agreed that such things sounded strange, as did some of these smaller groups' teachings. 'Adventists believe only twelve people go to heaven,' one woman explained. Someone responded in rebuking tones, 'But then if there are more than twelve in a service, they'll know *they* won't!' Everyone laughed, and conversation became general. I asked one man where his village was, and showed my surprise when I heard he was not Acholi – I had not realized. 'Ah but as Anglicans we do not differentiate. We are all just welcome, you come to church and you are accepted like that. You come to church, it is like you come home.'

At the *ladit*'s home, we were led into the sitting room and seated under the gaze of portraits of Uganda's president Yoweri Museveni and old black-and-white photos of the *ladit*, his family and Anglican reverends. Crowded on couches and armrests and the floor, we struck up a song as we waited for the *ladit* to freshen up, join us and join in. After he introduced his family, one of the choir members recounted the key point of the day's sermon: our God is a humble God, who arrived not on a grand warhorse, but on a humble donkey. After some praise choruses, everyone was invited to pray in their own words. These rose in intensity until the loudest prayer bound the Devil, cast out the demons causing the sickness, and called upon the Lord to heal, ending in a concerted diminuendo and the prayer leader's words, 'Lord, you have promised that those who lift their voices to you, you will hear. Hear us.' We were served some soda, after which we chatted for a while with each other and our hosts before bidding them farewell and heading home to the chores and families awaiting us.

The times that I spent with the Town Parish choir produced some of the most profound insights of this study. Seven years after the visit described above, what captures my attention in the fieldwork diary I have written of the event are not the Leso Maria procession or the choir's charismatic healing prayers, although such things have been the focus of many, if not most, researchers in the anthropology of Christianity (Vähäkangas and Lauterbach 2019); rather, it is the non-Acholi choir member's statement that going to church is like going home, and the row of portraits and photos in the sitting room where we sang. In my notes, I merely mention them, but I returned later to speak with the man who, in one of the old pictures, stands beside influential Anglican Acholis from Kitgum: Archbishop Janani Luwum, who was to be killed by Idi Amin, and Bishop Macleod Baker Ochola, who was to lose his daughter to suicide after rebels gang raped her in 1987, and ten years later, his wife to a landmine blast. Strikingly, as a member of the Acholi Religious Leaders Peace Initiative (ARLPI), Ochola was one of those to most fiercely advocate for forgiveness for the rebels, and for dropping the ICC indictments against LRA leaders in favour of reconciliation. On the other hand, as I describe in detail in later chapters, Ochola also had a central role in a conflict that dragged most of the Town Parish Choir out of Saint Janani Luwum Church for a number of years before reconciliation was effected.

Placed together, the old black-and-white photo, the president's portrait beside it and the choir's gathering beneath them to pray for healing, offer a snapshot of everything this book addresses. They speak of the social, political, cosmological and material embeddedness of churches. They witness the power of religious narratives and the practices that emerge from them to bring people together. But they also recall how narratives proclaimed from within embedded churches can tear people apart. Over the coming chapters, I explain how.

The Catholic and the Anglican Churches form the largest religious communities in the Acholi region; the largest pieces in a complex mosaic of religious plurality. Compared to the national average, Acholi has a considerably lower-than-average number of Muslims, and a comparatively greater number of Catholics. Recent years have seen the growth of PC churches, a phenomenon many argue was hindered by the war, but which has steadily grown in importance (L. H. Williams 2019; L. H. Williams and Meinert 2020). Community Church, one of Kitgum's biggest PC churches, was started, along with a school, by Australian missionaries during the war, and in the course of fieldwork, I encountered white missionaries from America, Britain and coincidentally, once even my home country Finland. Although the Catholic Mission was handed over to the local Catholic diocese by the Comboni missionaries in 2015, Western missionary priests from other orders stay at the mission in a supportive role, and transnational connections remain an obvious aspect of the religious scene in the region.

The same holds true for Islam, which entered Acholi with slave traders from Egyptian-occupied Sudan in the second half of the late-nineteenth century, decades before Christian missionaries. Yet Islam had less of a lasting impact in Acholi than in the neighbouring West Nile region, and more in western than in eastern Acholi, where Muslims remain a small minority (Atkinson 2010; Girling [1960] 2018, 251; Kasozi 1974, 224–6). The recent refurbishing of a small mosque in the centre and two on the outskirts of Kitgum town was funded by a Turkish development organization, and during the outbreak of nodding syndrome, a debilitating chronic condition whose origins are debated, Islamic teachers and healers from other parts of Uganda came to Kitgum to offer their diagnostic and therapeutic services to nodding patients (van Bemmel 2016).

In my observation, while differences in religious views and practices cause occasional tensions, in Kitgum they are overwhelmingly accommodated: in friendships, in families, in workplaces and in neighbourhoods. Although churches compete in the same religious marketplace, their cooperation in ARLPI points to their at least occasionally amicable relationships with each other, despite the occasional dispute and division (many of the town's PC churches have emerged out of splits). Yet religious division has been fundamental to the development of the social and political climate in Acholi: namely historical tensions between Anglicans and Catholics. It is this history, and the prominent role these churches played in peace efforts during the war, that led me to privilege them in a study of politics and Christianity in the region.

This book draws largely on material collected from the pews of two churches in Kitgum, and from time spent singing with or listening to the songs of their members. On many mornings, I was woken by harmonies floating in through the windows of the 'Doctor's house' in which the Catholic parish priest at Kitgum Mission had housed me together with my husband and our four- and one-year-old boys. The songs rang out from early morning mass at the astoundingly beautiful church of Saint Mary of Lourdes, Kitgum's largest church, which gathered about 500 people for each of its Sunday services. Its whitewashed steeple, coloured glass windows, ornate wooden crucifix, elaborate stonework floor, and wall paintings of white prophets surrounded by black baby angels all evidence the financial and personnel resources invested in the mission's development and upkeep by Comboni missionaries since its opening in 1914. The church is the heart of a large mission station complete with parish hall, catechumenate and retreat centres, compounds for the priests and for the Ugandan order of the Little Sisters of Mary Immaculate, a nursery school and kindergarten, the district's largest and best-equipped hospital, two primary schools, and a secondary boarding school. The mission also controls a great swathe of land in which tree-planting projects have taken root in recent years (see Alava and Shroff 2019). Many of the people living near the parish descend from the initial converts, catechists and labourers from different parts of eastern Acholi who settled there in the early 1900s. This history has till recent times given this part of Kitgum town a distinctly Catholic identity.

The second parish in which I concentrated my fieldwork efforts was the home of the choir I have already introduced above – the Church of Uganda parish of Saint Janani Luwum, known more commonly for its location in the administrative centre of Kitgum as 'Town Parish'. I often walked there

Figure 2. Stonework floor of the church of St Mary of Lourdes, Kitgum. Photo by author.

for second service after first attending the early service at St Mary's, some kilometres outside of town; both of these services were in English. The church of Town Parish is tucked tightly between its primary school and the foundations of a much larger church which has been under construction for over a decade. Other than the simple wooden cross at the front, the white fabric draped over the reading pulpit and altar, and the tassel hanging from the ceiling, the church is bare of decoration. But on Sunday mornings, the small space fills to the brim for three services, with about 200 people packed inside and outside the doors and windows in order to catch at least part of the sermon and the singing, while over a hundred children gather in the adjacent classrooms for Sunday school. There is a striking atmosphere of intimacy in this church, packed in tightly as people are, the choir sitting sideways squeezed in next to the pulpit, and benches and large mats for children lined up to the altar. This feeling of closeness and community differentiated Town Parish from St Mary's, where the priest, the altar and the pulpit were so far from the back of the church that one had to have extremely good eyesight, or glasses, to make out the priests' facial expressions if sitting there.

Figure 3. Choir practice at Town Parish. Photo by author.

With the exception of politicians and clergy, I came to know most of my key research participants, including choir members, through their various voluntary service roles at church. Many of those sitting on parish pastoral committees, with responsibility for youth activities, or singing in the choir, were retired or active civil servants and teachers or young adults who were either working in businesses and local CSOs or helping out on family land while searching for employment that matched their degree qualifications. Most of my closest interlocutors were well-educated, and many well-off in local terms, members of the local 'salariat', as Jones (2014) has noted to be typical of church elites in rural Uganda, although education alone did not guarantee financial success or even stability (Meinert 2009).[9] Consequently, most of my fieldwork interactions took place in English. By the end of my fieldwork in 2013, my Acholi skills allowed me to participate in simple everyday chats and to understand the gist of more complex conversations, sermons and speeches, but for interviews and events that required fluent Acholi, I relied on the assistance of my main research collaborator, Chiara Lakareber. Chiara was a recently graduated secondary school teacher of history and religious studies, born and raised in a Catholic family in Kitgum. In interviews, it often mattered that Chiara was recognized as a Catholic. Likewise, in fieldwork, as in academia, it has often mattered that I am a Lutheran.

Ontologies of peace and violence: Between anthropology, theology and 'belief'

We had hardly sat down for our first meeting when [an established anthropologist] asked me why my English didn't have a Finnish accent. 'I grew up partially in Hong Kong, where my parents were missionaries', I replied. He grimaced and snapped, 'I don't like missionaries'.

(Research diary, 2011)

Joel Robbins (2003, 193) has surmised that Christians, as 'neither real others nor real comrades... make anthropologists recoil by unsettling the fundamental schemes by which the discipline organizes the world into the familiar and the foreign'. My own position has been one of traversing the boundary between the familiar and the foreign, much like a chameleon, navigating various insides and outsides throughout my fieldwork on religion (Lauterbach 2013). Along the way, I have been challenged from both sides of the anthropology–theology divide, and from development studies where I was formally trained: for my ability to study churches when I belong to one; my ability to study Christian marriage or pastors when I'm married to one; my engaging with theology when I'm not trained as a theologian; even for writing a dissertation on religion at all when I'm a social scientist. The need to protect disciplinary territory in the scuffle for funding in neoliberal academia is understandable, but it does leave scholars trying to transgress divides vulnerable to attack on many fronts. But there is obviously more at stake. Who I was and how I have been positioned by others have been influential both in the corridors of academia and during fieldwork.

Whereas my research associate Chiara's Catholicism was often pointed out by research participants, it mattered that I was neither Catholic nor Anglican; as a Lutheran, I was constantly appropriated as 'one of us' and, in a sense, as an ally, by members of both churches. Although I am a member of the Evangelical Lutheran Church of Finland (evangelical in historical name but not like such churches in the United States for instance), I could well imagine belonging to some other church instead. As a missionary kid in Hong Kong, I attended both Anglican and Catholic Church services, meaning that going to church in Kitgum felt a lot like going home. There, being identified as a Christian distinguished me from most *muno* (white foreigners) my research participants had encountered. It also mattered that I was not 'born-again' in the sense understood by PC churches, since this category of Christians were considered competition, suspicious or both, by many (not all) of the Catholics and Anglicans with whom I interacted.

While I do not consider myself born again, I consider myself a committed member of my church, and as such, a member of a rapidly diminishing minority group among my age group of women in Finland, although, to date, the overwhelming majority of the population still belongs to the Lutheran Church. Even the frustration I experience with regard to churches' selective commitment to racial, social, gender and sexual justice feels similar in both Uganda and Finland – unsurprisingly, since my values, my faith and my ethnographic sensibilities are present in both. I feel my heartstrings tug during hymns, or communion, or joint prayer, in ways that I suppose could be labelled 'believing'. I say 'could be labelled' not to produce some kind of ironic distance, but because the strands of Christian theology to which I have been drawn since my early adulthood, with their roots in a nineteenth-century, pietist, *körtti*-Lutheran revival in Finland, emphasize divine mystery over human certainty or belief in a manner that has made it easy for me to adopt an attitude of what might be called committed methodological agnosticism – as opposed to mere methodological agnosticism (Droogers 2012; Ezzy 2004) – in my work. From such a position, in the years between conducting fieldwork and completing this book, I have drawn on my insights from Uganda to publish, in a Finnish online anthropological medium, critical feminist ethnographic commentaries on debates about Christianity, politics, marriage and church politics in my own church.

I feel little affinity either with scholars whose aim has been to expose Christianity to ridicule, or with those whose work has sought to prove God's existence via anthropological analysis – both types of scholarship having held prominent places in anthropology's history (Larsen 2014). Rather, I take my cue from Merz and Merz, who have invited post-secular anthropology to seek out 'an area where the self and the other, belief and disbelief, ignorance and certainty, possibility and impossibility, as well as the secular and the religious, meet, overlap and intertwine' (2017, 8): it is this area this book seeks to inhabit, and where I, as a scholar, find myself at home. Such an approach is also at the heart of my central argument, that whether churches advance peace, conflict or something else, is not a matter that calls for normative judgement. It calls for detailed and openly reflexive analysis.

In order to account for the theoretical and empirical focuses of this book – particularly its engagement with themes of suffering and hope – it should be acknowledged that my decision to study churches emerged from something resembling despair. My original plans – to explore further the depoliticizing effects of development aid in Acholi – became outdated when exceptional research was conducted and published (Branch 2011; Dolan 2009; Finnström 2008; Nibbe 2010) during the time I spent taking care of my first two babies. Moreover, I was somewhat repelled by the pathos of critical development studies in the early 2000s, driven as it was by the desire to expose how 'development' overwhelmed all attempts at genuine change while bolstering existing structures of fundamentally racist neocolonial power (Cooke and Kothari 2001; Escobar 1995; Ferguson 1994; Kapoor 2004; Keen 2008; Marriage 2006). I did not doubt this impulse, more so since northern Uganda appeared such a prime example of how far the rhetoric of 'aid' and 'international justice' could be from the reality. But I did find it deflating. So it was not just because of a need to find a new ethnographic location other than 'aid', and the dawning realization that Acholi churches had at that point not been studied much at all, but also a desire to locate hope in the midst of what had been coined the world's worst humanitarian crisis, that prompted the idea that I should join a church choir for my fieldwork.

For anthropologists of Christianity, Meretoja's (2014) description of the narratives of violence and fragmentation adopted by poststructuralist authors may sound familiar. It resounds with Joel Robbins's (2006) article on the uncomfortable relationship between theology and anthropology in which he claimed that the latter was 'not a discipline much given to finding radical otherness in the world or to using that otherness as a basis for hope' (ibid., 292). With the notion of resistance proven naive, anthropologists had become 'resigned... to serving as witnesses to the horror of the world, the pathos of our work uncut by the provision of real ontological alternatives' (ibid.). Robbins's inspiration for his argument came from Anglican theologian John Milbank's *Theology and Social Theory* (1990), which claimed that the ontology of modern science and politics is fundamentally violent, whereas Christianity, grounded as it is in the transcendent, embodies an ontology of peace (Kemppainen 2016).[10]

In his later call for an 'anthropology of the good', Robbins (2013) argued that a critique of 'othering' discourses in anthropology (Trouillot 2003) provoked anthropologists to take violence and suffering – specifically 'trauma' (Caruth 1995) – as their central concern. While Robbins quotes neither Milbank nor his own article on anthropology and theology in his call for an anthropology of the good, his call retains significant traces of Milbank's thinking. Robbins writes, 'if part of the point of the anthropology of the good is to return to our discipline its ability to challenge our own versions of the real, then we have to learn to give these aspirational and idealizing aspects of the lives of others a place in our accounts' (Robbins 2013, 458). In a key text of the anthropological debate on 'the good', a basic premise of Radical Orthodoxy – that 'our' (presumably secular/Western) 'versions of the real' are in need of being challenged by the 'aspirational and idealizing aspects' of an 'other' (ibid.) – is transported from what Furani (2019) describes as the 'theosphere', into a supposedly de-theologized space of the 'anthropodome'.

Since Milbank's seminal book, Radical Orthodoxy, a largely Anglo-American school of thought, has promoted theology as the lens through which society should be interpreted, and Christianity as the normative ground upon which it should be built. Among scholars to take on this task is the Ugandan, US-based theologian Emmanuel Katongole who, in *The Sacrifice of Africa* (2011), distinguishes three roles that churches have adopted vis-à-vis politics: emphasizing individual spiritual transformation; focusing on the pastoral role of community service; or accentuating the prophetic promotion of justice. These views, Katongole holds, are premised on the faulty Western assumption of religion and politics as distinct realms, whereby they add up to mere attempts to *improve* politics and the nation state (ibid., 50).

Adopting a strong narrativist position, Katongole suggests seeing 'politics as dramatic performance grounded in a particular story that requires, and in the end shapes, particular characters' (2011, 3). He thus calls for Christianity to undo and replace the stories of colonial and postcolonial violence: to *be* the story on which social reality in Africa is built, rather than a mere commentary on other stories. To this end, he narrates the stories of people and organizations that in their lives and actions have replaced violence with peace; one among them is a Catholic Acholi mother, who advocated for the safe return of children abducted by the LRA and for forgiveness for their captors. Yet as evocative as Katongole's stories are, they beg the question: what would a Christian peace ontology look like if applied on a broader societal level, beyond anecdotal case studies? This question can be explored from at least two directions, specifically: what public do Christian political ontologies address, and what difference do they make for reality?

To answer the first, we can turn to Michael Warner, who, in theorizing publics, has argued that 'when any public is taken to be *the* public, [its limitations] invisibly order the political world' (2002, 77). What the talk of an ontology of peace in Radical Orthodoxy risks occluding is that its vision is grounded in a narrowly defined Anglo-Catholic God. Indeed, critical theologians have raised issue with Radical Orthodoxy's blindness to different forms of oppression (Zlomislic 2012); its misguided denigration of political liberalism and religious tolerance (Insole 2004); its radical Eurocentrism (Vuola 2006); and its dismissal of the pressing issues raised by eco, liberation, feminist and postcolonial theologies (Ruether and Grau 2006).

It is perhaps not surprising that Robbins's Milbank-inspired clarion call for anthropological engagements with theology does not include such critical viewpoints. As Merz and Merz (2017, 8) have pointed out, anthropology's engagement with theology has so far largely involved a discussion between two disciplines that share a common Judeo-Christian root, with insufficient critical attention to the epistemological and West-centric underpinnings of mainstream academic theology (see also Daswani 2021). Most of the ethnographic scholarship that has engaged with non-mainstream theology has more often than not been based somewhere other than anthropology, even while interest in such work is growing among anthropologists as well (Lauterbach and Vähäkangas 2019; Lemons 2018, 2019). A recent example is Adriaan Van Klinken's *Kenyan, Christian, Queer* (2019), which was given an entire colloquium in *HAU*, a journal of ethnographic theory. One commentator, with refreshing honesty, states that 'as an unbelieving anthropologist' he has 'no idea' what he is supposed to make of van Klinken's unelaborated quote of an African theologian reflecting on the meaning of seeing one's body as belonging to the Body of Christ (Kulick 2020). The comment leaves me wondering how often anthropologists also use metaphorical language that only makes sense to their own? Ought secular anthropology not be familiar enough with the basic metaphors of the world's largest religion to be able to interpret simple theological statements? My answers to these questions would be: 'often', and 'yes'.

To reflect on the second question, that is, the actual relevance of ontologies to actions, it is crucial to note that Robbins's propositions for an 'anthropology of the good' (2013) and his call for recognition of multiple ontologies (2006) diverge from the radical ontological turn in anthropology (see, e.g., de Castro 2015; Henare, Holbraad, and Wastell 2006). Rather, it employs the concept of ontology in a manner akin to philosophers and theologians, that is, as a discourse about the nature of being (Graeber 2015, 15). Lurhmann (2018) makes a similar argument when she asks anthropologists to take god seriously, not because of god's reality, but because faith in the goodness of god, despite all the evidence against it, changes believers, and can thereby change the world.

That said, the arguments Graeber (2013) makes against the ontological turn are useful in assessing the relevance of 'ontologies' (Milbank), 'founding stories' (Katongole) or 'political imaginaries' (Andrews) of social reality. For Graeber, it is the naturalization of certain discourses about the order of reality that makes for an important object of analysis, rather than debates about the 'true' nature of reality as such (2013, 229). Surprisingly perhaps, it seems that Graeber's value-driven critique of ontological radicalism, and his activist, normatively anarchist, scholarly commitment to unpacking narratives used to naturalize political orders, bear a kinship of sorts with the theological ontologists I have discussed above.

To conclude what has been said thus far, this book occupies a middle ground vis-à-vis debates on the power of narrative: political narratives (to use Andrews's term), or ontologies (to use Milbank and Katongole's term) do not condition modes of action, but by moulding what is thought to be possible and worth pursuing they may enable or delimit them. Whether ontologies (in the sense implied by theologians) or narrative imaginaries (in the sense implied by scholars like Molly Andrews) provide absolute scripts for social existence, or whether they are contrived post-script to make sense of and justify political orders, they are relevant objects for anthropological analysis. Not as objectified 'stuff' mobilized for explanation in the sense critiqued by Latour (2005), but ethnographically, with an eye to what is done, and an ear to the stories told about it. The narratives that I have found most compelling, both in my fieldwork material and in anthropological theory, and the ones I suggest hold promise in analysing Christianity and politics in a location characterized greatly by violence, are those concerning 'the good'.

Anthropologies of hope and other 'goods'

While many have followed Joel Robbins' call for anthropology to engage with 'the good' (Robbins 2013, 456), others have challenged the very notion (Venkatesan 2015). For Veena Das, the turn's inclination to philosophical ponderings is 'symptomatic of a certain tiredness of having to deal with the quotidian forms of suffering in anthropology' (Das in Venkatesan 2015, 433). But does an interest in the good really have to rule out an interest in the quotidian forms of suffering? Ortner, for instance, has insisted that the anthropology of the good, and what she terms 'dark anthropology' be kept 'in active interaction with, rather than opposition to, one another' (Ortner 2016, 65). Hope and the things that disappoint it or foreclose it – fear, silence, suffering, and the historical and ongoing structural and political constraints it cannot escape – appear in this book as I argue they do in everyday lives: as fluid, abiding beside each other, one uppermost at one moment and another at the next. Writing of hope and peace in the way I do is thus not an attempt to turn away from suffering, which, it is clear, has been and remains profound in Acholi. To do so would be unethical. But not to speak of hope would be likewise, since, as Cheryl Mattingly argues, structures of violence, however repressive, do not preclude the possibility of human striving towards a better life, or the work of building and rekindling hope regardless of everything. As she reminds us, 'it is not more real to disclose our imprisonment within everyday life than to disclose the possibilities for transformation that this life also admits' (Mattingly 2010, 39).

This book's turn to confusion strikes a balance of complementarity between the positions espoused in the Das/Robbins debate, acknowledging that at the heart of much human experience is the simultaneity of suffering and good, pain and hope, violence and peace, and how people deal with the uncertainty that follows. Ethnographers of uncertainty have referred to this as subjunctivity (Cooper and Pratten 2015, 13), the subjunctive mood referring to a mood 'of doubt, hope, will, and potential [which is not] a quality of life, or of particular persons, but a mood of action: a doubting, hoping, provisional, cautious, and testing disposition to action' (Whyte 2005, 250–1); as such, it is also at the heart of imagination, which always deals with envisioned possibilities rather than certainties (Andrews 2014, 13; see also Bruner 1986, 26).

A particular variant of the anthropology of the good has been research focusing on hope, which has emerged simultaneously with a broader interest in hope across the social sciences (see, for instance, Bloch 1986; Browne 2005; Crapanzano 2003; Hage 2003; Zournazi 2002), and in partial resonance with parallel discussions around the theology of hope (see, in particular, Moltmann 2002). In an overview of this literature, Jansen (2016) makes a useful distinction between intransitive hope, which refers to an affect of hopefulness as opposed to hopelessness, and transitive hope, which orients towards an object or objects, as in hopes *for* something. Drawing on this distinction, two prevalent streams in the anthropology of hope can be recognized.

The first focuses on the 'political economy of hope': that is, how the distribution of hope by the state (Hage 2003) or by other institutions such as churches (Turner 2015) is always fundamentally political, and functions as a form of governing. The second focuses on hope amidst indeterminacy or hopelessness. In a key example, Hirokasu Miyazaki (2006) draws on Ernst Bloch's *The Principle of Hope* (1986), to argue that the essence of hope is its orientation towards the future, whereupon the task for the anthropologist is to replicate moments of hope in ethnographic writing. For Miyazaki, a 'method of hope' generates future-orientation and indeterminacy rather than the closure and backward-orientation typical of critical social science (Miyazaki 2006, 127). Besides Miyazaki, a flood of anthropological work on violence, sickness, and precarity has focused on indeterminacy and uncertainty, often treating them as productive of 'new social landscapes and social horizons' (Cooper and Pratten 2015, 2).

Yet Kleist and Jansen (2016) call for caution, noting that scholars who turn to Bloch to highlight indeterminacy as a prerequisite of hope mostly ignore that for Bloch, indeterminacy was a prelude to the very determined political project of communism. A scholarly desire to identify hope and rekindle it risks precluding recognition of hopes which the scholar does not wish to rekindle (Jansen 2016, 451–3). Instead of hope's replication, Kleist and Jansen advocate approaching 'hope as an ethnographic category in critical analysis rather than a normative banner in manifestos of optimism' (2016, 373–4). In this undertaking scholars would recognize the diversity of people's different hopes, 'only some of [which] will be in tune with any author's own' (ibid. 380). The caution is certainly worthwhile, particularly as I acknowledge that locating hope has been a driving force behind this study. But why would 'advocating hope' and 'analysing hope' have to be mutually exclusive alternatives? Instead of adopting an unnecessarily strict opposition between hope as an object of analysis, and commitment to a replication of hope as a scholarly disposition, it is my hope (!) that this book will show that the two can be combined.

Navigating hope and suffering in Acholi: The book outlined

What is the relevance of debates on hope, on 'the good', on suffering, on ontology and on narrative, for a book on churches, politics and *anyobanyoba* in northern Uganda?

Ever since the groundbreaking work of Sverker Finnström (2008), and often referencing Susan Whyte's work on subjunctivity in eastern Uganda (2002, 2005), uncertainty and ways of managing it have been a mainstay in anthropology on Acholi. A number of scholars working in this region have, I sense deliberately, skirted around the pitfalls of 'suffering slot' anthropology in a variety of ways: by focusing on how people existentially, cosmologically and morally navigated the realities of war (Lagace 2018; Meinert 2020; Victor 2018); by examining how individuals and communities come to terms with and live beyond experiences of sexual violence (Porter 2016; Schulz 2018, 2020); and by addressing how meaning is made in and through PC religious and social practices in the region (Williams 2019). Yet, despite the nuance in these and many other accounts, I have the sense that, as a whole, scholarly literature on northern Uganda has served to assign Acholi people to precisely the kind of 'suffering slot' that Joel Robbins (2013) describes.

While it is impossible to 'prove' this impression objectively, a search for 'northern Uganda' on Google Scholar indicates its origins: page after page of articles include words such as 'war', 'trauma', 'suicide', 'orphans', 'abduction', 'terror' or 'violence' in their title or key words. As David Mwambari has noted, '[o]utsiders interested in studying sensitive contexts tend to conduct research in response to international media coverage of crisis… In conducting their fieldwork, they often prefer respondents who are survivors of abuse' (Mwambari 2019, 4). Few scholars choose to conduct their work in Acholi for the region's music, childbirth and lactation traditions, or landholding structures alone, but more often than not because it was the site of a terrible war, thereby frequently reproducing a story that has already been told (Finnström 2019; see also Harris 2017, 3).

Acholi history of course goes a long way to justify a focus on suffering; all the horrors listed above have taken and are taking place, and are worthy of attention. But my suspicion is that the focus has also been a political move. In place of the government's official war-time discourse of the Acholi as the ultimate 'other' (see Atkinson 2010; Finnström 2008; Chapters 2 and 3 in this book), local and international academia, as well as religious leaders and other civil society actors, have created a narrative that essentializes the region's population into a homogeneous group – 'the Acholi' – and designates for this group the slot of the suffering subject. But a discourse of suffering can serve to create distance and otherness in much the same way as a discourse of savagery (Ahmed 2000). Moreover, as many scholars have argued before me and as I do in more length in Chapter 3, a discourse of suffering does not do justice to the way in which life actually unfolds in the midst of war and its afterlives.

In his recent introduction to the compiled ethnographic studies on Acholi by Frank Girling and Okot p'Bitek, Tim Allen characterizes the present time in Acholi as 'a moment of renewed hope and possible new beginnings' (Allen 2018, 42). The tentativeness of the wording – *possible* new beginnings – strikes me as exceptionally apt, and resonates with what I set out to do in the coming pages. The analysis in this book is grounded in the belief that it is possible to combine critical analysis of hope – its distribution, its transformation and its failures through time – with a normative commitment to balancing ontological presuppositions of suffering with those of 'the good'. This I aim to do by way of the replication of hope in both its intransitive and transitive senses. Thus, while many of the book's chapters pick up themes beyond those discussed in these theoretical orientations, as a whole, the book seeks simultaneously to analyse the distribution and the rises and falls of hope in Acholi, and to replicate the hopes for peace that were voiced in and by the churches I studied. As I discuss in the chapters to come, these hopes emerged both in formal narratives and in the practices of church members: blossoming and floundering within churches that were complexly embedded in the social, material, cosmological, and political realities of post-war Acholi and that also functioned as sites of political imagination and provided their members with resources for imagining community.

Chapters 1 and 2 provide a reading of the historical context against which the analysis in subsequent chapters is set. Chapter 1 traces the relationship of mainline churches and the colonial state in Uganda, and develops a model for analysing three primary forms of church embeddedness. Examining how the deaths of two Catholic Acholi catechists in the early years of missionary activity in Acholi have been re-signified a century later, the chapter closes with reflection on how the past continues to influence the present. Chapter 2 turns to the relationship between politics and mainline churches from the run-up to independence until the era of Yoweri Museveni's NRM. It also utilizes previously unused archival sources to trace how fraught relationships between churches, rebels and the state unfolded during the war.

In Chapter 3, I introduce Kitgum as a town emerging from war. Through reflection on how my own interpretation of the 'sense' of Kitgum has changed, and how my reading of silence and trauma has evolved, this chapter also elaborates on what I mean when suggesting that the notion of 'confusion' holds epistemological and ethical weight. I reflect on the difficulty of studying silence; on the risk that in studying silence one is breaking something that should instead be protected; and on what it actually means for research to be 'ethical'. By alternately foregrounding analysis of Acholi as a site of 'trauma', and my encounters with the limits of research ethical ideals, as well as my own ability to live up to them, the chapter suggests that discussion about 'ethics', 'method', 'truth' and the absolute centrality of reflexivity for all of them is just as pressing today as it was at the beginning of anthropology's reflexive turn.

In Chapter 4, I turn my attention to contemporary Acholi conceptualizations of politics. I show how an understanding of politics as *cung i wibye*, or standing atop an anthill, prevails in everyday discussion and notions of politics in Kitgum, and analyse a particularly elaborate moment of *cung i wibye* – the burial of a prominent opposition politician – as an example of how the Ugandan state is performed and negotiated in church settings. Chapter 5 develops the argument made in Chapter 4, asserting that the efficacy of public performances of politics draws from the fear, silence and ambivalence that underlies the everyday in post-war northern Uganda. While in Chapter 3 I focus on silence and confusion as they related to the past, Chapter 5 argues that silence and confusion also grow from silenced political and communal tensions in the present.

Chapter 6 mirrors the movement that I argue characterizes Acholi lifeworlds in the post-war moment, by turning from fear and ambivalence to peace, forgiveness, hope and moving on. I show how mainline churches have provided alternative, less violent, imaginaries for the future in Acholi, and discuss how these churches and their members orient towards peace, forgiveness and moving on in everyday lives. Utilizing analytical concepts from utopian studies, I argue that a Utopia of Peace has emerged as a response to the ambivalences and conflicts of the post-war moment, yet conclude by showing how peaceful narratives can be performed against a backdrop of excluded 'others' in ways that are at times profoundly violent.

Chapter 7 discusses moments when contests over power and resources unsettle the utopian ideals of unity and peace described in Chapter 6. It shows how the 'confusion' that results from the material, social and political embeddedness of churches in the local community provides the driving force for the Utopia of Peace yet, paradoxically, also sets the Utopia its insurmountable boundaries. The chapter also begins to show how, as I elaborate in the Conclusion, attempts to deal with confusion can end up creating more of it. One of the cases of 'confusion in the church' that I detail is the mysterious sickness and miraculous healing of Philip Odwong's daughter, Oyella Irene.

The path leading from the Catholic Mission to the family home where a thanksgiving celebration was arranged after Irene's recovery runs alongside mission buildings that sheltered people displaced during the war. It then skirts past the catechists' homes, and meanders through homesteads, small vegetable plots and cattle kraals; past circles of young men passing time under the shade of trees; beside lines of children with jerry cans waiting for their turn at the water pumps; along the edge of the land farmed by the Catholic parish despite protests from some neighbours; and past homes of local dignitaries from across political and parish political lines. Every time I walk this path, as I have done repeatedly in 2012, 2013, 2015, 2016 and 2019, it seems to speak to me more deeply. As years have passed, I have come to understand some of the layers of traumatic historical events that took place here; now unseen, but not unremembered; and I have more sense of the disputes, feuds, friendships and allegiances that crisscross over the path, and far beyond it. I would wish for every reader to be able to walk that path, and all the other paths and roadsides that I have walked in Kitgum, accompanied by those who, walking with me, have shared stories of Christianity, politics and the afterlives of war in their own lives. But since that cannot be, it is my hope that this book can at least begin to unpack some layers of these stories, and to finally, in the Conclusion, draw together the meandering lines of thought set out in this Introduction and carried through the pages between.

1

The gun and the word
Missionary-colonial history in Kitgum

When driving into Kitgum with my family in 2012, my mental map of the town had grown blurry since my last visit six years prior. We stopped the car and I asked a lady at a market stall: '*Mission tye kwene?*' Alongside everyday greetings, this question – 'Where is mission?' – was just about all the Acholi I could muster at that point. But it sufficed, and we were directed to the Catholic mission station, which in Kitgum is simply known as 'the Mission', whereas the area around the old Anglican mission is referred to by the Acholianized name 'Mican'.

This chapter answers the question '*Mission tye kwene?*' by tracing the processes through which the Catholic and Anglican Churches have become materially, socially, politically and cosmologically embedded into the landscape of present-day Kitgum. In so doing, it provides a contextualization for the analysis in coming chapters, and begins to unravel the ways in which churches are entwined within the violence, disputes and uncertainties captured by the notion of *anyobanyoba* [confusion] introduced in the Introduction. As we will see, Christianity was an important component in dynamics that built up through the colonial and postcolonial era, and ultimately erupted in 1986 as the northern Ugandan war. However, rather than beginning from the war, this chapter begins from considering the broader significance of missionary Christianity in contemporary Acholi. It's primary claim is that while it is a historical fact that the Catholic and Anglican Churches were introduced to Acholi by foreign missionaries, it is a comparable fact that for their adherents, the churches are rarely thought of as foreign impositions. Rather, they are complexly part and parcel of Acholi society and Acholi lives – they are embedded and owned.

Establishing 'good luck' and order among the Acholi people

In August 1912, colonial officer J.R.P. Postlethwaite arrived at Pandwong hilltop. With him he had forty Nubian askaris and plans for the pacification of eastern Acholi. The crux of Postlethwaite's plan was the establishment of a modern town, for which he brought the Acholi name: *kit gum*, or 'good luck' (Ocitti 1966, 39). The town's administrative centre was positioned on the northern flank of the hill, in the favourable bend created by the small river Pager as it skirts the hilltop. The location promised to be defendable in case of attack, which was likely to have been a priority, since the Acholi had proven difficult to convince of the necessity and advantageousness of succumbing to colonial rule (Dwyer 1972; Postlethwaite 1947).

The first attempt to establish British colonial dominion over what was to become the Acholi region had ended in disappointment in 1907. The colonial base, which was run together with the Church Missionary Society (CMS) mission station in Patiko, was closed after it was essentially isolated and cut off from supplies and workforce by the local chief's creation of a 'no-man's-land' around the white men. A year later, the CMS station also withdrew, leaving behind a handful of converts shunned by their community.[1] This turn of events came as a serious disappointment to the CMS, which had initially been invited to Acholi by the most powerful of Acholi chiefs at that point, Rwot (Chief) Awich of the Payira clan.[2] The CMS missionaries had written spirited and enthusiastic accounts of these first trips (Cook 1904; Kitching 1904; Lloyd 1904), although, as it turned out, high expectations turned to disappointment. Whereas CMS missionaries insisted they were being invited to Acholi due to the chiefs' desire to abandon their old ways and find 'good food that shall strengthen [their] souls' (Pirouet 1978, 150), Acholi elders later recalled Awich's primary interest as having been in the ability of missionaries to read and write (ibid.). Lloyd, one of the first optimists to arrive in the region some years earlier, described their departure from Patiko in the following way:

> [T[he people hearing we were off, hung round us like vultures, waiting for the little bits of rubbish we might throw aside while packing our odds and ends. Of course, as we expected, the Acoli refused point-blank to carry our loads to Uganda [Buganda], and we were obliged to send off to Hoima and Masindi over a hundred miles away, for Banyoro [the neighbouring people to the South of Acholi] to come to our help... A very few of the Acoli boys came to say goodbye... Only one soul from among all who had called us friends accompanied us

upon our way, and we almost thought there was a sign of pleasure on the faces of some as we passed from them in to the darkness...
>
> (letter from Lloyd, quoted in Onono-Ongweng, Holmes, and Lumumba 2004, 22)

During the withdrawal of the CMS and the British colonial government from Acholi, the first Roman Catholic Verona missionaries, whose religious order was based on the vision of the Italian priest, Daniel Comboni, to spread the Gospel to the source of the Nile, reached northern Uganda via what is now South Sudan.[3] By the time the CMS returned in the wake of the colonial government's second attempt to establish control in Acholi, the Verona missionaries already had a strong presence in the area. This second phase of British expansion to Acholi culminated in the establishment of Gulu town in 1911, in the face of opposition from Rwot Awich on whose clan's land the town was built.[4] During this time, traditional *rwodi* all over Acholi were disposed of – imprisoned, publically humiliated and some of them killed – and replaced with new colonially appointed *rwodi kalam* (chiefs of the pen, as opposed to *rwodi moo*, anointed chiefs)[5] as the Acholi called them. As Dubal has noted, '[w]here violence, committed against primitive resisters, was performed to meet colonial objectives, it was neither immoral nor against "humanity"' (Dubal 2018, 44). Among the sorest of the people's many grievances towards the new colonial district commissioners was the confiscation of Acholi weapons (Karugire 1980, 118, 125).

Prior to the establishment of the British protectorate of Uganda, slave and ivory traders from the Zanzibari coast and from Sudan had already been active in the region. Eventually the Sudanese established numerous trade posts in Acholi territory, where, after an initial phase of slave raiding among the Acholi, they increasingly collaborated with the Acholi to raid neighbouring groups (Atkinson 2010, 267–72; Girling 1960, 129–33). Interaction with the traders and administrators from Egyptian Sudan served to entrench divisions between Acholi chiefdoms and clans, enabling certain groups to emerge as stronger than others (Dwyer 1972, 39–57). Unlike in the large kingdoms of Central Uganda, the Acholi clans, which had settled in northern Uganda through successive migrations over a long period of time, existed fairly independently of each other (Crazzolara 1950), even within the chiefdom structures that ultimately emerged (Atkinson 2010). In the wake of the flow of small arms to the area, escalating tensions broke out in increasingly violent ways (Adimola 1954; Karugire 1980, 56–8).[6] Having replaced the Sudanese slavers with their own, often rogue, Sudanese soldiers – and so as to establish effective control over the

Acholi region – the British argued, with missionary backing, that it was in the best interests of the Acholi that their guns be taken away.

In 1911, members of the Lamogi chiefdom, joined by malcontents from other chiefdoms, informed the British that they would neither surrender their arms nor bow to colonial rule, and stocked up a network of caves under the Guruguru hills in preparation for war. Resistance to colonial rule was widespread, and the Assistant District Commissioner in Gulu wrote to his supervisor at the beginning of the Lamogi rebellion: 'This infection appears to be spreading… I consider that a final lesson should be given these people… they require to be brought to their senses in a very effectual way' (quoted in Adimola 1954, 172). The British captain, responsible for the siege of the hills that eventually followed, noted down the complaints shouted out by the fighters: 'Our fathers carried your loads! We will never work for any Mzungu! We will fight till we kill one Mzungu! We don't want peace!' (cited in Cisternino 2004, 375). Colonialist forces eventually cut the supply lines and access to clean water of the soldiers in the Guruguru hills. Ninety-one Acholi warriors were killed, three hundred died of dysentery and over a thousand Acholi were taken prisoner (Adimola 1954, 175). According to Cisternino (2004, 375), thirty-four Acholi traditional chiefs who had been sympathetic to the Lamogi resistance were permanently deported after the rebellion was quelled, and new chiefs were named by the British in their place. This would not be the only or the last event of its kind.

The establishment of Kitgum town in late 1912, just six months after the Lamogi rebellion, broadened and strengthened the dominion of the British Empire over this part of Uganda. This was almost two decades after the initial establishment of the British Uganda Company in areas contemporarily referred to as Central Uganda in 1888, the subsequent Uganda protectorate in 1894 and the full-fledged colony in 1905. In the coming decades, the development of Kitgum followed the prescripts of modernization: a cotton ginnery was established on the eastern side of town, and quarters for the civil servants and staff of the ginnery were built next to the town's administrative centre (Ocitti 1966). Cotton provided people cash with which to pay their violently imposed taxes, and the colonial government revenue with which to finance itself (Karugire 1980, 130). While direct colonial governance, in the form of the district administration and a police force, was executed from the flanks of Pandwong hill, an integral part of the colonial civilizing mission was deployed from the northern side of the Pager River, where mission stations were established by both CMS and Verona missionaries.

Cosmological embeddedness: *Rubanga, Lubanga* and *Jok*

In an article published in the missionary magazine of the CMS, the *CMS Gleaner*, in 1919, Reverend Wright, a member of the society, reflected thus on the first years of missionary work in Acholi:

> The mass movement in the Gulu district is not to be likened to an earthquake, or a river in flood. Still, there is a beginning, the commencement of a landslide, or the flowing of a stream. The ground proved very hard and barren when work was begun among the nude, wild tribes in 1903. The people lived away in the bush and spent their time in hunting and feasting, without a desire for anything spiritual.
>
> (Wright 1919, 134)

Wright's condescending characterization of the Acholi people with the biblical metaphor of hard and barren ground was further emphasized by the caption under one of the photographs included in the article: 'An old man of Gulu. A hard nut to crack'. The notion that the Acholi were hard to 'crack', that is, to convert, appears repeatedly in missionary accounts from the early years, and is, interestingly, often still alluded to by both Anglican and Catholic priests today.[7]

In the historical narratives, two issues are raised to explain this matter, the first of which is succinctly phrased in CMS missionary Kitching's observation that 'independence [is] perhaps the most marked characteristic of the Acholi race' (Kitching 1904, 816; see also Crazzolara 1950, 70 for similar characterizations). In centralized societies missionary efforts focused on the conversion of kings and their subsidiary chiefs, through whose influence large amounts of people could be at least nominally attracted to the new religions (Peel 1977, 77). In contrast, the independent chiefdoms and clans in Acholi posed a headache to colonial administrators and missionaries alike: each *rwot* and clan elder had to be individually convinced of the supposed benefits of submitting to both colonial and divine power (Dwyer 1972, 95–6). The second issue at stake is what Wright referred to as the Acholis' lacking 'desire for anything spiritual' (Wright 1919, 134).

Much later, in what is certainly a simplification but conveying something important nonetheless, the Acholi anthropologist Okot p'Bitek claimed that the Acholi do not think metaphysically, by which he did not refer to lacking intellect, but rather to his observation that in contrast with the European missionary tradition, 'one does not find among the Acoli a barren preoccupation with

An Old Man of Gulu
A hard nut to crack

Figure 4. Illustration in *CMS Gleaner* article about their work in Acholi (Wright 1919: 135). Reproduced with permission from the Church Mission Society archives.

certain kinds of abstract questions' (Imbo 2008, 371). Wright's claim that the Acholi were uninterested in the spiritual obviously rests on a culturally specific conceptualization of 'religion' and 'spirituality', which is assumed to necessitate a fascination with a particular type of metaphysics. Yet ethnographic studies by missionaries, later colonial anthropologists, and p'Bitek, all show clearly that prior to missionization, the Acholi already had an elaborate cosmology, and ways of engaging with the cosmological, which, I argue, Wright could have understood as 'spiritual' matters, had he not been so intent on understanding spirituality in a very narrow way.

In p'Bitek's (1971a, b) view, the key problem was that the concepts through which explorers, missionaries and later colonial anthropologists sought to describe the characteristics of, or the presumed absence of, Acholi 'religion' were ill-suited to the task. While I fully agree with this argument, I take it seriously enough also to refrain, contrary to p'Bitek himself, from using the concept of 'religion' to characterize what I refer to above as Acholi ways of engaging with the cosmological. As Cannell (2006) and Englund (2011) have argued – the notion of 'religion', as of 'faith' and 'belief', is premised on culturally specific epistemological presuppositions that are ill-suited to the task of describing the introduction of Christianity to Acholi lifeworlds. In place of what is referred to as Acholi 'religion', 'tradition', 'superstition' or 'witchcraft', depending on the source or research participants' personal views on the matter, I follow Letha Victor's (2018; see also Victor and Porter 2017) use of the concept of *tic Acholi;* 'Acholi work', to refer specifically to Acholi 'ritual work'. There are two reasons for this choice. First, as p'Bitek himself notes, the word 'religion' has no local equivalent in the Acholi language, hence the Arabic-originating *dini*, which is used in Swahili to refer to 'religion', was also borrowed into Acholi to refer to both of the region's imported religions: Islam and Christianity, as has commonly been done in contexts of mission in Africa (Vähäkangas 2008, 115–16). A second reason for not referring to *tic Acholi* as 'Acholi religion' is that many of those I interacted with, particularly Catholics, did not see Christianity and *tic Acholi* – or certain elements of it – as mutually exclusive or irreconcilable (see also Victor and Porter 2017).

A wealth of studies on historical and contemporary *tic Acholi* show that one of its central aims is the identification and remedying of causes of misfortune and ill-health (Baines 2010; Finnström 2008; Harlacher et al. 2006; O'Byrne 2015; Victor 2018). As p'Bitek has argued, in pre-Christian Acholi custom 'there was no ultimate power, one responsible for the sum total of man's sufferings and life' (p'Bitek 1971a, 85); however, the causes of misfortune and ill-health could be attributed to *jok* (plural *jogi*). Defining *jok* is highly problematic, for as O'Byrne notes, 'often the translation seems to confirm the assumptions and suspicions of the translator rather than giving an accurate rendering of the jok' (O'Byrne 2015). Compared to the notion of an ultimate power, the *jogi* were and are perceived as multiple: some are attached to particular places, chiefdoms or sub-clans, while others are 'free' agents capable of roaming and also of possessing a human being (Atkinson 2010, 87–9; Baines 2010; O'Byrne 2015; Victor and Porter 2017). As O'Byrne notes, based on research among the Acholi-speaking Pajok in present-day South Sudan, what apparently was the primary understanding prior to Christianity – that both fortune and misfortune could be attributed to *jogi* – has largely been replaced with the view that *jogi* are essentially problematic (2015, 9). This development is profoundly connected with processes of translation upon the initial encounters between missionaries and the Acholi.

p'Bitek shows how the terms with which missionaries conceptualized the world translated poorly into Acholi concepts, and vice versa, leading early CMS and Verona missionaries (both of whom produced their own Acholi versions of Christian texts), into constant dilemmas of translation – made all the trickier by the missionaries' initial reliance on translators and catechists from language groups neighbouring the Acholi. Furthermore, the missionaries translated on the basis of their own ontological, normative and religious givens; for instance, they were adamant that there had to be a supreme being among the *jogi* who was also the creator (p'Bitek 1971a, 49). In p'Bitek's view the Acholi did not have a word for 'create' or 'creator', whereby

> the question that the missionaries asked was not meaningful, because the imagery of man being moulded from clay did not exist in the language and the thinking of the Central Luo until the missionaries told them the story of Adam and the talking snake. But the choice of Lubanga [for the word to denote 'God'] is interesting, in that it was this Jok that breaks people's backs and 'moulds' the shape of a man.
>
> (p'Bitek 1971a, 45)

In p'Bitek's reading, the Acholi word ultimately adopted by the Verona missionaries for the Christian God – *Lubanga* – was a *jok* the Acholi believed to cause spinal tuberculosis, which moulded the patient into a hunchback.[8] Well before p'Bitek's scathing analysis of the failure of missionary translations, Crazzolara, a Verona priest, linguist and ethnographer, had described how the Acholi with whom he had spoken when he arrived in the region in 1911 had answered his questions about the world's creator (a notion Crazzolara claimed could be expressed with the Acholi word *cweo*) in ways that led him to conclude that *Jok* would be the most suitable translation for 'God'. The priest in charge of the Verona mission had, however, refused to adopt the translation on the grounds that the word *lajok* connoted black magician or, as it is translated at present, 'witch' (Crazzolara 1940). Thus the notion the Acholi had to refer to a supernatural power, deity or spirit – *jok* – was relegated to referencing the ultimate Evil in Christian cosmology. The Lugbara term, 'Ruhanga', as well as various other alternatives that were experimented with, disappeared over time, and the words *Lubanga* and *Rubanga* became the standard names for the Christian God[9]: indeed – names in the plural. Due to the borrowing of different pronunciations of the same word from neighbouring Bantu languages, the two missions adopted different versions of the name for God, so that to this day one can differentiate Christians on the basis of whether they depart with wishes of *Rubanga okony* (God bless you) if Catholic, or *Lubanga okony* if Anglican.

The befuddlement caused by all that was lost and confused in translation is captured in p'Bitek's *Song of Lawino*, where Lawino, the wife of a man who has become a staunch follower of the white man's ways and beliefs, ponders:

> The Hunchback/Where did he dig the clay/For moulding things?
> Where is the pot/He dug the clay
> For moulding Skyland/And the clay for moulding Earth?
> From the mouth of which river? (p'Bitek 1972, 138)

The process of translation not only concerned words, but also ideas. As p'Bitek has argued, in a spirit of early inculturation, missionaries had a keen interest in proving that some of their ideas were actually not so foreign to the Acholi. One of the notions that has been most persistently pressed is that of a supreme deity. Twenty-five years after the commencement of missionary work in Acholi, the Verona missionary Boccassino (1939) gathered texts on Acholi 'traditional' beliefs, and on the basis of these argued that belief in a supreme creator God had been endemic in Acholi prior to missionarization. The answers Boccassino reaped were, however, 'the harvest of the ideas that the earlier missionaries had sown' over the preceding quarter of a century (p'Bitek 1971a, 45). Consequently, for Boccassino to claim that the Christian notion of a creator was endemic to Acholi was in fact a form of intellectual smuggling. In p'Bitek's scathingly critical view, similar processes are evident in studies by Catholic theologians over subsequent decades, such as that by Kihangire (1957), who systematized what he claimed were ten traditional Acholi rules of conduct, which appeared strikingly akin to the Ten Commandments in the Christian Bible (p'Bitek 1971a, 48).

The lasting repercussions of the shortcomings of translation, and of the endeavours of missionaries to find family resemblances between Acholi cosmology and Christianity, were also evident during my fieldwork. For instance, the 'Acholi ten commandments' were cited to me both by a retired Anglican bishop and by an avowed traditionalist and public criticizer of the Christian churches. Many Catholics and Anglicans also explained to me that *Jok* should really have been the word that missionaries selected for God, although it was invariably considered too late to change the word now. Many Catholics and Anglicans alike also told me with conviction that there had already been an idea of a supreme God in Acholi prior to Christianity. On a wall beside the chapel at the Catholic mission hospital in Kitgum there is a painting conveying the extent of the naturalization of concepts originating in the work of missionaries: 'natural death' is translated *too pa Rubanga*. 'Death by God'.

Culture, custom and doctrine are never immutable, and what is or was the 'pure and original' is an impossible question to solve, but it is also rather irrelevant to my analysis of the embeddedness of Christianity in contemporary Acholi. What is more relevant for the argument I present in this chapter is the simple recognition that missionary endeavours in Acholi have had cosmological repercussions: not only in the sense that missionaries have introduced a wholly new religion, of which localized interpretations and translations have emerged, but also that missionary work has moulded the views among the Acholi about what was and is their 'own' cosmology, tradition and ritual work (for a similar argument on Sonjo cosmology in northern Tanzania, see Vähäkangas 2008). In this sense then, missionary churches in Acholi can contemporarily be seen as

Figure 5. Painting on the wall of the Catholic St Joseph's hospital. Photo by author.

cosmologically embedded in complex ways that also impact on what is seen as desirable, and as possible, in the aftermath of war.

Political embeddedness: Mission and state in colonial Uganda

Religion has been a crucial component in the evolution of Uganda's political system, and remains so today. From the national to the 'grassroots' level, Christianity has become deeply politically embedded, in that religious and political considerations, religious and political institutions, and communities engaged with religion or politics are enmeshed with one another or, when it comes to individuals, are often one and the same. The initial parameters for religion and politics in Uganda were set down during the early decades of the colonial era, and it is these that I focus on in the following; later developments will be discussed in further detail in Chapter 3.

Missionaries were a crucial component in the process of colonization, to the extent that the political historian Karugire has quipped that he is 'justified in classifying [explorers, missionaries, and the actual agents of imperial rule] as but part of the same process of colonialism quite simply because they were' (Karugire 1980, 62).[10] In many areas, Christianity was seen as first and foremost an aid to military expansion and abuse (Crichton 2017). Yet as elsewhere, the relationship between missionaries and the colonial establishment in Acholi was far from straightforward. Both CMS (Crichton 2017; Hansen 1984; Pirouet 1978) and Verona missionaries (Cisternino 2004) constantly had to weigh their short-term and long-term goals, as well as their different allegiances – to the competing mission, to *rwodi* and clan leaders, and to the colonial state – so as to ensure their survival and maintain their right and ability to continue their work. Throughout the decades of the Uganda Company and the protectorate, which preceded the colonization of Acholi, and under the colony thereafter, the colonial state establishment also deliberated on how best to arrange the relationship between state and religion. Alternatives ranged between religious liberalism in the style of the United States, implying a strict separation of state and church, to models based on a UK-style, closer union between church and state institutions (Hansen 1984).[11] These early deliberations remain central to understanding Ugandan political institutions and debates to this day.

As with elsewhere in the British Empire, the limited resources of the British colonial administration rendered it dependent on missionaries to fulfil integral roles in the colonial project (Hansen 1984). Unlike colonial officers, missionaries tended to stay in the same area for a long time, learning the local language and becoming familiar with local customs and culture, making them crucial intermediaries between *rwodi* and colonial officials. In Acholi, the Verona missionaries had a clear advantage in that their previous experience among other Nilotic groups in southern Sudan had paved the way to their learning the Acholi language and familiarized them with the culture, while for the CMS, whose prior experience was among Bantu people, Acholi was in many ways new and foreign. Furthermore, as Pirouet's (1978) study details, due to the relative unimportance accorded to the Acholi region, the spread of Anglicanism in the area was largely carried out by catechists from neighbouring groups, rather than English missionaries.

Securing colonialists' support was particularly crucial for the primarily Italian and Austrian Verona missionaries who, due to their nationality, were on the wrong side of the battle lines in the two World Wars. In contrast, CMS missionaries shared language, nationality and (typically) denomination with the representatives of the colonial power. But they were insufficient in number to provide all the services the colonial government expected of them and, in any case, the Brussels Act of 1890 obliged Britain to allow Verona missionaries to work in its colonies. Yet suspicion was rife in state–mission relations. During the World Wars, Italian and Austrian missionaries were heavily restricted by the British, and interned at the Catholic seminary in Gulu (Mugarura, Mwaka, and Lanek 1998, 36–7).

The practical priority for both the CMS and the Verona missionaries was the opening of schools and the provision of education; the 'magic' of writing was what people wanted to learn, and literacy was also a priority for the colonial government, to which end missionary education was supported with government grants (Gingyera-Pinycwa 1976, 21; see also Willis 1914, 7). Both missionaries and colonialists believed that Western education was the essential tool for imparting the skills, attitudes and habits necessary for 'development' to take root in the colony, but missionary schooling also assisted in rooting out those forms of local belief which were seen to constitute a form of opposition to colonial rule, such as the opposition posed by Acholi *ajwaki* (spirit mediums), who mediated relations to powerful chiefdom *jogi*. Provision of formal education remained in the hands of missionaries until 1925, at which time the government, following the spirit of the Phelps-Stokes Commission on indigenizing education in Africa, set up a governmental department of education to complement missionary teaching (Tiberondwa 1977, 82).

However, the colonial government's investments in education in northern Uganda paled in comparison to those made in other parts of Uganda (Karugire 1980, 70–1) and subsequently, the majority of schools in Acholi were Catholic. Theoretically, the schools were open to anyone, but the expectation was that students would convert to the religion of the founding church, causing great concern for the colonial government which, in its 1940 Secondary Education Policy Committee Report, encouraged the CMS to establish schools with a 'more definitely British character' in Acholi (quoted in Kabwegyere 2000, 160). Ironically, the colonial government was simultaneously concerned that the division between Anglican and Catholic schools might provide a ground for the development of entrenched political divisions (Gingyera-Pinycwa 1976, 21–35; Hansen 1984; Tiberondwa 1977, 74), a concern that was to prove well-founded.

As the primary focus of missionary activities in Acholi, education was also the arena for the fiercest competition between the two missions (Gingyera-Pinycwa 1976). Intense rivalry between Catholics and Anglicans in Uganda had already begun during the early scuffle for favour with the Kabaka's court in Buganda in the late nineteenth century. The religious wars of that time ended with British soldiers under Captain Lugard coming to support the Anglican contingent to remove Catholics from positions of authority (Ward 1991).

In Acholi the colonial government showed many kinds of preferential treatment towards the Anglicans. District commissioners often sided with the CMS in land disputes between the two missions, and CMS missionaries, unlike their Verona equivalents, were involved in choosing and installing new chiefs – thirteen of the altogether thirty-six Acholi baptized before 1913 became *rwodi kalam* (Pirouet 1978, 165). All of this caused resentment among Catholic missionaries (see Cisternino 2004 for ample examples of missionary rivalry).[12] The Verona were, however, far more numerous and endowed with better financial resources, since reaching these parts of Africa had been at the very core of the vision and dream of their founder, Daniel Comboni (Comboni Missionaries Uganda N.D.). In contrast, despite the vision of individual CMS missionaries of increasing their efforts in the north, the authorities in London did not provide substantial support for the CMS's work in the area (Onono-Ongweng, Holmes, and Lumumba 2004, 26); at least until 1926, the whole of Gulu, Kitgum and Lango districts had just one British reverend to oversee church activities (H. G. Jones 1926, 152). By 1967, the greater northern region (encompassing Acholi, Karamoja, Lango and West Nile) had thirty-two Catholic mission stations, served by ordained missionary priests, compared to the Anglicans' four. Although the CMS had few well-resourced mission stations with foreign missionaries, 'where there was a Catholic station there would generally be some kind of Anglican station too, however small' (Onono-Ongweng, Holmes and Lumumba 2004, 26), but their presence was far more humble, and has remained so up to this day.

One can imagine that from the perspective of the Acholi, it was often hard to tell missionaries and colonial officials apart, particularly in cases when missionaries took on tasks of the colonial administration (see Pirouet 1978, 157). Often, however, missionaries opposed or criticized colonial officials' use of violence (see, e.g., Cisternino 2004; Shepherd 1929, 161–3), to the extent that the Anglican missionary Lloyd's complaints against colonial officials led to him being referred to in government correspondence as 'the notorious Mr. Lloyd' (monthly report by colonial officials, cited in Dwyer 1972, 115). Due in part to the criticism they frequently received from missionaries, some colonial officials were actively unsupportive of missionaries' efforts (Cisternino 2004, 27 see also; Dwyer 1972, 112–21), and at times individual missionaries were called away after finding themselves on bad terms with the responsible colonial district commissioner (Hansen 1984, 314). In sum it seems likely that, as Hansen writes more generally about CMS missionaries in Uganda,

> [Even] when the mission defended African interests it was done on the basis of an acceptance of the colonial system. The aim was to secure reasonable and decent conditions for Africans within the colonial order, but it was not the mission's place to question that order's existence as such.
>
> (Hansen 1984, 313)

Overall, it seems missionaries were most likely to speak on behalf of the Acholi when doing so served their interests of establishing or maintaining influence among local communities. The Verona priest Vignato, for instance, is said to have characterized his relationship with the district commissioner in Kitgum in the following way: 'They say that I polish the Englishman's shoes. Not only will I polish them, but even kiss them if the Mission's survival is at stake' (quoted in Cisternino 2004, 410). As Whitmore (2013) has argued based on his reading of *Lok pa Acoli Macon* – a brief history of the Acholi authored by a Verona missionary (Pellegrini 1949), which is still used in schools today – the quandary facing missionaries was that to speak or write strongly against the colonial empire would have risked expulsion. This was also the case in Kitgum.

This silence has effects. As we will see, following a description of the social and material embeddedness of these churches, the way Acholi martyrs are commemorated suggests that churches have effectively eliminated politics and violence from the story of Acholi's missionary-colonial past.

Social and material embeddedness: The growth of Kitgum town and its missions

The first missionaries settled in Kitgum a few years after the town was formally established by the colonial government in 1912, and a few years after missions opened in Gulu. The Italian Verona missionaries established a well-manned mission station in Kitgum in February 1915 (Gulu Archdiocese 2012, 7), whereas CMS missionaries were sent to Kitgum at some point between 1913 and 1915 – sources differ on the exact year (Onono-Ongweng, Holmes, and Lumumba 2004, 43) – to a district where CMS missionaries described the local residents as being 'wilder than in Gulu' (Wright 1919, 134). Ever since then, and up till 2015 when Kitgum Mission was handed over to the local Catholic Diocese (see Chapters 5 and 6), the Catholic Mission remained one of the strongholds of the Verona (later Comboni) missionaries in Acholi, and was served by expatriate missionaries. In contrast, the Anglican Mican had white missionaries only very briefly in the early years; these were soon replaced with native catechists and clergy, first from other parts of Uganda, but later increasingly from Acholi.

The evolution of Kitgum town, from a tiny village to a substantial district centre, was accompanied by a growth in the town's population,[13] a considerable part of which clustered around the new mission stations which were established approximately two kilometres from the district administrative centre, and separated from each other by a similar distance (Cisternino 2004; Ocitti 1966). As explained in detail elsewhere (Alava and Shroff 2019), the land on the left-hand side of what later developed into a road from Kitgum towards Palabek was allocated to the Anglicans, while the Catholics were allotted land on the eastern side of the pathway to Mucwini. At the time, eastern Acholi was sparsely populated, and the specifics of who exactly gave the mission land, and how much of it, were not really at issue. Since then, population growth and increased land pressure have, however, brought these questions to the fore in ways that highlight the historical roots of contemporary church embeddedness (ibid.).

Churches were thus from the beginning embedded in relations within and between local communities, and the negotiations between missionaries, colonial officials and local communities continue to resonate up to today. Notably, when missionaries arrived in Kitgum in the early 1900s, they were given rights to land *both* by colonial authorities *and* by elders of the Lemo clan, which had used the area in question for grazing. There are no official documents of the original agreement between the Lemo and the Catholic missionaries; what is known is based on what elders involved in the negotiations told younger clan members, now elders, who are still alive today. The colonial administration eventually gave the missionaries a document leasing the church the right to 50 acres of land for forty-nine years, which has since been extended. This Temporary Occupation Licence, or TOL, covered less than 10 per cent of the land area that Lemo elders, Catholic clergy, former neighbours of the parish, and the local land officer consider to this day to be the land granted to the mission by the Lemo (for a full account of the mission land, see Alava and Shroff 2019).

The history of the missions' establishment also underlines how the churches contributed to the emergence of new types of sociality, new communities and new class distinctions. In Kitgum, CMS and Verona missionaries invited converts from all over eastern Acholi to come and settle around the missions. The missionaries also had work for the migrants to do, particularly at the Catholic Mission: some of those who moved worked on constructing the hospital and church, others came to work at the clinic, others to train as catechists, while yet other converts were drawn to the location to make a living in affinity with the new religion and the modern healthcare and education it promised. These original neighbours of the missions – who were usually described to me as 'committed Catholics' by their descendants, and 'foreigners' by the Lemo – built their homes alongside the Mission, had children and settled. They became the first members of a wholly new type of community, one based on religious affiliation rather than clan. Drawing on the archived diaries of the Catholic Mission in Kitgum, Cisternino describes how one Verona priest, sent to take care of the Mission in 1918

> [was] trying to put some order into the management of the station, transforming it on the model of his previous station… turning it into a Christian village with its own mayor… installing married couples there, catechumens with young families, exclusively Christian, so as to create a kind of social mini-climate inspired by Christian tradition and management, and in which the strong anti-Christian traditions of Acholi society were supposedly very much reduced.
>
> (Cisternino 2004, 475)

The separation of converts from their clan and chiefdom communities, and hence from their duties towards them, enabled a separation also from what were considered 'pagan' ritual practices by the missionaries (see Kallinen 2014, 161–2). A cornerstone of this separation were the attempts to inculcate 'Christian' gender norms in converts, that is, to abandon polygamy, cease payments of bridewealth and establish male superiority – only the last of which transpired

(Alava 2017a; Harris 2017). Outside of this new 'Christian village', Acholi was being hit hard by disease, drought, famine, and the forced labour and violence imposed by the colonial government. In contrast, in the communities that grew up around the missions in Kitgum there was a chance of some assistance in the form of income, clothing, food, or – particularly after the Verona Sisters started a clinic at the Catholic Mission in 1925 – new medicines at the mission dispensary.

As discussed further in Chapter 7, the missions have provided certain privileges to some of the families settled in their vicinity. The 'social mini-climate inspired by Christian tradition' that Cisternino (2004, 475.) describes has also proven resilient over the past century. The identification of certain parts of Kitgum town as predominantly Anglican and others as Catholic was actively upheld during the colonial era by both missionaries and their adherents, and this denominational demographic differentiation has to some extent persisted up till this day. Many prominent Catholic families continue to live around the Mission, and Anglican families around Mican. However, while the area around the Catholic mission was identified as predominantly Catholic during my fieldwork, the people living in the area surrounding the Anglican Church were increasingly of mixed denominations. This was partly due to many Anglicans' having shifted mainly to born-again churches as a result of the conflict within the Church of Uganda (see Chapter 7). But the change had also come about as a result of the war, during which all residential areas near the urban centre were packed with people seeking the comparative safety of town. These developments, and the ways in which they were described to me, highlight something of how the churches have become embedded in the social fabric and the narratives with which ideal sociality is described in contemporary Kitgum.

As my research participants often told me, 'all sorts of people from the villages came around' during the time of the war; for instance, numerous people claimed that witchcraft practice and alcoholism had increased during this time. The 'original' committed Catholic and Anglican residents and their descendants in these areas were typically seen as having been less likely to engage in such activities. Elders who lived near the missions repeatedly described to me how good life had been in the neighbourhood in their childhood; all the people had gone to church, and the relationship among the people, and between the people and the priests, had been very close. Compared to their nostalgic reminisces, things now seemed more confused, the young people more disorderly and the state of things at the churches also a bit too mixed up for most of the elderly adherents' liking.

The narratives against which the present, the past and the future are measured in contemporary Kitgum, whether political, cosmological or something in between, are profoundly entangled with the history of missionary work in Acholi. In the final part of this chapter, I return to consider the entanglements of Christianity and politics and argue that the sense of ownership that many Acholi Catholics and Anglicans experience regarding their churches is achieved in part through a troubling silencing of the political and violent aspects of these churches' past.

The martyrs in Paimol: Re-interpreting the missionary/colonial past

The death in 1918 of two Acholi catechists, Jildo Irwa and Daudi Okelo, in Paimol, some 70 kilometres east of Kitgum Mission, has become a powerful symbol for the contemporary Catholic Church in Acholi.[14] They are, in the words of Joseph Okumu, the Acholi priest responsible for gathering the evidence required for the martyrs' beatification, 'models of freedom, apostolic zeal, truth, justice, responsibility, forgiveness and reconciliation' (Gulu Archdiocese 2012). According to the story of the martyrs as told in Catholic accounts, the two young catechists were so determined to spread the Good News to yet unreached parts of Acholi that they departed for this distant destination despite the cautionary words of the Verona priests at Kitgum Mission who had baptized them. The catechists taught reading, writing and catechism to all those who wanted to learn, and held prayers in the hut granted to them by the local sub-chief. A small hand-out about the martyrs that I was given at the commemoration of their beatification in 2012 explains their deaths in the following manner:

> People who opposed the new religion took advantage of socio-political unrest to stop the preaching of the Gospel in Paimol. The two catechists were hounded, threatened, ordered to give up their activities, and finally speared to death.
> (Gulu Archdiocese 2002)

There was indeed socio-political unrest in the region. Resistance to colonialism did not end with the quelling of the Lamogi rebellion discussed above, or the establishment of Gulu and Kitgum towns. I suggest, therefore, in contradiction to the official Catholic interpretation, that the introduction of the new religion must be understood as *part* of the socio-political unrest, rather than

Figure 6. Painting of the martyrs of Paimol on the wall of a parish office at Kitgum Mission. Photo by author.

the latter being seen as a veil beneath which opposition to the new religion could take place. A closer description of the case, and reflections on how the martyrs were commemorated in 2012, provides an illustration of how the colonial and missionary past is re-interpreted in the present.

The death of the catechists Jildo and Daudi occurred amid a widespread revolt against foreign rule and influences in eastern Acholi in which people in the area, who had been harshly hit by an epidemic of smallpox in 1917 and a serious drought-induced famine in 1918, were demanding an end to the enforced labour and taxation imposed by the district governor on top of their other sufferings. Many blamed the drought and the epidemic on the catechists, who were leading people to neglect *tic Acholi*. Anger came to a head when the anointed *rwot*, Lakidi, and his *jago* (sub-chief) Ogwal, who had been leading anti-colonial struggle in the region, were deposed. The British replaced them with a *rwot kalam* – 'chief of the pen' – who was not a hereditary *rwot,* but a warrior from the neighbouring Lira Palwo chiefdom, who had gone to Anglican boarding school and was more amenable to the policies of the colonial government (Cisternino 2004, 475–90; Webster 1969).

In mid-October 1918, revolt broke out. The deposed *Rwot* Lakidi's followers attacked the new *rwot kalam*, while the children of the deposed *jago* attacked the compound in which the Catholic catechists were staying and speared them to death. In nearby villages, foreigners as well as local Catholic converts were killed, and Lakidi's men retreated to the hills. Within a few days, Ugandan troops led by a British colonial officer quenched the rebellion using similar measures employed six years earlier in Lamogi. *Rwot* Lakidi and his *jago* were captured and taken to prison in Kitgum to await colonial justice. One of the rebels was publically hung on Christmas Eve while the rebellion still continued, and once others were caught two more shared his fate, 'with… solemn ceremonial, after receiving Baptism from Fr. Cesar' at Kitgum Mission (Cisternino 2004, 487). According to a letter written by a Verona father, *Rwot* Lakidi told the priest prior to his own execution:

> I was only against the Miri [government] that had unjustly dethroned me, and with one pretext or another stripped me of my livestock and kept me for months imprisoned in Kitgum. I had promised to send my son to the Catholic Mission, and if he did not come it was because the karani [clerk] had told me that the Miri wanted the Chiefs' children to be sent to the Anglicans and not to you. (Letter published in the Verona missionaries' magazine *La Nigrizia* in May 1919, quoted in Cisternino 2004, 487)

According to missionary sources reproduced by Cisternino, local Catholics in Paimol had from the beginning seen Daudi and Okelo as having 'died for the cause of Religion' (Cisternino 2004, 490; Gulu Archdiocese 2012). The Verona missionaries were, however, slow to come to agreement on the matter among themselves. While some of the priests of the time agreed that the two catechists were indeed martyrs, the priests at Kitgum Mission did not collect the bodies from Paimol to give the catechists a Christian burial in the mission graveyard. It was only in the 1990s that steps were taken to call for their beatification, which eventually took place in 2002, since which time the martyrs of Paimol have become a powerful symbol for Acholi Catholics.

Based on the accounts provided by Cisternino, it seems fair to say that the martyrs were killed not only for their faith, but as an outcome of widespread resistance to the disruption of social, political and cultural life that colonial rule was bringing to Acholi. Cisternino argues that rather than resisting the new God and his emissaries, the people resisted the colonial government, and all those who were associated with it: the tribes of *bongo* (European clothing) and *waraga* (paper) (Cisternino 2004, 484). Yet while the correspondence between Verona priests after the event, as well as official documents gathered in support of the beatification, takes careful stock of the political context of the Paimol rebellion, the story most often produced of the martyrs in northern Uganda contemporarily is detached from this broader historical and political context. For instance, at the commemoration of the martyrs in 2012 which I attended in Paimol, not a single reference was made to the political context within which the martyrs were killed: not to the imposition of colonial order, or the forcefully imposed new religion brought by the missionaries, or the killing of the many Paimol rebels at the hands of the colonial government.

During my fieldwork, people who openly expressed (to me) any resentment towards the missionary heritage were few and very far between, and I never heard Catholics speak of the martyrs as part of a story not only of Christian courage and resilience, but also of colonial conquest and religious expansion. While individual clergy were often keen to engage in 'inculturating' Catholic practice to resonate with Acholi custom, the body of the Catholic Church, that is, its members, never expressed to me the kind of postcolonial critique of missionary work that permeates, for instance, Okot p'Bitek's razor-sharp analysis and prose about the missionary enterprise in Acholi (p'Bitek 1971a; p'Bitek 1972). In the Anglican Church, this type of sentiment was even more strikingly absent, including among the clergy.

Those who criticized contemporary Catholic missionaries usually did so on the grounds that they felt the missionaries were partial in their granting of assistance or jobs. Some also said that they saw it as positive that the Comboni missionaries were finally leaving and the church could be in the hands of their own priests. But even in these cases, the sharpest edge of the criticisms was never directed at the churches as such. For the Catholics and Anglicans among whom I did my fieldwork, the church was their church, not the church of the white men: a church to which they belonged, whether firmly or not, not a church imposed upon them by others. Within the Kitgum Catholic or Anglican public, I found no discussion about the violent history of the colonization of Uganda and the role of missionaries in this project. This is also evident in how the story of the martyrs of Paimol is interpreted within the Catholic Church. To corroborate this claim, I return to another retelling of a historical story, and to the interpretation offered by Todd Whitmore of the Verona priest Pellegrini's *Lok pa Acholi Macon* (hereafter '*Acholi macon*'), or 'stories of the Acholi of old times' (Pellegrini 1949). This little booklet remains the most widely available book on Acholi history in the region, and is still used in schools.

Based on his analysis of Verona missionaries' personal diaries and letters, Whitmore holds that following advice to be 'prudent', the missionaries who worked in northern Uganda during the early decades of colonialism opted to remain publicly silent about colonial atrocities that they had witnessed and which they condemned in private (Whitmore 2013, 23). Eventually, Whitmore argues, the Verona missionaries, swayed by their gratitude to the Pax Britannica that had brought respite to their colleagues after the Mahdist War in Sudan, as well as their fear of expulsion in the aftermath of the Second World War, replaced this stance of careful silence with active support for the colonial project. Whitmore bases this claim on his critical reading of Pellegrini's *Acholi Macon*, in which Pellegrini 'rewrote salvation history' (Whitmore 2013, 4). The saviour in this story was the British explorer Samuel Baker, whom the Verona missionaries' founder, Daniel Comboni, had decried in an early letter to his superior as carrying out in Acholi a 'violent invasion', during which 'many thousands of Africans were killed' (Writings of Daniel Comboni, quoted in Cisternino 2004, 80). In contrast, in Pellegrini's *Acholi Macon* Baker is described as having come to Acholi to banish the Arab slave trade, and being received with jubilation by the people in Gulu (Pellegrini 1949, 37–41).[15] I argue that a similar depoliticized reading of the past as that recognized by Whitmore in *Acholi Macon* – a reading in which violence is silenced and a perceived victory of good over evil celebrated – can be seen in prevailing Catholic narratives concerning the Acholi martyrs.

The silencing performed by the Vatican is even more stark than it is in accounts that I heard and read in Uganda. The formal Vatican announcement of the martyrs' beatification (The Holy See 2002) describes how Daudi Okelo, who volunteered to replace the previous catechist of Paimol, is cautioned by a Verona priest about the difficulties he is to face, such as 'frequent in-fights of the local people, instigated also by gangs of raiders and traders of slaves and gold, sporadically visiting the area'. The Vatican directory does acknowledge that there were some 'tribal and political disputes' since 'submission to the British government was often followed by ill-concealed intolerance'. But the specific dynamics of this submission and intolerance are obfuscated, and a vague reference to (non-British) raiders and traders is left to fill the void. In this vein, the disposal of the anointed *rwot* Lakidi and his replacement with a 'chief of the pen', and the outrage it triggered, is described and diluted into the following statement:

> [D]ue to an unhappy decision taken by the District Commissioner, there rose a serious tension. Raiders, Muslim elements and witchdoctors took advantage of the violent situation to get rid of the new religion brought by Daudi.
>
> (The Holy See 2002)

In essence, the Vatican account dismisses the entire project of colonization, in all its dehumanizing violence, as nothing but one individual 'unhappy decision' by one colonial officer. The deposed local chief's sons, who actually speared the catechists, are described as 'raiders, muslim elements and witchdoctors (ibid.)'. In this oversimplified version of what led up to Daudi and Jildo's martyrdom, there is no upheaval of a cosmological balance, no hut tax, no forced labour, no loss of customary authorities – not to mention any culpability of the church as the handmaid of colonization.

While the martyrs' story *could* be interpreted and utilized to advance a postcolonial critique of the violent roots of colonialism in Acholi, and the ways in which missionary work served the violence of empire, it is not. Rather, the martyrs have been transformed into a symbol that simply answers questions that are of immediate relevance to Christians and the Catholic Church in Acholi today. This came out eloquently in the sermon given by a Comboni missionary at the commemoration of the martyrs in 2012. Every year in October the commemoration attracts thousands of pilgrims – and hundreds of merchants selling food, drink and Catholic trinkets to the pilgrims – to the place of their death, which was renamed Wi-Polo (in Heaven) by local residents after their martyrdom. In the sermon, given in English before it was translated into Acholi, the priest first re-told the official story of the martyrs with no reference to the political context in which their deaths took place, after which he analysed it in the light of the Bible readings of the day. Just as the martyrs had come to this remote spot, the pilgrims had, so the bishop declared, come to find meaning, and a sense of worthiness:

> Here we are among simple people. Here where we look at the beauty of the mountains, we see something beautiful... Tomorrow we will again be confronted by the crisis of faith. The crisis of family, the crisis of politics. There is crisis everywhere! There is confusion, corruption, drugs. People have lost the meaning of existence. This is crisis! They are looking, but they don't know for what....
> Here,... these two young men, Jildo and Daudi, lost their lives for the Gospel. We need their courage, we need their faith.
> (Fieldwork notes, 20 October 2012)

The bishop ended his sermon with a request that all pilgrims renew their faith and commitment to the Church, and a call for young people to serve as catechists, as priests, as sisters, as brothers, as dedicated Christians and as the future heads of Christian families.

By pointing out the way in which the violent past is silenced (see also Alava 2019) in this re-telling of the story of the martyrs, I wish to make two points. The first is not that I consider these contemporary readings false, or unimportant. Clearly, the search for meaning, direction and hope is an important one for Catholic Ugandans, and the search for committed staff members and supporters a vital one for the Church as an institution. But I do argue that considering the violence of the missionary-colonial past, the degree to which contemporary forms of political violence have their roots in these historical legacies, and the extent to which religion has been employed to legitimate political violence in both Uganda's distant and more recent history (see the following chapter), the Catholic Church in Acholi – as well as the Anglican – could well draw self-critically on its own key stories to deal with issues that desperately need addressing in contemporary Uganda.

The second point shifts my focus from the bishop who told the martyr's story to the crowd gathered to listen to him. The request the bishop made for young people to commit themselves to the service of the church was essentially the same as that made by the missionaries and the martyred catechists one hundred years ago. Yet it was blatantly clear to those gathered under the heat of the sun in Paimol that everything had changed. Acholi had been transformed in innumerable ways by half a century of colonial rule and a century of Christian mission. However much there was in social, cultural and individual lives that remained untouched by the Christian message in the ways the missionaries would have liked them to be touched, on the hill of Wi-Polo the heaven that touched the pilgrims was not considered an alien imposition or a foreign influence. The joyful ululating of the thousands in the crowd, the radiant smiles on the faces of the young liturgical dancers, the Small Christian Communities and delegations from neighbouring parishes lining up to bring offertory gifts – it was to their martyrs that they sang praise and gave: their God, their Church.

A Comboni missionary once lamented to me that for a hundred years, the Comboni had worked in northern Uganda, yet the Acholi were still scheming against each other, still not getting married in church, still jealous, still fighting each other. Not unlike the Italians, almost 2,000 years after Christianity reached them, I realized in hindsight. In some ways, the elderly missionary's feeling that nothing much had changed was spot-on. Individuals and cultures are indeed resistant to change. But the idea that mission had had no effect on Acholi society was clearly wrong. From the written form of the Acholi language, to the language in which people in contemporary Kitgum talk of development or forgiveness, to the way in which politics and church entwine, even the layout of Kitgum town –

missionary impact in northern Uganda has been immense. Through complex processes of adaptation, resistance and change, mainline churches have become cosmologically, politically, socially and materially embedded.

By delineating the history of missionary Christianity as a (at times reluctant) partner to colonial violence in Acholi, this chapter has provided a historical groundwork for the remainder of this book. As the next chapter moves from the time of colonization towards the postcolonial era and the catastrophic northern Ugandan war, this chapter serves to remind that when Joseph Kony named his rebel group the 'Lord's Resistance Movement/Army' he was referencing not *only* the generic 'Lord' petitioned in the Lord's prayer by Christians the world over. As anthropologists of Christianity highlight, religion in social context is contextual: the LRA's name referenced the God of *Christianity as it was embedded* in Acholi. It is in the light of this historical embeddedness that the book's aim – to interpret the Catholic and Anglican Churches' statements, actions, silences and inactions concerning politics, war and peace – can be pursued.

2

Church, state, war

In late 2019, I returned to Kitgum for a brief visit. It was dark when I stepped out of my car to open the gate of the Catholic mission and I almost walked into Mr Orom, a local politician on his way home from a parish meeting; we hugged with happy exclamations. During our ensuing conversation, he mentioned his ambition for 2021: to get back into power at the district level and displace the Anglican who had defeated him in 2016, thus securing the future of Catholic schools in Kitgum.

This meeting sets the scene for this chapter, one concerned with the interrelations of church, state and war in Uganda. In the previous chapter, I delineated how missionary churches infiltrated and influenced Acholi during the colonial era. Following on its heels, this chapter provides a condensed chronology of Ugandan history from the immediate pre-independence era to the present, with a focus on how churches were involved in, or positioned themselves relative to, political dispute and outright war during these decades. The chapter thus considers how churches' embeddedness, described in the previous chapter as resulting from the colonial era, can be employed to explain the impact of Christian institutions and practices both on the northern Ugandan war and on attempts to create peace in its midst and its aftermath.

Any Anglican or Catholic church, chapel, choir or community is part of a bigger whole: a diocese, an archdiocese, a national synod or episcopal conference. What happens at the 'grassroots' of Christianity, therefore, is never fully detached from events at the churches' national (and even global) level. Starting from these basic premises, this chapter seeks to illuminate the complex ways in which the histories of church, state and war resonate in contemporary attitudes towards politics, and churches' roles in politics, in Kitgum. This casts light on why my encounter with Mr. Orom, whose ambition was to topple his Anglican adversary, deserves pride of place as this chapter's opening anecdote. As one chain in a link of encounters at the gates of Kitgum Mission – my own and those told to me in stories – it encapsulates the themes addressed in this chapter.

The first part of this chapter describes how Ugandan church-affiliated political parties were formed, dissolved, re-established and eventually marginalized under Museveni's reign. It also reflects on church–state relations in contemporary Uganda, and on how patterns of past political configurations continue to mould people's political imaginaries in Kitgum today. The second part returns to 1986, when the Acholi region was shoved out of the story of Uganda's national development and onto a violent and destructive trajectory of its own, analysing how the northern Ugandan war affected the positioning and response of mainline churches through prayer, aid and advocacy. Finally, I argue that the matter of national bodies' largely leaving Acholi churches to fend for themselves reflects broader trends of church–state relations and the militarized ethnopolitics of state-building in Uganda.

On the same evening I bumped into Mr Orom, I received permission from the Mission's parish priest to look through a dusty pile of books and papers that I had discovered in my bedroom cupboard. Amongst the books – mostly in Italian, on subjects like Combonian theology, trauma counselling and the compatibility of African religion with Christianity – I found a pile of *Familia Comboniana* (FC) newsletters from the 1980s and 1990s. I had never before come across these thin, non-descript pamphlets in which snippets of news sent in by Comboni missionaries in different parts of the world are gathered together and distributed monthly to staff and sponsors the world over: at that time, alternating between English and Italian. Reading through the Uganda pages of these newsletters while I sat on the mission floor surrounded by the noises of night-time Kitgum – crickets, barking dogs and the din of Acholi pop from the loudspeakers of nearby bars – I was taken back thirty years in time in a way I had experienced very rarely during my fieldwork. As I describe in Chapter 3, in 2012–13 it seemed to be impossible, unpleasant or simply uninteresting for many of my interlocutors to dwell on memories of the war. In my previous work (Alava 2017b, 2019), I have explicitly chosen not to describe in detail events which people in Kitgum left untold, rather drawing from Taussig (2011) to argue that for the anthropologist, there is at times wisdom in muteness. But the FC newsletters changed this. They opened a window onto the sounds and stories of war, told as the war unfolded. Before I turn to these memories, and to the events that engulfed Acholi after 1986, it is necessary, however, to step back to an even earlier era, when the greater North in Uganda was not yet known for its war, but as the centre of political power.

Fighting for schools and jobs in the run-up to independence (1950–62)

As the previous chapter showed, religion, politics and ethnicity were intricately enmeshed with one another in colonial Uganda, in ways that impacted on the political institutions and patterns of thought that emerged as the country prepared for independence from Britain. One of the central contentions during this time was how relations between the state and churches should be arranged, and the place that church-founded schools would have in the independent nation (Hansen 1984). Schools started by Anglican and Catholic missionaries were key sites of both political education and political mobilization, and thereby of interest to all parties wishing to weigh in on the country's political future. The leaders of most early pre-independence political parties were from Anglican-founded schools and, by 1960, these parties merged to form the Uganda People's Congress (UPC). The UPC developed a strong nationalist stance, lobbying for limitations on the power of colonially endorsed chiefs, and independence from missionary-established churches.[1] Both demands were a cause for concern for the Catholic Church, as were the UPC's purported communist and atheist leanings. Catholics channelled this concern into support for the establishment of the Democratic Party (DP), which built on a model of European Christian Democracy (Gingyera-Pinycwa 1976; Ward 2005). Although both the DP and the UPC sought to portray themselves as representing all Ugandans, by the time of independence in 1962, the DP was popularly known as Dini ya Papa[2] (religion of the Pope), and the Uganda People's Congress (UPC) as the United Anglicans of Canterbury (Ward 2005, 112; Welbourn 1965, 18–20).

In Acholi, Catholic concerns were voiced in two publications by the Verona missionaries: in 1952 the bi-monthly Luo-language (thus legible for Acholis as well as in neighbouring Lango) *Lobo Mewa* ('Our Land') had a circulation of 12,000, while the monthly English-language *Leadership* magazine had a circulation of 8,000 (Gingyera-Pinycwa 1976, 175). Both were distributed mainly through schools, whence they spread to teachers' and students' villages. Catholic schools were fundamental to the missionaries' aim of nurturing the Acholi towards what they perceived as spiritual, moral and political maturity, and the departure of the colonial authorities, with whom the Verona missionaries had negotiated in the past, would render political parties the key to their continued control. Generating support for a loyally Catholic DP was thus essential. The church's institutional concerns coincided with those of lay Catholics, who were growing restless due to their experience of Anglican domination. A 1958 issue of *Lobo Mewa* articulated this clearly:

> The dispute concerning religion in Uganda is not over doctrinal differences but about JOBS AND SCHOLARSHIP. The Catholics feel aggrieved and wonder why such important posts like that of county chiefs, or subcountry chief, and others are held by Anglicans.
> (Quoted in Gingyera-Pinycwa 1976, 52; capitalized in original)

In Kassimir's words, the DP's 'raison d'être was far more for the social mobility of lay Catholics than the promotion of a Christian world view or the protection of church privileges' (1998, 64). While Catholics argued that Anglicans had long had preferential access to important jobs because of systemic colonial government practice, Anglicans largely claimed that their success was the outcome of a specific mentality instilled in them by their education. Young Anglicans, the argument ran, were being coached in personal initiative and leadership, as opposed to the docility and obedience typical of a Catholic education (for a preferentiality argument, see Karugire 1980, 135–6; for a mentality argument, see Welbourn 1965, 9–10, 13–15).

Claims about denominational abilities and preferential treatment intertwined with issues of ethnicity and locality. As Uganda prepared to gain independence from its colonizer, divisions between Ugandans were becoming increasing entrenched, not only in terms of religious difference, but through the politicization of ethnic boundaries manipulated by colonial policy (Atkinson 2010; Karugire 1996; Laruni 2015; Mamdani 1996). The divisions between the north and the south of the country, which were to provide fuel for bitter political conflict for years to come, were constructed both through ethnically stereotyping colonial rhetoric and the unequal allocation of colonial investment. Northerners like the Acholi and the Langi – who were on average taller than their southern and western counterparts, and who had been branded in colonial literature as 'warlike' – were seen as a suitable reserve for military recruitment (Postlethwaite 1947, 71), so that by the 1960s, 60 per cent of the national army were from Acholi (Omara-Otunnu 1987). Conversely, the bulk of colonial investments in economic development and education targeted Buganda, where – following decades of interaction – the British established their colonial capitol long before extending colonial rule to northern Uganda. Areas far from the capital such as Acholi, particularly east Acholi (including Kitgum), were under-served and under-developed (Ocitti 1966). The combination of economic sidelining and the military experience many northerners gained through their service in the King's African Rifles led to growing desires for political influence in the northern region (Leys 1967, 17–18).

Exactly who ended up in league with whom was far from clear-cut: alongside ethnicity and region, political allegiances were heavily influenced by religion.[3] For instance, many northerners turned to the UPC in hopes that its leader, Milton Obote from Lango, would bridge the gap between the north and the more developed south (Atkinson 2010, 8). Yet the UPC was also firmly associated with the Anglican Church.[4] The DP – in some ways an obvious political choice for church-educated Catholic northerners – was made less appealing by the fact that the party's leader was Benedicto Kiwanuka, a Muganda (for a detailed analysis of Kiwanuka's significance for Uganda, see Earle and Carney 2021). At the same time, many Anglican Baganda supported the Bugandan nationalist party, Kabaka Yekka (KY), which had a more Anglican orientation than the DP, despite the fact that its leader was from the same region.

Ethnicity, locality and religion played out at the local level throughout Uganda, including in Acholi. Both colonial and missionary investments had centred on western Acholi and particularly Gulu – partly because the colonial government had granted the *rwot* of the largest pre-colonial Acholi chiefdom, Payira, the title of paramount chief (Komujuni 2019; Paine 2014), exacerbating pre-existing differences between Acholi's eastern and western halves. Still, as Leys (1967) notes, while certain villages and towns were predominantly DP or UPC, including the Verona and DP stronghold of Kalongo, east of Kitgum, the more common pattern was for party and religious allegiances to cut across villages, clans and families, as reflected in the Acholi nickname for 'religion': *apokapoka*, division (Finnström 2008, 246). Formal party politics under the flag of independent Uganda would entrench – and complicate – these divisions even further.

Religion and troubled nation-building (1962–86)

Uganda gained full independence on 9 October 1962 with the Anglican Milton Obote, from Acholi's neighbour, Lango, as its prime minister. A year earlier, the DP had won the most seats at Uganda's first Constitutional Conference, making Benedicto Kiwanuka prime minister of the interim National Assembly. The defeat of the Catholic-leaning DP by an alliance of two Anglican-leaning parties, the UPC and KY, entrenched religious division as a fundamental aspect of politics in the newly independent nation. While the common narrative highlights religion as division in newly independent Uganda, church historian Jay Carney (2017) importantly notes that churches were also part of the project of nation-building: they too were seeking to establish themselves as national institutions. Furthermore, church leaders in 1960s Uganda were heavily influenced by a deepening of ecumenical relations throughout the region, epitomized in the 1963 establishment of the All Africa Council of Churches (ibid., 773). In Carney's words, the 1960s saw Ugandan churches advocating for 'politically quiescent social development' (ibid. 767), particularly through the newly formed Uganda Joint Christian Council (UJCC). Obote's decision to nationalize church-founded schools against the wishes of the UJCC left many Catholics bitter, and increasing numbers of members of both churches grew increasingly disillusioned, as ethnic and regional divisions grew and Obote became staunchly identified as a 'northern' president (Ward 2005). Regional allegiance among 'northerners' was itself tenuous, however, and divisions both within and between neighbouring groups were manipulated to garner political support (Laruni 2015).

In 1971, dissatisfaction with Obote's increasingly authoritarian leadership erupted in a military coup led by General Idi Amin (Lofchie 1972). Amin, a Kakwa from West Nile, was the first and, to date, the only Muslim to have headed Uganda. Initially, Amin sought to court the favour of religious leaders, many of whom were optimistic that Amin would be an improvement after Obote's devout anti-church stance. Bishops from northern regions like Acholi, which bore the brunt of Amin's reprisal against the people who had been Obote's military backbone, were unimpressed. Over years of increasingly erratic and abusive rule that ruined Uganda's economy, Amin sought to provoke divisions within church bodies, yet religious leaders also collaborated with each other to lobby for change: through regular private interactions with the president, and ultimately, increasing public reproach (Carney 2017). This came to a head in February 1977, when Amin's troops ransacked the home of the Anglican Archbishop Janani Luwum, an Acholi from Mucwini near Kitgum (see Chapter 7), claiming to discover guns and a purported plan to kill Amin and reinstate Obote – the truth behind the accusations is debated up till today (Carney 2017; Niringiye 2016; Olara Otunnu 2020; Ward 2005). Eleven days later, Luwum was detained and murdered in what was thinly disguised as a traffic accident, together with his fellow Acholi, the former Inspector General of Police Erinayo Oryema, and the Minister of the Interior Charles Ofumbi, from the likewise Luo-speaking Jopadhola group (Kaufman 1977).

In 1979, Amin was ousted in a multi-force attack from neighbouring Tanzania, led by Obote's Uganda National Liberation Army (UNLA). In the two chaotic years that followed, wanton violence against civilians and political opponents by different factions almost equalled the worst of the Amin years. Obote returned to formal presidency in 1980 through a rigged election that should have in fact been won by the DP (Kasfir 1998, 49). In the midst of the chaos, a group of Ugandans allied with Rwandan refugees calling itself the National Resistance Army (NRA) launched a rebellion known as the Bush War against Obote's UNLA. Its leader was Yoweri Museveni, a Munyankole from western Uganda, who had fallen out with both the UPC and the DP, and unsuccessfully contested the presidency in the 1980 elections. Museveni established national resistance councils to win over the hearts and minds of civilians (Museveni 1997), and blamed the largest group of UNLA – the Acholi – for their use of brutal anti-insurgency tactics: some sources put the death toll in the region hardest-hit by the fighting, Luwero, as high as 300,000 (Mutibwa 1996), with the NRM also appearing to have committed many atrocities, sometimes masquerading as UNLA (Atkinson 2010). The churches' 'prophetic presence', as Carney (2017, 788–92) characterizes their advocacy for peace and stability in the tumultuous years between 1979 and 1985, ultimately faded as the Bush War increasingly divided the country, and clergy, into two sides. As the war waged on, Obote's troops became increasingly disgruntled and, in 1985, an Acholi UNLA officer, Tito Okello, ousted Obote. Okello invited the numerous armed groups operating in Uganda at the time to peace talks in Nairobi. A peace agreement was signed in December 1985 but never implemented, and a month later, in January 1986, Museveni overran Okello and marched into Kampala, where he has held power ever since.

The extremity of violence during these first post-independence decades to some extent brought the historically antagonistic churches closer to each other (Ward 1991). Yet the twists and turns of political power, and the waves of ethnically targeted state violence during the rules of Obote, Amin, Obote again, and later Museveni, have put national churches in an awkward situation, since the churches are divided by the same ethnic alliances that have divided the regimes of presidents from their opponents. Through much of the tumultuous early period of Uganda's independence, these divisions, and churches material and political dependence on the state, led them to play a circumscribed and cautious political role. While preferential treatment by the ruling power of one church could trigger the animosity of another, the same was also true within churches: statements of individual religious leaders were easily framed as ethnically motivated, leading to a kind of internal handicap that often kept churches from speaking out strongly on sensitive issues (Ward 2005).

For instance, as Catholic theologians Waliggo, Katongole and Ssettuuma (2013) show, the Ugandan Catholic hierarchy did not issue a single pastoral letter between 1962 and 1979, when Amin was overthrown. Under Amin, Churches were effectively scared into silence by the killing of the Church of Uganda's archbishop. Yet even during this public silence, churches' grassroots activities, such as arranging burials for prominent victims of violence, led them to be 'cast in the role of the opposition' (Pirouet 1980, 21). In an important corrective of the much-repeated narrative of churches' divisionary tendencies, Carney (2017) highlights that *despite* the many internal and external pressures, churches have at various times found common ground, and used it to speak out forcefully on contentious political issues, and argues that in many situations, silence can be a sign of prudence, patience, non-violence or resistance (ibid., 795). While I to an extent agree, and have made similar arguments elsewhere (Alava 2019), I believe it important to acknowledge the particular location from which such an assessment is made. For those suffering the brunt of state terror, churches' silence about that terror may appear less as virtue, and more as neglect.

Remnants of past patterns in the present

Before turning to an analysis of the ways in which dynamics of politics and religion have changed under Museveni and the NRM, this section stops to consider how, despite the considerable shifts in Uganda's political landscape, old patterns of division – between east and west Acholi, and between Catholics and Anglicans – continue to appear in discussions of politics and church politics in Kitgum.

The division between 'upper' (higher and drier) eastern and 'lower' western Acholi (see Finnström 2008, 33) continues to have contemporary relevance within churches today. The administrative centre of Catholic power in Acholi is at the seat of the archdiocese in Gulu, which also hosts the minor and major Catholic seminaries, major Catholic schools, and the head of the Catholic Church's development arm, Caritas. That said, many notable Catholic leaders are from eastern Acholi, and have received substantial career support from Comboni missionaries. Through their Comboni connections, some of these priests have been able to foster ties to benefactors abroad, prompting grumbling about preferential treatment among younger priests, particularly those from west Acholi. Eastern Acholi Catholics' aspirations for a separate Kitgum diocese to be splintered off as an independent diocese within the broader Archdiocese of Gulu, also reflect this east–west division. So far, these plans have stalled, which some of my acquaintances in Kitgum attribute to the purported greed of western Acholi. In the Anglican Church of Uganda, this split has already occurred, as Kitgum and Gulu are separate dioceses.

A second division is that between the Catholics and the Anglicans. The issues that pitted Catholics and Anglicans against each other in the run-up to Independence – schools and jobs – continue to sour relations. I encountered countless young and old people – both Catholics and Anglicans – who, when asked about religion and politics, raised concern over access to government jobs and positions of political authority. Whereas Catholics commonly claim that anti-Catholic attitudes are systematically engrained within all governance structures in Uganda, Anglicans tend to assert more specifically that they do not stand a chance of getting jobs whenever particular offices are held by a Catholic. The position of the education officer seems particularly vital, since, as I discuss in more detail below, an education officer is said to be able not only to give and take jobs, but to influence the designation of schools' founding bodies, and even to manipulate records so that a school established by one church can be claimed by the other. During my research, I have heard detailed accounts of such cases and claims from representatives of both mainline churches.

Anglican-Catholic animosities bind local and national debates together. Many Catholics with whom I have spoken in Kitgum have referred to the nominally Anglican Obote becoming independent Uganda's first prime minister over the Catholic DP's Kiwanuka, and the fact that Uganda has never had a Catholic president, as proof of anti-Catholicism at the heart of Uganda's political system. Anglican research participants, on the other hand, refer to Catholics' failure to make it to presidency to illustrate how Anglicans are more willing and able to adopt positions of authority. Such stereotypes, which Welbourn (1965) described as common in the 1960s, have remained prevalent. Some people willingly acknowledge they are stereotypes, but others assert the purportedly greater success of Anglicans in politics and procuring jobs reflects genuine differences in the way in which students are brought up in church schools, churches and Anglican/Catholic homes.

Stereotypical perceptions by Anglicans and Catholics of each other have at times meshed with broader speculations pertaining to the division between the two mainline churches. Many of my interlocutors, for instance, suspected that the British, who had always supported Anglican over Catholic missionaries, had

had a hand in replacing Kiwanuka with Obote in the second of the 1962 elections. A notable number of Catholics, including many young ones, claimed that some kind of bigger geopolitical game must still be in play, for, as the argument went, how else could one explain that a Catholic had never become president despite Catholics always being in the majority? Similar conspiracy speculations lingered among Anglicans. One highly educated elderly Anglican man, for instance, furnished me with copious details purporting to prove that the Comboni missionaries' actions in contemporary Kitgum, such as the building of new chapels, were all part of a bigger plot whereby the Catholic Church, with Italy behind it, was preparing to colonize Uganda. I was never presented with any proof of this, nor for the claims over discrimination on the grounds of religious affiliation at the local district level; nor was I able to ascertain whether there was any truth to them. Yet even if they simply circulate so densely as to appear true, I believe they speak of the way in which the historical divide between Catholics and Anglicans has continued to resonate in Ugandan politics, even when the parameters of the game have undergone two dramatic shifts.

The first of these relates to the shift in church–state relations under the NRM regime: currently, the UPC and the DP, which embodied the church–party unions that coloured Ugandan politics for decades, have become completely marginal. In the 2021 elections, the DP and UPC both won only 9 out of 336 parliamentary seats, that being 6 less and 3 more than in the 2016 elections. Although the NRM is considered to lean more towards Museveni's own Anglican Church, where his roots are in the Balokole-revival (see Ward and Wild-Wood 2012), and the Pentecostal churches to which his family members have close ties (See Valois 2014, Chapter 7), the NRM is not considered a 'church party' and never has been.

The second shift of importance concerns demographics: political debates framed around the Anglican–Catholic divide are increasingly debates among the older, outgoing generations of politically active citizens. Political analyses of a younger generation are made on different grounds. Every time Uganda goes to vote, the proportion of voters who have experienced, or have memory of, politics prior to the NRM grows smaller; the 'Museveni babies' now make up 78 per cent of the population (see Reuss and Titeca 2017). For many of these young people, the UPC and DP are ancient history; furthermore, many of them are drawn to Pentecostal churches, leaving the Anglican and Catholic churches in which they may have been baptized as children. The discussion I had with a highly devoted Anglican man in his forties reflects this shift. Knowing the general theme of my study, he first spent a long time describing the UPC–DP division in Uganda's history. Once he had concluded, I asked him to explain the present, adding, 'If the DP were Catholic and the UPC were Anglican, what is the NRM?' He answered, 'They are the Pentecostals. And some Anglicans, and all those Catholics who love their stomach more than they do even their country.' It is to changes in the national political arena upon the NRM's coming to power to which we now turn.

Patronage, sidelining and threats: Churches under Museveni (1986–2020)

For decades, the division between Catholics and Anglicans played a huge part in Uganda's politics. In this section, I discuss the transition to NRM rule in Uganda, and the shift it signalled for church–state relations at a largely national level; the different view of the world from Acholi will be the focus of the following section.

One of the outspoken goals of Museveni's National Resistance Army, and the subsequent 'no-party movement regime' of the NRM, was to promote peace by countering ethnic and religious divisions in the country. Indeed, for a long time the Movement system was lauded for just that, both by its supporters in Uganda and by many international donors and political analysts (Carbone 2008; Hauser 1999; Kasfir 1998; Mwenda and Tangri 2005). Years of widespread, state-perpetrated violence under Amin and the second Obote regime had been characterized by increasingly politicized ethnicity. Museveni's rhetorical insistence on breaking down divisions and building a new political system for Uganda seemed a turn for the better, yet, as I will show, Museveni's rhetoric of unity hid a grim reality in the country's north and east. Before looking at that, however, a few thoughts on how Museveni's regime has affected the religious field. Three interrelated aspects are worth highlighting.

First of all, Museveni's 'no-party movement regime' replaced the earlier largely religion-defined party political set up, in which Catholics and Anglicans were on opposite sides of the party line. By the time parties were again allowed, after a referendum in 2005, the DP and the UPC came back considerably weakened. By this point, many Catholic and Anglican politicians had spent years gaining influence within the NRM system, and had become staunch supporters of the Movement. Hence, it was not from the old league of UPC and DP politicians that the most serious opposition to the NRM arose, but from within the ranks of the NRM itself. This became clear when the Forum for Democratic Change took a leading role in Uganda's political opposition under the leadership of Museveni's former ally, Kizza Besigye.

Second, since Museveni's coming to power, with the expansion of religious freedom in Uganda that followed, PC churches have proliferated and grown.[5] These provide the older churches with stiff competition in the religious market, thus altering the tone of political debate in the country and leading to the birth of what Bompani and Brown (2014) refer to as a 'Pentecostalised public sphere'. This is most clearly evident in public outcries over sexual morality: churches and individual clerics may become the focus of public scorn if they do not echo the condemnatory tones of the fiercest Christian activists (Alava 2017a).

Third, the NRM decades have shown an evolving choreography of distance and closeness between the state and institutional churches. The dismantling of political parties under the 'no-party movement system' initially kept both the older churches at arm's length from State House (Gifford 1998; Ward 2005). With time, the NRM stance on churches softened until 'gradually both Museveni and the Movement have recognized that the churches are such a prominent part of the fabric of Ugandan life that they cannot be ignored or sidelined' (Ward 2005, 116). Ward also notes that Museveni's takeover resulted in a notable improvement for Catholics who, while adamant supporters of the return of multiparty politics during the 'no-party movement system', still had more political space under the NRM than they had ever had under the UPC (see also Twesigye 2010, 210–13). With Museveni in power, those clerics who have not openly opposed the government have found it relatively easy to operate without intervention or restraint, and those with large followings have also attracted state funding and presidential visits (Alava and Ssentongo 2016). This trend within churches reflects Museveni's successful use of patronage to secure support, including in former opposition strongholds, such as Acholi (Atkinson 2018).

In the past decade, politicians have often reminded religious leaders not to interfere with politics, while, somewhat paradoxically, religious leaders inclined towards the NRM have been appointed by the president to political positions of power.[6] The tone of these reminders recalls the violence that underpins political imaginaries in Museveni's Uganda, as evidenced in a striking speech the president gave in 2010 at a celebration of the restoration of the Bunyoro kingdom (Ekitibwa Kya Buganda 2010; Ssekika 2010; *The Observer* 2010). Museveni began by explaining that the NRM had restored traditional kingdoms because the chiefs had now realized that leadership was not only passed from father to child; one could also gain power through elections. Given that Museveni came to power through the gun, and that his electoral victories have repeatedly been bolstered by security forces (see, for instance, Titeca and Onyango 2012), the statement was ironic. Museveni continued:

You Banyoro call it *olubimbi*. When people are in the garden digging, each one uses a hoe to till their portion (*olubimbi*). There will be no problem if each concentrates on their portion. Now, if you suddenly jump into my *lubimbi*, I [might] cut your head and there would be no case [to answer]. When they (authorities) come to investigate, they will ask: 'How was his head cut?' [The answer will be], 'He crossed from his *lubimbi* to mine and I wasn't seeing him. I was digging and he suddenly appeared from there.' Now, mature people who know what to do can handle this matter well. (*The Observer* 2010)

The president then explained why, although he was a Christian, it was not his place to baptize anyone. When he went to church, he had only to remain humbly silent and allow the officiating priest to place the bread in his mouth at communion. Finally, the president thanked those traditional leaders who had not transgressed the boundaries of their *lubimbi*. This was important, because 'the problems we had in the past, in the 1960s, resulted from people moving from their lubimbi' (ibid.).

Already almost a decade earlier, Museveni had made a similar comment about the relationship of churches and the state, to which a Catholic priest responded:

Our political leaders are so inconsistent on issues between Church and State that it is impossible to rely on them. For them the Church is right when its leaders support them but the moment the Church speaks out in disagreement, then it is meddling into politics. It is then told to stay out and concentrate on spiritual affairs.

(Kanyike 2003)

Kanyike's description encapsulates state–church relations in Museveni's Uganda to date. As I have argued with Jimmy Spire Ssentongo (Alava and Ssentongo 2016), the state has steered churches into silence and acquiescence through the gift of cars and other donations to religious leaders.[7] These gifts are made more efficacious by being reinforced with threats, such as that presented in the president's speech quoted above: those reaching out from their own religious *lubimbi* to the *lubimbi* of politics face the threat of accidental decapitation. Physical force and its threat were particularly familiar to religious leaders in Acholi through the years of chaos and war that ensued upon Museveni's capture of state power. And, in facing that chaos and conflict, Acholi clerics told me, they felt abandoned.

One Catholic priest specifically recalled his non-Acholi clerical colleagues declaring to his face, at a public gathering, that the war in the north was strictly a northern problem, on which the Catholic Church as a national body had no reason to take a stand. Yet the sources I have had access to, and the claims I have heard during my fieldwork, give a very mixed picture of the extent to which, and the time at which, national churches responded to the war. Three non-Acholi Catholic scholars (Waliggo, Katongole, and Ssettuuma 2013) claim that the pastoral letter of 1999, written to celebrate the 50th anniversary of the Declaration of Human Rights, was the first to do so. Yet it does so very indirectly: without detailing the violence it is referring to, or the parties responsible for that violence, the letter calls all parties to commit to peace, expresses a depoliticized solidarity with those suffering from violence, and asks for Christians to show generosity to the victims through donations (Uganda Episcopal Conference 1999). Ward (2001, 208) notes that in 1996 Catholic Cardinal Wamala pleaded that Kony (not Museveni) stop the violence, but it was only in 2004 – sixteen years after the war began – that the Catholic hierarchy issued a clearly phrased pastoral letter on the matter (Uganda Episcopal Conference 2004). How long it took for such pastoral letters to be penned is striking, considering that the Church's highest authority – Pope John Paul II – had visited Gulu in 1993. Yet a dossier of documents I received from a Comboni priest (see below) just before finishing this book suggests that it is a mistake to focus on pastoral letters alone. A 'Statement to the press by the chairman of the Uganda Episcopal Conference', dated 15 June 1991, which is written following a national bishop's meeting in which the situation in northern and north-eastern Uganda was discussed, and signed by archbishop Wamala, states:

> Rebel activities and civil war always bring about difficult human situations to which it is not at all easy to find the right solutions. Notwithstanding all the sympathy they may have for those who are faced with such problems, the Bishops consider it their duty to voice their concerns at the flagrant violations of human rights perpetrated in the course of trying to solve them. Combatants on the Government side as well as on the side of the rebels are guilty of them. It must be said very clearly... that acts of terrorism committed by lawless people can never be justification for a Government and its armed forces to commit similar acts in retaliation.
>
> (Wamala 1991; included in Donohue 1991)

This unequivocal condemnation of NRA's violence by Uganda's Catholic bishops contrasts strikingly with the accounts I have heard, repeatedly over the years, about the national churches' failure to voice their concerns over the war. This is not to say that the experiences of Acholi clergy of having been left to fend for themselves are mistaken. But the document – which I myself was stunned to read, since it went completely against the grain of what I had thought I knew – also speaks volumes to how simplifying narratives take hold in the midst of immense complexity. A similar complexity characterized Anglican responses.

Whereas Anglican leaders *within* northern Uganda took an active role in political advocacy over the war (see also Taylor 2005) – particularly as part of the Acholi Religious Leader's Peace Initiative (ARLPI) (see Chapter 6) – outside of Acholi the Church of Uganda remained noncommittal on the subject. A rare exception was a conference of northern CoU bishops in 1998, which was attended by the bishop of Luwero Diocese (Ward 2001, 208–9). The retired Anglican bishop, Zac Niringiye, has noted that, following Archbishop Luwum's death, the Church of Uganda as a national body remained equally silent about brutal anti-Acholi violence during Amin's reign of terror (Niringiye 2017). The CoU's reluctance to take a stand reflects a more general tendency as, in comparison to the Catholic Church, it has 'exert[ed] a more discrete, behind the scenes, influence in public affairs, reflecting both their traditional sense of being part and parcel of the institutions of the state, and their continued consciousness of the fragility of their own unity on political issues' (Ward 2005, 116). While, for the first two decades of the NRM regime, bishops and church leaders in Kampala were busy navigating the political situation so as to maximize institutional survival, their members and staff in Acholi were grappling to survive.

War crashes down on northern Uganda

Father Marcus led me by the hand to meet a young man who had no hand. It was slashed off during the war, the priest told me. 'These are the ones whose stories you need to hear.' The young man's stare did not invite questioning, so I left his story to him, and we stepped away.

(Fieldwork notes, 2012)

On the day I wrote these notes, it was Father Marcus himself whom I had wanted to ask about his work during the war. But, rather than embarking on his own tales, he took me to the young man and, before hurrying off in an evasive manner to some important business, sighed, 'It was a confusing time. Difficult to analyse.' For years, these words seemed to be all I could, or wanted, to write about the time of the northern Ugandan war (Alava 2019). Reading the FC newsletters reminded me why: it *was* a confusing time, difficult to analyse.

Retrospective accounts of the northern Ugandan war recreate timelines, pick out themes and provide their readers with much-needed overviews. Yet such overviews, from a bird's eye perspective with the clarity of hindsight, do not always make clear how in the midst of things, there was no timeline, no knowledge of how tomorrow would be, there was little other theme than chaos, and no birds-eye perch from which to grasp the big picture.

So far, I have used wide brushstrokes to delineate some patterns of church–state relations during Uganda's first decades of independence and how they continue to influence contemporary Kitgum. Museveni's coup d'état, however, led Uganda onto two parallel trajectories: that of increasing stability, peace and development in south and central Uganda, and war and chaos in much of the north and the east (Shaw and Mbabazi 2007). Yet as I will discuss at length in Chapter 3, I heard fairly few stories about the war during my fieldwork in 2012–13, partly because I chose not to ask for them, which is why here, I build to such a large degree on the Comboni newsletters.[8]

It is impossible to tell in a short space the whole story of a war that was embroiled in complex local, regional and global processes. Even a timeline of the war, which evolved through cycles of alternatingly intense fighting, peace negotiations, internal displacement and humanitarian intervention, is difficult to establish. Instead of attempting either of these approaches, I follow three aims in the remainder of this chapter. First, I focus on the early years of the war (roughly 1986–92) as recorded in the FC newsletters, to describe how churches sought to position themselves vis-à-vis different warring parties and their claims to religious authority. Due to the centrality of religious revival to the rebel movements operating in Acholi at the time, this period deserves particular attention, and through it, themes emerge that are relevant for the entire war period.

Second, I draw on sources from various periods of the war to describe how churches sought to respond to it – through aid, prayer, and at a later stage, advocacy – and how differently the Anglican and Catholic Churches were placed, both politically and financially, in their attempts to do so. Set against the preceding account of church-state relations at a national level, my unraveling of the dynamics of churches' public engagement in war-time Acholi speaks to the increasingly ethnopolitical and militarized core of Museveni's Uganda.

A war over souls, spirits and survival: The early years of war in Acholi

Museveni's Bush War against his opponents came to a formal end with the capture of Kampala in January 1986, but rather than conflict ending, it shifted. The FC of March 1986 (FC 1986 # 407) acknowledges the NRA's capture of Kampala, noting that numerous mission stations in the north had been looted, although not by whom. In April (FC 1986, # 408), the newsletter states that Acholi-Bur and Pakwach in Acholi were 'liberated' (ibid.) by the NRA and describes a wildly cheering crowd in Kampala welcoming the president to the national celebration of the Uganda Martyrs in Namugongo: 'After the bloody episodes of the civil war, the peace and security now enjoyed by the country was emphasised and seen by all as a special gift of grace granted though the intercession of the Uganda martyrs' (FC 1986, # 414).[9] But the tone of the letters quickly changes from celebratory to deeply concerned.

While peace seemed to descend in Kampala, armed groups were looting and attacking various parishes in Acholi in 'premeditated and cold-blooded attacks against the goods and people of the Church, things never seen before in this area and which are becoming very worrying' (FC 1986, # 415, 10). A report published in December (FC 1986, # 417) provides an example of the general tone of the newsletters, and of what life was like amid what was to become a twenty-year war:

> The last months were marked by severe disorders which hit, in particular, the area of Kitgum, Nam-Okora and Patongo, causing casualties, wounded, looting and destruction of villages. There has also been a real outburst of terrorism recently in Kalongo and vicinity. In general these disorders are caused by violent confrontation between detachments of ex-soldiers and those of the new army. On the morning of November 2 [1986], a true hurricane of violence broke out around the Kalongo mission... The situation became calm again at about 11 o'clock and only then was it possible to celebrate, in the presence of a small number of people, the Holy Mass for the dead. The next day a first count was made of what had happened: the casualties were in the tens, the wounded some hundred.

The newsletter then recounts details that speak of the extent of the Catholic Church's service delivery in the region:

> The Kalongo hospital was relatively spared, also because a group of Christians had engaged in its defence. All public means of transport disappeared, resulting

in serious difficulties for the sick who can no longer be brought to the hospital. Some of them are known to have died in their villages. The hospital's activity in 1985 was: 119,296 medical examinations; 6.889 patients hospitalized; 1,001 operations; 6,929 cases of assistance in pregnancy; 1,760 deliveries; 480 blood transfusions. The people are left with a sense of fear and insecurity. There are rumours about clashes, with casualties and wounded, in the district of Kitgum and elsewhere... However, one has the impression that things are slowly returning to normal.

(FC 1986, # 417)

The impression was to prove false. In February 1987, government soldiers forcefully evacuated all Comboni communities to the east of Kitgum, citing 'insecurity of the region, where the people refuse to submit to the government' as the formal reason (FC 1987, # 420). Even at the few missions that were allowed to remain open, priests were forbidden to travel to rural areas to administer sacraments (FC 1987, # 422). The real reason for these limitations was likely a desire on the part of the NRA to prevent missionary hospitals from attending to wounded rebels, as well as limiting the numerous missionaries, almost all foreign nationals, from witnessing what was going on across Acholi. Throughout the 1970s and 1980s, there were well over one hundred Comboni missionaries working in Gulu diocese, and the number dropped below one hundred only in the 1990s.[10]

What was going on was, in Adam Branch's words, NRA's 'counter-insurgency without the insurgency' (Branch 2003, 10). The Comboni newsletters recount a number of NRA brutalities, among them an attack in Nam-Okora in 1986 where, as Akullo and Ogora (2014) have detailed, the NRA's 35th Battalion killed seventy-one people. The Comboni priest of the local parish, who lived at Kitgum Mission at the time of my fieldwork, was only able to organize the gathering of the victims' remains two months later, burying them in a mass grave with the assistance of an Anglican reverend (ibid.). FC newsletters also provide detailed accounts of NRA involvement in cattle raids across the greater North (see, e.g., FC 1988, # 429). In the wake of the army-facilitated raids, which ripped away the social and economic backbone of a cattle-rearing, mixed-farming people, rebels had an easy time garnering the support of a population, including numerous disenfranchised former soldiers, among whom '[p]overty, humiliation, deep resentment and mistrust [were] growing' (ibid., 14).

The NRA brutalities (see Dolan 2000 for accounts from Acholi survivors) spurred complex waves of rebellion. Large numbers of Obote's former UNLA soldiers regrouped in Sudan to form the UPDA (Uganda People's Defence Army), and took a strictly military approach to fighting Museveni. Alongside them, however, other groups emerged under the spiritual leadership of erstwhile civilians, which also attracted former UNLA soldiers. Over the course of the war, these groups split and merged, at times collaborating with one another, at other times fighting both the national army and each other. During 1988 alone, Comboni newsletters mention attacks in different parts of Acholi by Alice Lakwena's (*Lakwena* being the Acholi word for 'Messenger') Holy Spirit Movement; her father Severino Lukwoya's Rubanga Won ('Our Father'); and Joseph Kony's group, which is referred to first as Lakwena II and later as the Holy Spirit Movement. Additional attacks and incidents of violence are attributed to cattle raiders from Karamoja, unidentified smaller groups of armed robbers and the new national army, Museveni's NRA.

Later research has provided detailed information on government atrocities, and detailed the lineages of the various groups that emerged in Acholi to counter government violence (Atkinson 2010; Behrend 1999; Branch 2003; Lamwaka 2016; Schulz 2020). What the newsletters evoke, however, was the utter chaos and confusion that characterized much of this early phase of the war (see also Dolan 2000). A further layer of complexity was added by the fact that the groups of Alice Lakwena, Severino Lukwoya and Joseph Kony all incorporated religious elements. Nuanced analyses of the cosmological, spiritual and ritualistic elements of the rebellions have been provided elsewhere, and I will not repeat them in detail.[11] What is important to note is that the rebels' claims to religious authority put the churches on the spot: they had to take a stand on what the rebels were teaching their parishioners about spirits – the Holy Spirit in particular – God, creation and the powers of nature.

Part of the purported aim of Alice Lakwena, Severino Lukwoya and Joseph Kony was to purify Acholi of *cen;* the spiritual pollution perceived to have first tarnished Acholi soldiers during the Bush War in Luwero and then affected the entire Acholi people upon the soldiers' return. Among the spirits that were to lead the rebels in this purification were the (Christian) Holy Spirit, but also at various times, a deceased Comboni missionary and Archbishop Janani Luwum, an Anglican. Christian symbols and practices – hymns, prayers, Bible reading, candles and crosses – were also incorporated into the movements, with the rebel leaders drawing from their personal archives. Severino Lukwoya had served as a Catechist of the Church of Uganda, his daughter Alice Lakwena converted to Catholicism as an adult and Kony had been an altar servant in the Catholic Church (Allen 1991; Behrend 1999, 132). Kony's Lord's Resistance Movement/

Army (which was earlier named the Holy Spirit Movement and the Uganda People's Democratic Christian Army), Lakwena's Holy Spirit Mobile Forces (HSMF) and Lukwoya's Lord's Army all portrayed themselves as standing on the side of the Christian God against the evils of paganism. Kony's forces did this particularly brutally, killing the *ajwakas* and destroying the *abilas* – diviner healers and ancestral shrines – to which the Acholi had customarily turned to confront adversities (p'Bitek 1971a; Finnström 2008).

At times, these prophetically led rebellions – Helen Nambalirwa Nkabala (2021) analyses how many LRA members interpreted the Old Testament in a way that suggested Joseph Kony was Moses – explicitly challenged the missionary-established churches.[12] The rebels' anti-church sentiments, or what could be read as their attempts to wrest moral authority from the churches, also come across clearly in the FC newsletters. A report written by the chairman of the parish pastoral council in Kalongo describes the tug of war over souls between the church and the rebels during the first years of the war:

> Very many Christians accepted his teaching out of fear, even a number of Catechists. In fact Severino Lokoya even 'anointed' one Catechist as Bishop. He said that the Holy Spirit had revealed to him that Priests, Brothers, Sisters etc. would not return to Kalongo; the hospital would not re-open. Black people of his religion would be the ones running the affairs of Kalongo. For two Sundays after his preaching in the area, very few people attended the service in Church. Several meetings were then held with faithful Christians and Catechists to try and explain the danger of accepting Lokoya's teaching; all were warned not to enter the new movement… Most of the claims of Lokoya about cures and miracles did not materialize, and the people left en mass and there was a consoling return to the Church.
>
> (1988, # 432, 15)

The letter's tone and its assumption of the consoling return of Christians (whether consoling for the people or the church is unclear) speaks amply of the positionality of the Comboni newsletters. So does a comment made later that year, when priests in Kitgum sent a letter warning parishioners of what they deemed the 'pseudo-religious contents' of Severino Lukwoya's movement (FC1988, # 432, 16). Lukwoya's group retaliated by kidnapping three priests whom they attempted to convert to what was described as 'an absurd cocktail of christian biliefs [sic]; pagan traditions and superstitions and personal inventions' (1988, # 433, 9). Eventually, the NRA attacked Lukwoya's group and carried the three unharmed but tired priests back to Kitgum mission.

The tenor of the Comboni newsletters suggests that the missionaries' attitude towards the spirituality of Lakwena's and Lukwoya's rebels was fundamentally hostile. However, other sources, as well as comments made in passing during my fieldwork, suggest that clerical support, particularly for the early stages of anti-NRA mobilization, also had varying degrees of religious undertones. Behrend (1999) describes Anglican reverends holding services in Alice Lakwena's church in the early stages of HSMF mobilization, while Allen (1991, 393) tells of Catholic sisters who believed Alice might be a genuine prophet, and both Anglican and Catholic catechists are known to have joined the groups. A report by Kitgum Catholic Deanery in March 1987 concluded that the popularity of Alice Lakwena's group 'reveals the fact that there is in the heart of many people a deep and religious sense' (cited by Lamwaka 2016, 78). Despite the clergy's fear that Lakwena's movement could develop into a dangerous sect, it was credited with contributing to a genuine spiritual revival, and to 'greater unity and solidarity among people of different clans and religious denominations' (ibid.).

From these and similar accounts throughout the newsletters, a couple of things emerge. First, church personnel were divided amongst themselves over how to respond to the different warring parties, particularly to their spirituality. Secondly, although churches did not begin organized advocacy campaigns until much later in the war, they actively took stands vis-à-vis the different armed groups, making these stands public to their members, and rebels were thus obviously very aware of clergy resistance.

In October 1987, the NRA defeated Alice Lakwena and her forces, and a peace agreement was struck between the UPDA rebels and the NRA in 1988. At the same time, attacks by Joseph Kony's group were increasing, leading one Comboni missionary to deplore that it was increasingly 'impossible to see a way out of this bloody and useless conflict' (FC 1988, # 438, 12). In an attack on Pajule Mission, for instance, Kony's group killed thirteen civilians and catechists, burned granaries and homes, and looted countless items. In this case, as in many others to follow, the rebels accused residents of cooperating with the Catholic Mission and the NRA, both of which had spoken critically of the rebels (1988, # 434).

In January 1989, Museveni's army launched Operation North – the first in what was to be a string of military campaigns purportedly against the LRA, but experienced by the population as directed against them, as the missionaries noted:

> The army is intent in massive mopping up operations in the villages forcing everybody into the town... with the intent of identifying the bandits. Whoever

is found in the village is killed and the villages, crops and woods are all burnt up. Famine is foreseen for the beginning of the year.

(FC 1989, # 440 11)

Suffering the brunt of Operation North, and with limited access to provisions, the LRA became 'particularly hard against catholic [sic] institutions in Gulu and surroundings, like schools, missions, hospitals, convents, looting and stealing' (1989, Jan 440, 11). Similar accounts pepper newsletters in the following years, until an event in late 1990 indicates missionaries were being targeted not only for loot, but as possible conduits for LRA propaganda.

In December 1990, an Italian TV team, accompanied by a Comboni priest and a representative appointed by the NRA government, travelled to Kalongo Mission to film a documentary. On the way, Kony's rebels intercepted them, abducted some of the group, and demanded they shoot footage that would be aired on the BBC. Two days later they were released, but were immediately arrested by the NRA military and accused of collaborating with the enemy. Two weeks later, with all their footage of the rebels destroyed, the team was finally released (FC 1991, # 462, 13). The story highlights the claim that the rebels had an agenda which the government was keen to suppress (Finnström 2008). It also highlights that churches, alongside Acholi civilians, were stuck in the middle of the warring parties, suspected and targeted by both the rebels and the state.

Prayer, aid and advocacy amid the confusion of war

So far, this account has focused on the first phases of the war, and on the complex ways in which churches were entangled in it. But despite and partially because of that entanglement, churches also acted within the conflict context – through prayer, aid and advocacy. Churches have been praised as peacemakers in northern Uganda (Apuuli 2011; Hoekema 2019b; Jordhus-Lier and Braathen 2013; Ochola 2008; Soto 2009), but what is often forgotten in these accounts is that religious leaders' concerted peace advocacy came into the picture quite late in the war. Initially, the main focus of churches was providing people with spiritual assistance and, where they were able, material aid (Rodríguez 2002).

Writers of many of the Uganda excerpts in the Comboni newsletters describe the simultaneity of existential crisis and spiritual revival in the region during the war. In the few discussions I had about churches during the war, my interlocutors both recalled churches as emptying out as people lost all interest in

God, and as having been full of people seeking solace or at least entertainment during the war. One youth leader described the particular popularity of wartime gatherings where Christian educational films were shown, such as *The Jesus Film* (Sykes and Krish 1979), which tells the story of Jesus's life, death and resurrection and has been dubbed for evangelization purposes in hundreds of languages. Others claimed that the increase in attendance in places like Kitgum was simply a consequence of displacement-induced population growth, and that many people stopped attending church altogether. As far as I have been able to discover, there are no statistical records of church attendance during the war.[13] The newsletters make it clear, however, that amidst the chaos of war, church celebrations were treasured as attempts to hold on to some semblance of normalcy. For instance, a newsletter from 1988 first recounts a long list of brutal attacks, and then provides a joyous account of the re-opening of Kalongo Mission after a government-forced shutdown. The event was led by an Acholi priest whose home was in the area: he celebrated his first mass, and joined fourteen couples in Holy Matrimony (CF 1988, # 438).

The newsletters repeatedly describe the despair of the missionaries in the midst of their parishioners' impossible life circumstances. Despite difficulties, foreign missionaries and local church staff mostly stayed at their mission stations, hospitals, schools and small outstations, even when their superiors gave them the explicit option of leaving (see similar accounts in Comboni Missionaries 2019; Obol 2012; Soto 2009; Whitmore 2010a). In the midst of all the uncertainty and confusion of the war, those Christians who remained close to the mainline churches, as well as their staff, turned to the spiritual and theological resources those churches had to offer. Whitmore (2019) draws on extensive ethnographic research to describe the spiritual practices developed by the Little Sisters of Mary Immaculate, the Ugandan order of nuns established by the Comboni missionaries, to maintain hope amid the war. But churches did not just pray. The Comboni newsletters show clearly how, beginning early in the war, the Catholic Church's second and third responses – aid and advocacy – were built on theological grounds. A statement in a newsletter from 1988 encapsulates this:

> We are aware it is a complex situation with historical, social and political roots. Besides praying to Our Lord and Our Lady for peace, which would give a definite solution to the problem, is there anything else that we can do to alleviate so much suffering. The [Comboni] community of Ngeta [in Kampala] offered Msgr. Leo Odongo, coordinator of immediate relief, a first contribution for medicine and

food. Our Founder D. Comboni, was also faced with the terrible problem of slavery and reacted very strongly. As an emergency plan he bought freedom for many slaves. But, above all, he untiringly strove to involve all religious and political authorities for the abolition of slavery.

(FC 1988, Jan 429)

FC newsletters speak of donations to help missions provide relief aid in different parts of the conflict-affected north from the early years of the war, long before the international humanitarian community would acknowledge the prolonged crisis in the region. To illustrate the longevity of the church's service provision in the region, recall the newsletter excerpt I quoted earlier: in the single year preceding Museveni's take over, 1,760 babies were delivered and over a thousand operations were conducted in Kalongo hospital. Once war hit, individual priests used their personal networks to gather funding for direct assistance, while the church in Kitgum, for instance, worked in close collaboration with the Catholic-founded Italian NGO, AVSI, to provide relief aid. At times of heightened insecurity, Catholic institutions and parishes provided shelter and basic supplies to thousands of displaced people and night commuters. Ironically, because the mission stations were usually able to restock after looting, the military repeatedly claimed that the Catholic Church was supplying the rebels, a claim that sometimes got clergy into serious trouble.

The material situation was very different for the Anglican Church in Acholi, which CMS missionaries had left largely in Ugandan hands from the early years of colonialism. During the war, the new Church of Uganda diocese in Kitgum did establish some direct contacts with the Church of England and with Lutheran Churches in Germany (see also Taylor 2005), but these connections were far narrower and less monetized than those enabled through Comboni networks. Overall, during the war, the Church of Uganda had meagre resources, and its staff often lived alongside people in the displacement camps – as did most Catholic catechists – with little if anything more to live on than their neighbours. In a 2007 interview (Odoi-Tanga 2009, 246), the bishop of the Church of Uganda in Gulu described church officials having to chase people back into the camps when they moved to the vicinity of churches in large numbers, since the churches had no help to offer and the crowding led to outbreaks of sickness.

Yet even with their sometimes scant ability to provide hands-on assistance, the two mainline churches had an institutional presence in Acholi throughout the war that was simply incomparable in scope and strength to any other organization save the military. As Ward (2001, 201) puts it, churches had 'means of access to people that the government does not', which enabled them to provide 'a channel by which local opinion can express itself' (ibid.). This embeddedness in the realities of people's everyday existence in the midst of the war eventually became the grounds from which religious leaders were to launch into their third arena of action: advocacy.

In 1997, leading Catholic and Anglican clerics in Kitgum, soon joined by the local Muslim leader, gathered in response to a brutal massacre in the district to discuss what they could do to promote peace (Apuuli 2011; ARLPI 2009; Lumumba 2014; Rodríguez 2002). One step was to start attending each other's religious services, something that had never occurred in the churches' history in the region. The first formal joint peace meeting was called by the Acholi Religious Leaders Peace Initiative in Gulu the following year, and the formal organization was formed in 1999 (Hoekema 2019b). Yet even during the earlier years of war, clerics sometimes negotiated with rebels for the release of captives, or approached the military with requests for negotiation (see, e.g., FC 1988, # 434). Peace prayers were also arranged in Gulu prior to the establishment of ARLPI, at least as early as 1991 (Dolan 2000). Behind the scenes, the Catholic Church provided support for local advocacy groups: human rights abuses were documented and legal aid was provided both by the churches' own Justice and Peace Commission, and by the Gulu-based Human Rights Focus (HURIFO), which was initiated in talks around a priest's dining table.

A key issue for churches was how to position themselves vis-à-vis the warring parties. As already mentioned, the attitude of both LRA rebels and the government towards the churches was ambivalent. Ward (2001) claims that the NRM considered the Catholic Church a more credible ally than the Anglican, which had had such a close relationship with the Obote regime. However, the Catholic Church had a long-standing position as 'the church of opposition', and this did not change with the NRM's coming to power. Furthermore, as my interlocutors reminded me, the Catholic Church was rendered highly suspect in the eyes of the government by factors such as the willingness of church hospitals to provide health services to anyone who was wounded, including the rebels; the international connections of foreign missionaries; the historical identification of many Comboni missionaries as opposition-minded agitators; and, at a later stage, certain priests' attempts to remain in contact with the rebels in order to persuade them to engage in peace talks (see particularly Soto 2009). The situation also evolved as the war dragged on. With the exception of individual, staunchly anti-NRM clergy like Bishop Ochola, the Anglican Church in Kitgum, for instance, has come to be viewed as much more closely identified with the

NRM than its Catholic counterpart. In the following, I elucidate the complexity of these entangled relationships and animosities through a closer look at an event that took place at Kitgum mission in 1991.

'A confusing time. Difficult to analyse.'

In April 1991, a Catholic priest was whisked away by soldiers in the middle of celebrating Holy Thursday mass at Kitgum mission. The question of why this happened, and what it was all about, is, as Father Marcus put it, 'difficult to analyse'. It is even harder to decipher because my access to information about the incident is partial: I have been able to learn only the Catholic – rather, *a specific* Catholic – side to the story. The people who initially told me the story in 2013 swore me to secrecy, and asked me to protect their safety, as well as my own, by not asking questions that might trigger the wrong kind of interest in my research. Since then, the situation has changed: first, because one of those involved, *ladit* Philip Odwong, has written and is seeking to publish his memoir, and has given me permission to write about the things he describes in it (Odwong 2019). Secondly, this memoir inspired me to track down Father Paul Donohue, the Catholic priest who was hustled away from Kitgum, and who now works for the Comboni missionaries in New Jersey, who also shared with me his copies of what appear to be official documents concerning the case. With Father Donohue's permission, I share his account of what happened as he narrated and interpreted it. I believe the story is worth discussing in detail, for it perfectly elucidates the *anyobanyoba* of how church, state and war were – and remain – entangled in Uganda.

> I was taken away from the church at 5.15 PM during the second reading of Holy Thursday. Easter came early that year. A few days before, Philip [Odwong] came to tell me some people had been arrested, and warned me he thought something was going to happen. And then when I was celebrating mass, the [government] soldiers circled the church, they pointed at me, and they told me to go out. And I said no, and they pointed at me more forcefully. They told me I was not being arrested, but Betty Bigombe [the Minister of State for the Pacification of Northern Uganda; herself an Acholi] wanted to see me, and take me to Lira, where general [David] Tinyefuza would interview me, but they would bring me back tomorrow. So I went and took off my vestments and grabbed a few things in a bag in my room, and that's the last time I was in Kitgum.

So I flew with Bigombe to Lira, and never saw the general. On Easter Monday, I was driven by a car to Kampala. After one night at a hotel, they said it is too expensive to keep me there, so they told me to stay at the Comboni house in Mbuya, and demanded I hand over my passport. I had two passports, since I had reclaimed my Irish citizenship, and I have American. So I gave them the Irish passport, and that saved me in a certain sense. They took me to Mbuya, I was debriefed with the provincial superior, who called the Minister of Foreign Affairs at that time, Semugerere, who worshipped at our church. He knew that I gave them my Irish passport, and that I had been detained under house arrest, so when the Minister of Internal Affairs called Paul Semugerere to tell him that could he please inform the American embassy that I was going to be expelled, Semugerere said 'I can't do that, he's Irish. Don't you read: you have his passport'. So the whole thing collapsed.

According to the account he has shared with me, Father Donohue remained in Kampala from Easter Monday until the 16 June. During this time, people (Father Donohue says to this day he does not know who they were) started to deliver envelopes for him at the place of his residence containing a total of ninety pages of documents concerning the dispute over the school. Father Donohue wrote a dossier in which he explained how he understood the documents, which he delivered to the American ambassador, the British High Commissioner, the Nuncio (the papal representative in Uganda) and the Provincial Superior of his missionary order. When a family emergency called Father Donohue home, he went to collect his passport from the British Council, which handled Irish affairs. It was given to him with a diplomatic letter from the Ugandan ministry, which, Father Donohue was advised, equated with, 'you can't come back'.

Father Donohue's answer to my question as to why he thinks this happened contains two parallel and interlinked stories: of local dispute over a Catholic-founded school, and of national-level political intrigue. Here is the first:

The headmaster of the Anglican school, Gipir [a pseudonym I have given him following an Acholi tale about two vengeful brothers], who headed what was later to become the girls' section of Kitgum High School, was stealing money from the school. Complaints were made by a group of committed Catholics on the board, and a team was sent, from [the Ministry of Education in] Kampala, to review the school finances. The headmaster responded by burning the school down. In the meanwhile, another Anglican, Labongo [pseudonym] had asked Gipir to lend him some land for storing his sesame harvest. But Gipir sold it all off, and Labongo had him arrested and put in jail. Other Anglicans intervened, and said it is not good for two members of the church to fight each other.

> Labongo refused to have Gipir released before he paid him back. So Gipir took all of the money from the school PTA [Parent-Teacher Association], of which he was the chairperson, and he wrote a cheque to Labongo that was something like 5000 US dollars at the time.

According to Father Donohue, all this took place when he was away on holiday. When he returned, he went to the bank, saw the signatures, realized what had happened, and publicly denounced the principal. 'That's when', he told me, 'the fight began.' His next description begins to hint at the second level of 'why':

> What they did was very clever. They sent the Vice President [of Uganda] to the school, and so I was there meeting him. In the meantime, the Anglican members of the education committee for the district had a meeting that didn't have quora, but they wrote minutes. And in those minutes they said that I was working with the *olum* [literally 'bush people', '*lum*' meaning bush; a commonly used euphemism for the rebels], and that's something very serious. And then they went to Kampala, and gave these minutes to the Ministry of Defence, the Prime Minister, they just disseminated them everywhere. That eventually is what got me in trouble.

Similar accusations had been made against other Catholic priests in earlier years, leading to one deportation shortly after the NRA took power (see O'Kadameri 2002), and were to be made in years to follow (see Soto 2009). Father Donohue believes that accusations of his collaboration with the rebels were just a cover for what was really going on – just as accusations of plotting a rebellion were, according to Philip Odwong, a convenient way for people with high stakes in the fight over the finance troubles at Kitgum High to get him and other Catholic defenders of the school out of town and into prison, or to settle scores against persons with growing political standing in the town (Odwong 2019, 169–80). Yet, according to Father Donohue, it was not just about the school. He continued:

> You know, I still have these documents, all 90 pages of them. And from them, I got the idea that some people high up [he mentioned names but I am withholding them] were preparing to take the cream off the milk, if you know what I mean. They knew the British were going to fund the rebuilding of northern Uganda, especially amongst Acholi. I think they thought I had figured out that they were setting up this group of people who would bring the money, or a good portion of it, in. Basically that's what I wrote in the dossier.

What Father Donohue appears to be referring to is the Northern Uganda Rehabilitation Program (NURP), which began in 1992, the year following his effective deportation. Both NURP and the subsequent Northern Uganda Social

Action Fund (NUSAF) have been shown to have been profoundly corrupt: massive portions of the funding went directly into the pockets of government and military officials (Atkinson 2018; Golooba-Mutebi and Hickey 2010).[14]

The 1991 events are also described in the FC newsletters. Following Father Donohue's sudden departure, all the foreign missionaries at Kitgum Mission were taken in for questioning, and 'accused of favouring the cause of the rebels and threatened with expulsion' (1991, # 466, 15). The accusation was striking in its irony. At the time, Kony's rebels were systematically looting Catholic missions, sometimes, 'while government troops... stood watching' (ibid.), doing nothing to help. The newsletter recounts:

> One of the worst and sad things is the political intimidation of the Catholics, and several prominent Catholic lay people have been arrested on unspecified charges. All this is happening under the very eyes of the military who are either totally passive or, with their wrong[ly] timed interventions, seem to give tacit approval to the destruction of Catholic institutions, the only institutions left to care for the people, who are caught up between the warring factions.
>
> (1991, # 466, 16–17)

Among the leaders and elders mentioned here as having been rounded up by the NRA in 1991 were Tiberio Okeny Atwoma, whose 2012 state burial provides the background for my analysis in Chapter 4, and *ladit* Philip Odwong, whose life story I recount in the book's opening pages. Those detained were accused, without evidence or proper legal process, of plotting to overthrow the government (Amnesty International 1991). Eventually, as detailed by Caroline Lamwaka (2016, 261–3), a public outcry prompted Uganda's inspector general of government (IGG) to look into the case, finding that the arrests had not been based on sufficient inquiry, and that the prisoners had faced torture during their detention. After a year spent in custody, they were released.

According to Fr Donohue's dossier, as well as the unpublished memoirs of *ladit* Odwong – in which letters, receipts and reports related to the case are reproduced, many of them identical to those contained in Father Donohue's dossier – among those arrested, tortured and kept for months without their families knowing whether they were alive or dead, were four people who had raised the alert about school funds being misappropriated at Kitgum High. But the backdrop against which Father Donohue now, almost thirty years after the event, situates the disputed issue of Kitgum High and his deportation extends beyond the suspected theft of aid money to northern Uganda. Instead, he comments on the entirety of the war as not being what it seemed:

> There were several thousand [soldiers] stationed in Kitgum, [but] they never really tried to get the rebels. In June of 1990, they just disappeared, they disappeared. And two days later you hear about the invasion of Rwanda, supported by Museveni. And Paul Kagame became the leader. So that's a fact: they disappeared, all of them, overnight, all of them, left. So I see that as their training. So that's my opinion, I can't prove it. But the coincidence of timing, and the reappearing in the border with Rwanda, it's too much.

Father Donohue's accusations of Museveni's using the Acholi as training fodder for his soldiers and Rwandan allies in the NRA and (as discussed elsewhere in our interview) government peace efforts as not being genuine are not unique to him. Other people's memories of the early years of the war include many similar conjectures (Dolan 2000). The links between war in Acholi and broader dynamics – such as the war in Rwanda (Prunier 1996), Museveni's intrusion into the Democratic Republic of Congo accompanied by massive looting of gold and other precious minerals and the proxy war between Sudan and Uganda (Mwenda and Tangri 2005; Prunier 2004, 2008; Schomerus 2012a), and US support for Museveni's purported fight against terrorism (Finnström 2012; Titeca 2013; Whitaker 2007) – were often well grasped by Acholi living in the midst of it.

But my purpose here is not to take a stand on what exactly went on in the shadows of war, what actually happened at Kitgum High, or whether the fight about the school was indeed the reason for Philip Odwong's arrest or Father Donohue's deportation, for I cannot. Already, a comparison between the story as detailed by Father Donohue and that by Philip Odwong shows that whatever took place was immensely complicated, and mired in rumours and allegations at an extremely fraught time of war. But a few points of the story are worth pausing to consider, even if its details are controversial, unclear or might even be denied.

The story elucidates how different levels, from the very local to the national, become imbricated in a single event, something that I claim characterizes the very nature of churches' relationships with each other and with public authorities in Uganda. The dispute between two men – the pseudonymous 'Labongo' and 'Gipir' as narrated above – was also a dispute within the Anglican Church and likewise divided the Catholic Church between the likes of Father Donohue, who wanted to bring what he believed was the truth into the light, and those who advocated minimal intervention and maximum silence.[15] The debate was also between the two churches, which both had an institutional interest in retaining schools and their funds under their own wings. District-level politicians and authorities became involved, as did those sitting in high offices in Kampala; at all these levels, religious affiliations and connections materialized in phone calls, petitions and help given or withheld. If it is true that members of the district education committee made the accusations against Father Donohue, it appears that a conflict over mismanagement of school funds eventually attracted the interest of both the military and highest levels of government authority to Kitgum Mission.

Yet, while tentacles of the dispute were debated and discussed in ministries, embassies, dioceses and military barracks, the conflict over Kitgum High also affected a community of parents desiring quality education for their children in a war-torn region. At the end of the day, it was these children and their parents, regardless of their religious denomination, who paid the highest price, not only for the abuses committed by individuals against the school, but also for the inability of the two churches, as institutions and as communities, to work together to fix it. When I asked Father Donohue in 2020 why he thought this was, he remained quiet for a long time, sighed and said it was a good question.

As I have shown, the relationship between the two churches in Kitgum was extremely strained at the time, and, as this chapter has discussed, the tension went back decades. It was only much later, after hundreds had been killed in brutal massacres in Kitgum, that Anglican and Catholic clerics in Kitgum sat down together with their Muslim colleague, to discuss what they could do, together, to address the plight of their people.

Northern Uganda as a window onto church–state relations in Uganda

This chapter has discussed how churches have positioned themselves in relation to the state, at both national and local levels. I have shown how the multi-ethnic nature of Uganda's mainline churches has led them, as national bodies, to often remain silent in the face of decades of shifting patterns of war. Furthermore, I have noted that when churches did speak out, they were repeatedly ordered by the state to remain within the boundaries of their spiritual mandate or face the consequences. Within Acholi, this was particularly true. Focusing more on the Catholic Church than its Anglican counterpart, I have shown that Acholi churches did not breathe the winds of change that brought stability and development to much of the country following Museveni's coming to power. In the midst of a war, wherein multiple rebel groups rose to resist the plunder and destruction wrought by Museveni's NRA, churches struggled to position themselves vis-à-vis the conflict parties, and to assist their members with what spiritual and material resources they had. In this, they were both enabled and constrained by their complex embeddedness in the community. Eventually, but only after decades of bitter dispute between them, the sheer brutality of the war forced mainline churches to put aside their disputes and find common ground as advocates for peace.

Finally, I claimed that both national patterns of church–state relations and local histories of war continue to influence the arena of churches and politics in Kitgum. To illustrate this, it is time to return to the story with which this chapter opened: my meeting with Mr. Orom, the Catholic politician, at the gate of Kitgum Mission. At the time, he told me he was vying to return to power so as to ensure Catholic schools remain under, or are returned to, Catholic management. Thirty years before, that same battle got people deported and gaoled. More recently, in villages outside Kitgum, the dispute over schools has led to fistfights, with someone even being killed in a fight over a church-founded school in western Acholi. Mr. Orom comes from a hard-core Catholic family, and the generation before him stood staunchly with the Democratic Party. He himself has taken a different road, however, and after a short stint in one of the rebel groups that opposed Museveni, he has aligned with the NRM.

Mr Orom's concern about churches' control of their schools was shared by numerous others. During the short time I spent in Kitgum in 2019, Catholics told me of the manoeuvres they claimed were being instigated under the new Anglican bishop to grab schools from the Catholics. In a mirror image, my Anglican friends told me of the lies that Catholics spin to get their hands on schools that were established on Anglican land and thus intended to be Anglican. Debates of old are at play. And entangled with them, in stories at least as complex as that of the 1991 deportation, are decades of war, with patterns of allegiance, betrayal, family rupture, access to funding, and religious and social ties all forming a kaleidoscope of *anyobanyoba* that, even after years of seeking to understand it, I often feel I am scratching only the surface of.

While the past continues to shape political debate in contemporary Kitgum, it is vital to acknowledge that the underlying patterns are changing, and in many ways have already drastically changed. Elderly Catholics in Kitgum claim the area around the Mission is staunchly Catholic – as do Anglicans of their *Mican*. But many young men who live in the area, and drove me to and from the Mission with their *bodaboda* motorcycle taxis, rejected these labels as old people's talk: times were changing. Mr. Orom did not get through his party primaries in 2020. His concern with church schools is not the main concern of young generations, increasing numbers of whom are turning away from the Catholic and Anglican

Churches to the more vibrant music and preaching of born-again churches, away from the old church-related parties' opposition to Museveni to the thin promises of the NRM. Old patterns of churches and politics remain, but they are fading out of memory, as are stories of the type I have told in this chapter: of attacks, of abductions, of schools changing hands in complex and murky conditions. The past is being left behind, whether because of memory fading, or deliberate silencing, or new pressing issues pushing old grudges off the agenda. The next chapter turns to consider this fading and silencing in more detail, and to describe Kitgum as a town emerging from war.

3

Learning to listen to silence and confusion
Fieldwork in the aftermath of war

In this chapter, I describe Kitgum as a town emerging from decades of violent conflict. During my longest stretch of fieldwork in 2012–13, six years had passed since the war shifted territory to neighbouring countries, leaving northern Uganda free to breathe after almost twenty consecutive years of warfare. Contrary to what I expected, the war was rarely on people's lips, and the atmosphere of the town was characterized by a profound sense of normalcy and recovery. On paper, the transition from war to peace was largely complete: thousands of formerly abducted children and former LRA soldiers and wives had passed through integration centres, the large displacement camps had been closed and people had moved back to their villages after years of forced displacement. Humanitarian agencies had largely been replaced by more development-oriented NGOs, and even many of these were in the process of scaling down and leaving.

I could hardly recognize the Kitgum I was experiencing with my family as the same town I had visited in 2006. For instance, in 2006 the mental image I had of young Acholi men drew from the vacant stares of what I imagined to be former child soldiers gathered at street corners in Kitgum town, but in 2012–13 this image was replaced by young men enthusiastically practising old Anglican hymns in choir practice, lovingly taking care of their toddlers, or sitting in a DVD library exchanging views on the latest movies and discussing possible job openings. Although many people were struggling with poverty, the town I had expected to encounter as one painfully recovering from war felt almost untouched by it.

It was only gradually that it dawned on me how little the war was spoken of. In the first few months of fieldwork in 2012, the majority of people I met, talked with informally, or interviewed, said nothing of the war unless I asked direct questions about it. For reasons I will discuss in this chapter, I usually did not.

A shroud of silence concerning the war also lay over the pews in which I sat in the churches I was studying. The absence of stories of war became particularly pronounced when, after some three months of fieldwork, I started conducting interviews with young adults at the two churches I was studying. More often than not, these stories were told with almost no reference to anything related to the war I knew (or would later come to know) the interviewees had lived through. In part this related to my particular research participants (see Introduction), many of whom had escaped some of the worst fates of war in the region. Most had not been abducted, and some had avoided even seeing live battle. But they had all heard it, lived in the midst of it, run for cover when sounds of shooting neared their side of the town. Everyone had been affected. As I came to eventually know, almost everyone I interacted with on a regular basis had lost a family member – a parent, a child, a sibling, or a cousin brother or sister – during the war. They all had family members or personally knew people who had 'been with the rebels', or who were somehow not coping well with their memories of war.[1] But more often than not, these things were hidden in silence.

As it became clear to me that the war was a topic that many people wanted to avoid, I was puzzled how to proceed. I could not help but wonder what the silence could tell me. Were people not talking about the war only because I was not specifically asking about it, or were they actually not talking about it to each other either? If I had done fieldwork in a village outside of Kitgum, or somewhere other than the churches, would people have spoken more about the war? What was the ethical way to treat the silence as an ethnographer? Was there any way of studying it without breaking it, after which it would no longer be? Eventually, I decided to ask people I had come to know more closely whether the silence concerning the war only extended to me, or whether people also did not talk to each other about the past. Through the answers I received, and with insights gained from research on silence and trauma, my reading of the silence I met with in Kitgum has transformed considerably, not only during periods of fieldwork, but in the spaces in between, when I have read and re-read my fieldwork notes and interviews, explored memories, and returned to reflect on preconceptions I myself had about silence, trauma and healing.

The chapter has two aims, addressed in parallel throughout the coming pages. First, by drawing from studies on trauma and silence to describe the evolution of my own interpretations of the silence I encountered in Kitgum, I illustrate what it is that I refer to as the afterlives of war, and how traces of war-time violence shape lives in northern Uganda in the present. This lays the groundwork for analysis in subsequent chapters of how mainline Christian churches, as institutions and communities deeply embedded in Acholi society, have influenced the contours of political imagination in the region. Second, through a focus on embodiment and relationality, the chapter raises questions concerning the ethical and emotional implications of conducting fieldwork in a society recovering from war.

What might silence say (other than 'trauma')?

I have grown to believe that silence is polyphonic: it consists of multiple, at times discordant and contradictory sounds, and cannot be consigned to single-cause explanations such as 'trauma' or 'recovery' (Alava 2019). Yet my initial ideas about why so few people talked about the war in Kitgum were influenced by my own pre-held understandings about silence and trauma. They were also influenced by my close proximity to the churches I was studying, particularly the Catholic Church, at which I spent more time in the first half of my fieldwork than at the Anglican. Many of the priests with whom I discussed my observations of peoples' silence concurred that people did not talk much about the war; for most of these priests, this silence was a cause for grave concern. It signalled a deep trauma, and what some of them termed people's inability to 'deal with' what had happened. The priests' concern for their non-talking parishioners to a certain extent reflected their theological training, through which culturally specific notions of trauma and healing had been embedded into the mainstream vision of Catholic pastoral and psychosocial work in northern Uganda.[2] This was evident in the plans for a new Catholic University to be launched in Acholi, where it was planned that course units on counselling would be integrated into all programmes. As someone involved in the project explained to me, 'Whether you're working in IT or something else, the people you are dealing with will all have suffered trauma'. Since then, the university has started off with two departments: IT and counselling, with the aim of 'addressing the needs for healing, reconciliation, moral integrity and development of the region' (University of the Sacred Heart Gulu 2020).

In many ways, the clerics were right to believe that everyone in northern Uganda has been affected by the war. In a survey conducted at one of the worst peaks of the war, 79 per cent of respondents had witnessed torture, 40 per cent had witnessed killing, 5 per cent had been forced to physically harm someone, and 62 per cent of the women interviewed had said they were thinking about committing suicide (Médecins Sans Frontières 2004). During my fieldwork in

2012 and 2013, suicide cases were common in the region, and were generally attributed to repercussions of the war (see Kizza et al. 2012). Catholic priests had encountered thousands of people who came to them for the spiritual consolation and emotional relief offered by confession during and immediately after the war, and some still met regularly with former abductees who kept coming back to beg the priests to pray for their nightmares to end. Yet, although I was hearing these stories from the priests, all I myself witnessed or heard in my first months of fieldwork was what to me appeared as normal, everyday life.

I thus interpreted silence through the prism of what I expected the silence to be suppressing. As the months passed, I became increasingly aware of what I took to be hints of deep, dark and troubling currents underneath the silence and the surface of everyday life. The label I attached to all this was the same as those around me were attaching to it: trauma. As Fassin and Rechtman (2009) have argued, 'trauma' has become a marker of our time. Since the last decades of the twentieth century, understandings of trauma have morphed in Western psychiatry, with the suspicion characteristic of many previous treatment regimens replaced by empathy for the victims of traumatic events. Although clinically trauma is understood as 'overwhelming emotional experiences that cannot be coped with and integrated into the person's existing inner world' (Maček 2014a, 4), the notion's extension into other genres of writing, clinical practice and social advocacy has led to its incorporation into particular frames of moral politics: 'As a tool of a politics of humanitarian testimony, trauma contributes to constructing new forms of political subjectification and new relations with the contemporary world' (Fassin and Rechtman 2009, 216).

Today, individuals and communities – even nations – impacted by armed violence have almost automatically come to be interpreted as collectively traumatized (Hamber and Wilson 2002); so also northern Uganda. In Kitgum, adoption of the trauma narrative was particularly noticeable among those who had worked with humanitarian agencies during the war, at a time when humanitarian aid around the world was pervaded by an elaborate discourse that constructed 'psychosocial support' as the ultimate treatment for 'trauma' (Fassin and Rechtman 2009, 158).

One impact of this discourse has been that silence in post-conflict situations is typically read as a pathological sign of untreated psychological wounds – although this view is increasingly critiqued. Drawing in part from roots engrained in Western culture through Catholic confession (Foucault 2012; Landry 2009), both advocacy and scholarly epistemologies of violence and trauma – whether the violence of the Holocaust, the Rwandan genocide or

Apartheid – commonly 'prescribe public verbal articulation as the key to healing' after traumatic events (Kidron 2009, 50; see Tankink 2007 for an example from Uganda). Indeed, verbal articulation in various forms is essential to a number of different approaches to post-war 'healing': retributive or restorative justice; commemoration through memorial plaques or special services; truth-telling or peace and reconciliation commissions; or spiritual or psychological counselling. Looming behind much of the scholarship that supports these proscribed solutions to 'trauma' are Freudian views of the detrimental effects of repressed memories on the psyche, although newer approaches, less influenced by Freud, also underline the imperative of re-living through telling, and hence overcoming (Harnisch 2016). When informed by such views, silence may be read as a sign of pathological avoidance and repression, negative secrecy, or hegemonic silencing and subjugation (Kidron 2009).

Alternative views of silence that step beyond the imperative to speak out are, however, possible, and I argue often ethically justified. Thesauruses commonly define 'silence', first, as an absence of speech, but also as referring to a state of standing still and not speaking out of respect for someone deceased, or as referring to a moment reserved for prayer. Rather than silence implying a kind of failure, it can also be a culturally appropriate coping mechanism (Burnet 2012), and a political act that is in fact full of agency (Das 2007; Eastmond and Selimovic 2012). Moreover, as Marjaana Jauhola has shown, the audial space that silence creates may fill with alternative modes of expression (2016). The crucial point here is that these different views of silence are not mutually exclusive. Rather, as I slowly came to realize during my fieldwork, different meanings of silence exist alongside each other and it is not necessarily easy – or even necessary – to pinpoint one specific reason for people's hesitance to talk about the war.

At the same time as I was becoming aware of what I experienced as disturbing undercurrents of violence, trauma and fear, I was also becoming aware of the sometimes pronounced, sometimes subtle ways in which they were addressed and dealt with in everyday lives. These types of undercurrents, both traumatic and healing, are often enveloped in a silence that Burnet describes as 'cling[ing] to a normalized reality' (2012, 78). A particularly poignant analysis of this double-sided nature of silence is found in Veena Das's work, and her notion of a 'descent into the ordinary' (2007). In her ethnography, Das powerfully shows that the violence of significant events does not disappear with the absence of words but, rather, meanders into and through the fabric of everyday social life. As past violence is incorporated into the ordinary, it may continue to wreak havoc on the victims of violence, leading the victims – both individually and communally – to turn the violence in on themselves. This process has been described with the metaphor of the destruction of the social fabric (e.g. Burnet 2012), and it was evoked also in northern Uganda. One of the young active Anglican women with whom I discussed the issue elaborated this point when, months after my initial interviews with her, I asked her about the silence I had experienced:

> And now you see that there's a lot of trauma. You see that? That is it. They don't want to talk about it, but it is affecting them. They know it; others were raped, they did not talk about it. Nobody knew about it. Everyone has been, in a way, affected... Like there's a man here, the daughter remained there [with the rebels] until today; they don't know whether she's alive or she's dead. But they will not talk about it. Unless they hear someone talking like war, then they become, and maybe they'll even keep quiet. Now, that gives it. People become angry so fast. Their emotions is disturbed. You, you just trigger it. That is why there's a lot of violence. There's too much violence here. Wives killing the husbands, husbands killing wives, children. So, that is the result of it. Eh? Because talking, choosing not to talk about it, does not mean that you don't know and it's not affecting you. And because you even don't talk about it, you want to put yours in action. Anyone who triggers it, it comes all and [snaps her fingers]. Lot of trauma.

My friend's description evokes a sense of trauma that permeates the weave of the ordinary, and of memories that may be triggered and spill out uncontrollably; as 'contamination that seeps into [the affected person's] immediate environment – his family and home' (Meinert and Whyte 2017, 284). This is one side of a descent into the ordinary. But the other face of what Das describes suggests inhabiting the life that was shattered by violence as a precarious movement towards healing: an acknowledgement of what has happened, coupled with the acknowledgement that life can and must go on despite it.

I believe it is here in particular that over-reliance on the dominant trauma paradigm can lead to misconceptions about the meanings of silence in post-conflict societies. Not all memories of the past are traumatic; rather, for many, memories and experiences *have been* integrated into the person's existing inner world (Maček 2014a, 4), in which case not talking about the past does not necessarily imply negative avoidance but, rather, a precarious movement towards healing.

This weave of life, wherein the past is present, albeit not necessarily or often spoken of, can be conceptualized as a culture of silence (Eastmond and Selimovic 2012) wherein 'silence may hold important meanings and carry agency in making and upholding vital relationships' (ibid., 505). As sociologist

Elina Oinas (2001) has shown in a different context, for girls to avoid talking about things they experience as uncomfortable does not necessarily imply repression or avoidance, but can rather indicate an attitude of pragmatic coming to terms or of 'constructive normality' (ibid., 84), whereby a set of 'embodied and often unconscious social skills [allow for] surviving day-to-day life as a social being' (ibid., 87). As Burnet (2012) has argued for Rwanda, however, silence can simultaneously be a culturally appropriate, voluntarily adopted coping mechanism, *and* hegemonically enforced. In the same vein, I argue that silence in northern Uganda can be understood and should be respected as a coping mechanism. But coping mechanisms have repercussions, and as I show in Chapter 6, the careful monitoring of what can and cannot be spoken of inhibits much-needed societal and political critique.

For now, however, I wish to explore the methodological implications of these alternative readings of silence. If memories and knowledge of the past may be effectively conveyed without words – that is, embodied in practices, in deliberate silences, in gestures, and inscribed in bodies (Burnet 2012; Kidron 2009) – it becomes necessary to focus one's attention on something beyond words. As Kidron, Das and Burnet have all argued, sensitivity to non-verbal cues tends to increase with time spent in the field. What also tends to increase with time is trust; in Burnet's (2012) case, it took years of building rapport and proficiency in the language for people to trust her with their most intimate and painful memories of the Rwandan genocide. My own experience during fieldwork was that both sensitivity to reading non-verbal cues and progress in trust and friendship changed what people kept silent and what they would share.

One day towards the very end of my fieldwork, as I was cooking with a neighbour with whom I had spent a lot of time over the previous months, she suddenly, for no apparent reason, pointed to the scar on her arm. I had often seen it but only barely registered it (see Jauhola 2018 for an account of a similar experience). She told me it was from a bullet, and then went on to list a number of people related to her who were killed during the war. We continued with our tasks in silence for some time after that, until I ventured to say that when I was there in 2006 and the war was still going on and people were at the camps, everybody was talking about the war, but that now, few do.

> **Grace:** Because now the rebels are away, they're in Congo.
> **Henni:** Yeah. But still, people don't talk about that time, it's like they don't want to remember.
> **Grace:** They don't. Even I, I don't like to talk about it. I don't.

Although she said she does not like talking about it, I did not feel she was telling me to pull back, particularly as the initiative of mentioning the bullet wound had been hers. I thus said that I had been wondering whether it was just that people did not want to talk to me about it, or whether they did not talk with friends or family either. 'They do not,' she responded. But then, pausing what she had been doing, Grace started talking. Throughout her narrative, I was stirring a pot of rice to keep it from burning, and as she continued, merely shook my head from time-to-time in empathy and disbelief, but she did not need prompting. It seemed that once the floodgates opened, there was no stopping the memories: A cousin's brother from a neighbouring house had been killed. Her friend had been abducted along with a group of other girls, and of the entire group, this friend was the only one who came back. She had been impregnated by the rebels, the child had died, and now the woman had HIV. One time they had seen rebels just outside the house, and a hundred of them ran to the church for shelter. By nine the next morning they had become so desperate that someone had dared to go out to fetch them water. Grace told of a Christmas they had spent hiding in their huts, listening to the rebels moving around outside. There had been shooting and bomb blasts everywhere; even her father's compound had been bombed. During the war, there had been public video showings with images of breasts and penises cut off, of chopped limbs boiling in pots, but nobody wanted to go to see them.

I continued stirring the rice, concentrating on the task so as to counter the surreal sensation of bearing witness to the heart-wrenching memories of someone I had always thought of as so happy and 'free' – as the Acholi often describe those with an open and friendly demeanour towards others. At the end of this long list of memories, Grace returned to the incident that had scarred her arm:

> I was carrying the baby with my other hand. If it had been a stronger gun that they fired, we would all have been dead. The rebel was carrying two guns. I went in, my hand, it was broken, I didn't feel a thing, there was just blood flowing. I went to another room, they tied it from here. We really suffered. We really suffered. It was just too much.

Memories of the war in northern Uganda are everywhere; they trickle into the everyday, and to such an extent that there is nothing spectacular about them, they are simply part of the weave of life. As many of my friends explained to me, once I asked them, there was no need to talk about the war, 'Because as one friend explained it you know you've experienced the same thing. So it's useless to talk about it. After all, the other person has experienced it. It was our normal way of living.' Breaking into laughter, she continued, 'So talking about it is even monotonous.' This sense of the war being nothing particular to talk about, of becoming so entirely ordinary for those who had lived through it, was repeated in many of my later interviews, and seemed particularly prevalent among those who had no memories of life before the war. One boy told me that he grew up thinking houses are for living in during the day, and that at night everyone everywhere slept in a church. When war becomes normalized, it is unnecessary to talk about it among those who share that sense of normalcy.

Yet, although this silence can at times be read as a sign of healing and overcoming, there are also times when the absence of words is a signal of something quite different. As Koselleck has written:

> There will occur events, or chains of events, which are beyond the pale of language, and to which words, all sentences, all speech can only react. There are events for which words fail us, which leave us dumb, and to which, perhaps, we can only react with silence.
>
> (Koselleck 1989, 652)

Jenny Edkins (2003) has argued that scholarly reference to unspeakability may be the chosen escape for the academic who cannot deal with the gravity of the events for which she seeks words. In Edkins's view, it is almost too easy to say that some things are simply too terrible for words. But, how then should one, as a researcher, and as a human being, deal with genuine failure of words, when one is left numb, when one would rather turn away from something than engage with it, or write about it?

Ethics in encounters with silence

In a book dedicated to contemplating the ethical and emotional challenges of fieldwork in contexts affected by war (Thomson, Ansoms, and Murison 2013), transitional justice expert Lino Ogora (2013) provides an arresting account of his encounter with an elderly Acholi man. The man was a survivor of one of the worst massacres experienced during the northern Ugandan war, someone whom Ogora approached in the course of his work for a research and advocacy NGO. The man refused to answer Ogora's questions. Researcher after researcher had come to interview him, and time and time again he had recounted his story, yet he had never benefitted in any way whatsoever from sharing it. Ogora, himself an Acholi-speaker, suspects that the absence of a language barrier and, probably, also of the historically constructed racialized power structure that inevitably posits a white researcher as a potential patron in Acholi (Whitmore 2011) allowed the elderly man to express his true feelings about how researchers had treated him. It empowered him to refuse Ogora to extract his story from him once more; it enabled him to choose silence.

It is an ethical imperative that research should not cause harm to its participants. Yet the cumulative effect of numerous research projects had clearly caused the old man both hurt and annoyance. In 'research hotspots' – places like northern Uganda, and in particular their fairly easily accessible and comfortable urban centres – this cumulative effect can be considerable. I am tempted to name this the 'Café Sankofa effect' after one of my family's favourite places of respite in Gulu town, where we went for a few days' break about once a month throughout the time we lived in Kitgum. Similar places exist elsewhere: places with cool beer, brownies and espresso; places that pull in a crowd of MA and PhD students and research consultants from the Global North, often in the company of their local friends and colleagues, jointly searching for a break from the emotional toll of studying the aftermath of war. In 2013, over coffee in one such place, Lino Ogora estimated that ever since the final years of the war, five new researchers had come to visit him *every month*. It seems clear, as Mwambari (2019), for instance, has analysed, that these flocks of researchers leave a complex print on the society they study. It was clear to Ogora, and had become even clearer to him after his encounter with the elderly man. Even among those of my Acholi friends who had not themselves been interviewed by countless researchers, there was an awareness that people were growing tired of researchers, particularly those who wanted to hear about the war: a kind of collective research fatigue. But what should those of us who belong to this flock of researchers – who have been to such 'research hot-spots', made friends in them, and invested years of our lives in understanding them – think of this? Should we return for more but make sure we do not overburden those individuals who have already been burdened by previous researchers? Should we focus our research on peoples' desires in the present and for the future, rather than wear them down with questions of the past? Or should we stay away, and allow the Acholi to save their stories for their children?[3]

I don't think there are easy responses to such questions, but despite my inability to answer them, I feel they need to be posed. The question I wish to address here concerns the ethical ways to recognize and respond to silence when we encounter it in the course of our research in the aftermath of war: when should we break it, when protect it? Arguing against the kind of objectification of ethics that we increasingly see around us in academia – the kind of 'ethics' that can be assessed by way of the mechanized check-boxes of many ethical assessment committees – I wish to draw on the sorts of experiences recounted in the reflections above to speak of fieldwork ethics as a form of everyday, or in Lambek's (2010) rendering, 'ordinary ethics'. He argues that the human condition renders it impossible for us to escape the fact that our acts, down to our most simple gestures and words, are subject to being judged against criteria defining what is good. This condition is universal although the criteria are not – as shown, for instance, by my discussion about different approaches to understanding silence.

Action research scholars Lundy and McGovern (2006) have argued that 'in situations where political violence has occurred and marginalized groups have experienced social injustice, it is ethically impossible and morally reprehensible for social researchers to remain detached and silent' (ibid., 49). Yet, on a totally different note, Kidron (2009) claims that studies of silenced memories risk becoming the political or moral mission of scholars seeking to liberate the perceived victims of silence. Referring to Hayden's (2007) analysis of how the moral visions of ethnographers may impair their analytical insight, Kidron argues for particular care when 'vocal, and politically liberated' researchers engage in research concerning societies recovering from war: the researchers' charged moral underpinnings 'may wreak havoc with our observations and findings, reflecting our own worldviews rather than the lived experience of our subjects' (Kidron 2009, 18).

In contrast to Lundy and McGovern, for whom the option lies between action research and remaining 'detached and silent', I argue that the two – silence and action – are not each other's opposites. To refrain from immediate action does not imply the scholar's detachment, nor does it need to mean silence. The choice between 'breaking the silence' and 'protecting it' is a thoroughly ethical one, but it can only be resolved situationally. This situational ethical analysis, which is not a one-off exercise, but rather needs to be cultivated as an in-built and ongoing process of ethical reflexivity throughout the research process, requires acknowledgement of temporality, and of the relational character of the research process and of silence itself. Situations change over the course of a research project, and even over the course of a single day of fieldwork. What one research participant may be unwilling to discuss at one point might be an acceptable topic at another, and may also be precisely the subject on which another wishes to spend hours sharing her experiences. Or as I myself have noted, what might be acceptable for someone to say about the northern Ugandan war in far-away, middle-class Entebbe might be very different to what is possible and acceptable for someone to say in a village context where perpetrators of wartime violence live as each other's neighbours. And what a research participant might be willing to divulge to one scholar might be something she would never discuss with another, whether because of age, gender, a language barrier, or affection or dislike.

This aspect of relationality is crucial, for silence takes two: it is never born solely of the researcher or those she researchers, but in the relationship between them (Alava 2016a). The researcher's positionality and the constantly evolving webs of relationships she has with her research participants influence the shape, extent and tone of silence – and of its absence. What is particularly at stake is the transformation and unfolding of these relationships over time. As Finnström's (2015) analysis of secrets kept and later broken during more than ten years of research in northern Uganda shows, issues that have been veiled in silence may be unveiled much later. Changes in the external political context, in the participants' desire to speak out, in the researcher's orientation and wish for impact, all have bearing on the relationship between the researcher and her research participants, and on what this relationship carries. Each of these issues influences the others in countless ways, and as the variables change, so do the ethical questions that silence and its breaking posit to the researcher. No institutionalized and bureaucratized 'ethical clearance' procedure can cater for questions of this order. To use Lambek's (2010) term, the ordinary ethics that cut through the everyday of fieldwork as a matter of living (Malkki 2007), escape control and order.

Empathetic listening – and acquiescence at the limits of an ethics of encounter

Sarah, a young woman with whom I spent much time in Kitgum, once said something that has stayed with me to this day. She was one of the liveliest and most active people I knew, often joking, laughing and smiling, and it took me months to realize that she had had an extremely hard life. Her perseverance through it all to find herself standing on her feet, with a respectable job, and a respected position in her church, was remarkable. Yet she had suffered immense loss, and eventually shared with me memories of things she had seen during the war that shook me to the core. One day, sometime after these memories had been shared, Sarah told me that a member of her family had lost a baby. I offered my condolences and sighed that she had had a tough life. She answered, with a small firm smile on her face: 'I'm strong. On the outside. But if you looked in, you wouldn't survive.' I believe she was in some very real sense right. There was such pain, not only within her, but within northern Uganda as a whole, that it is difficult for the ethnographer to survive the encounter emotionally.[4]

Arguing for ethnography as the practice of cultivated empathy, Burnet (2012) suggests that the ethical alternative for researchers encountering people who have witnessed violence may in fact be to hold back, noting that respecting people's choices not to talk is a way of giving them back the agency taken from them during the violence they have endured or witnessed. Burnet's view resonates strongly with my own sense that to impose the topic of war on people whose everyday lives I was researching would have been inappropriate and unethical of me. But I must also acknowledge that by protecting the silence of people I was interacting with during my research, I was also protecting myself. It was easier for me to stay silent, to avoid head-on engagement with the war; to pick a topic of research that did not have the war at its apex. In notes from the final weeks of my 2013 fieldwork, I reflected that while I was to an extent drawn by harrowing stories of war, I had also been very drawn to protecting the silence. As I noted, 'the apparent peace (= silence) actually suits me very well. It's less emotionally draining. *And this is exactly the same reason that the people here are silent*' (Fieldwork notes, February 2013, emphasis in original).

Dealing with the kinds of atrocities and violence that the northern Ugandan war unleashed rightly forces researchers to reflect on the complex motives that drive our research. To what extent is research in former war zones driven by a voyeuristic impulse? It is a painful question to ask, but one that cannot be lightly bypassed. We know that violence sells headlines, and there is no reason to assume that a similar fascination with the unspeakable does not also promote academic publications.[5] Yet the kind of research that dwells on the horrors of mass perpetrated violence without giving readers any tools with which to contextualize or come to grips with it has rightly been criticized for being 'pornographic' (Maček 2014a, 20). Fieldwork in contexts shattered by decades of war and violence is thus mired in multiple ethical and emotional pressures and dilemmas, making what Hoel (2013) writes about it particularly pertinent. She argues that while we as researchers

> *partake* in power and in the construction of relationships of power... we also engage in research that requires a high level of personal commitment, giving of

yourself in particular research encounters – not because of what you might gain in return, but because this is also an ethical and human interaction that is taking place, the building of trust, and embodying unfamiliar and at times challenging local environments. Through these imbricated nodes, the notion of being vulnerable emerges as a delicate embodied response to research relationships that generates emotional and affective sentiments.

(Hoel 2013, 42)

This passage, framed with accounts of encounters from Hoel's own fieldwork among Muslim women in South Africa, provides a touching image of a profoundly ethical, embodied fieldwork encounter – one between a vulnerable researcher and vulnerable interlocutor – which may even have a healing effect for the interlocutor (ibid.). But does the sharing of pain in fieldwork encounters always have a healing effect? Recall the encounter I had with Grace where, as we cooked, she suddenly began sharing with me her memories of the war. As I recall the moment in hindsight, I can see that it was in many ways painful, for both of us. It was clearly painful for my friend and I felt like a witness to something I had no way of really understanding: a witness to pain that I could not console. All I could do was be there and listen, and show by my gestures and small intonations that I was listening. But I had no way of knowing whether re-telling her story eased my friend's pain.

The life story interview I conducted with Daniel, someone whose family had shared two separate personal incidents with my own, which connected us in a special way, tells a somewhat different story. Daniel, whom I had already known for about half a year when I formally interviewed him, began his story by briefly mentioning a rebel attack he had witnessed as a child. Soon both the tone and the topic of the interview changed, and for almost three hours we spoke in a very relaxed way about all sorts of things: children, friendships and dreams for the future. At one point, far into the interview, I asked him about his first memories as a child. When he did not quite understand what I meant by my question, I gave an example of some of my own memories from early childhood, of being stung by a bee, and of walking under falling leaves with my father. Daniel responded by telling me the first two things he remembered. The first was when, as a three-year-old, he had succeeded in sowing, caring for, and eventually harvesting his own small plot of groundnuts. The second was when, at the age of four, he had to watch at short range the rebels beating someone he knew almost to death. Without my asking, he told me a detailed account of the event and its aftermath: how he had felt and how he still carried the memory with him.

I told Daniel that half a year into my research, he was a rare case, since many of the people I interviewed said nothing about the war, and asked whether he was surprised to hear that. He said absolutely not, since people generally did not talk about the war. Other than his wife I had been the first, and would be the last, to hear his story. I asked Daniel why he had told me. He answered, 'Because I love you,' and laughed. This was not a romantic moment in the slightest; rather, the feeling was an evocation of the particular relationship enabled by the out-of-the-ordinary situation. The interview encounter, and the telling of his life story, drew us to discuss things which, as my friend explained to me, would usually not be considered appropriate to share in a friendship. As he explained, the young urban Acholi man and woman learn to shield what is on the inside: 'God for us all, man for himself. So, we can share other things, eh? We can share God, but now, when it comes to the inner part of me, I will not say it out, so that you should not know.' The interview, which was embedded in a family friendship that had developed over shared experiences of sickness, fear and happiness, allowed a break in the norm of keeping things in and produced a particular kind of trustful fieldwork encounter, which Daniel characterized with the surprising but perhaps apt concept of love. Similarly, Meinert (2015, 124–8) describes how it was only years after beginning her research in northern Uganda that some interlocutors told her about what they had experienced during the war: the required trust was built slowly.

But such a relationship does not – far from it – develop with every interlocutor; countless relationships in the field never include trust, sharing or friendship, let alone love. While Hoel evokes the notion of embodiment to call for ethical and human interaction in research encounters, I feel a focus on embodiment also helps in coming to terms with situations wherein stories of exemplary ethics cannot be told, and where the researcher's limitations affect the spaces between self and other where silences are formed, kept or broken. These embodied limitations may relate to situations in which research participants expect the researcher to feel comfortable with something when she is not; those created by embodied roles, such as motherhood; and by the researcher's traits – quick-temperedness, stubbornness, irritability, or as Maček (2014b) has noted, an inability to deal with the emotional strain of encountering the pain and trauma of people one encounters.

Many roles, characteristics and abilities enable certain kinds of understanding, but as I learned in relation to silence, they may also disenable. They may be the cause for silence. When my friend said to me, 'If you looked in, you would not survive,' I thought she was referring to the harshness of what she held within her.

In hindsight, I realize her statement was also an assessment of me, and of what I, as a person and as a researcher, was in her eyes capable of bearing.

Unshackling the preconceptions: Re-reading silence

Coming to re-read silence as I have in the course of this study was not at all self-evident or easy. I found it extremely difficult to understand the insistence of so many of my friends in Kitgum that talking about the past even with close friends or family was completely unnecessary, when for myself, the sharing of painful experiences signals intimacy and closeness. As a Finn, I should, stereotypically, value silence as a subtle form of communication (Carbaugh, Berry, and Nurmikari-Berry 2006). Yet I am, perhaps, not a very stereotypical Finn but, rather, emotionally outspoken, very talkative and tending to prefer ceaseless banter to silence. For me, intuitively, the 'natural' and 'good' response to painful memories would seem to be to express distress and sorrow – to talk until the pain lessens. Learning to identify and verbalize emotions is a prime concern for young adults in my social settings, and a skill in which parents like myself also train our children. The public psychotherapeutic culture of the contemporary West also spurs on what could almost be called a genre of emotional confessing. In Kitgum the same did not hold, and the expression of excess emotion was not considered appropriate in many such situations where an emotional outburst in my own cultural setting would have been considered fair enough.

Speaking out about everyday emotions and speaking about traumatic memories are of course two different things. But the cultural frames and narratives surrounding silence in general influence the ways in which an ethnographer comes to interpret silence encountered in fieldwork. In my case, the cultural frames I carried with me from Finland intermingled with the ways in which the Catholic priests made sense of the silence they witnessed among their parishioners. Partly, the shift in my view of silence came about through a fusion of horizons with people I encountered in Acholi, particularly through learning about their horizons in unverbalized ways: in situations where people reacted to my or my children's expressions of emotion by signalling that they were considered strange, for example. I will dwell, in some detail, on two such encounters in which this type of emotional learning took place, and which have profoundly influenced my reading of silence in Kitgum.

One afternoon, a visitor appeared on our porch just a few minutes after the death of my son's puppy. I was exhausted after many long days of fieldwork and

Figure 7. Group photo after a baptism service to which an Anglican reverend invited my family at his home village. Photo by author.

long nights of writing fieldwork notes, so when my homesick four-year-old son cried uncontrollably about the loss of a puppy I had forgotten to get injected for rabies, I was quite the emotional wreck. In my fieldwork diary, I wrote:

> Once I get the boys to sleep, Hassu has died. Just as I am washing the dead puppy so that the boys can say farewell and bury him after their nap, [a visitor] arrives. He can probably not quite understand what he sees: me crying over a dead puppy, washing away its bloody vomit. I go to wash my hands and gather myself a little, cover the puppy with an old newspaper, and sit down by the visitor on the terrace. He has come to agree on a time for an interview... I try to keep myself together, struggling between not crying and finding words in which I might explain myself. I try to say that my son has been missing home so much, the dog meant a lot to him. But it doesn't seem to really make much sense, and I can't do it without my voice breaking. So I suggest we meet for an interview in the afternoon, and try to explain myself by saying "sorry, I'm an emotional woman." [The visitor] leaves, and I go in and burst into bitter tears, angry at myself for not arranging for the vet on time, sorry for my son who has to deal with his friend dying, and at a loss for words for explaining the disparities in the worth of human or canine life in different

corners of the world. I wonder what [the visitor] must think of me, and what everyone else thinks of me.

(Fieldwork notes January 2013)

While the encounter says much about the different cultural expectations concerning human–canine relationships – puppies in Kitgum are taught to be tough guard dogs, not cuddled – it (and similar incidents) also taught me, more importantly, that my preconceptions about appropriate reasons for expressing emotion had to be recalibrated. Similarly to what Burnet (2012, 116) writes with respect to Rwanda, silence in Acholi is a culturally appropriate coping mechanism for dealing with painful memories and, as I realized when observing my children playing with our Acholi neighbours' children, also for dealing with physical pain. Even very small boys were taught not to cry and boys the same age or a bit older than my four-year-old would bite back tears and concentrate on breathing deeply rather than expressing their pain, even when seriously injured. Burnet (ibid.) notes that in Rwanda, recalling memories that might make a person cry, particularly before a relative newcomer like an ethnographer, was not considered appropriate. A similar cultural norm likely also influenced my encounters with people in Kitgum, and explains in part the increase in people's reference to war as I came to know them more closely.

But more than this, the incident with the puppy seemed to reinforce the assessment my friend had made a few weeks earlier. If I had a hard time dealing with exhaustion, my child's homesickness and a dead dog, how could I survive looking into the horrors of war that people around me carried in their memories? The encounter with the man and the puppy shares a nook in the halls of my memory with an encounter I had seven years earlier, on my first visit to Kitgum in 2006, which began with a trip to one of the most congested displacement camps in the district. That first visit plunged me into shock. The day was scorching hot, the camp was crowded and noisy, children were dirty and many looked gravely ill, and my overall impression was one of beyond inhuman living conditions and utter despair. After the half-day visit to the camp, I returned utterly shaken to the comfort of my hotel in Kitgum town. In my thesis, I describe what happened next in the following way:

> Despite the comfort of a hot shower and the imported chocolate I had waiting for me at the hotel, the only thing I could think of at the time was that I needed to get out. Luckily there was no flight out of Kitgum for two days, for I am sure I would have run away had it been an option. Shock with the circumstances at

the camp, anger with humankind for allowing such suffering, profound doubt in my own capacity to do any meaningful research in such overwhelming surroundings – the feelings came in torrents, as did the corresponding tears. Having heard me crying in my room, Evelyn, the young receptionist at the hotel [who had been among the survivors in a group of schoolgirls abducted by the LRA], came knocking at the door to ask me what was wrong. At the time, her words gave me little comfort, but during the following days the words spurred in me a shame-filled resilience that pulled me through the rest of my fieldwork: 'But think about us, we have lived in these camps all our lives.'

(Alava 2008, 18–19)

I felt a similar kind of shame after the encounter with the man over the dead puppy, particularly as he turned out to be one of the few exceptions to the rule of people not talking of the war: in the interview I had with him later in the day I learned that he had been the only survivor of a rebel ambush in which he saw many of his friends killed. Crying over a puppy was, in this light, completely out of proportion. While in 2006 it was a 'shame-filled resilience' that pulled me through my fieldwork, what upheld me during the longer period of living with my family in Kitgum was the exponentially more complex web of my and my family's relationships with research participants, acquaintances and friends, and the myriad emotions attached to them – all of which shaped the way I listened to the silence that had largely fallen on the town since the war's end.

Acknowledgement of how circumstances and personal characteristics delimit the possibility of ethical, embodied fieldwork encounters leads me to some disconcerting reflections. What can and should one do if, as a researcher, one wishes to show commitment to a different kind of ethics of research than seemingly allowed by the context and the scholar's own embodied limitations? What if the scholar's inability to hear stops her research participants from speaking out as they would wish?

I feel there are no easy answers to such complex questions. What seems clear, however, is that while research participants may rightly refuse to answer questions, and communities may rightly wrap past violence in a shroud of silence, we as researchers cannot similarly silence questions about the ethics of engaging with such communities and individuals. Openness to the challenge these questions pose has led me to attempt to adopt through various stages of my work what Page (2017) has recently described as a form of vulnerable writing:

[W]hat is at the heart of vulnerable methods and vulnerable writing are ongoing questions about what unsettles, about relations to the unfamiliar and strange, and about the erasure of the complexities of subjectivity... This unsettled uncertainty of the research process, rather than foreclosing on further understandings, provides space for new forms of unknowing and continued attempts at understanding the stories of others.

(ibid., 28)

As Page notes, and as I reflected when I chose in my dissertation to mirror the silence of my interlocutors and to not provide a detailed narrative account of the horrors of the northern Uganda (see Alava 2017b, 2019), such an approach goes against the grain of the desire to know, expose and explain. It also draws attention to questions of writing as representation.

Ethics in writing and representation

So far I have argued that the ethics of researching silence must always be pondered on the relational level, that is, in encounters we have in the field with our interlocutors. In the final part of this chapter, I turn to weighing in the ethics of research on a representational level. The two levels are not entirely separate, since the ethics of representation relates not only to how we plan, conduct and write about our research, but also to how the language we use in doing so structures our thoughts and acts, and hence positions us in relation to those we study (Alava 2019). Here, I follow the view of the existential anthropologist Michael Jackson, who writes:

> Whether we admit it or not, every cool act of analysis is also a creative act initiated within our particular personality and explicable in terms of our biography. In my view, true objectivity in interpretation does not consist in repressing, masking, or setting aside this biographical field of choice and intention but in revealing it clearly as it interacts with history, producing new syntheses in the shape of a poem, an essay, or even a revolutionary act.

(Jackson 2013, 88)

Such a view of ethnography, which founds itself on moral, aesthetic and political commitments rather than epistemological certainties (ibid.), also foregrounds the question of how pre-theoretical commitments (Moore 2004) guide our interpretations of silence. As Fassin and Rechtman (2009) have argued, the language of trauma, healing, and speaking out is entangled within a politics of representation and morality – something which also has profound, ethically questionable implications for research. As Kidron writes:

> As Euro-Western discourses of hegemony and subjugation, human rights, victimhood, and trauma take on a moral register of universal truth, enlightenment, and progress, our personal and professional vision of what should be remembered and articulated, as well as how, where, and by whom, is in my view at odds with the ethnographic imperative of 'sustained engagement' with our subjects 'on their terms'.
>
> (Kidron 2009 in author's responses to comments to article)

The overwhelming moral weight of the 'trauma paradigm' leads to places like northern Uganda being ascribed the labels of post-conflict, traumatized, or war-affected, when might they not also be described by words such as recovering, elastic, dynamic or even just relieved? These words matter, for many reasons, one of which is that they position the researcher relationally. What, for instance, might be implied by saying northern Uganda is 'aggrieved', rather than 'traumatized'? Would it not call the scholar away from the role of the benefactor or liberator, into that of the mourner? To mourn does not require speech. To mourn can mean to stay silent together.

The question of why labels like 'traumatized', 'post-conflict' and 'war-affected' are so common in our research proposals and publications is a complex one which I cannot address at greater length here than to suggest one explanation. I suspect that the practice follows in part from how so much of the research on 'post-war societies' takes war as its starting point and then often focuses on the very worst aspects of it: child soldiers, former abductees, or the victims and perpetrators of atrocities. There are many good reasons for this and I am not suggesting it should cease. But I think there is serious reason to consider whether the version of the world thus constructed does justice to the societies described. Holly Porter, whose research has explored communal and individual responses to rape in Acholi, writes of this beautifully:

> Rape is an aberration – the uglier side of the elephant, as an Acholi illustration goes, but not the whole animal. If you make up your mind about the nature of elephants based only on this vision you would decide that they are a rough, wrinkly and gray animal with no mouths or eyes – but you would only have looked at an inch on the left buttocks. Then again, if you really want to understand the great beast, you will need to look at it in its entirety, hairy bottom included.
>
> (Porter 2013, 48)

Any study in a post-war context will have to take account of the war itself and, regardless of her chosen angle of analysis, each scholar will have to find words with which to describe the traces of the violent past in the present. Yet my research experience shows that it is possible to research a war-affected community in a meaningful way while refraining from taking the war as the primary point of reference, and while problematizing the assumption that silence after war signals 'trauma'. Choosing not to break the silence after war but, rather to focus on what people themselves find meaningful and wish to discuss can facilitate description of how people come to terms with the past, how they make meaning in the present, and how they seek to materialize their dreams for the future. As Blaufuss has argued, our final authority as authors 'narrows the ability to present multiple truths and narratives, various narratives that had been part of what felt like an extensive conversation, as told and lived in the field' (2007, 14). The ethical challenges of researching silence thus follow us through from the moment of selecting topics, through each and every fieldwork encounter, to the final challenge that lies at our fingertips as we choose the words with which to describe the atmosphere and feeling of the 'field' where our ethnographies are set.

Closing and moving ahead

This chapter had two aims. First, it sought to describe Kitgum as a town emerging from war, one characterized by silences and their occasional breakings, and as I describe in more detail in chapters to come, by an oscillation between fear and hope. I argued that it is essential to differentiate between multiple reasons for silences, and advocated analyses' looking beyond the category of 'trauma' as an explanation for societal dynamics in the aftermath of war. And, as future chapters will further elaborate, it is not only the past that leaves Kitgum heavy with silence at times, for silence also arises from uncertainty about the political present, and from ambiguity concerning the future. Furthermore, silence is not always destructive; it may be precisely what enables life to continue and people to move on.

Second, through reflection on my own fieldwork encounters and my evolving interpretations of them in Kitgum, I considered the ethical implications of researching societies in which violent pasts are veiled in silence. Ethics as institutionalized in the bureaucratized processes of academic ethical clearance committees has little to offer for navigating everyday fieldwork encounters in such contexts. Instead, I highlighted the need to commit to sustained engagement with the 'ordinariness' and situationality of ethics. Furthermore, I argued that there is a need to pose difficult questions about the cumulative effect of research in 'hot-spots' like northern Uganda, even while I myself acknowledged a failure to provide answers to many of the questions I raised.

In the following chapters, the notions of silence, trauma and memory will return, and I will suggest other, parallel readings of them. In Chapter 4 I begin an analysis of the public performance of politics in churches in Kitgum, and argue that their efficacy rests on that which is neither seen nor heard. It is this unseen and silenced that Chapter 5 delves into, arguing that the politics of fear and uncertainty links with silence in essential ways, for fear makes people silent, and silence makes people uncertain. In Chapter 6, where I turn to analyse Christian utopias of peace in Acholi, I turn another leaf, and suggest an alternative, partially contradictory reading, of silence, showing how silence about the past may also enable moving forward. Taken together, the chapters to come will recapitulate the claim made in this one: that silence is relational, and its making, maintaining and breaking must be understood and analysed as occurring within the web of relationships that define its limits. Understanding the afterlives of war, anywhere, yet alone designing politics, policies and practices that enable individuals and communities to cultivate hope of less violent futures, requires sustained consideration of the complexities, contradictions and confusions, of which silences speak.

4

To stand atop an anthill
Performing the state in Kitgum

People say *cung i wibye* [to stand atop an anthill] because they feel politicians stand above them to talk to them, rather than standing at the same level. That is what politics is all about: about wanting power. When the British came, that is how they ruled, and that is how 'politics' came to be translated in this way. When we realised that it was possible for us to get rid of the British and for us to be free; for *Uhuru* to come; 'politics' became associated with freedom. But now, people have realised that it has gone back to being all about getting power; that these ones who want to climb up to the anthill, they will do anything to get power. The politicians are just lying. They are all full of lies.

(Elderly man in Kitgum, November 2012)

In this chapter, I elucidate the relationship between Christianity and politics in Uganda by focusing on the kind of politics played out at public church events, what in Acholi is referred to as *cung i wibye*, literally to 'stand on an anthill'. As explained by the man I quote above, the term's roots lie in the colonial era when men like J.R.R. Postlethwaite climbed onto anthills to address the crowds. Postlethwaite himself believed that his Acholi nickname, *Bwana Gweno*, which translates roughly as 'chicken lord', was given in reference to his frustration over the difficulty of procuring chickens for his meals (Postlethwaite 1947, 61); a difficulty described from the Acholi perspective simply as Postlethwaite 'violently seiz[ing] chickens from people' (Ogenga Otunnu 2016, 12). But those I heard the story from in Kitgum in 2012–13 claimed the name was coined so as lighten up the turmoil of colonial rule; to ridicule Postlethwaite's manner of strutting about in his fancy colonial garb. What was never mentioned in the stories told to me was the extent of this turmoil. Historian Ogenga Otunnu, for instance, describes how, in an attempt to crush Acholi resistance against the colonial demand for unpaid labour and taxes, Postlethwaite gathered a large crowd of people in Kitgum to observe how the chief of Pajule was lowered, 'with his head down, into a pit latrine until he died' (Otunnu 2016, 122). Violence has thus historically been deeply engrained in *cung i wibye* – and I claim, it continues to be.

The historical roots of the notion of *cung i wibye* were unknown to many young Acholis I spoke with, whereas political leaders insisted the word was ignorant slang. Instead, they claimed, 'politics' should be translated as something like *lok kom loc lobo*, that is, 'the way the world is ruled'. While most people acknowledge, when asked, that *cung i wibye* in its contemporary use relates to the politics of rallying, particularly in the run-up to elections, the word is, alongside the Acholianized *politik,* the most common translation for 'politics' in Kitgum. Something that almost everyone agreed on was that *cung i wibye* absolutely cannot and should not happen in church. But it did.

Public church gatherings in Uganda function as arenas for party politics and the politics of the state. In these situations, the churches are the anthills upon which politicians stand to present their agendas, confront their opponents and woo their supporters. Besides offering large crowds prayer, music, preaching and a church-sponsored full meal, such celebrations provide their organizers with opportunities to 'rub shoulders with the big shots', as one of my Catholic acquaintances phrased it. Notable politicians are routinely present, and public functions allow clergy to consolidate their relationships with political leaders, to whom glossy invitation cards are routinely distributed well in advance. Politicians are also keen to join the organizing committees of these events, where they at times wield considerable influence.

Some of these events, including those on which I build this chapter, also offer people a unique chance to witness national-level political drama. At the core of my analysis is the 2012 state burial of Acholi opposition politician, Tiberio Okeny Atwoma. Alongside it I draw on insights I gained throughout my fieldwork, particularly the resonances between Atwoma's burial and the handover of the Catholic Mission, and the commemoration of Saint Janani Luwum, which I attended on consecutive days in 2015. For residents of Kitgum, these three events, for which the president of Uganda travelled all the way to their town, were spectacular and highly out-of-the-ordinary occasions. In the midst of my own fieldwork as well, they appeared as episodes of particular importance: as 'heightened examples of existing social and political relations' (Madison and Hamera 2006, xvii).

By providing an analysis of the public relationship of churches and politics in post-war Acholi, the chapter weaves together insights from earlier chapters: on how the interconnections of Christianity and politics have evolved through Uganda's postcolonial and colonial history (Chapters 1 and 2), and on how silence and trauma colour the everyday in post-war Kitgum (Chapter 3). The approach I adopt contends that church events not only reflect, but actually reproduce the state: '[p]ublic cultural representations and performance of statehood crucially shape people's perceptions about the nature of the state' (Gupta and Sharma 2006, 18). Following J.L. Austin (1975) and Judith Butler (1993), I consider these events to be performative, that is, capable of creating and constraining the phenomena – in my analysis the state – that they produce (ibid., 3). Butler emphasizes that words can be re-signified, and that speech acts may hence transform reality, yet she remains cautious about the possibility of individual actors enacting substantial change through speech, because speakers are inextricably embedded in their historically and discursively constructed subjectivities (Butler 1997, 49, 55). In a similar manner, it is difficult for speech at political events to escape the speech tradition in which the speeches are made, particularly in situations embedded in legacies of violence. Yet while there is much in the performance of *cung i wibye* that refers to existing genres of violent political discourse, these performances are not entirely scripted. At public church events, negotiations and contestations take place between different interest groups and their diverging visions of what Uganda is and should be.

A resonant perspective can be found in the view that rituals not simply represent or symbolize a reality outside of them, but are capable of altering non-ritual realities (Kapferer 2004). Kapferer argues that the time of ritual relates to the time of the ordinary everyday 'as depth to surface' (ibid., 37). This idea resonates strongly with my experience of the public church events in which I participated in Kitgum – and with the metaphor of the anthill – but with a crucial twist: in Acholi, I argue, the public rituals of state-making bear a connection to ordinary lived reality as a visible surface that excludes from sight the largely unseen underside of the anthill. To borrow the language of Jenny Edkins, it is the deep, chaosmatic everyday of 'the political' that is held in abeyance when 'politics', in its most visible form, rises to the surface (2003). While Kapferer argues that what goes on in ritual is commonly more akin to that which goes on behind the scenes of theatre rather than in the limelight of the stage, I suggest that at events like Atwoma's burial, the altar, the pulpit and the microphone stand are the stage on which the ritual of church and state are performed. As I argue later in the book, however, the ritual of state-making in post-conflict northern Uganda is completed, to draw on Kapferer's distinction, behind the scenes.

While Uganda under President Museveni has been described as a hybrid regime, which skilfully combines elements of liberal and totalitarian governance (Carbone 2008; Perrot, Makara, and Lafargue 2014; Tripp 2010), and as an 'arbitrary state' which 'allow[s] for pockets of civic organization and pathways for citizens to make claims... [but makes] these spaces fragile by intervening in them violently and unpredictably' (Tapscott 2021, 3), I find the most resonant characterization to be found in Cecilie Verma's work: a 'conquest state with a democratic face' (Verma 2013, 176). For Ugandan citizens, the outward markers of liberality are assessed against personal and communal experiences of encountering the state's totalitarian face (Alava 2020). Both of these aspects were visibly present at Atwoma's burial, of which I now provide a detailed account before setting out to analyse what it tells us of the nature of politics in Uganda, and the role churches play in it.

The state burial of 'a nationalist and a man of God'

Tiberio Atwoma had in his day been one of Kitgum's most renowned politicians. An early member of the Democratic Party, Atwoma had represented the Acholi region at Uganda's Constitutional Conference in London in 1961 and was later one of the Acholi representatives in the 1992 Constituent Assembly. In 1991 he was arrested together with a group of Acholi elders under suspicions of plotting a rebellion – the same group as Philip Odwong, whose case I have discussed earlier, and released months later once all accusations were found false (Amnesty International 1991).

The role Atwoma had played at historical moments granted him the honour of a state burial. The fact that this was no ordinary burial was obvious already before Chiara and I arrived on the scene, as the road from the presidential helicopter's landing site to Atwoma's homestead in Oryang village, near Kitgum town, treated as it was with a fresh layer of flattened muram, was smoother than any other in the town. The homestead itself was surrounded by soldiers and policemen, and all guests were required to have body checks and pass through metal detectors. The ceremonial ground was typical: tents filled with rows of plastic chairs are placed to form three sides of a rectangle, with each tent reserved for a particular group: local participants; district, political and religious leaders; priests, nuns and brothers; and visitors from neighbouring districts. Rather than crowding into the tents, Chiara and I found spaces among a group of women who were allowed to spread large raffia mats in front of the tents, in the shade of a mango tree.

The sometimes very long gap between the announced time of beginning and the actual event starting serves an important preparatory role. During this time, North American praise songs and hymns on keyboard organ are played over the sound system, and interrupted to signal the gradual arrival of dignitaries. This time is also used by the master of ceremonies (hereafter MC), usually a priest or former Catholic seminarian, to prepare the audience for what is ahead. At Atwoma's burial the MC, for instance, announced that the president would not be shaking any hands due to an outbreak of Marburg disease in a distant part of Uganda. He also warned that there would be a gun salute, during which the audience, whom he acknowledged were very used to gunshots, should remain calm. Finally, the MC disciplined the audience:

> After the blessing, police will carry out a solemn procession. Let us give attention to what is going on. Maintain silence, please, as the blessing of the body is going on. Maintain order. If you are not ready to stay here, then please get out. You must give Tiberio Atwoma the dignity that he deserves. And for us, we interpret this as the dignity that God has given him and we must be respectful of that.

Yet the solemn silence that the Catholic clergy in particular always requested was seldom present. With the exception of short moments when the crowd is absolutely silent and listening to the speaker, public masses and the political rallies that follow them are often lively participatory events, where the crowd refuses to remain passive and silently appreciative spectators. This time was no exception; as the priest called on the mourners to rise, the women sitting around me on the ground started talking and broke out in a great deal of the local sound for disapproval: 'Tst-tst-tst'. 'Please, let us remain silent!' the MC begged, as the crowd became louder and louder. Eventually the procession of priests entered, and a local parish priest welcomed all visitors:

> We know that Mzee [an honorary title for elderly men] was a believer, who was working for the government to help the Acholi people and Uganda at large... Let us give a mighty clap for the gift of Atwoma. He was a nationalist, and he was a man of God.

And so the celebration of Mass was underway, and the event framed as a commemoration of a deceased nationalist and man of God – and concurrently, a celebration of a nation and a Church that outlived him. In his sermon,

Archbishop John Baptist Odama narrated a vision of a united Uganda, and of a global community of responsible humans of different ethnicities, tribes, religions and political parties, together seeking unity through forgiveness and love under the eyes of a loving, caring and forgiving God. The greater the political prestige of the event, the more both Catholic and Anglican sermons and prayers in Kitgum tended to emphasize the responsibility of political leaders to steer Uganda towards peace, unity and God. So also here:

> We pray that you unite us to remember Tiberio Atwoma, who had respect for human rights, and who brought peace. Give these gifts to other leaders. Let them use politics to unite, and not to divide people... We pray for peace in our hearts, because we don't have peace in our hearts or in our communities. Bless Uganda with good leaders.

In preparation for Communion, all those gathered were asked to greet their neighbours with the words, 'Peace be with you.' The choir struck up a song which we all joined, requesting that the Lord bind us together with love and hope that cannot fail. Just as communion was about to end, a helicopter flew low over the compound: the president was about to arrive. The arrival of Museveni signalled a shift of tone: from the clerically led emphasis on Christian reconciliation and unity, to one of open party political contest.

The president arrives – and the *cung i wibye* begins

As the line of the president's vehicles approached the ceremonial ground, the police brass band struck up the national anthem. Only a handful of people joined in the singing, while others muttered and tried to peer over each other's shoulders to see Museveni behind the big black cars and open-top army trucks loaded with soldiers in full combat gear that escorted him. The president and his company took their seats in the NRM-yellow tent emblazoned with the national emblem of Uganda which had been empty up until this point, and the line of bulky vehicles drove away. The mourners who had been selected to lay wreaths were now called up by the MC in an ascending order of hierarchy. A group of senior citizens, followed by local councillors, district council chairpersons (LC5s), resident district commissioners (RDCs), and representatives of the three major opposition parties each said a few routine words of farewell to the deceased.

The chairperson of Atwoma's Democratic Party (DP), Norbert Mao, followed the farewells with an emphatic statement: 'Democracy must be founded on justice. Uganda will never be peaceful if it is not led with justice and peace!' To this, the crowd responded with enthusiastic applause and ululation, after which hundreds joined Mao as he sang the DP anthem into the microphone. Next in line to lay their wreaths were the ministers and the deputy speaker of parliament, the president, and finally the archbishop. After a short moment of silence, the speeches began, again in hierarchical order, starting from the bottom rung.

The first to speak was the chairperson of the organizing committee, who, like practically all those following him, addressed his words primarily to the chief mourner:

> Your Excellency, President Yoweri Kaguta Museveni, we extend our heart-felt appreciation for your joining together with the Acholi people and the Acholi sub-region in mourning. This is a simple act of love and care for humanity and for the Acholi people. As the saying goes, a leader in a moment of need and sorrow is a friend indeed. Our grateful thanks.

Very few people clapped in response, and the MC invited one of Atwoma's sons to give a speech on behalf of the mourning family. In it, he said:

> We are actually very grateful to the government, for what they have decided to do, because at a time like this we were very uncertain, at a time like this you can be so confused, but the state chose to give this fantastic burial, so thank you Your Excellency.

On behalf of Atwoma's family – his two wives, eleven children and over seventy grandchildren – the son then requested a tractor to assist them in their farming work, a bursary to support the education of the grandchildren of the deceased and a school to be constructed to respect Atwoma's legacy. His requests were received with 'tst-tst', and subdued ripples of laughter from different parts of the audience; as I later learned, many people, including some members of the family, had found the man's behaviour a travesty. After listing his requests, the man shouted out, 'Long live the president. Long live NRM!' A few people ululated and clapped in the tent closest to the president and his entourage, but the rest of the crowd of thousands remained silent. Another son gave a speech of thanks, and concluded by stating it was up to Atwoma's children and grandchildren to ensure they lived exemplary lives, so donors could trust them.

The MC then invited the local village councillor to speak, and instructed him to keep his speech to two minutes, to which the crowd responded with a burst of laughter. After listing all the necessary protocol, the local councillor congratulated Museveni 'for being the first ruling president to step on this soil'. He then told the president how in 1986, a group of soldiers in Museveni's National Resistance Army had stormed their village, killed thirteen people, and left behind widows and orphans who had had no chance for education. The elder continued:

> Here we are actually good Christians, every year we commemorate with special prayers the victims of 1986. Those prayers are no longer about grievances and such things, but to commemorate and remember the victims. Next year, on the 20th of September, Your Excellency, if you do not have anything particular, we ask you to come and join in the prayers.

A wave of laughter and cheers swept over the crowd; the man's politeness towards Museveni was easy to interpret as taunting. He continued:

> Construction of a church is underway here now. Altogether 800 million shillings are needed for the construction. The government can help, so that growing children, youth, can be brought to the church to be taught, so that there will be no more loss of innocent life as was here. We shall not in fact allow you to pray. We shall be praying for you!

And again the crowd laughed and cheered the LC on. Finally he declared that locals expected the government to help provide for three kindergarten classrooms, an office and a store in memory of the dead: 'Long live Uganda! Long live the NRM!'

After LC chairpersons had announced how much each of them would give to funeral expenses, the line of speeches by male speakers, which had already taken hours by this point, was interrupted with the first female parliamentarian's speech. At the time, the woman MP for Kitgum district, Beatrice Anywar (pronounced 'anyewaar'), who at that time was a member of the leading and largest opposition party, the Forum for Democratic Change (FDC), was known as an outspoken and popular member of the Acholi parliamentary group. Anywar politely raised a number of concerns to the president's attention: the awful quality of roads; the low level of government sponsorship for Acholi students' university fees; teachers' unpaid salaries; the lack of care for victims of the nodding disease[1]; the lack of drugs at Kitgum government hospital; unpaid soldiers in the army; and unpaid death claims for the family members of deceased Acholi soldiers. Before giving a closing list of specific requests, Anywar decried restrictions on the freedom of press in Kitgum. She mentioned no details, but the audience knew she was referring to a recent incident in which a local radio station had been forced to temporarily expel some of its staff or face closure after its reporters had criticized members of the government for stealing money meant for northern Uganda.

After Anywar, it was time for speeches by representatives of opposition parties. First among them was the party president of the Uganda People's Congress, Olara Otunnu, whom the audience cheered like a rock star. In contrast to all the other speakers before him, Otunnu, an Acholi from the village of Mucwini in Kitgum, began his speech in the local language:

> Leaders of Acholi, of Uganda, I greet you, and thank you for being here. We have gathered here to pay our last respects to Tiberio Okeny Atwoma. God has given a gift to our leader, and that gift was different. He didn't give it to many people. Fear was not given to Atwoma. He stood by truth until he died… As we gather here today, we show our respect to someone who was high. So we should dance, sing, and in all ways show him the respect he deserves. Some things he told me, I will now tell the president.

Otunnu switched to English, and slowly, with calculated emphasis on every word, hailed the president. The crowd responded to each name with increasing jitters of laughter, and each twist and turn of the speech that followed drew waves of affirming response from the audience:

> My special brother… His Excellency… General… Yoweri… Kaguta… Museveni… seated here in the land of my ancestors! You see those hills there? My ancestors, they are resting at the foothills. You relax! I have no worry about them! Now that you are here, make sure you have plenty of *malakwang*, of *odii*, of *boo*, of *lakerokoro*.[2] My special brother… We met to discuss with Atwoma. At one point he went to Kampala to see your doctor, and I gave him a lift. So we were talking on the way, and the first thing he said over and over again, was how this land, this people, this civilisation [with more and more emphasis on the words as the list went on], has produced so many outstanding people to the world: Daudi and Jildo! Janani Luwum! Matthew Lukwiya! Okot p'Bitek![3] People of such great talent, that this place gave to Uganda, who then gave them on to the world. Who will take their place?

After discussing the deplorable state of education in Acholi and demanding Museveni, with the power and resources, do something about it, Otunnu returned to the land of his ancestors:

> And then, finally, kindly. The issue of land. The issue of land. The issue of land! The issue of the land of our people, of Acholi, of Uganda. He [Atwoma] wanted it to remain in the hands of us! I guarantee, my brother, that nobody is more interested in genuine development than the Acholi. Nobody welcomes

> genuine investors, not the fake ones from the State House, but genuine investors, as warmly as the people of Acholi. Madvhani group,[4] if they are interested in investing and producing, why are they not interested in lease arrangements?... Don't let anyone deceive you that land is not an issue here. It is! It is! It is a matter of capital importance.

Otunnu's comment about deceiving statements referred to one made by an army general, widely reported in national media and discussed also in Kitgum, that contrary to what Acholi opposition politicians and civil society actors said, land was not really a burning issue in northern Uganda. After people stopped laughing and cheering, Otunnu carried on:

> After the existential threat in the concentration camps,[5] people have come out with nothing in their hands but the land. The land! My people must and they will defend their land. Today, tomorrow, always! Respect their land! Let them develop it peacefully! So again, I welcome you my brother, to the land of my ancestors. I was going to shake your hand, but I understand you are deeply concerned and scared for the ebola [sic] phenomenon, so I will leave it for a later time.

At this, and for lack of a more fitting way of expressing what occurred, the crowd absolutely cracked up, and I with them. Once everyone eventually calmed down, Otunnu concluded his speech with:

> So Atwoma, travel well. And my brother... his Excellency... General... Yoweri... Kaguta... Museveni...

The roar of laughter, ululation and cheering that erupted from the crowd drowned out the rest of Otunnu's words, and continued until after he had returned to his seat. The crowd seemed to be entirely elated by Otunnu's entertaining and cleverly confrontational style, yet, entertained as I was myself, there was also something slightly disconcerting in the way in which Otunnu magisterially manipulated the moods and reactions of the crowd. The ferocious critique that lay between the seemingly polite lines of Otunnu's speech, the casual way in which he mocked Museveni's fear of shaking hands, and the apparent elation of the people when he mocked the president, all slightly unnerved me.

The audience muttered and chatted while the FDC's vice president read a letter from Kizza Besigye – it was the speaker after him for whom everyone was waiting. Norbert Mao, the party leader of Tiberio Atwoma's DP, was escorted to the podium by the audience's rhythmic clapping and extremely loud cheering. After litanies of introduction, Mao began:

> I want to tell you: Things are changing. When it is dark, light is coming. When you cry, it helps, but it doesn't stop the cause of the crying. There's a beginning and an end to everything; not *pakalast*.

People erupted in cheers and laughter at the reference to the slogan Museveni had used in his 2011 election campaign, which had been adopted from the name of the most common mobile bundle in Uganda. The slogan, fiercely critiqued by opposition at the time of the elections, meant 'until the end', and was seen as a reference to Museveni's wish to remain president until his death (see, e.g., Rice 2011).

> Your Excellency, on the part of the DP, we think we are in this together. If the vehicle you drive is crashed, the driver with the seatbelt may be okay, but the people sitting in the back of the pick-up not so. We have thus come here to make sure that you deliver us to the goal.

Mao then confronted the president with a list of grave problems in Ugandan public administration, and then addressed the audience:

> When you hear all of us here talking like this, you wonder why there is no top forum for top leaders to really discuss about these issues. We have a problem in this country: when we try to address the population, the police come with teargas! That is why we come to funerals, we come to weddings, and to graduation parties. A funeral is not the place to discuss these issues!

Mao then turned to the 50th Jubilee year of Ugandan independence which had been celebrated only a few weeks earlier:

> In the Bible, in the Jubilee year, everything is forgotten: you forgive us, and we forgive you. Otherwise, there's no way we can go forward, because we can't change the past. But the future we can. Your Excellency, take the opportunity this year to surprise even your worst opponents. I am still young. It is true, I have 48 years to go before I reach the age of the deceased. We the young generation: we will support any programs that contribute to the general development of Uganda. We are committed to see that nobody need to rise to presidency by walking on the blood of the former president.

Mao was given generous applause, and MP Beatrice Anywar came to request that the crowd also clap for Museveni. Her efforts incited only half-hearted claps here and there, and many people did not bother to join in at all. The first representative of government to speak was Henry Okello Oryem, a member of parliament for Kitgum district and the State Minister for Foreign Affairs of Uganda. Oryem, who is the son of Tito Okello (the army general who ousted Obote from presidency in 1985 and was in turn ousted by Museveni's NRM/A in 1986), had been a lawyer in the UK where he had studied until running for MP on an NRM ticket in 2001. In his speech, Oryem rejected, issue by issue, grievances raised in preceding speeches by claiming there was nothing about which to be aggrieved. He concluded:

> It is thanks to the achievements of the NRM that a number of things we have witnessed have taken place. Olara Otunnu had a platform here to directly address his president. And brother Mao, he also had a platform here to address his president, freely and without fear. Thank you, brothers, for freely talking, and for paying respect to the president. Let us thank the NRM for these achievements, which are in accordance with the spirit which the NRM cherishes. If the time comes for Museveni to end his reign, Otunnu or Mao can take over. I will not take sides. If the time comes, one must step down.

Oryem received some claps and cheers from the tent for NRM supporters that was pitched near the president's tent, and was then followed by another NRM man, the deputy speaker of parliament, Jacob Oulanyah. Also from Acholi, Oulanyah originally joined parliament on a (UPC) ticket and switched to the NRM after losing his seat in 2006. He launched into an even more pronounced attack against the opposition and song of praise for the president than Oryem had before him:

> In this Jubilee year, we celebrate the life of Atwoma. But your Excellency, there is no other Ugandan Jubilee president. Only you! Uganda has been independent for fifty years. There is a question I have really been troubled by, and I want to request humbly that you, the Acholi people, help me to answer this question. Why, I have to ask, why were there 9 presidents, violent coups, and bloody looting, in the first twenty-five years? And why, in the last twenty-five years have we had one president, no violent coups, and no looting. Why? Truly I would like to find out the answer, why? I tell you. It is because President Yoweri Kauguta Museveni got something right. He got something right about Uganda. About these people. There was no looting. No bloody coups.... Your Excellency... committed your life to achieve this dream!... All these people should focus on the same vision, because it has kept the country together. Never again shall we subject Uganda to chaos, to war, to demonstrations that destroy property and cause chaos.

Once Oulanyah concluded, the stage was set for President Museveni himself. The speech, which was simultaneously translated from English into Acholi, opened with Museveni's declaration that he had not come to talk about politics, which he immediately followed by stating that the deputy speaker of parliament had been correct in his assessment that the NRM had succeeded because of its disavowal of sectarianism. After briefly dwelling on his familiar arguments (see, e.g., Museveni 1997), Museveni criticized a suggestion Atwoma had made during the run-up to independence, that the country be called 'The Nile State' rather than 'Uganda', which referred to the nation's largest kingdom, Buganda. 'We in the NRM opposed this. Our reason was – and this is my theme – that Uganda is one.' In a surprising move that crossed the national media threshold, Museveni then continued with an apology:

> I'm sorry mistakes have been made by the NRM. I would like to apologise for the mistakes of the NRA. This thing of 13 people being killed, I have never heard of it, I have heard of the massacres in Mucwini by the LRA, of mistakes in Namukora by Battalion number 35.[6] But of this massacre I have never heard. I apologise. I am sorry. We have bad people in all groups. The difference, and where I would like to challenge my younger brother Olara Otunnu, is that NRM has mistakes, but also the capacity to overcome those mistakes, and not collapse like the UPC has done so many times. That is the difference. I apologise sincerely for the mistakes. One of the mistakes made was to arrest these elders, like this one, Mzee Atwoma. Some of our fellows in the NRM panicked, they thought these people were in conspiracy to overthrow the government. However, because NRM has got bad but also good people in it, it works as a system. And eventually the good system came in and acquitted the charged. And again I apologise for those mistakes.

The president then recounted all the reasons why Atwoma had deserved a state burial, and promised that a technical school would be constructed in Kitgum in his memory. That said, he continued:

> For the families of our pioneers, as long as I have the authority of president, what I can do is provide some positions. That is what I did with Henry Okello Oryem [the son of Tito Okello, whose speech preceded Museveni's]. Now, the son of [late President Milton] Obote is in parliament.[7] If Tiberio Okeny Atwoma has some educated children, I would like to see how I can deploy you. As to Mao, I support his call, we should all work together, have a forum. There actually is a forum that I innovated in 2006. FDC's Besigye boycotted it; he has been giving a lot of trouble really. Mao gets it wrong saying we give them teargas. That's right, teargas is the easiest way, the softest way to deal with troublemakers.

When someone wants to trample the tomato sellers' tomatoes, and the police say no and they don't listen, what do you do? The best thing to do is to fire some teargas into their eyes so they stop. It's not us who want teargas, it's Besigye, although one time, Mao, you also joined in. But on the opposition part, Besigye has been boycotting the forum. The National Resistance Movement, we were ready before, and we are ready now, to meet with national leaders. Now I don't want to talk about politics, the only thing I want to take up is the Gulu-Kitgum road. It will be tarmacked.[8]

The crowd, which had been increasingly muttering disapproving 'tst-tst' sounds, shouted out, '*Goppa, goppa!*' meaning 'lies'. Museveni responded: 'You say I am lying, but I tell the truth!' The president wrapped up by saying there was no time to address other issues, or to personally meet the family of the deceased, be he would leave them 10 million shillings (about 2,500 euros) for burial expenses.

The crowd's response was almost aggressively passive, with only a handful of NRM party enthusiasts cheering in their own tent. Museveni's explanations did not go down well with members of this audience, who looked to me mostly to be tired, unimpressed, even angry. A procession was formed to escort the coffin to the grave, followed by a group of Acholi *bwola* dancers with drums. Odama swung the censer over the grave, after which the body was lowered into it. By this point, hardly anyone was paying any attention to what was still going on. Instead, there was a lot of laughter, and the English words 'state burial' fluttered through the crowd's chatter. Above the ceaseless prattle, I could just hear Odama reading into the microphone the final words of blessing at the graveside. Few people seemed to notice that the police were going through an elaborate series of signals and gestures, so when the police fired their guns in a salute, hundreds of people jolted and screamed in panic. In just a few seconds, people seemed to remember that they had been warned, and broke out in relieved laughter.

With his final words, the archbishop addressed the president: 'May this gesture of your being with us, and this reconciliatory gesture with the other parties here, be the way we move as this country, and may Tiberio Okeny Atwoma lead us in this.' The president's cars arrived, and he and all his companions filed in and drove away. As evening was already falling, most people ignored the invitation to line up for food, and instead headed home, exhausted as we were from almost seven hours with no food and too much sun. Mass was over, as was a remarkable show of political debate and entertainment.

Performing personalized, gendered and neopatrimonial power

Major public church events in Kitgum both reflect and reproduce Uganda as a hybrid regime in which liberal and authoritarian elements are merged, where power is highly personalized and gendered, where political deliberation is largely submerged by neopatrimonial logics and politicized ethnicity, and where the relationship between mainline churches and the state remains important. The performance of statehood at these events is not, however, in the form of a monologue; rather, the state that emerges is the result of contestation and negotiation between numerous participants and their diverging political imaginaries. These negotiations continue in everyday lives, after the festival grounds are cleared up, and everybody has gone home. The state, while not all-powerful, provides critical boundaries within and against which political imaginaries in post-war northern Uganda can be crafted. In the following, I discuss in turn each of the characteristics of the Ugandan state that I mention in the core argument above.

The first point to make concerns the extent to which the state performed at these events materializes in the persona of the president. A striking characteristic of this and other similar events is that regardless of what was actually being celebrated, the president was their centre of attention. Rather than to the audience or the government, not to mention the bereaved family, all speeches, save that of Museveni himself, addressed the president – the embodiment of state power in Uganda. When confronted with pleas for assistance, or with a request to make Saint Janani Luwum day a national holiday, the president does not respond by saying he will request administrative staff to prepare a motion to be discussed in parliament. He responds by making a personal promise, which he then puts into motion (as in the case of the Janani Luwum memorial day), or forgets. The personal promise of the president is not a guarantee – two years after Atwoma's burial, his relatives complained that none of the things the president had promised had materialized. However, Museveni's word is as good a guarantee as Ugandans can get; his opinion sways the ruling party, dominates a large part of the press and to a large extent manipulates the parliament (Goodfellow 2014; Tripp 2010). Part of this personified power emerges from the way in which the president distances his regime's actions from himself. The apology that he made for NRA atrocities in Oryang is a case in point. The president claimed never to have heard of the plunder, which seems unlikely: the NRA was under his command, and even if word of their actions had not reached Museveni in

1986, they are sure to have reached him by 2012, and far earlier, since Atwoma had taken the case to a civil court and, according to Father Paul Donohue (see Chapter 2), been threatened with death unless he withdrew the case (Donohue 1991).

The second point to make concerns the extent to which power is gendered. The fundamentally patriarchal character of politics in Uganda was highly evident in Kitgum, where both the public performance of politics in moments of *cung i wibye* and political affairs in general are largely dominated by and structured around men (for a detailed analysis of women in Ugandan politics, see Tripp 2000). Notice that the speakers I cited at Atwoma's burial were almost all men. Even those speakers whose brief speeches I bypass in the account I give, such as LC5s of other districts, were male. The only and notable exception to the rule of speaking men at Atwoma's burial was the woman MP for Kitgum, FDC's Beatrice Anywar. Even more notable was the way in which she was addressed by the president in his speech, when he described how it came about that Atwoma was given a state burial: 'So Honourable Minister Okello Oryem came to me, and it was suggested to me also by my daughter Beatrice' – to which people responded with spontaneous laughter. The Member of Parliament for Chua County, Kitgum district (male), was referred to by his title of *Honourable Minister*, whereas the Member of Parliament for Chua County, Kitgum district (female), was allocated her place with the patronizing use of the label of 'daughter'.[9] Although at times contested, the imagery of the president as benevolent father, and the predominance of men in public arenas are profoundly influential templates for Ugandan politics. As Sylvia Tamale has noted, female politicians, despite their remarkable creativity, 'have to execute their political agendas within a historically entrenched male paradigm' (Tamale 1999, 63).

The third characteristic of the Ugandan state that becomes apparent at these events is the extent to which Museveni's power is embedded in neopatrimonial relations (Mwenda and Tangri 2013; Titeca and Onyango 2012; Tripp 2010; Wiegratz, Martiniello, and Greco 2018). I use the notion of neopatrimonialism not in the sense employed in 'good governance' discourse (for a critique, see Abrahamsen 2000), but to distinguish contemporary neopatrimonialism as a form of governance from patrimonialism (Beekers and van Gool 2012, 17). The space of *cung i wibye* is used for the unconcealed and unabashed procurement and consolidation of patronage relations. At Atwoma's burial, local politicians requested the president to provide services for their electorate, and simultaneously reminded the electorate that it was they who were lobbying for schools, hospitals and tarmacked roads – services for which the NRM state then took all the credit. Moreover, the president publically promised descendants of the deceased positions of power. In exchange for the president's goodwill and benefaction, speakers appealed to Museveni as the father, benefactor and protector of his people, and in turn, promised to pray on his behalf.

The fourth point to draw out is the way in which these events signify the relevance of churches for the Ugandan state, and the way in which churches are embroiled in the same neopatrimonial relations and, by extension, legitimize their perpetuation (Gifford 1998). In this sense, it is already in itself significant that such considerable space is given to *cung i wibye* at public church events, and that there are such close connections between churches and politicians (Alava and Ssentongo 2016).[10] In 2015, at both the handover of the Catholic mission in Kitgum, and at the commemoration of Luwum in Mucwini, Museveni donated 30 million shillings (some 900 USD) to the local parishes. It was not clear whether the envelopes came from his personal finances, or whether they were under some kind of state budgetary control. Nonetheless, the overwhelming majority of the audience greeted the president's envelopes with massive cheers and ululation. One young Catholic man explained to me that since the war

> the issue of money has come in seriously, and it is the controller of very many things. Even politics. Let me say like the NRM people, most of them they poured money, like during the election, when you go and attend a rally, you are dished with 5,000. So when you go to the village, some people they cannot afford to get 50,000 in a month, or 10,000 in a month, so, when you give such kind of person 5,000 shillings, they will become very happy and, ABC, oh yeah, they vote for you. Because you have given them what? Money. People just select money.

While this particular young man believed that support for the NRM was suicidal in that the ruling regime was clearly unable or unwilling to deliver on its promises, for many, the calculation was more pragmatic. It was rarely the neopatrimonial character of the state *as such*, or the status of the president as 'father of the nation' *as such*, that was critiqued at public church events or in discussions with my research participants. Rather, the crux of the critique was often that the spoils of neopatrimonial governance were not being doled out in sufficient quantities to Acholi. This is why people cheered wildly when Museveni announced he would contribute money to the parishes. Increasingly, the attitude towards Museveni in Acholi seems to be: he may have mistreated us in the past, but if we vote for him now, at least he might give us 'something little'. This argument resonates with that of Karlström who, drawing on research in Central Uganda's Buganda, argues:

Discourses of 'eating' and the size of political 'bellies' are thus anchored in a moral economy of politics, in which the engorgement of politicians' bodies takes place within a social matrix of substantive reciprocities, and thus confirms the legitimacy of their authority. This relational matrix is experienced by many rural Baganda as more reliable and effective than the abstract mechanisms of distribution and legitimation of the modern 'rational'-bureaucratic administrative system and the liberal democratic state, in so far as these have been operative in Uganda.

(Karlström 2003, 68)

The irony here is that while the performances of *cung i wibye* at church events reproduce and re-endorse imaginaries of a 'moral economy of patronage', these events also endorse the detrimental neopatrimonial governance that characterizes Museveni's Uganda, which has repeatedly left northern Uganda outside of the social matrixes of substantive reciprocity at a national level.

Imagining and performing (dis)unity

In recent years, criticism towards Museveni's regime has in some arenas deepened, while limitations for his power have been removed. It is not often that spaces emerge for the kind of political debate that I witnessed at Atwoma's burial, since, as the opposition politicians speaking at the event put it, in public spaces other than those of burials, weddings and graduations, the risk of teargas looms large. What then, is the meaning of speeches held at them, and more broadly, of state-making rituals like this one? I claim that church events were about imagining community and its boundaries, and thus productive simultaneously of both unity and disunity.

At events like Atwoma's burial, there was constant signalling towards a community beyond those gathered: through their participation, Acholi spectators were, ideally, to be re-born no longer as 'mere Acholi', but as Christians and as Ugandans; as Acholi members of the Church and the Nation. This was already evident in the language used; in contrast to local parish events, events attended by the president were conducted almost exclusively in the *national* language English, with translation into Acholi provided only for the sermon and for the president's speech. At Atwoma's burial the rhetoric of unity and oneness ran through the speeches of both Odama and Museveni. The archbishop called for recognition of the global community of humans (what I analyse as a reality-altering utopia in Chapter 6), while the president emphasized the oneness of Uganda, to which end he repeated his well-rehearsed arguments about the linguistic affinity between Uganda's Bantu southerners and westerners, and Nilotic northerners.

What this narrative of unity leaves out, however, is the deep anti-northern sentiments that have cut through Museveni's rhetoric and actions ever since the Bush War, and the continued importance of anti-Acholi sentiments and more generally, of politicized ethnicity in Ugandan politics. Just saying things are different does not make them so. While on the face of it the political church events I attended perform a state and a nation that extends beyond ethnic boundaries, I claim they inadvertently re-make Uganda as a state in which ethnicity continues to be deeply politicized and imbricated within both structural and explicit state violence. Many Ugandans begrudge Museveni's home region in western Uganda, as well as the capital city, for their inordinate advancement under Museveni's reign. The feeling is particularly accentuated among northerners, whose awareness of their region's lagging development combines with personal experiences. The name of my neighbour's son disappeared from the list of recipients of government scholarships at Makerere University and, according to the mother, was 'replaced by the name of some Baganda boy'. Against this background of lived experience, Museveni's claim that 'Ugandans are one' at events like Atwoma's burial rang hollow, at best. At worst, the blatant lie of unity made the disunity all the more apparent.

A similar point can be made about the opposition leaders' speeches. UPC's Olara Otunnu said to the president: '*Museveni*... seated here in the land of my ancestors! You see those hills there? My ancestors, they are resting at the foothills. You relax! I have no worry about them.' Norbert Mao, on the other hand, assured listeners that the DP was 'committed to see that nobody need to rise to presidency by walking on the blood of the former president'. In citing the potentiality that ancestors or forces seeking to depose the president might turn violent, the speeches brought the cited threat to the arena of debate even while denying it.

The question of threat in political speech is, however, multifaceted. What is crucial to an analysis of speech acts is acknowledgement of their embeddedness in pre-existing relations of power, that is, to take into account 'the dimension of social power that constructs the so-called speaker and the addressee of the speech act in question' (Butler 1997, 55). While public church celebrations transform the temporary outdoor space of the church into a battleground for competing political groups, the competing groups are not in equal positions: the playing field is not level, since the party in power has both the money and the military capacity to crush its opponents (Tapscott 2017; Titeca and Onyango 2012).

Yet rather than performing Uganda as a hegemonic authoritarian monolith, church events do at times function as arenas for explicitly political debate. Opposition politicians spoke fiercely on the appalling state of education in the sub-region, the limitations on the press and freedom of speech, the unprotected state of their land, and the poor quality of government healthcare.[11] The fact that such critical issues were raised is notable, yet what is equally essential to note is that the space for critique was circumscribed. Because opposition leaders spoke first, NRM representatives, culminating in the president, could close down the debate by revoking crucial points of the opposition's critique and ignoring the rest.

Moreover, the space for critique in Uganda does not remain stable through time. Two years later, in the run-up to the next election, church celebrations in Kitgum offered no space for the opposition whatsoever. Indeed, when I returned to Kitgum two years after the end of my longest stretch of fieldwork, and again in the run-up to presidential and parliamentary elections, it seemed that many of the illiberal characteristics of the Ugandan state had become more pronounced and visible, including its deep militarization (see Chapter 5).

Cung i wibye and imaginaries of the state

The Acholi notion of *cung i wibye* captures the nature of politics as it takes place at public church events in Kitgum to perfection; politicians use churches as 'anthills' from which they address the crowd with their campaigning and internecine conflicts. I suspect that the notion of politics as *cung i wibye*, and the frequency with which this particular notion is used to describe politics, captures something crucial about conventional political imagination in Acholi. Politics is a matter of men (it is almost always men) standing on top of anthills, telling people below them what to do, and when necessary, forcing them to listen. Politics is also the process through which men compete for their place on the anthill, partially through wooing, buying or bullying, the favour of those below. What is notable is that entrenched in this notion of politics is the potential for violence, since where there are those standing above ruling others, there will be those below who resent being ruled. A prominent politician in Kitgum explained his view on the relationship between churches and politics like this:

When something goes wrong with the government, religious leaders can come and say, 'Sir, we feel it should be ABCDE.' They shouldn't say to people, 'Okay, come into the streets, begin marching, begin demonstration; I think the government is doing wrong, take up the spears, take up the guns!' But politicians who know the craft of politics can do that because that one is in the line of politics.

What relevance do church events have as sites of cultural performance and as arenas of political imagination in a context where going into the streets to march and demonstrate, and taking up spears and guns, are all in the line of politics? To answer this question, I suggest considering these events through Kapferer's theorizing on rituals, which he conceives of as a temporary slowing down of the tempo of everyday life (Kapferer 2004, 48). As I elaborate in the next chapter, it is the always shifting and changing, fractal-like and crosscutting reality of *the political* (Edkins 2003) – the 'continuously flowing, merging, and flowing' character of life in post-conflict Acholi – that is temporarily slowed down in rituals of state performance. These spaces of ritual, I hold, may be conceived not only as a space whose dynamic interrupts prior determining processes but also as a space in which participants can reimagine (and redirect or reorient themselves) into the everyday circumstances of life (Kapferer 2004, 47).

If we think of public church events in these terms, the preceding analysis leaves us asking to what extent this 'phantasmagoric space of ritual' enables participants to reimagine, redirect or reorient into the everyday circumstances of life. The question is an ambiguous one, as the following two chapters will show. The events described in them are very different, and can be seen to fall on different points of a continuum between repressive and hopefully imaginative. At some, like Atwoma's burial, the atmosphere is highly confrontational; at the 2015 events even the space for confrontation was closed off (see Chapter 5), while at others, the narrated utopia of unity meets practically no resistance (see Chapter 6).

Even when the presence of the military, people's fear, and the power used by the state to steer events, narrow down the space for political deliberation, they allow for speakers to tell stories about what is and what is not working in society: what Andrews calls the lifeblood of politics (2014, 86–7). The stories told from pulpits and podiums engage the speakers' audience, and allow for the audience to weigh in on the offered alternatives, take part in their performance, and reimagine and reorient themselves accordingly. Writing of poorer Brazilians being pushed to the margins by the increased commercialization of the carnival in Rio, Sheriff observes that *carnaval* is

> a ritual of intensification in which Brazilians celebrate their own vision of themselves as an amorous, optimistic, unified, and color-blind nation. People on the morro [i.e. favella or slum] might sneer at the notion that their country is a 'racial democracy', yet, during carnaval, they have traditionally conspired in the production of a nationalist illusion. They have done so not because they are the victims of false consciousness, as some have suggested, but because they honor the dream, delicate as it may be, on which carnaval, as a festival of national unity, is based. For poor people of color, the carioca carnaval is less about Brazil as it is than about Brazil as it ought to be.
>
> (Sheriff 1999, 22)

It is something akin to this that I suggest takes place at major church celebrations in Kitgum. While all participants are aware of the darker underside of politics, which are the focus of the coming chapter, these public rituals, and the religious speeches performed at them, evoke an imaginary Uganda: one in which fear is unnecessary, where societal and economic development is imminent, where freedom of speech is respected, where community is forged through forgiveness and love rather than necessity and force, and where the president really is a benevolent father who loves all his children in equal measure. To echo Sheriff, people living in the margins of the state as the Acholi do, may be sceptical of the government, and sceptical of the Ugandan nation-building project, but on occasions of religious celebration, they still partake in the performance of Uganda as they feel it ought to be.

5

The underside of the anthill
Crafting subdued citizens

In February 2015, two and a half years after Tiberio Atwoma's burial (see Chapter 4), Kitgum town prepared for President Museveni's arrival to two different church events: the handover of the Catholic Mission to the local diocese after one hundred years under Comboni missionary administration, and to the first national commemoration of Janani Luwum, the Anglican archbishop martyred by Idi Amin. The town thus expected another round of high-level *cung i wibye* (standing on anthills), but in a strikingly different mood to that I witnessed in 2012. It was only a year until national elections, where the president would be re-elected and new parliamentarians and local council members selected. And the fever was rising (see Alava and Ssentongo 2016).

In the days prior to Museveni's arrival, a rumour circulated in town that 'some people' – in one variant I heard these were 'men from Kampala' – had been inciting people to insurgency against the government in a remote village in eastern Acholi. As the rumour had it, numerous army trucks had appeared and people had been forced to burn their own huts and the surrounding bush so that the soldiers could search for weapons purportedly hidden by the purported rebels. There was no reference to such events in the national media, but the various people who mentioned the rumour to me all insisted they had heard it from acquaintances with relatives or friends living in the affected area. The details in the story were somewhat vague, which was not surprising. As one man put it when I asked him for details: 'Here, it is hard to know what is actually happening.'

While there was no way for me to verify whether the rumour was grounded in fact, what is noteworthy is that the villains of the piece were not the purported rebel group but, rather, the government soldiers who came to bully the locals and force them to burn their huts. As such, the rumour resonated more with people's memories of the government's anti-insurgency activities during the war than with the violence perpetrated by the LRA (see Chapter 2, as well as Atkinson 2010; Branch 2003, 2011; Dolan 2009; Finnström 2009; Whitmore 2019). It was thus not a coincidence that the timing of the rumours coincided with the president's arrival. Having soldiers en masse in Kitgum to 'secure the town' for Museveni's visit, as my friend described their presence, reactivated memories of a commonly experienced but silenced past, and led these memories to spill over as rumours in the present.

Since the end of the war the presence of overt state violence in northern Uganda has, for the most part, and for most of the time, significantly decreased. Despite the fact that insecurity of various sorts continues to be a pressing issue (Abonga et al. 2019; Allen 2015; Divon & Owor 2021; Tapscott 2017), the lives of most people I have interacted with over the years were permeated by a sense of relative physical safety and security, in vivid contrast with the time of the war, when people's physical safety was constantly under threat from soldiers and rebels alike. However, life is still commonly characterized by a profound sense of uncertainty, ambivalence and fear, in ways that influence perceptions of politics, and of the ruling NRM regime and state in particular.

In the previous chapter I argued that public church events function as sites of politics as *cung i wibye* (standing on anthills), and can be read as arenas of negotiation over the contours and narrative underpinnings of political life in Uganda. In this chapter I suggest that the public performance of politics *on* the anthills of churches gains its efficacy from the rumours, fears and unknowns that remain wrapped in silence *under* them. As the previous chapter showed, at times some of the confusion and silence that characterizes the political in everyday Acholi is held in abeyance; politics is performed as if it were not mired in rumour and suspicion, and the state is performed as if it were not as violent and repressive as people often know or feel it to be. Yet even in moments when the space for political imagination appears enlarged, such as at Tiberio Okeny Atwoma's burial (see Chapter 4), what lies beneath the anthill does not disappear, but is rather pressed underfoot.

In part this is achieved through violent repression by the state, but in part through the participation of the spectating crowd. A turn to the undersides of the anthills thus signals a turn from the performances of *cung i wibye* towards their audiences. By providing arenas for the at times violent production of the state, and through inculcating particular approaches to political leadership, churches often – not always – contribute to producing a subdued citizenry. To make this claim, I turn to theorizing on postcolonial statehood and citizenship.

As a lineage of scholars since Fanon (1967) has argued, the violence of colonialism left its marks not only on the structures and trappings of the state, but in the minds and bodies of citizens. Writing of China, Kleinman and Kleinman for instance observe:

> Bodies transformed by political processes not only *represent* those processes, they *experience* them as the lived memory of transformed worlds. The experience is of memory processes sedimented in gait, posture, movement, and all the other corporal components which together realize cultural code and social dynamics in everyday practices.
>
> (1994, 716–17)

For Achille Mbembe, the relationship between rulers and subjects (dubbed states and citizens in independence constitutions) is 'inscribed in a largely shared symbolic order' (Mbembe 2006, 159). Because the symbolic order is shared, the subjects of power themselves participate in creating and upholding the regime to which they are subjected. In this view, state-craft builds on the combined power of compelling images and the state's ability to apply pain (Mbembe 1992, 4). This sense of the state as imagery is also conveyed by the opposition explored by Cecilie Verma (2013) between the Acholi notions of *wang* or 'face', and *cwir*, or 'heart/liver' which is used to denote the difference between the appearance of politics, and its deep, hidden and violent essence. The concept of *cung i wibye* captures precisely this relationship between that which is apparent at the surface level, and that which lies beneath.

Here, the question posed of Foucaultian analysis in general remains pertinent: is there any space for agency in Mbembe's vision of the postcolony? Although he acknowledges the potential for citizens to call attention to the vulnerability of state power through their participation in its ratification, the overall tone of Mbembe's analysis remains bleak. Criticizing Mbembe's analysis of ceremonial patterns of power as intrinsically pathological, Karlström argues that political ceremonies in Buganda may in fact provide 'resources for popular critical consciousness' (2003). In my view, these different interpretations are in part dependent on the specific relationships between the state and its citizens (Alava et al. 2020). In some places more than others, at some times more than others, the state forces citizens into submission to a degree where little or no space for critical consciousness or its expressions remains. Therefore, to analyse the political import of church events, it is also vital to consider the particularities of their context, and changes that occur over time. That is what this chapter seeks to do.

Moments of *cung i wibye*, particularly of the level I chanced to witness both in 2012 and 2015, are rare occasions in Kitgum. Between the burial of Tiberio Okeny in 2012 and the 2015 events, Museveni had not visited the town. Yet, just as anthills are joined by the ground on which they stand, so moments of pompous state performance are connected through the interludes between them. Drawing on analysis of moments of strikingly subduing *cung i wibye* in Kitgum in 2015, on my discussions with research participants, and on my own experiences of fear, silence and ambivalence during my fieldwork, this chapter highlights the constraints placed on political imagination by the afterlives of war, and the memories of violence, fear of violence, and general *anyobanyoba*, confusion, that they entail. In the closing of the chapter, I argue that many Acholi have adopted a subjunctive mood in relation to the state (Whyte 2002; Whyte 2005, see also Introduction), that is, a mood that is 'responsive to the if and maybe of experience and looks to an uncertain future with both hope and doubt' (Werbner 2002, 15). In Chapter 6, I will argue that the Christian Utopia of peace is crafted precisely in and against this context of confusion, and furthermore, that while it provides an important alternative to the violent politics of state-making, the beliefs and practices inherent to this Christianity of utopian peace contribute to nurturing subjunctive moods towards existing political reality in its adherents.

Silence and suspicions

In a place where war and violence are in not so distant a past, it is easy to stoke rumours like the one with which I opened this chapter, just as it is possible that the rumour had truth to it. Legacies of violence clearly affect political imagination. But violence and rumours of violence colour political imagination throughout Uganda, not just places dubbed 'post-war' regions like Acholi.

In December 2012, a twenty-four-year-old NRM Member of Parliament, Cerinah Nebanda, died upon her arrival in a Kampala hospital. A government-sponsored autopsy found traces of alcohol and cocaine in her body. Numerous MPs from both the opposition and the NRM, including the parliament speaker, Rebecca Kadagga (who at the time was believed to have ambitions to replace Museveni as the party head), publicly questioned the autopsy results and accused government operatives of killing Nebanda. The young MP, although a representative of the NRM, was known as a bravely outspoken critic of the state. According to a reporter who went through hours of archived videos of parliamentary debate, Nebanda had fiercely challenged the president on the day before her death (Epstein 2014). The president threatened to have anyone spreading rumours about the government's involvement in the death arrested, and two MPs were taken into custody. Speculation about the cause of death intensified, however, when state security officials arrested a doctor who, at the request of the family of the deceased, was attempting to take samples from Nebanda's body to South Africa for independent assessment (*Daily Monitor* 2012).

Sometime after Nebanda's death, I asked two people with whom I was sharing a meal in Gulu, whether there had been much talk among their acquaintants about the matter. One of them fell quiet, drank his water and left without saying a word. After a while, the man remaining said, 'People are learning not to comment.' I sighed and said things did not sound good, to which he replied, 'Yes. These things are happening. And they're going to keep happening. Uganda is moving towards totalitarianism.' After a moment's silence, he sang the first lines of the Ugandan national anthem's second verse:

Oh Uganda! The land of freedom,
our love and labour we give.
And with neighbours all
at our country's call
in peace and friendship we'll live.

In the context of a nation buzzing with rumours about a purported political murder, the irony of the anthem's words could hardly have been more glaring. For many, including in the context of the churches I studied, 'Oh Uganda' resounded more as a prayerful lament, rather than as praise. In addition to the experiences of war, which had cast their shadow on the anthem's glowing portrait of the nation, the image was tarnished by rumours of deaths like Nebanda's, and by the fears that percolated through everyday lives, none of which lent credence to the notion of Uganda as a land of freedom or peace.

Among the most oft-cited of such fears were rumours that the government had spies keeping an eye on anti-government talk and activities in every village, every local council, every workplace and every church (see Alava and Ssentongo 2016) although people practically never spoke of the stories as rumours, but as facts. These reports intensified at certain times: in 2015, for instance, as the country began to prepare for the 2016 elections, when my friend Orom explained the unlikelihood of Museveni losing in the following way:

You know here, there is a system already in place, everywhere. The state intelligence has officers all over, even in this village here, they are there. I could be a security officer, and you would never know. Or you could be, and none of us would ever know.'

'Even here?' I asked, pointing to the serene scenery of houses and fields through which we were walking. 'Yes,' Orom answered with a serious look on his face. 'If you start talking too much against the government, they will report you, and one day the army will come to your door, and you will be taken away. And never be seen again.' While recent, documented cases, other than those of prominent politicians like Cerenah Nebanda, were seldom referenced as reasons for such fears by my interlocutors, Cecilie Verma's longitudinal study spanning a number of years during which she followed the lives of former LRA rebels who were re-trained and recruited as so-called 'NRM cadres', suggests that Orom's fears were not unfounded. Rather, she writes:

> I no longer doubt the very dense presence of spies and government agents scattered over even the vast peripheries of Acholiland – possibly the whole country – in the name of internal and external state security and in the form of a range of different networks and cells to which you can belong as different ranks or categories of informers. That makes for a constant flow of – and a constant suspicion of – information and questions that are considered a matter of or as scrutinizing 'politics' and 'security'. (Verma 2013, 48)

As argued in Rebecca Tapscott's research on non-state security provision in Acholi, there has been speculation as to the actual capacity of such security initiatives and possible spy networks, yet what makes them effective is their very arbitrariness (see Tapscott 2017, 2021). Indeed, from the perspective of Kitgum, and my research participants, none of whom as far as I ever learned were themselves involved in such networks, the question of how efficient state security networks *actually* are, was somewhat irrelevant. Rather, the crucial issue seems to be that many people *believe* state security to be extremely and dangerously effective; they believe the state to have, as one of Tapscott's (2017) interlocutors put it, such 'long hands', that were they to take up any kind of anti-government activities, the information would quickly reach the ears of the state, with grave repercussions.

Past and present, intermingled

In the beginning of this chapter, I used the example of rumours of rebel mobilization in Kitgum in 2016 to illustrate my argument that fears in the present intermingle with memories of past violence. For elderly people, particularly those who had been personally involved in party politics prior to Museveni's time and who had been harmed or had lost family members in the waves of political violence that have swept across Uganda since its independence (see Chapter 2), this was true in a particularly transparent way. But the intermingling of past memories and current fears was also true in less obvious ways in everyday lives.

In a focus group discussion about politics with a group of adolescent altar servants at Saint Mary's, one of the boys said, 'These days, people don't have so much fear.' Another immediately interjected, stating, 'No, people are fearing. If you talk, bad people can come and kill you.' That the notion of 'bad people' was not defined in any way in the conversation (and nor did I prompt clarification) was illustrative of a more general tendency for comments relating to security, violence and terror in northern Uganda to be fundamentally vague. Often, it was hard to figure out what was purportedly going on, and who exactly it was that was seen to pose a threat: former rebels, for instance, or the police, or the state, or the unidentified assailants who featured in stories I was frequently told of murders committed in particular parts of Kitgum town (for a detailed analysis, see Finnström 2009).

A similar sense of uncertainty related specifically to the fear of state security. For example, in the discussion quoted above, my friend Orom commented that speaking out against the government would at times be tolerated, adding, 'They know that a barking dog doesn't bite. So they will let you shout out as much as you wish, and it will be allowed. But if you start talking seriously, then you're taken or assassinated.' As Orom and many of my other research participants explained, the tricky if not impossible thing was to know when one was crossing the line; hence, it was generally regarded as better to stay quiet and not speak about politics at all in public, or with anyone other than one's closest friends and family.

All this added up to a pervasive sense of uncertainty, one captured by the Acholi term for confusion – *anyobanyoba*. In an interview with a woman in her thirties in 2013, I mentioned that I felt like there were undercurrents around me that I could not quite understand. Martha heartily affirmed this sensation, and continued:

> – The way it is now. It will remain like that, eh? People will pretend it's not there. I'm telling you. Unless there is something that has happened in relation to the silence that people have kept... It will remain the way it is; that's just things will sort itself.
> – But will it? I mean, does that happen, do things just sort themselves?

– What people now treat are the outcome of the unseen silent – that is what is being handled. And that is why I've told you there's a lot of murder. There's a lot of hatred and jealousy. Because sometimes others have got opportunity to get something out of it [the war]. Others have gone down completely.

Martha placed her hands, palms facing up, in front of her, and put them at two different levels:

Here, a clear reason [is] known to each other. That you are here [at the low level], and I know why. Because maybe all your children were killed, and no-one will talk about it, and you remain. This one also knows that you are [at the higher level] because you are being supported by the rebels. Or you took advantage and got rich. So you send your children to school. And maybe, I did not send mine to school because their father was killed during the war, or their mother.

Moving her hands to the same level, Martha explained this was the reason why it was impossible for Acholis to reach a shared understanding:

There is noooo any discussion that will end without chaos here… If you went to the village, you could have sensed it, even if you are not hearing. You see that? Those are the things.

The village Martha referred to was one I had visited on the invitation of her elderly relative, unaware that my visit had been timed to coincide with a meeting in which a community dispute was to be discussed, and where my presence would serve to bolster the argument of one of the parties involved. In my fieldwork diary, I described the meeting in the following way:

The situation is tangibly tense, and tensening by the second, although outwardly everyone's demeanour is calm. Voices are slightly raised. The only one talking on top of the others, or grumbling, is at times *ladit* [the elderly man I had travelled with]. It's as if there's a gas leak, and if a match were struck, the whole place might blow. It does not feel scary as such, just tense, very, very tense.

While everyone at this particular meeting was outwardly proper, the discussion that ensued was full of veiled complaints and threats, and the atmosphere felt explosive. It is in moments like this that the weft of silence, and the potentiality of crisis and confusion that it contains, comes to the fore, refusing to remain unnoticed. Yet it is also moments like this that Martha insisted required such vehement silencing: 'What is here is there because people even don't want to provoke it. They say *wek gwok ma oneno, oneno*. Let the sleeping dog lie. Yes.'

The things that Martha believed should not be provoked were, importantly, not divisions and conflicts between the government and the Acholi, but among

Acholi, which had often been created or exacerbated by the war. This is an important aspect of the afterlives of war – that is, that the silence and ambivalence that lingers under the anthills of political performance is not solely about fears and uncertainties related to the state or the possibility of new rebellion. In a society tinged by recent war and state-perpetrated violence, a sense of the distant violent state, and of violence in everyday lives, is intimately enmeshed. Jointly, they contribute to the ambivalence and confusion that undergirds moments of political performance.

Fears rise as the president comes to town

Although fears and rumours and violence were issues that people occasionally (and only occasionally; see Chapter 3) mentioned in everyday discussions and in interviews, it was only through my own experience that I really grasped how fear – and the feeling of having the state under one's skin – operates. This learning did not take place so much or so forcefully during my initial fieldwork, however, as when I came back to Kitgum in 2015, a year prior to the presidential and parliamentary elections.

Whereas in 2012 the potholes on the road from the helicopter landing site to the homestead of the deceased Tiberio Atwoma had been filled just prior to the president's arrival on the scene, by 2015 such emergency repairs were not necessary. World Bank funds and Chinese contractors had been utilized to initiate a huge construction project to improve the road from Gulu to Kitgum town, and from there past the Catholic Mission, via Mucwini, towards the border of Sudan – all in order, many claimed, to buy Acholi votes for the NRM (see Lagace 2018). Chatting with my friend Isaac at his office a few days prior to the celebrations, we were interrupted by the sound of huge trucks driving by along one of these newly repaired roads, and Isaac's colleague popped in to tell us that they were army vehicles.

There had been military vehicles driving by their office for a number of days, because, as Isaac observed, UPDF soldiers always came in to 'secure the area' at least a week before the arrival of Museveni. Just before the army trucks passed the windows of the office, Isaac and I had been grinding our teeth about our modems not working. Both of us used the same mobile operator, and our modems had been unable to pick up a 3G signal since the previous night. After leaving Isaac's office, I received a call from someone in the operator's service centre who told me that, according to their technical officers, there was no 3G

Figure 8. Posters for politicians lined walls and trees in the run-up to the 2016 elections. Photo by author.

network in the area where I had tried to use the modem. I was annoyed and frustrated: the network had worked just the day before, why not now?

And then the thought struck me with almost nauseating force: what if this had something to do with the presidential visit? I knew absolutely nothing about mobile networks, but as I had never had this kind of trouble with the internet in Kitgum before, it seemed like too much of a coincidence that the trouble had started just as the trucks with soldiers were rolling in to 'secure the area' for Museveni. The intermittent paranoia I remembered vividly from earlier fieldwork trips to Kitgum in 2006 and 2012–13 returned. I became convinced that all my text messages and phone calls were being tapped, and worried that this would somehow get someone I had interacted with into trouble. While I could rationalize that my research could not possibly be a matter of concern for Ugandan state security, and while I suspected that I was totally overreacting, the nagging sense of uncertainty was unsettling. A few days later, my technically skilled friends figured out that my internet problems were due to my outdated modem and not the network. Somebody may well have been eavesdropping on everyone's calls in Kitgum, even without the president's being there, but my modem failure had nothing to do with it.

Yet the fear that the incident had re-triggered in my mind lingered. A few days later I was chatting with a close-knit group of friends, one of whom, Kidega, I knew well. The young people had spent a few hours talking about politics and speculating about the trajectories of Uganda's political development in years to come. The conversation turned to the police and to secret spy networks, and the sense of shared confidentiality led me laughingly to admit that during previous fieldwork I had at times wondered whether Kidega had been recruited by security officials to keep tabs on me. The group of friends all laughed at me teasingly, then the conversation turned to other topics. Both laughing at such matters with close friends and knowing when to shift the conversation from spies to sports are essential aspects of everyday sociality for people living under a violent state. They serve to moderate both the level of risk and of the stress related to living surrounded by it.

My feeling unnerved and unsettled when the president came to Kitgum was thus not an insular, individual experience. Rather, it reflected the ambivalences, suspicions and feelings of *not-really-knowing* that colour people's sense of politics in northern Uganda. As Meinert has written, in post-war Acholi, 'the trick [is] to expect distrust, and then possibly, and carefully, to unfold a sense of trust over time; trust which might, however, later revert to distrust' (2015, 126). This sense of fundamental distrust is foundational for the way in which the state is experienced. And as I now turn to show, the everyday experiences through which the resulting subdued and subjunctive citizenship moods become engrained within people are complemented in moments of extraordinary state presence – what Mbembe (1992) calls the carnivals of the postcolonial state.

Cung i wibye on NRM terms

To illustrate how this under-the-skin sense of fear and uncertainty functioned to enforce the power of the state's performance at public church events, I turn to the two notable occasions of this sort for which President Museveni arrived to Kitgum in 2015, a year prior to his eventual re-election. As detailed in the previous chapter, Museveni was openly challenged at Atwoma's burial in 2012. In 2015, at both the Mission handover in Kitgum and Luwum's commemoration in the nearby Mucwini on the following day, the playing field was completely cleared in the president's favour, so that no speakers representing the political opposition were allowed onto the podium.

At Atwoma's burial, Museveni's speech had addressed the criticism levelled at him in the numerous speeches preceding his by his political opponents. In contrast, in 2015 the many speeches that preceded the president's were either utterly apolitical, or sang his praises. With nothing critical requiring extemporary response, Museveni was thus free to craft his speeches as he saw fit. To begin, after congratulating the event organizers, he tallied the achievements of the NRM in northern Uganda. To this end, he appropriated what he judged to be achievements of Janani Luwum and of the Comboni missionaries: just as Janani had stood up against injustice, the NRM had stood up against the injustice of the previous regimes; and just as the Combonis had started schools and hospitals, the government was now providing its people with many good services.

The longest segments in Museveni's speeches at the events focused, however, on reprimanding the Acholi. To this end, the president employed a gimmick he regularly uses while travelling around the country, that is, he emphasized his key point through the application of a few select words in the local language. At the handover of the Mission in Kitgum, these words were *lotuko* (players) and *loneno* (spectators):

> For football, you need both... But when you have got *lotuko* and *loneno* in the economy, that's a big problem. According to the 2002 Census, it showed that 32 of homesteads were *lotuko*: they were in the money economy. 68% were *loneno*. They were just spectating.

At Luwum's commemoration on the following day, Museveni developed the argument further. He mentioned that the previous day someone had complained to him that the problem in Acholi – the reason why they are not *lotuko* – was that people are poor. But, the president insisted:

> You cannot be poor if you have land. The problem isn't poverty, the problem is sleeping. Archbishop Sentamu [a Ugandan cleric currently serving as the Bishop of York, who officiated at the service] can tell you how many people there are in the UK with as many acres of land as you. Poverty is not the problem but sleeping. People must now all be *lotuko*.

To make sense of the weight of Museveni's claims, they need to be analysed in context of the political economy of northern Uganda. Previous chapters have outlined the north–south divide that has cut across Uganda since colonial times and, to this day, almost a decade after the end of the war, the income disparity between the north and the rest of the country remains conspicuous (UNDP 2015, 21). That disparity was cemented when many Acholi lost practically everything they owned due to the war. Most notable among these losses, both economically and psychologically, was the loss of cattle which were of crucial importance to them: as capital, for tilling the soil, for manure, and for forging social cohesion and security through bride price (Alava 2017a; Porter 2016). Alongside the loss of cattle, people in the region have undergone years of physical and psychological torment in a war in which Museveni and his soldiers were far from innocent (Atkinson 2010; Branch 2011; Dolan 2009; Finnström 2008; Lamwaka 2016; Whitmore 2019). The majority of Acholi people continue to rely on low-technology subsistence agriculture (UBOS 2014), a state of affairs for which there are many reasons: unclear, insecure land tenure and intense land grabbing pressures (Atkinson and Latigo 2020; Hopwood 2021, Hopwood and Atkinson 2013; Martiniello 2015; Martiniello 2019; Sjögren 2014), low-yielding soils and difficulty accessing external markets (Gollin 2010), and limited access to credit – none of which were mentioned by Museveni in his speech. Arguably, many of these are issues that the government could have influenced to a greater extent than it has; for instance, the most recent agricultural census conducted in Uganda showed that only 6.2 per cent of northern Ugandan farming households had access to credit, in comparison to 14.4 per cent of those in President Museveni's home region of western Uganda (UBOS 2010).

Museveni concluded his speech by announcing that because so much of the money he had so far sent to the north had been devoured by what he called 'clever people', he had decided he would no longer allow civil servants to run development projects in the region.[1] Instead, from now on, special army officers would distribute building materials and farm inputs in what was called 'Operation Wealth Creation'.

Two things stand out in the announcement. First of all, building materials and farm inputs do not go far towards solving the bigger issues of the political economy of subsistence agriculture and high levels of poverty in northern Uganda (Wiegratz, Martiniello, and Greco 2018). As Branch and Yen (2018, 86) aptly put it in their analysis of neoliberal reconstruction efforts in Acholi: 'the idea that the massive structural causes of poverty in the north could be effectively addressed by shifting the agency for transformation to the displaced Acholi peasantry was nonsensical'. Secondly, with this announcement, Museveni narrated himself into the role of the benefactor, placing all the blame for the appropriation of northern Uganda's billions of shillings of aid money on people below him, while simultaneously circumventing claims – and evidence – of corruption by the NRM government and politicians and the Ugandan army (see Mwenda and Tangri 2013; Zeller 2013).

In light of all this it seemed there were good reasons for people to be angered by the president's words, and to express their anger. But no-one did. In contrast to the crowd's annoyance that I had witnessed at Atwoma's 2012 burial, in 2015 there were no sounds of 'tst-tst' or shouts of '*goppa!*' (lies!) directed at Museveni, nor gleeful ululations at the opposition's subtle ridiculing of him – just unbroken silence and thousands of eyes staring in the president's direction.

My question is: what had changed to so load these events in Museveni's favour, and how was it that the audience seemed to accept Museveni's berating without the slightest indication of protest, when a few years earlier they had jeered and called him a liar?

The first issue to be considered in exploring this question is the opposition's absence at these events. Their absence, and the president's presence, as well as the negotiations that had gone into making it so, highlight the considerable extent to which party politics are intertwined with the administration of Ugandan churches (see Chapters 2 and 4). According to people I knew on and near the organizing committee of the Mission handover, high-ranking local NRM members had forced their way onto the committee and, once entrenched, had announced that prominent members of the opposition should not be allowed to speak at the event as they would 'spoil the day'. Some of the ordinary committee members had tried to ask for clearer justifications for the directive, but had been brushed aside by NRM heavy weights and, ultimately, no opposition members were given the floor. While there may have been other instances, I have only ever heard of one major public church event in Acholi, where an adamant and respected priest managed to keep politicians of all stripes away from the microphone.

At the Luwum commemoration in Mucwini, the absence of members of the political opposition was perhaps even more striking, since one of the key people behind escalating the Luwum memorial from a local to a nationally celebrated event was Olara Otunnu, the (then) chairperson of the Uganda People's Congress (UPC), who had incited the crowd to such glee with his anti-Museveni political oratory at Atwoma's burial. Although Otunnu's father had been Luwum's close friend – as sons of the same village and committed members of the Anglican Balokole revival – Otunnu did not reach the microphone at the Luwum memorial (see Chapter 7 for further analysis of the event).

Phoebe Luwum, the late archbishop's daughter, spoke on behalf of the family. Rather than suggesting that her father – who died criticizing the government's over-stepping its lawful boundaries – might have had something to say about the deteriorating state of democracy and human rights in Uganda, she maintained a grateful demeanour towards Museveni. The tone of her speech, which startled me at the time, made far more sense when she announced some months later that she would run in the 2016 NRM primary elections, at which the party's candidate for MP from the Mucwini area would be selected. (She lost, amid rumours of serious, state-bolstered intimidation, to the standing minister and Museveni's long-term stooge in Acholi, Henry Oryem Okello).

It is tempting to speculate about possible incentives provided to Luwum's daughter, or to others involved in the organizing, to enlist their support for Museveni. As I mentioned in Chapter 4, the president has had no qualms about openly inviting his former opponents, and their children, into his ranks. But while it can be suggested that the absence of opposition to Museveni's *loneno/lotuku* speech can be interpreted as the outcome of manipulation of the playing field at the events in question, and of the political playing field in Uganda more generally (see Titeca and Onyango 2012), I believe there is more to the story.

Perhaps even more significant in the end was the spectators' silence at the events in question. Relevant to this point is that the president's speeches were not novel, but, rather, drew from a well-rehearsed repertoire of anti-Acholi sentiments. In particular, they resonated with the official discourse by which Museveni has internalized the problems of northern Uganda *into* Acholi throughout the past three decades (Alava 2008). This builds upon racist colonial representations of the Acholi people as essentially warlike and unpredictable and, particularly since the war, as both lazy and shackled by dependency syndrome (Atkinson 2010; Finnström 2008). The speeches were thus a continuation of a dynamic and narrative that was evident throughout the northern Ugandan war.

The key argument I wish to make in this regard is that I believe state rituals like those described in this and the previous chapter, figuratively and literally, guide Acholi bodies towards submission. They create not only a particular kind of state, but subdued citizens (Alava 2020). While this submission is at times reversed, as when the audience at Atwoma's burial responded to Museveni's rhetoric with shouts of 'lies!' and critical tut-tutting, overall, a submissive habitus has been engrained among many Acholi during the course of Museveni's rule, extending over decades of war and its aftermath. Following Mbembe (1992), this submission cannot be seen simply as a case of coercion and lack of opposition. Rather:

> [i]n the postcolony, an intimate tyranny links the rulers with the ruled, just as... vulgarity [is] the very condition of state power. If subjection appears more intense than it might be, it is also because the subjects of the *commandement* have

internalized the authoritarian epistemology to the point where they reproduce it themselves in... daily life.

(Mbembe 1992, 22–3)

A profound indication of the humiliation intrinsic to such internalization was provided at the Mission handover, where the LC5 chairperson humbly thanked the president for a cattle-restocking programme in which only 798 cows had been given to farmers in the district as compensation for the more than 100,000 lost to the Ugandan army, neighbouring cattle rustlers and rebels during the war (Finnström 2008). I quietly asked a friend sitting beside me how many cows his family had lost in the raids, which he, like many others, believed had been condoned if not orchestrated by Museveni to snap the backbone of the Acholi (see Chapter 2). He answered, 'Three hundred'.

In discussions about the relationship between the Acholi and Museveni's state, expressions such as 'we have been forgotten' or 'we don't exist' are commonly used. The most concise and harsh of such statements that I heard during my fieldwork was made by a well-educated Catholic man in his forties, Komarach, who described the state's attitude to the Acholi thus: 'We are like condoms; we're used and thrown away.' Komarach's likening of the Acholi to condoms which, as he explained, are used for others' pleasure and then discarded poignantly illustrates the intensity and intimacy with which the relationship with the state is experienced, as well as the sense of humiliation and abandonment that colour the relationship.

I believe the lack of expressed annoyance by the crowd listening to Museveni's speech can be read as a result of a submissive habitus tinged by shame that many in the region have adopted in relation to the central state, and that builds upon the earlier violence of colonization (see Chapter 2). Mbembe holds that the postcolonial bodies which submit to playing the part of submissive citizens cheering the state do so 'precisely in order to better "play" with it and modify it whenever possible' (1992, 22–3). There are certainly moments when this play is evident, as I mentioned in the previous chapter analysing Atwoma's burial in 2012. A Mbembeian interpretation of all three functions – of the large numbers of people who crowded to take part, of the excitement that the events engendered among spectators and of the laughter the opposition leader's speeches at Atwoma's burial triggered in the crowd – might suggest carnivalesque enjoyment as a central aspect of public church events and of the performances of *cung i wibye*. But at the events attended by Museveni in 2015, there was none of the playful mockery of the state apparatus that Mbembe describes. Neither did I see such play in the weeks after the clampdown on opposition protests in 2016; nor in the silences into which many retreated as soon as the politics of the state – the army, or state security officials – were raised in discussion.

From this it appears that the ludic resources available to the subjects of the postcolonial state are more available for some than they are for others, and at some moments than at others. In contemporary post-war Acholi, these resources are limited by the vulgar and obscene violence of postcolonial performance (Mbembe 1992, 29–30) coupled with the less symbolic and more direct violence of the gun. Indeed, Museveni's transfer of 'development initiatives' to the army gave him the perfect reason to employ the military to rural areas (Vokes and Wilkins 2016, 592). At times of heightened security in particular, such as the run-up to elections, there is very little space in northern Uganda for the kind of laughter Mbembe claims to be subversive. When faced with the inevitability of a gun, that laughter dies.

This threat had practical implications for the rationales by which people judge politics. In the previous chapter I discussed my research participants' view that many people in Acholi were choosing money over political deliberation because of the pragmatic consideration of the acute emptiness of their pockets. A similar pragmatism seems to be at play in people's choice to remain silent in 2015: even though there seemed to be no immediate threat of violent retaliation were people to stand up and protest, one could not be sure. Opposing the president might turn him even more firmly against the Acholi – just as voting for him might enable more lenient treatment (Atkinson 2018). Thereby, rather than rallying in anger, it was better to respond with silence.

'What can I do at the moment'?

So far, I have argued that the violent core of the NRM state inserts itself into the private realm of people's homes, lives and thoughts in Acholi, so that even in the absence of overt state repression, and in the intervals between the state's public appearances, an under-the-skin sense of the state prompts people into submission. This cautious habitus is the outcome not only of the sense of an external and potentially violent state, but also of often war-related tensions and divisions among the Acholi, which are pressed underfoot and veiled in silence.

But is that grim diagnosis all there is to say? By way of conclusion, I wish to point to yet another aspect of the story, echoing insights of previous scholarship on the pragmatic and life-affirming adaptations Acholi people have adopted to overcome the violence they have endured (Finnström 2008; Porter 2016; van Bemmel 2016; Whyte, Meinert, and Obika 2015; L. H. Williams 2019), and of those who have lived through it themselves and shared their story (Amony 2015; Cakaj 2016). Running parallel and even counter to the apprehensive sense of uncertainty and confusion in contemporary Acholi is a down-to-earth commitment to the everyday. A comment by an articulate and well-educated friend, Rubangakene, concerning the violence and suffering in his childhood and the challenges he was encountering in the present, captured a ubiquitous approach to life in Kitgum.

> I think one of the things that I have learned, and I think this is written for me everywhere, is that with life nothing continues forever. Even if the moment is very exciting, even if the moment is so painful, nothing continues forever… All this is the moment we have, all these transitional things at that particular time, they will pass… Also, I should know that at any point anything can happen. Sometimes when I tell even my wife, I say, 'You see, this life of ours you see, it's very painful, or it's very beautiful. At one point the contrary will be there; if it is very beautiful, you know that the painful moment will be there. If it is very painful, then the other one is also there.'
>
> The only thing is, whatever you can do, whatever you can do at that particular time to make life continue, that is the thing we should do. Other than worrying that, you know, '[My employers] have not paid, how will I live with this? – no! 'What can you do?' is the question I always ask. 'What can I do at the moment?' instead of saying, 'Why this?'

Rubangakene, and many of my other acquaintances, bore witness to the power of the subjunctive mood (Whyte 2002, 2005), which focuses on action, on making uncertainty manageable, and 'acknowledges contingency' while evoking 'possible futures' (ibid., 254). As I discussed in Chapter 3, such sentiments also bear witness to what Das (2007) describes as a descent into the ordinary.

Not dwelling on the past or the uncertainty of the political future, even during moments of heightened political tension, but rather taking life as it is given, focusing on the present and on building a future for themselves and their children, is a powerful sign of resilience and healing in the face of the unspeakable horror of the past, one to which the Christian emphasis on forgiveness grants a special additional colour. Jenny Edkins (2003) has suggested that this kind of focus on the detail of the everyday, through which human beings come to terms with the fundamental insecurity of life, can be seen as an alternative to logics of violence and retaliation, one that enables alternative responses:

> [P]erhaps the only response to the realisation that nowhere is safe, might be to insistently carry on with the mundane activities on which we are mostly engaged most of the time: bringing up our children, engaging in small acts of courtesy, living our lives, dying our deaths.
>
> (Edkins 2003, 228)

Such a response was also evident in the days prior to Museveni's visit to Kitgum Mission and Luwum's commemoration in Mucwini in 2015. Rather than spending their days speculating over rumours of new rebel groups, or feeling paranoid about their phones being tapped, most people I encountered were taken up by concerns of a wholly different order. Women were busy preparing food for the thousands of pilgrims expected to sleep in parish members' homes and in nearby schools, and the choirs were busy practising their musical pieces. Similarly, at the events themselves, the friendly banter of people in their colourful Sunday best made repressive state security fade from one's mind soon after passing through the metal detectors and body checks.

The adoption of a subjunctive mood and an orientation towards the future were as palpable in Kitgum as the fear and confusion that at times broke through the quotidian concerns of everyday life. Ultimately, in the midst of war's afterlives, the sense of politics – which provides the scaffolding and boundaries for political imagination – is lodged in this ambivalent space between secure and free, and repressed and threatening. Churches are also ensconced within this space; they are not *external* to the dynamics of political imagination and practice, but *embedded* in them.

Churches' messages of forgiveness, peace and moving on (Chapter 6) – as well as their common, though not ubiquitous, teachings of subservience to political leadership (see Alava and Ssentongo 2016) – feed into subjunctive citizenship moods. Simultaneously, churches enable and contribute to the continuation of a political system grounded in fear and repression. They do so both inadvertently, by providing arenas for the carnivals of violent state-making, and deliberately, through choices to maintain silence when it suits their institutional self-interests (see ibid., as well as Chapters 2 and 3).

Yet the picture is not this simple. The material presented in this chapter suggests that the violence, confusion and silence that lie beneath the anthills of political performance in Acholi render social projects hesitant and vulnerable to disruption, and make it difficult to believe that the violence that has ravaged the region for decades could ever be replaced by genuine peace. However, as I demonstrate in the following chapter, amid the confusion inherent to the afterlives of war, and despite the ongoing violence of repressive state-making in the present, hope and imaginaries of peace *are* crafted: in publicly delivered utopian narratives of peace, in peoples' embodied practices of worship and prayer, and in their simple acts of living their lives, of asking, as Rubangakene and his wife strive to do: 'What can I do at the moment?'

In turning to speak of utopian narratives of peace, I shift tone in a way I claim mirrors a movement I have often witnessed in Kitgum: from fear and violence to forgiveness and hope. Yet this shift does not indicate a break. The next chapter harkens back to Catholic Archbishop Odama's sermon at the national burial of Tiberio Atwoma, analysed earlier in this book. By emphasizing peace, national unity and forgiveness, the sermon, which preceded a litany of political speeches, aimed to tame the narrative violence of *cung i wibye,* and the physical violence that undergirds it, thus partaking in the creation of a Utopia of Peace. I turn now to analyse this vision, and the consequences of its promotion by mainline churches, before finally, in Chapter 7, shifting focus again, to how 'confusion in the church' reveals the peaceful utopia's limits.

6

'My peace I give you'
Utopian narratives of inclusion and boundaries of exclusion

> God said through the Prophet Isaiah, 'He will rule over the nations and settle disputes. They will beat swords into ploughshares. Nations will plan for war no more... Let I and you, each and all, be builders of peace. War never again in Uganda. War never again in Africa. War never again in the world.'
> (Archbishop John Baptist Odama, Gulu town, September 2012)

There was much talk of peace in Kitgum. Words like those of Archbishop Odama were at the time of my fieldwork familiar to anyone familiar with the churches involved in the Acholi Religious Leaders Peace Initiative (ARLPI). But there was also much talk of the absence of peace in the post-war era. As I described in the Introduction, the elderly Anglican *mego* Atenyo described it as the people having 'gone mad' in the displacement camps. Likewise, Komarach, a middle-aged Catholic man quoted earlier for his analysis of collective humiliation, saw Acholi society as having been 'reduced to debris' as a result of the war, its population drinking, dancing and using drugs in an attempt to find 'consolation for unacceptable death in mass form'. Among the devout Catholics and Anglicans with whom I spent time, war-time displacement was commonly seen to have undermined a common moral framework that had previously ensured harmonious co-existence in Acholi, a process that in many people's eyes, particularly those of the elderly, was exacerbated by modernization and the influx of new 'liberal' (a)moralities (Alava 2017c; Vorhölter 2014). In the description Archbishop John Baptist Odama gave me in an interview, these two explanations merged:

> The Acholi now, its moral code... has been corroded. Such that the way elders were being handled and being looked at as a source of not only information, but as source of guarantee of the ethical and the traditional code is virtually broken. [Now] they don't have much impact, not much, because the influence of the elders and the parents and so on, was around the fireplace: what they used to

call *wang oo*; this was where really their authority was, and then from that one to the chiefs and so on. It used to be easily seen, and directed the whole social life of the people in the proper way, but today it is not so! This factor of technology and modernisation has come in... Especially the younger generation has access to the other worlds elsewhere through the computer, through this telephone things, through this television... So people have got a lot of mixed, how do I call it, mixed outlook. And in that way, I could say the identity of the Acholi as such, is being played low.

In the social space of the mainline Christian churches I studied, lamentations over the loss of harmony and order, and analyses of the reasons for all this confusion were not the end point. Rather, they were the sounding board for visions of a brighter future: the dark canvas upon which bright images of a peaceful future were painted.

This chapter shows how, in response to the northern Ugandan war and the sense of societal and individual confusion that has followed it – confusion traced in preceding chapters – a Utopia of Peace has emerged within mainline Christianity in the region. This Utopia, which I distinguish from other utopias

Figure 9. Archbishop Odama and two Comboni missionary bishops at the commemoration of the Paimol martyrs. Photo by author.

I discuss in the chapter by capitalizing the term, can be conceptualized, following Andrews (2014), as an evolving field of individual and collective social imagination, in which certain narratives gain particular traction due to the power with which the institutions crafting them – in this case mainline churches – are endowed. On a public level the Utopia of Peace presents an image of harmonious co-existence in the past, alongside a Christ-inspired vision for a harmonious future that will overcome the decades of violence in Uganda and Acholi during and since colonialism. On a personal level this Utopia helps make sense of painful experiences, and allows for the re-orientation of the temporality of knowledge from retrospection to anticipation (Miyazaki 2006).

The Utopia of Peace is most clearly articulated in the visions of the ARLPI and its long-term chairman, Archbishop Odama. The core of this vision was also present at the burial discussed in Chapter 4, at which Odama presided to speak of national unity enabled by God-given peace and forgiveness. However, the Utopia of Peace emerges not only from the pulpits and statements of religious elites, but also in the fragments of visions for a better future that are articulated amid everyday life. These aspects of the Utopia – its formal and everyday variants – share certain features: first, an understanding that pre-colonial and pre-war Acholi society was more humane, peaceful, just, and harmonious – as a whole, less confused – than at present; secondly, they express the hope for, and belief in, the possibility of a more peaceful future for the region; and finally, they posit that the Christian God can play a beneficial role in advancing the coming of this brighter destiny.

The Utopia of Peace is seen as the opposite of, and the antidote for, the confusion and disorientation that have followed decades of war; it is against this confusion that the Utopia of Peace is narrated, and from which it gains its momentum. In earlier parts of this book, I have described the relationship of churches and politics in Acholi through the metaphor of the anthill, foregrounding violence, silence and fear as foundational for these relations. In turning to utopia and peace, this chapter may thus appear as a disjuncture. Yet it is a purposive disjuncture, which seeks to illustrate how political theologies of peace, and the violent contexts within which they are spun, relate to each other.

The 'peace' of the Utopia of Peace transcends all the different aspects of 'peace' that I heard referred to in Kitgum: 'peace' as the absence of war, as an internal sense of peace, as spiritual peace, as unity, and as a sense of social harmony (see Porter 2013). As such, it resonates strongly with the Christian theological concern with peace (Gehlin 2015). A transcendent, God-given peace powers the utopian vision of Archbishop Odama with which I opened this chapter: a Utopia in which swords will be beaten into ploughshares, and there shall no longer be war.

In the most meticulously articulated and publicized version of the Utopia of Peace, that of the ARLPI and Archbishop Odama, humanity is bound together by the love of God. Everyone, regardless of colour, gender, ethnicity, creed or political affiliation, is joined together in a peace that overcomes all hate, hurt and desire for vengeance. Here the Utopia of Peace emerges as the opposite of war and violent division, as capable of strengthening and expanding a sense of inclusion beyond boundaries of religion and ethnicity. Yet I argue that, as previous renditions of powerful utopias in northern Uganda's history show, the crafting of inclusion always carries with it the violence of boundary work.

To make these claims, I combine insights from recent work on narrative imagination and the anthropology of hope with the work of scholars in the multidisciplinary field of Utopian Studies. After outlining central theoretical debates in these fields, the first part of the chapter focuses on the peace theology of Archbishop Odama and the ARLPI, in particular on how it evokes ideals and images of unity. I then analyse the ARLPI's Utopia as part of a continuum of utopian thought in northern Uganda, arguing that it resonates profoundly with the utopian visions that underlie the violence it has set out to counter. I suggest that because of its embeddedness in structures of power, the Utopia of Peace inadvertently strengthens many of the boundaries from within which it is narrated.

From analysing the ARLPI's publicly articulated Utopia, I turn to the fragments of everyday imaginaries of hope and peace, and to the way in which the Utopia of Peace allows its adherents to reorient themselves from the past towards the future. I close the chapter with reflection on how peaceful the Utopia of Peace actually is, and the extent to which it and its mainline Christian setting have touched and influenced societal co-existence in Kitgum.

The emphasis of the chapter is on the views of those who suffered the real impact of the war. Yet it is also important to point out that the story of religious leaders coming together to make peace amidst the ravages of war is alluring to outsiders; it provides a sense of hope for the war's observers, that despite the terrible things human beings do to each other, they can also do good. In recent years, emphasizing the role of religion in peace-building has been highly fashionable: for scholars, an emphasis on religion as a peacemaker provides a means to counter 'clash of civilizations'-type analyses; for faith-based development actors, it provides a means of much-needed self-re-invention amidst critiques of the depoliticizing effects of development and the push to channel aid increasingly through the private sector rather than NGOs. I suggest that these broader trends also explain part of the hype over ARLPI, the funding it has gained, and the overly positive scholarly accounts of its importance.

ARLPI broke important new ground for peace efforts in Acholi, which comes out clearly in first-person accounts such as those by Soto (2009) and Obol (2012); in Apuuli's (2011) work on ARLPI's role as one of the Acholi civil society actors demanding local rather than international criminal justice solutions to the war; and in Whitmore's (2019) work, which highlights that religious practice was less about sustaining ARLPI, than it was about supporting individual church workers in their commitment to stand beside the people they served through the war. These and other accounts (Jordhus-Lier and Braathen 2013; Lumumba 2014; Ochola 2008) make the power of ARLPI's story amply clear. Yet, particularly when narrated by its prominent spokespersons, it can also lure the observer into over-interpreting its importance: for all its merits, the ARLPI most certainly did not 'end Uganda's civil war', as Hoekema (2019a; see also Hoekema 2019b) has claimed. It is between the unrealistic promise of the churches' Utopia of Peace and its limits that this chapter seeks to strike a balance.

Utopia as theory and method

Many definitions and often-negative connotations have been attached to the concept of utopia since it was crafted in 1516 by Thomas More from the words 'not' (the Greek prefix *ou*), and 'place' (*topos*) (More [1516] 2001). Classically, utopia is conceived as a social imaginary that looks both back towards an idealized past, and forward to a future in which society has been perfected or at least improved. In this sense, utopias are essentially paradoxical: they speak simultaneously both to that which is no longer, and to that which is not yet, straddling an imagined past and an envisioned future. It is from a sense of disquiet with what is, and a desire for change (sometimes a volte-face) towards something better, that utopias gain their power, for which reason they often arise in contexts of extreme social breakdown and crisis (Moylan and Baccolini 2007).

Partly due to the widespread association of utopic thought in general with socialist utopias in particular, 'utopia' was long discredited as a concept within mainstream social science: critiqued, on the one hand, for being the stuff of worthless daydreams, and on the other, somewhat contradictorily, as dangerous instigating political programmes which, when followed, inevitably lead to totalitarianism (Levitas 2013, xiii). 'Anti-utopians', such as John Gray (2008), define utopias as visions that reject human nature by holding on to the belief that harmonious co-existence is possible, and that society can be perfected. Since such delusions unavoidably lead to violence, Gray suggests abandoning utopian projects like liberal humanism and universal human rights, and instead resorting to calculated realism in politics (ibid.).

Yet what defines itself as realist political thought is typically silent about its own underlying visions of the good society. In sociologist Ruth Levitas's view, Gray's anti-utopian stance leaves unanswered the question of who would make the calculated choices realists call for – and how – if, as Gray demands, humanity were to abandon the belief that 'political action can bring about an alteration in the human condition' (Gray 2008, 21). In the end, Levitas (2013, 7–11) argues that the recipe offered by anti-utopians like Gray is fundamentally conservative: they propose that there is no alternative to the current world order, as if the current world order were not to some extent the outcome of particular visions for society that preceded it and undergird it.

Speaking against the view that visions, dreams, hopes and desires for a better world are naive and useless, scholars in the field of Utopian Studies have called for the acknowledgement of the utopic elements of thought embedded in *all* political thought, not only socialism (see, e.g., Levitas 2013; Moylan and Baccolini 2007). This body of scholarship draws heavily on the philosophy of Ernst Bloch who, in *The Principle of Hope*, argued that utopia is an anthropological given, since across time and cultures human beings have always had a propensity for imagining and longing for a different life (Bloch 1986). Despite being grounded in a Marxist tradition, Bloch argued that even established religion or bourgeois culture, dismissed by Marxist ideology critique, can contain unrealized cultural ideas, desires and visions, which could transform present and future society, and which therefore should be salvaged (Kellner n.d.). In this view, utopia appears 'an unavoidable and indispensable element in the production of the future' (Levitas 2013, 6).

Following the distinction made by Kleist and Jansen (2016), I suggest that enmeshed within the Utopia of Peace is hope, in both a transitive and intransitive sense. On the one hand, the Utopia of Peace is heavy with an intransitive hopefulness, that is, a positive sentiment implying desire for and hesitant belief in positive change; on the other, it conveys transitive hopes *for* particular steps that would revive the envisioned peace. I suggest, however, that particular aspects of the social imaginaries embedded within the Utopia of Peace, particularly as narrated by religious leaders, ultimately constitute boundaries of exclusion, thereby producing the grounds for new forms of violence.

Hirokasu Miyazaki's (2006) work on hope, which also draws from Bloch, resonates interestingly with the arguments of Utopian Studies scholarship. For Miyazaki, the essence of hope is its anticipatory orientation towards an indeterminate future; interpreting hope as an outcome of preceding events, or treating it as an object of philosophical or social scientific inquiry, thus renders hope void. In this view, the method of hope is to create indeterminacy in situations where established knowledge appears to eliminate the possibility of maintaining hope (ibid., 69–85). Whereas the method of philosophical contemplation, and of much social scientific critique, looks backwards and tends to reify the past as a coherent whole (ibid., 13–16), the method of hope replicates moments of hope in the distant or near past, thereby inheriting and rekindling hope in the present (ibid., 130–40). Despite Miyazaki's critique of social critique, I argue that his view of a method of hope in fact bears a close resemblance to Utopian Studies scholars' view of utopia as a particular method of social critique. For many of these scholars (see, e.g., Browne 2005; Gardiner 1992; Levitas 2013; Moylan and Baccolini 2007), utopia, as an orientation towards the *not-yet*, is open, processual and transformative, rather than fixed, ready-made and final. Rather than *absolutist utopias* (Eskelinen, Lakkala, and Laakso 2020, 4), the cornerstones of utopia as social critique are what Moylan (2014) calls *critical utopias*, which reject utopias as blueprints, yet retain them as dreams.

In sum, I suggest that utopias can be analysed as a particular kind of political narrative and social imaginary, which derive their specifically 'utopian' tone from the fact that they are infused with both transitive hopes *for* particular outcomes, and the intransitive *affect* of hopefulness (Kleist and Jansen 2016). From this it follows that there are two edges to utopias as I approach them in this chapter: on the one hand, through an expression of an affect of hopefulness, they orient towards a not-yet; on the other, by virtue of the specific hopes embedded in them, they may promote pre-determined and at times violent blueprints for society.

To illustrate, consider Emmanuel Katongole's political theology. In light of the classical definition of utopia given above, Christianity in general can be seen as utopian in its very structure, in that it extends between the mythical creation (prior to the Fall of mankind), and the new creation in the future (at the return of Christ). As I described in the Introduction, Katongole sees Christianity as an alternative to the violent narrative of the nation-state that now undergirds African politics. In his vision, '[t]he salvation promised by God to God's people, to which the birth, life, death, and resurrection of Jesus is a witness, is not merely spiritual: it is a concrete social, material, political and economic reality that is ushered into existence by God's revelation in history' (Katongole 2011, 59). Katongole's vision can be seen as bearing both of the marks of hope's centrality to utopia: in the intransitive, affective sense, hope is deeply embedded through all his work (see also Katongole and Rice 2008), as through Christian theology in general (Moltmann 2002). It is a transformative orientation towards the not-yet, one crafted not with blueprints but with contextualized re-readings of how the biblical promise of an ultimate transcendental future unfolds amidst the lived realities of communities that have created paths of peaceful co-existence in the midst of societies wrecked by conflict. Yet Katongole's vision is also a very specific, transitive hope *for* something: a community that puts into practice the hope of an imminent second coming of Christ. In this sense, it conveys a blueprint for society.

Drawing from these different perspectives on utopia, I suggest in the following that the Utopia of Peace in mainline Christianity in northern Uganda conveys aspects *both* of utopia as a method of hopeful social transformation *and* of the inherent violence of utopian social imagination.

'My tribe is humanity'

Considering the bitter war experienced in northern Uganda, and the decades of political violence that preceded it, much of it pitting one ethnic or regional grouping against another, it might appear unrealistic to insist that Ugandans can be united. Yet this is precisely what the ARLPI has lobbied for, most prominently in the figure of the Catholic Archbishop John Baptist Odama. Odama, himself from Arua in West Nile, was consecrated bishop of Nebbi in 1996 and archbishop of Gulu in 1999, in which role he acted as the ARLPI chairperson from 2002 to 2010. During this time, the ARLPI, which had originally begun as an informal meeting group for religious leaders in Kitgum, began visibly lobbying for a peaceful resolution to the war. For instance, Odama led a group of religious leaders to sleep in Gulu bus park in solidarity with the thousands of children who were sleeping under verandas and under the stars in towns and trading centres to avoid abduction by the LRA.

Odama's sermons and speeches, which I heard on numerous occasions over the course of my fieldwork in 2012–13 and again in 2015, sought to alter reality radically, resonating strongly with Katongole's (2011) vision of political theology, which claims:

> [T]he church's political existence begins with and is sustained through the discipline of lament. For lament is at once about memory and the formation of a community of memory, a community that constantly remembers God's story of creation and lives out in revolutionary anticipation the promise of God's new creation.
>
> (Katongole 2011, 101)

In such a spirit, Odama's speeches were typically structured so as to begin with lamentations on two themes: the general problem of humanity's failure to find God and all the suffering that has followed, and the specific problem of divisionism in Uganda. An example of the former is provided by Odama's opening words at the celebration arranged in Gulu when he was awarded the World Vision's International peace prize in September 2012:

> Paradoxically, as I take this prize, human beings are still entangled in searching for good life. Human beings are hating human beings. Human beings are abusing human beings. Human beings are defiling human beings. Human beings are dealing and robbing human beings. Human beings are fighting human beings. Human beings are repressing human beings. Human beings are enslaving and killing fellow human beings. All such conditions continue to exist in families, in villages, and in the whole world.

An example of lamentations over lack of unity appears in the words Odama spoke at the state burial of Tiberio Atwoma (see Chapter 4):

> [Atwoma's] passion for the unity of the country, for the unity of tribes: this was correct. Because if we are divided, we fall apart. Unity is fundamental. In Uganda, we need it badly. It all started badly. Now disunity has come everywhere: to politics, religion, clans, even families. In a family, the husband can be UPC and the wife NRM. Some refuse to eat together because they belong to different parties! I am not lying [the crowd responds affirmingly], I am telling the truth! We must hear the prophetic voice of anyone who speaks of unity.
>
> (Fieldwork notes, October 2012)

Rather than simply lamenting, however, in each of his sermons Odama moved towards crafting a utopian vision of what Uganda, and humanity, could become. For Odama, this vision rested on his belief in the unity and equality of all humanity, and the possibility of comprehensive peace – between nations, between tribes, in families, and in society – that this belief enabled. In his speech at the World Vision International Peace Prize celebrations, Odama told a story that he often repeated:

> Someone once asked, it was a lady, 'Where are you from?' I answered, 'I have found out that my tribe is humanity.' 'Where in Uganda is it?' she asked. I said to her, 'You know, I have travelled all over the world, and everywhere people say welcome, welcome, be at home. Which then is my home? I have found out my home is the family of humanity.' I have found my job is to teach humanity we are all one people.[1]
>
> (Fieldwork notes, September 2012)

Although he never used the term himself, the content of Odama's theology resonated with the legacy of African Ubuntu theology, both in its evocation of the sense of one shared humanity and in its emphasis on reconciliation as the only pathway to the future (see, e.g., Hankela 2014; Haws 2009).[2] At Atwoma's burial, Odama elaborated on two metaphors for his vision of the unity that could exist between members of humanity: a bouquet of flowers and the Ugandan flag. As Odama explained, both have many colours, both would also be reduced in worth were even one of the colours to be removed. Each person has something to give, something unique, Odama insisted that nobody else of the seven billion people of Earth can contribute to the good of humanity.

Questions of unity and diversity, and inclusion and exclusion, have long been debated in the social sciences and philosophy, and also in theology. Emmanuel Katongole's (2011) view of the topic is a radical one: he declares that when a person and a Church is 'in Christ', it becomes ridiculous to think of such a person in terms of ethnic categories such as Hutu or Tutsi. Yet considering ethnicity ridiculous would be unthinkable for the majority of my research participants. In fact, Archbishop Odama and one Ugandan Catholic priest were the only people with whom I talked, or heard speak of ethnicity in Kitgum, who did not verbally display an explicit sense of ethnic pride; interestingly, neither were Acholi.

Amy Finnegan has argued that a strong sense of collective identity has emerged naturally from the collective trauma suffered by the Acholi during the war (see Dolan 2009), but that this collective identity has also deliberately been fostered in order to reposition the Acholi in relation to both Museveni's anti-Acholi narrative and the victim narrative of the international complex of aid and retributive justice (Finnegan 2010). The necessity of integrity was elaborated by the archbishop of the Church of Uganda, Henry Luke Orombi, when he visited Kitgum in October 2012. In his speech at the opening of a village church, Orombi said,

> My Christians… We live in Kampala, but we come from the northern part. When a bird begins nesting, it builds a nest. Many sons in Kampala do not know

about home. They do not know about brothers and sisters. They know no home. But Acholi is for Acholi! Nebbi for Nebbi! Why do you look down upon your home? I have been to East Uganda, to Central Uganda, to the West. And I can say: we northerners have a problem! We ask God to save us from this problem. We don't love our people! We don't love our home!

(Fieldwork notes, October 2012, Opete, Kitgum)

As Finnegan (2010) argues, religious and cultural leaders have played a pivotal role in the fostering of a collective Acholi identity. Although Odama (himself from Arua) was far less invested in cultivating a strong sense of 'Acholiness' than, for instance, the retired bishop of the Church of Uganda in Kitgum, Macleod Baker Ochola, his stance on ethnicity was also quite distinct from Katongole's radical disavowal of it. Rather than an erasure of ethnic, regional or clan identity, the metaphors Odama invoked – of the bouquet and the multi-coloured flag – speak to a vision of unity that accommodates diversity. Yet neither Odama's nor Katongole's visions answer the practical question of how this Utopia should be put into practice. How should the bouquet be constructed, for instance, when allocating the national budget, or deciding on quotas for parliamentary representation? How many of each of the different flowers should there be in the national bouquet? And how, concurrently, would the 'national cake' – to use the euphemism so commonly employed in Ugandan political debate – be divided?

Rather than a blueprint for how society should be organized, I read Odama's variant of the Utopia of Peace as a challenge to individuals, churches and communities to think beyond the constraints of reality as we know it: to envision a different reality – a not-yet in which one could find one's primary identification in the 'tribe of humanity' – and to find ways to transform the not-yet into reality. Similar utopias of inclusion have been fostered elsewhere: by Bishop Verryn of the Central Methodist Church (CMC) in Johannesburg, for example, which for years housed thousands of Zimbabwean refugees in its premises. In her study of the limits of the ideal of Ubuntu at the CMC, Hankela writes:

> The rule of survival set limits on how far people were ready to go in caring and helping in the name of *Ubuntu*. The continuation of one's own group's existence as respected human beings and one's own religious identity surfaced as prerequisites for reaching out to the other in need.
>
> (Hankela 2013, 329)

Hankela's observation would suggest that the uncertainty many Acholi have felt over the past decades concerning the continuation of their group's existence as respected human beings places powerful restrictions on the extent to which the sense of a Utopia of Peace, and of national and global inclusion, can be fostered in this context.

As discussed previously in this book, Uganda's postcolonial history has been marked by the tension between the need to affirm empowering ethnic pride and cultural integrity, and the reality of a multi-ethnic nation. Katongole would say that the problem with all the visions that have been evoked in response to the challenge of state-making in Uganda is that they all take the nation-state for granted. In his view, churches have been socialized by the myth of the politically ethnicized nation-state in postcolonial Africa, and hence speak from within that socialization. But Katongole argues that the (Catholic) Church can and must transcend this socialization. Reflecting on my own experience of conducting ethnographic research on churches and politics in northern Uganda, however, I am not at all sure that this is possible. From the point of view of Acholi, the problem with a vision like Katongole's is that those in positions of overwhelming power over others within a nation-state are unlikely to relinquish such positions, however evocative the visions of another world may be.

There thus seem to be tensions embedded within the Utopia of Peace in northern Uganda: a tension between the demand for universal inclusion and an acknowledgement of the need for a sense of ethnic integrity, but also a tension between an understanding of peace as a state of settled reassurance and peace as a vision towards which one must struggle. For the rest of this chapter, this insight drives empirical exploration of how these opposing tendencies and tensions unfolded amid the lived realities in which the Utopia of Peace was crafted.

So far, this chapter has analysed the Utopia of Peace through a focus on the public speech of religious elites. Because of the institutional power of the institutions they represented, their narratives carried weight within the field of individual and collective social imagination in northern Uganda. Bishops and priests often live a very different life to that of their parishioners, but many of them also come from humble backgrounds and retain close connections with 'the grassroots' of the churches they serve, if only by visiting and caring for their families, many of whom live in rural areas. Hence, although their often-evocative speeches can be seen as distant from the everyday reality of their listeners, they are not completely divorced from it, and traces of the publicly recounted and preached Utopia of Peace could be heard in the speech of active Catholics and Anglicans in Kitgum. Many of my research participants employed the trope of

Utopian peace-thinking in our discussions, particularly when it came to unity, respect and peace between the religious groups of different churches – goals they almost unanimously attributed to the teaching and practical example given by the ARLPI. Furthermore, the provision of formalized narrative resources in sermons was not the only way in which mainline churches in Kitgum functioned as sites of hopeful social imaginaries. Before turning to these less formally articulated forms of the Utopia of Peace, however, I wish to draw parallels between the ARLPI's formal Utopia of Peace, and earlier forms of utopian thought in northern Uganda.

Predecessors of utopian thought in Acholi

Imaginaries of the past and the future can be considered as located on a continuum, and the Utopia of Peace is no exception, drawing on and influenced by the social imaginaries preceding it. Utopian thought did not emerge on the religio-political scene in Acholi with the ARLPI, for the violence of northern Uganda's war, which prompted the creation of the churches' Utopia of Peace drew, in part, from the utopian visions of the millenarian rebel movements that emerged in the region in the 1980s. Furthermore, as Allen (1991) argues, the visions of rebel leaders Alice Lakwena and Joseph Kony need to be seen as drawing, to an important extent, from Christian epistemologies and teachings, and also on the impacts of the legacy of missionary work on 'customary' Acholi understandings of good, evil, witchcraft and spirit possession (see Chapter 1).

The activities of Alice Lakwena and other similar figures in Acholi after the take-over by Yoweri Museveni's NRA can in part be understood as a mode of self-defence against the violence perpetrated on the Acholi by the NRA, but also as driven by the need to deal with the perceived cosmological imbalance triggered by the violent deaths meted out by Acholi soldiers during the Bush War (see Chapter 2). In Behrend's reading, the war of Lakwena's HSMF (Holy Spirit Mobile Forces) was a war against war, which aimed to 'put an end to violence in Acholi and to build a new, better world free of evil' (1999, 61). Driven by this vision, and by disillusionment with the ability of the technologies of war to address the cosmological problems that were plaguing the Acholi, Lakwena devised magical methods of warfare, such as stone grenades and sacred water that rendered the anointed bullet-proof. Through the adoption of these methods, she claimed, the pure would defeat the wicked, and society would be transformed (Behrend 1999, 61). In written testimonies, HSMF fighters expressed their belief that their 'victory would result in national reconciliation, removal of bad leadership and a return to multiparty democracy' (Allen 1991, 378).

The radical utopias of these earlier movements have left marks on Acholi society and patterns of thought. Although there is an enormous difference between the LRA and HSMF – both of which used physical violence and military measures to advance their goal of transforming Acholi society – and the ARLPI, which used prayers, peace mediation, public appeals and various forms of political lobbying to the same end, I suggest there are two notable parallels that merit attention.

The first of these is their recourse to, and production of, a narrative of social and moral decay and redemption. The ARLPI variant of this narrative prescribes forgiveness and reconciliation, a renewal of bonds of respect between elders and youth, and the crafting of unity across ethnic and religious divisions as the sources of redemption. Moreover, leaders of the ARLPI have consistently demanded that political leaders respect multiparty democracy, calling for national reconciliation. Many of these points parallel the early utopian visions of the HSMF and later the LRA. Behrend writes that '[t]he HSMF... developed their own interpretation of Christianity, which allowed Catholics, Protestants, and even Muslims to join the movement' (1999, 84). Contrary to later rebel movements in the region, Alice Lakwena succeeded in broadening her group beyond ethnic boundaries, albeit only among northern Ugandan Luo-speaking groups like the Iteso, Langi and Jo-Padhola (ibid., 84). Although the LRA never succeeded in this, and its core fighters have always been Acholi, the narrative of unity also figured importantly in Kony's teaching. As Behrend put it in an analysis written early during the LRA war, Kony said 'he had resolved to fight to destroy all those who wanted to fight. The struggle would last until no one had the wish to fight any longer', and that he 'wanted justice and righteousness to reign throughout the country' (1999, 179).

The second parallel, one also referenced briefly by Allen (2010, 257), concerns ritual practice. As the emergence of the HSMF, and to a less explicit extent also the LRA, was in part a response to the problem of *cen* (vengeful spirit, see Chapter 2) brought to Acholi by Obote's soldiers who had been involved in atrocities during the Bush War against Museveni, both Lakwena and Kony adopted rituals of cleansing and purification for those recruited to their ranks. Likewise, one of the key goals of the ARLPI was to establish, in collaboration with Acholi elders and the Acholi chief's cultural institution *Ker Kwaro Acholi*, a set of practices – drawing from pre-existing custom but with modification and new codification – that could be applied to facilitate the return of former LRA soldiers and abductees 'from the bush', and their resettlement into their homes (see Allen 2010; Baines 2010; Harlacher et al. 2006). The ARLPI, like the HSMF and LRA before it, drew on customary cleansing ceremonies, also adopting Christian elements and practices and working them into the rituals.

Christianity was by no means the sole driving force of the two rebel movements, but it moulded Alice Lakwena, Joseph Kony and the structure of their utopias in important ways. Alice's father, Severino Lukwoya, who took up Alice's mission after her troops were crushed trying to reach Kampala and she escaped to Kenya, was a catechist in the Anglican Church (Behrend 1999, 174–8).[3] Lakwena converted to Catholicism, and both she and Joseph Kony, who had served as an altar boy, drew heavily on Catholic symbolism in constructing the teaching and practices of their movements (see Chapter 2 for more on this point). In addition, the movements borrowed from the Church of Uganda's Balokole revival movement, which had gained particular momentum in Kitgum since its emergence in the 1920s (see Ward and Wild-Wood 2012). In Behrend's view, the teachings of certain Balokole leaders prefigured many of the later prophecies of Alice Lakwena and Joseph Kony: 'the Christian teaching in general and the Balokole in particular opened up a new dimension of time: the future. Hopes were... on a future millennium, which allowed for prophecies announcing the end of the world' (1999, 122).

Arguably, to many Acholi people, at least those old enough to remember the early days of the rebel movements, the similarities between the rebel utopias and the Utopia of Peace of the ARLPI are recognizable. I do not suggest that the ARLPI has consciously or even subconsciously 'borrowed' from the rebel movements' manifestos or ideologies. Rather, since the HSMF and the LRA share a cultural, social, political and linguistic setting with the ARLPI, it follows naturally that both the rebels and the religious leaders drew on similar narrative and ritual patterns to advance their aims of social transformation.

The violence of peaceful unity

From a very early stage, the utopian visions of the HSMF and LRA became entwined with brutal physical violence, which Alice Lakwena and Joseph Kony claimed was necessitated by the impurity of the external and internal enemies of the Acholi (Allen 1991; Finnström 2008). While the Utopia of Peace in mainline Christianity in northern Uganda has not adopted this form of violence, in the following I suggest that it too was imbued with the violence inherent in boundary-making between those already included within the sphere of harmonious co-existence, and those outside it. Furthermore, in terms that are strikingly similar to those used earlier by Lakwena and Kony, those outside the boundaries are often deemed impure and sinful.

At the Advent service of 2012, the presiding missionary priest at Saint Mary's emphasized Advent as a time for purification, for attentiveness and for concentrating on Christ. He spoke of how Jeremiah (29:11) had a vision for the future, and of how for us also, there would be a future, a way out of the terrible times our corrupt society was enduring, if only we looked to Jesus. The priest then shifted attention from the plural 'you' (originally the Israelites in exile), to the many individual 'yous' gathered to hear his sermon:

> At Advent, you must watch yourselves... Debauchery, drunkenness, cares of life: these are the things that take us away from God. It is like the teaching of modern society, of this so-called freedom, that you are free to do whatever. Like drunkenness, in all forms, not only alcohol. Also this dancing: the youth, they go to dance all night. Youth, you become stupid that way, it is like a drug. Jesus tells us: watch yourself, for in these easy ways we can spoil ourselves.
> (Fieldwork notes, November 2012)

The Utopia of Peace that has emerged within mainline Christianity in post-war northern Uganda posits societal and individual peace in Christ as the ultimate antidote to war, violence and 'confusion'. Ultimately, it seeks to (re)establish harmonious relations within the family and the clan, and to lead humankind to believe in Christ. The fundamental violence of this Utopia thus lies in the violence inherent to the construction of boundaries between inclusion and exclusion, and in the attempts to stabilize the moral order among those included.

Moreover, the Utopia of Peace is hostage to its embeddedness in particular constellations of moral, political, ethnic and religious power. Its potential to alter social reality is conditioned and circumvented by the influential role played by a fairly homogeneous group of old men in defining the content of public renditions of visions of peace. As Baines (2007) and Porter (2016) show, religious leaders, as well as cultural leaders such as members of the Acholi cultural institution Ker Kwaro Acholi, embody the patriarchy and gerontocracy of contemporary Acholi society. Similarly, the view that authoritative bodies have a particular responsibility in steering society towards fulfilment of the Utopian ideal is an integral component of the Utopia of Peace in northern Uganda. As Archbishop Odama himself put it at the end of his sermon at Atwoma's burial:

God says 'You don't know the hour! That is reserved to me, God. Be ready. That's all I ask. Do the good I've asked you to do with the rest of those who are my images!' This is a big challenge for leaders, whether they be religious, political, or cultural leaders. If we don't steer the people correctly to God, you are dooming them! Parents, if you don't steer your children, you are dooming them! Teachers, if you do not steer your students in the right way, you are dooming them!… At the final judgement God will ask you why you haven't done that!

(Fieldwork notes, October 2012)

Although I argue that the preaching on unity by clerics like Odama has been important for the construction of peaceful co-existence in the aftermath of war in Acholi, the quality of this peace is not identical for all co-existing members of society. The fact that religious elites are largely urban, male and materially well-off renders the Utopia of Peace, at least the religious elite's public renditions of it, a predominantly patriarchal, gerontocratic and, as I argue in detail elsewhere, heteronormative project (Alava 2017a). Holly Porter makes a related argument when analysing churches' responses to women's complaints about rape. In a reflection of pervasive moral norms in Acholi, churches have promoted dealing with rape *gang gang* (meaning 'close to home') by emphasizing forgiveness; they have put little effort into educating their members about gender-based violence, nor have they foregrounded the desire of individual women for justice and reparation after wrong-doing (Porter 2016, 165, 176–83). An emphasis on peace thus comes at a price. Furthermore, as I discuss in more detail in the following chapter, despite all its outspoken attempts to move in the opposite direction, the Utopia of Peace remains hostage to the social, political, class and gender locations from which it is promoted, and the boundaries surrounding them (see Introduction, and Warner 2002). Hence it re-constructs these very boundaries even when aiming or claiming to break them.

Churches as sites for hopeful orientations of temporality

Analysis so far has focused on elements of publicly articulated 'elite visions' as components of the Utopia of Peace in mainline Christianity in northern Uganda. But the Utopia of Peace was not moulded and evoked merely in public and through public address. In this part of the chapter, I turn to analysing the Utopia of Peace as it emerges from fragments of future-oriented hopeful imaginaries articulated and embodied in everyday lives. I argue that, for my research participants, it took the form of a sense of inner peace, of destiny and purpose, and of there being hope for a future where things would get better; thus, simultaneously it makes sense of the painful past and turns the minds of its adherents towards the brighter future possible in the not-yet. It allows individual Christians and church communities to overcome the violence of life during the war, and to concentrate on the ways in which things are getting better. While constantly relating to, and drawing from, an idealized 'better' pre-war or pre-colonial past, the Utopia is oriented towards a future in which social harmony is again re-established through forgiveness, a return to a proper morality, and, for my Christian research participants, through prayer, praise and God.

Kidega, a Catholic man in his thirties, explained to me that he rarely prayed on Sundays, but often went to morning mass during the week, saying, 'It keeps me organised. It gets me focused.' He continued by stating that 'Here, people go because that's what they do. You can't just fade out of it'. Going to church was a habit for many, followed without particular reflection, yet for Kidega it served a purpose since it helped him to keep organized and focused. For others, the purpose was different. Recall the young woman I introduced in Chapter 3, Sarah, who told me that she was tough on the outside, but that if I looked inside her, I would not survive. She had been through a lot of hardship in her life, both during her childhood in the midst of war and after the war ended, yet nothing in her demeanour suggested her experiences. When I asked her what made her volunteer hours of her time every week for the tasks she undertook in the church, Sarah answered:

> Aah, it's not something very big. I go there because that's the only place that can give me peace. I can get my comfort, I can see my faith. You get the point? I feel very safe when I'm in church. Very safe. Since from the time I started joining in Sunday school, I really love church. And if I don't pray, on any Sundays, really I feel bad.

It is remarkable that she first begins by asserting that 'it is not something very big', yet it is a practice that makes her feel 'very safe': 'safe' in fact being something rather big in her circumstances. The sense of safety and what I would call 'inner peace' was cultivated by both words and embodied practices in church services. Peace was a major feature of liturgy at these churches, most noticeably at the Catholic Church, where the Lord's Prayer was followed each Sunday with a prayer for peace: 'Lord Jesus Christ, you said to your apostles: I leave you peace, my peace I give you. Look not on our sins, but on the faith of your Church, and grant us the peace and unity of your kingdom where you live for ever and ever.'

Figure 10. Choir members and children during Sunday service at Town Parish. Photo by author.

Almost every Sunday, the prayer was followed by a hymn which many people, even some of those who rarely sang along to any of the others, joined in singing:

> May the peace of the Lord be with you – with your friends and your family, too. Let it be and let it grow and everywhere you go may the peace of the Lord follow you.

A sense of peace was not cultivated by words alone, but also by numerous aesthetic and embodied ritual elements of church services, also described in rich detail in Whitmore's (2019) analysis of the spiritual practices that, drawing on Combonian theology, were employed by Catholic sisters during the northern Ugandan war. The importance of these was rarely elaborated by people I interacted with, but, rather, indirectly referenced in comments about church services as moments of peace, calm and focus. The impact of the aesthetic and the non-verbally ritualized was manifest in the demeanours of the people I observed around me at church on quiet, calm Sunday mornings, when the early morning sun leaked in through the stained-glass windows, lighting the paintings and floor tiling at Saint Mary's church, or lending a sparkle to the year-round, red-and-silver Christmas decorations at the Town Parish. Each Sunday, the hundreds of bodies gathered in the churches seemed to fall into a joint rhythm of breathing, led by the elegance and precision of the movements of the priests, catechists and altar boys performing the Catholic liturgy, under the predictable and always repeated order of service at both churches. Amid the often hectic pace of fieldwork and family life, there was much that quietened my own mind and body in these embodied rituals, and a similar quietening was evident in those around me. My notes from church services often describe the expressions of calm, often of boredom, but also of happiness and elation, of those sitting beside me in church, singing along to the Catholic hymns, or clapping and ululating during the praise choruses at Town Parish. Through these embodied practices, mainline churches cultivated in their members a sense of internal contentment, peace and hope.

This sense was summarized by a praise song that was regularly sung at the Town Parish. As I discuss in more detail in the following chapter, this parish had recently overcome years of serious in-fighting and division, and in interviews and informal discussions, members of the parish often expressed excitement over how things were again moving forward in church. Even the choir was back in full swing, leading the parish almost every Sunday in a song that encapsulates a sense of hope and future-orientation that I think was a key to why the church was experienced as meaningful by its members. The English verses of the hymn, which was repeated in Swahili and English for minutes on end, went like this:

> Things are getting better, things are getting better!
> When the Lord is on my side, things are getting better,
> things are getting better, things are getting better!
> Things are already better, things are already better!
> When the Lord is on my side, things are already better,
> things are already better, things are already better!

Between services, I learned about the situations of some of the choir members: of their desperate search for work, and the frustration of those with work due to insufficient salaries – situations Hage (2009) aptly refers to as 'stuckedness'. I had heard the life stories of those singing, some of whom had shared with me horrific memories of war that they carried with them and, as I discussed in Chapter 3, I knew that similar and worse memories were carried in silence by others. Yet the same life stories made it easy to understand their conviction that things were getting better. Now the parish was singing without gunfire in the distance; people were cultivating their own food and were no longer dependent on food aid. Even the split in the church was being healed. Things *were* getting better, and for many of the Christians I knew in Kitgum, this was radical and insurmountable proof of the Lord's being on their side.

In the song, the reorientation of temporality was radical: rather than dwelling on the past, it was the future, and the future-oriented present, that was determined to be worth knowing and talking about (Miyazaki 2006).[4] A similar chorus that really got the Town Parish going, with people dancing, clapping and singing, the little church reverberating with the energetic acoustic praise, consisted of a short and to-the-point line, 'When Jesus says yes nobody can say no.' Never mind that Christians as much as other Acholis were confronted by one obstacle after another; that plenty of gatekeepers seemed to be saying no to them, blocking their plans and blighting their hopes. The peace of mind provided by the churches' proffered faith in a better future pulsated through the choir's energetic praise songs, into those of us singing, and into the parish we were leading in praise: the church was our peace. However, as the following chapter demonstrates in more detail, a spiritually endowed sense of peace mingled and merged with the material realities of Acholi Christians' lives, and played out within the moral economies of their churches.

Utopia – or critical utopia?

I have argued in this chapter that in the aftermath of war in northern Uganda, a social imaginary that I refer to as the Utopia of Peace has emerged in mainline Christian churches in the region. On an individual level, it has facilitated leaving the painful past behind and orienting outlooks and practices towards the future. On a communal and social level, the Utopia of Peace has enabled a move towards reconciliation and the bridging of ethnic and religious boundaries, thus contributing to post-conflict reconciliation in Uganda. I have, however, also claimed that this social imaginary functions through the creation of boundaries of exclusion, and that it is deeply constricted by its embeddedness in relations of class, gender and age.

In light of this, the question I explore in the final pages of this chapter is whether the Utopia of Peace is better conceptualized as the kind of utopia that provides a closed-off blueprint for society, or as an open-ended, transformational, critical utopia, as advocated by scholars like Levitas (2013), Moylan and Baccolini (2007) and Eskelinen (2020). To answer this, I return to the work of Hirokasu Miyazaki, who, employing insight from Ernst Bloch (1986), suggests that replicating hope in ethnographic writing demands the disavowal of teleological conceptualizations of the world: 'There is no God's plan, no essential disposition of the world that will automatically unfold' (Miyazaki 2006, 15). In this Blochian view, one similar to that of Utopian Studies scholars, the direction of change in the world is indeterminate, not predetermined. In contrast, the Christian vision of Catholic and Anglican Acholi clerics leaves far less space for indeterminacy: lying on the ultimate horizon of their visions is the imminent coming of Christ. Yet, as I have mentioned above, the precise content of how that day will come is never discussed; moreover, for the ARLPI, which brings together Anglicans, Catholics, Muslims and Pentecostals, the question is by definition avoided. Thus, despite its orientation towards an eschatological future in Christ, the focus of the Utopia of Peace in mainline Christianity is in fact ultimately on the present: the anticipation of the future is employed, as Emmanuel Katongole has contended in his later work (2017), in the task of lamentation and transformation – of selves, societies and the world – in the present.

Thus there is no conclusive answer to the question I pose – whether the Utopia of Peace is a closed-off and ultimately violent system as Gray (2008) argues all utopias to be, or whether it conveys the transformative potential evoked by Utopian Studies scholars (Levitas 2013; Moylan and Baccolini 2007). Instead, I suggest the Utopia of Peace, imbued as it is with hope of the intransitive and transitive sort (Kleist and Jansen 2016) – and since it takes the form of a field of imagination rather than a ready-made narrative set in stone – evades strict definition. Yet a number of points emerge.

To start with, the Utopia of Peace provides a model for a very different politics to that of *cung i wibye*: of harsh power play on anthills undergirded by lingering threats of violence (see Chapters 4 and 5). In contrast to the prevailing political climate in Uganda, in which nothing is left open for genuine political debate or negotiation, and in which there is very little forgiveness for past sins whether individual or collective, the Christian Utopia of Peace, predicated as it narratively is on forgiveness and reconciliation, turns its back on the past, and opens up towards the future.

In so far as the publicly articulated vision – the transitive hope – of the ARLPI promotes the strengthening of the gerontocratic and patriarchal order as the solution to conditions of 'confusion' in Acholi, its Utopia of Peace can be seen to reproduce violent structures in Acholi society. Yet the same Utopia also transgresses existing violent boundaries of exclusion, and seeks to create new communities of inclusion. Furthermore, through its nurturing of an intransitive affect of hopefulness, the ARLPI's vision of peacemakers and an end to war is one that individual Christians and communities wrecked by violence have drawn on to orientate their lives towards the future and out of the painful past.

In this context, the current crises for which Acholi society as a whole is seeking solutions should be born in mind. At present, there are serious concerns over alcoholism in Acholi, over violence in families, and over the loss of purpose and direction in young people (see Amanela et al. 2020 for a recent overview). Not only Acholi religious leaders, but also many of the people I have interacted over the years – young, well-educated, and actively practising Catholic and Anglican youth – were of the opinion that, in these circumstances, order was essential, because without it, there could only be more chaos (Alava 2017c). My young acquintances often articulated these concerns in different ways to the old, yet they agreed with their elders that *something had to be done*. This was particularly so among those who were struggling to make a living, meanwhile steering not only their own families, but also their younger siblings, some of whom were, in my friends' views, 'lost': unemployed, drinking, gambling or risking getting infected with HIV (see also Olsson 2016 173, 190–3). It is in this context of 'confusion' that the Utopia of Peace that I have analysed in this chapter has emerged among mainline churches – in the discourse of their leaders, and the practice of their members – in what I suggest be seen as an attempt to contribute to re-imagining community in Acholi society after decades of war.

Finally, however, while I argue that the Catholic and Anglican Churches have played important societal and political roles in Uganda, historically as well as in the present, I also argue there are very few grounds for claiming that their vision of peace has been adopted throughout Acholi society, or even noted. Not only is the 'peacefulness' of the Christian narrative of peace in northern Uganda problematic in ways I have discussed in this chapter, and the actual reality of inter- and intra-church relations often so ridden with conflict as to render words of peace rather hollow (see Chapter 7), there are also considerable limits on the significance of this narrative in the first place. Church teaching on peace was highly visible and audible in the largely ecclesiastic spaces in which I conducted my fieldwork, but it is far less so in other spaces, for instance in those less defined by Christianity. Furthermore, even *within* the 'highly Christian' social locations that I studied, the power of the church to define the ways in which its members orientate themselves towards life is notably constricted (see Alava 2017a). To elucidate this point, and to draw this chapter to a close, I return to a moment of important realization during my fieldwork.

The passing of the parade

In April 2013, just a few days before we left Kitgum to return to our home in Finland, the Catholic Church arranged an ecumenical Peace Week in Kitgum Town. The timing seemed impeccable, with the event allowing me to gather one last round of fascinating data on some of the core issues of my research. The event began with a procession headed by Catholic, Anglican, Muslim and Pentecostal clerics, who walked approximately two kilometres from the Catholic Mission to the event location on the other side of the town.

Just before leaving to join the procession, I decided to take my four- and two-year-old boys with me. The extempore choice turned out to be a disaster. The crowd of some 200 people, the announcements and music being played from the loudspeakers on the back of a pick-up truck in the middle of the procession, and the heat of the early afternoon soon broke my older boy's resolve and had him overwhelmed and sobbing by the side of the road. As the procession started down the hill, and just as I was despairing that I would have to return home with Eemil and miss everything, my husband drove past us and collected our sobbing boy.

Figure 11. Poster for the Gulu Provincial Peace Week. Photo by author.

Annoyed as I was at the time for missing the procession, these unexpected events drew my attention to something I would likely have overlooked had I walked into town in the middle of the singing and clapping group. In my fieldwork diary, I wrote:

> I start to walk to town with Wilho strapped to my back, imagining that I will catch up with the procession, but I never do; I am too far behind and they are walking too fast. The striking thing about walking a little bit away from the procession – slightly behind them at first, and in town along parallel streets so as to cut some corners – is realising how life remains at its normal pace on streets the procession doesn't pass through, and very soon resumes its normal pace on those it does, after the procession has passed. It's symbolic, perhaps, of how little this Ecumenical Peace Week touches the day-to-day life of the town. In one of the opening speeches at the event, someone says, 'It is clear that we will leave this place changed, it is unavoidable.' I'm just not so sure. Rather, I felt very cynical after today's experience at the Peace Week. I felt I had heard the speeches before. During the group discussion on peace, reconciliation, and politics, where I listened in on the group for religious leaders, I had to bite my tongue not to stand up and say 'Come on guys! How about looking into yourselves as well; into your relationships among the churches, into your own corruption, into your own injustices? How about working on those things before going on these rampages about the shortfalls of others?'
>
> (Fieldwork notes, April 2013)

It is these issues – the relationships among the churches and the politics within the churches – to which I turn in the final analytical chapter. Here, suffice it to say that although the event itself left me feeling cynical, looking back at the statement made by the Peace Week speaker with a few years' hindsight, I believe he was right. It is clear that the religious gatherings – Sunday services at which our choir sang at Town Parish; the public church events at which politicians and clergy offered competing political narratives for their audiences to embrace or denounce; or events for talking specifically of peace as arranged by the ARLPI – had left, and continued to leave, Acholi society changed. As performative practices and rituals, they matter. Without all these events, without mainline churches, and without the Utopia of Peace they have contributed to crafting, Kitgum, Acholi and Uganda would be a different place. But how different?

The ARLPI has rightly been recognized for its attempts to advance peace during the northern Ugandan war (Apuuli 2011; Hoekema 2019b; Jordhus-Lier and Braathen 2013; Ochola 2008; Soto 2009). However, to conclude, I claim that the analysis presented in this chapter offers a number of correctives to existing work on the topic. First, the 'Utopia of Peace' to which I claim the ARLPI's actions contributed, was far less straightforward than commentators have so far acknowledged. Since it has been a response not only to the war, but to more general patterns of societal transformation, and since it resonates profoundly with historical predecessors of utopian thinking in Acholi, it cannot be assessed merely as an antidote to violence between the LRA and the UPDF. The Utopia of Peace also contains ingredients that seek to bolster gerontocratic, conservative and patriarchal societal control in the region. Second, despite the role the ARLPI played, existing analyses of religious peacemaking more often than not fail to consider the limits to the ability of the ARLPI or individual churches to effect change: no matter what churches say, their words may well be unheard or disregarded as irrelevant, even by their members, let alone other societal actors. Third, in the context of war and its afterlives, it may be at least as important to analyse the effect of the Christian emphasis on peace on individual practitioners, as it is to conduct analyses of religion in the public realm: for churches to contribute to peoples' experiences of calm, trust, peace or hope in the midst of war and its afterlives is no small thing.

7

Confusion in the church

'This is Henni Alava. She's studying all the mess in the church.' The words with which one Catholic Acholi priest introduced me to another – although disconcerting at the time – capture something essential. Much of what goes on in churches in Kitgum that interested me – quarrels between factions; contestation over resources; rumours about theologically unsound teaching or the behaviour of one Christian or another; debates about the precise location of boundaries between churches' and their neighbours' land; speculation about the political allegiances of bishops; disgruntlement over the allocation of church scholarships, and so on – was looked upon as mess. While I intuitively categorized this mess as 'church politics', my Acholi acquintances told me the term does not translate directly into Acholi. The closest equivalent, I was told, would be *anyobanyoba i eklisia* if speaking with a Catholic, or *anyobanyoba i kanica* if an Anglican: confusion in the church. It is this mess and confusion, and how those who encountered it understood it and came to terms with it, which is discussed here.

The chapter has two aims: first, it draws together threads from earlier chapters to explore the precise nature of 'confusion in the church', and how it is addressed in the midst of war's afterlives in Acholi. By showing the limits of the Utopia of Peace, I illustrate how a focus on embeddedness scatters analytical light aimed at the relationship between 'Christianity' and 'politics', kaleidoscope-like, such that the boundaries between the two become refracted; politics skittering into Christianity and vice versa; in a manner aptly captured by the notion of *anyobanyoba*.

Secondly, and so as to achieve the first aim, the chapter takes issue with a claim made by Paul Gifford (2008; 2015) about the 'real' nature of mainline Christianity in Africa, which, he suggests, 'is not obviously about relating to the divine. [Rather] it is most obviously about access to Western resources and the whole range of things this brings: education, employment, modernization, global opportunities' (Gifford 2015, 278). Gifford makes a valid point in emphasizing the significance of the resource flows channelled by mainline churches in Africa (ibid., see also Beckmann, Gusman, and Shroff 2014; Christiansen 2010; B. Jones 2013). In a situation where the continent as a whole is becoming increasingly marginalized from and exploited by the global economy (Bayart 2000; Ferguson 2006; Harrison 2010; Nigusie and Ali 2020), the magnitude of external resource flows (e.g. for development or peace-building activities) sets them apart from other types of revenue to which churches typically have access, leading to very particular types of relations: what in Bayartian (2000) terms could be called the 'extraversion' of many African churches.

There are two points in Gifford's claims, however, that require attention. First, although external resources are clearly important, it is misleading to conceptualize foreign funding as something almost single-handedly shaping Christianity in Africa. Western resources are not a novelty, after all funding for 'development' was a building block of the colonial missionary enterprise. More importantly, the financial assistance churches receive from missionary or NGO patrons is but one aspect of the material embeddedness of religious institutions (see Chapter 1 and Alava 2016b) alongside, for instance, support from political patrons and local members (see, e.g., Alava and Ssentongo 2016; Bompani 2016; Lauterbach 2017), or attempts to secure church access to land (Alava and Shroff 2019; Baroin 1996).

Secondly, the case studies I present show that the opposition Gifford (2015) introduces by positing churches as sites of procuring access to power and resources, *rather than* as sites of accessing the divine, is misleading. While Gifford acknowledges that people may *also* find spiritual resources within mainline Christian churches in Africa, his division between the divine and the material is utterly foreign to much religious thought on the continent, wherein access to material blessings is a central reason for relating to the divine (Ellis and ter Haar 2004; Lauterbach 2017; Magesa 2002; Mbiti 1990). Rather than being in opposition, this chapter shows how 'the divine' *intersects* with the 'the mess': a result of the churches' being crosscut by, and embedded in, relationships through which power and resources are distributed. This intersection is clearly illustrated by the three cases of 'confusion in the church' analysed in this chapter, the ways in which 'confusion' is conceptualized and addressed by church members, and the resources on which they draw to address it.

The first case, which details a miserable day experienced by the choir of the Anglican Town Parish, provides a snapshot of a recent moment of confusion, which, as the second case shows, relates to over a decade of conflict between the so-called 'Concerned Christians' and the leadership of the Church of Uganda's

Kitgum Diocese. While the first two cases focus specifically on what was meant by 'confusion in the church', the third case, about inexplicable sickness and healing in a devoted and comparatively wealthy Catholic family, directs attention to explanations of, and engagement with, particular kinds of confusions in Acholi in the space between social status, witchcraft and God.

A pilgrimage turned sour

In February 2015 the field beside the small parish church in Mucwini, some 20 kilometres from Kitgum town, was to serve as the scene of the yearly commemoration of the death of a son of the village, Janani Luwum, after whom the Anglican Town Parish in Kitgum had been named. Luwum, who had been the archbishop of the Metropolitan Province of Uganda, Rwanda, Burundi, and Boga (Zaire), died while under arrest in Idi Amin's cells in 1977, after publicly reprimanding Amin for arbitrary state violence. Today, the global Anglican Church refers to Luwum as a saint, and his likeness is captured in a statue in Westminster Abbey, among other twentieth-century martyrs. In 2015, the day of his death was for the first time to be celebrated as an international day of commemoration. Choirs, traditional musicians, and dance groups were to travel from Gulu and Kampala to join local Acholi choirs, their performances augmented by that of a South African opera singer. Pilgrims were scheduled to arrive at the site from neighbouring countries, with the service to be presided over by the Ugandan-born John Ssentamu, who, as archbishop of York in the Church of England, was second in the church's hierarchy. Even the president would come.

When the director of the Town Parish choir, David, heard I would be in Kitgum in February 2015, he demanded that I also join the excursion to Mucwini as part of my old choir. Since November the previous year, the choir had gathered five times a week to practise a list of songs given to them by the organizing committee. In January, a new list had been sent, replacing all but one of the songs on the first list, so the choirs had been working extra hard to learn the new material. When I joined them just over a week before the big day – my skills in reading sol-fa notation *prima vista* stretched to the limit – excitement about the coming event was tangible. The choir dedicated hours in the evenings and weekend preceding the event itself to practising the twenty-plus songs to be sung at the commemoration: traditional Anglican hymns in English and Acholi, the Ugandan national anthem, the (little-known and rarely sung) Acholi anthem and Handel's Hallelujah chorus. They would join a busload of choristers from Gulu to travel to Mucwini the day before the event, and there practise the programme with choirs from Kampala, with socializing taking place at the school at which the choirs' accommodation would be arranged.

That was the plan. Reality was to prove different.

The day before the event in Mucwini, Kitgum Mission was handed over by the Comboni missionaries to the local diocese – a significant event for my Catholic acquaintances, and the reason I had arranged to be in Kitgum at this particular time (see Chapter 5). Knowing the event would stretch well into the evening, I opted out of travelling with the other choir members and arranged to ride to Mucwini the next morning with fellow-alto Sofia, her small baby and a mixed group of Catholic and Anglican women living near the Catholic Mission. We arrived a few hours before the service was to start, to encounter a number of disgruntled singers. No transportation had been arranged; no accommodation preparations had been made, and it had been well past midnight before it had finally become clear that there would be no joint practice, since the choirs from Kampala and Gulu would not arrive until the following morning. David, the choirmaster, was initially refused a copy of the order of proceedings for the service, and having managed to track one down, he learned that almost all the songs the Town Parish choir had rehearsed had been deleted. Our fellow singers had thus woken up annoyed, tired and hungry. And it was only going to get worse.

When Sofia and I arrived, tents were still being pitched around a large open space facing the small hill on which Janani Luwum's grave sat alongside the local church. In front of the grave a covered wooden podium and altar had been raised. No separate choir tents had yet been set up near the altar, so our group of some thirty singers headed for the tents nearest the altar, on the opposite side of the field to the yellow NRM tent in which the president and other distinguished guests would be seated. As we carried over piles of chairs and tried to settle into something resembling choir formation, a middle-aged woman clad in a dress of glossy fabric and flashy cut, a striking headdress and oversized sunglasses complained loudly that the front rows were for 'my girls', a group of young dancers from Kampala. The choristers tried to explain that the choir should be sitting together in formation, but the 'the woman from Kampala' (as my choir friends later referred to her) simply frowned and refused to budge. My friends exchanged annoyed looks, indicating to each other with rolls of the eyes and silent mutters that the woman was too full of herself. The impression was strengthened when we realized that she was Acholi-speaking, yet chose to speak English, even to those members of the choir who could only respond to her in Acholi.

In the meantime, David was going back and forth negotiating with the other choirmasters and the event coordinators and appearing increasingly annoyed. Over the next couple of hours, confusion and irritation was compounded by conflicting orders and counter-orders as our gradually depleting choir was chivvied from one uncomfortable spot to another; abused as terrorists by a member of the security team; refused a position in the space eventually allocated to the joint choir due to our lack of robes (we were wearing black and white as instructed so that all choirs would match); and, finally, sitting on the ground in the scorching heat of the dry season without shade or programmes.

Eventually the president arrived, and once he and other notables had paid their respects at the grave of Luwum, the service started. At one point a youth group from Kampala were given the microphones, and struck up praise songs in Swahili and English, which no-one in the Kitgum choir had heard before, and which also left the audience silent. As national TV filmed the joint choir, the Kitgum choristers alternatively looked sour and stayed mute, or looked around sheepishly, first trying to pretend we knew the songs and eventually catching on. We joined the Kampala choir when they reached out to hold our hands and wrap their arms around each other's shoulders during a song praising God and Christian unity, but from the looks on my chorister friends' faces, it seemed I was not the only one finding it hard to put my heart into it.

Archbishop Ssentamu's inspirational sermon on justice and the righteousness of Luwum, given in perfect British English, was rife with examples from life in the United Kingdom and intricate philosophical and theological metaphors. I was fairly busy taking notes, but it was clear his words had little resonance with the choir members sitting around me: people looked bored. Expressions were livelier during the performance of the skilful South African soprano – a classic opera aria in Italian, to the accompaniment of a playback symphony orchestra – during which the young men sitting near me first looked around incredulously and eventually cackled with glee. The opera singer also performed Handel's Hallelujah Chorus – alone – although the choir had spent hours, as advised, learning to sing it for the event.

By the time the service eventually reached an end, the choir members from Kitgum had all made their way into the shade of the nearby trees, now without hindrance from security officials. As the *cung i wibye* – standing on anthills – began, with a line-up of purely pro-government speakers (unlike the political confrontation I witnessed at the 2012 state burial, see Chapter 4), choristers chatted quietly while passing around water bottles and little snacks, all of us trying to rehydrate after many hours in the blazing sun. The audience on the VIP side of the field erupted in ululations when the president announced that he would donate thirty million shillings (about 7,500 euros) to the local parish, that a statue of Janani Luwum would be erected in Kampala and that 16 February would henceforth be a national holiday. My choir friends were slightly less enthusiastic, and the man next to me wondered, muttering, which budget would be footing the president's contribution. With everyone's spirits already dampened by the 'Kampala lady', the condescending visiting choirs and the dry season's sun, Museveni's speech, described in Chapter 5, seemed almost appropriate. Only minutes before he announced his contributions, Museveni had admonished the Acholi for their low integration into the monetized economy. In northern Uganda, he explained, 'You have too many *loneno*, spectators. You need to have more *lotuko* – players.'

The distribution of food was set up in a way that made it clear that only dignitaries were expected to enjoy it, despite prior promises of food for all. Once the speeches were over and the president had left, a deflated choir made ready to travel back to Kitgum. Sofia and I were relieved to be able to rejoin the group of Catholic and Anglican women, who spent the trip home engaged in a lively discussion about whether Anglican saints were really saints. Some of our choir friends managed to hitch rides on trucks, but by the time the three women choir members who had not found a place had walked the 12 kilometres to Kitgum, it was abundantly clear that, for the Town Parish choir, this was a pilgrimage gone sour.

The day after the event, the choir met at the normal time for practice. Very few of the members came, however, and since the nearby football arena was blaring music for a Charismatic crusade starting that day, we were unable to sing, so those gathered concentrated mainly on dispiritedly venting their displeasure over the previous day's events. A few weeks later David formalized the choir's annoyance into a nine-page report submitted to the event's central organizing committee, quoted here with his permission. The report, written in English, begins by establishing the importance of choirs and music in the Anglican tradition:

> Since music is what nurses souls, and only what can bring any person or group of persons closer to God before mentioning any word of prayer, choristers and all who have loves on and believes in music, treat choirs with all the respects and dignity they deserve.
>
> (Acellam 2015, 2)

After alternating sections of dry factual account and spirited theological argumentation, the report concludes with a list of recommendations, some purely technical, such as that local choirmasters should be involved in the National Organizing Committee and not just people based in Kampala, others flavoured with a touch of acidity:

> With the fact that musicians are intellectual enough to sing any language even that of birds, we therefore recommend that if there is need to sing any song in any language in such a function, give it to the choirs early enough and tune to listen.
> (Acellam 2015, 8)

Some of the choir members attributed the chaos to the president's presence. The security official's accusation that the choir members were terrorists and positioning the choir on the basis of presidential security certainly underlined that political considerations impinged on liturgical ones at this event – as at all other public church events (see Chapters 4 and 5). David, however, directly countered this interpretation in his report, stating that 'no... excuse should be on the coming of the president as far as the confusions are concerned because the president could not stop the committee from allocating a tent for all the choirs' (Acellam 2015, 8).

The most painstakingly elaborated argument in David's report, however, is that the event failed to be properly Anglican; notably, he used the official denominational label 'Anglican', rather than the term 'Protestant' more typical in lay speech in Uganda.[1] As he made clear in the report, David (a former keen member of the Concerned Christians; see the following case study) was all for ecumenical engagement but, like many ecumenists, he argued that proper relations between different denominations should not add up to sloppiness: to engage with others, one must first clearly articulate and embrace one's own tradition. Hence, David's report argues that singing Catholic hymns at the service without having managed to secure a Catholic choir, and the inclusion of non-Anglican praise songs, undermined a key objective of the event: 'The celebration of the life of St Janani Luwum should strengthen our faith as Anglican and to believe in our doctrine since it is the only doctrine that saved the entire country from Idi Amin Dada and his regime'. In David's analysis, the way the event was arranged indicated not only the National Organizing Committee's loose commitment to Anglican doctrine, but to non-material values in general:

> It was observed and realized that even elites in our society do value only hardware materials, and because music is [an] unseen and untouched subject that can

only be heard when performed, the choirs were unvalued in this function and left out. This is a very unfortunate situation especially for development of the memorial and if continued, then we are going to sell away St. Janani Luwum and the memorial to those with worldly wealth. But remember, Janani Luwum did not die for the rich, because majority of them had flown to seek asylum in other countries living [sic] behind the poor as preys to the monster.

(Acellam 2015, 7)

David's argument that Janani Luwum had not undergone martyrdom 'for the rich', but for the 'poor' who had been left as 'preys to the monster', was strikingly similar to that made by the bishop at the commemoration of the Catholic martyrs in Paimol (see Chapter 1). Luwum, like the catechists in Paimol, was a martyr for the ordinary people, those without material wealth, those struggling – like the majority of the members of the Kitgum Town Parish choir – simply to make a living. In this rendering, Luwum had given his life for those without the comfort of the oversized sunglasses of the 'woman from Kampala'. And, although it was not spelled out in David's report, it was clear that for Anglican Acholis, Luwum was a son of their soil, more so than of Uganda. This only added to the insult of the National Organizing Committee's bypassing the choir in peripheral Kitgum when planning an event to celebrate the patron saint of the town's very own church.

David's report – and many of the comments of the choir members with whom I discussed the event – can be understood in part as an attempt to grapple with a sense of humiliation, and being shamed. For its members and choirmaster, being in the Town Parish choir was a serious affair: they devoted considerable time to practising, not only to improve themselves as singers but, as some of my informants explained, because being in the choir helped them to be better people (see Alava 2017c). Their participation in an ecumenical choral event held a year prior to Luwum's commemoration, where they had met with choirs from various Christian churches across Uganda, socializing and singing with them, had been hugely meaningful. Plans for the conduct of the music at Janani Luwum's commemoration had also been made among the choirmasters at that prior event: plans that the sudden death of the joint choir project's coordinator and the take-over by the National Organizing Committee had humiliatingly brought to nothing.

Although it was not directly articulated in David's report, nor by any of my friends in the choir, their demeanours and the sum of tiny comments and choices of wording made it clear that the handling of the event by 'the people from Kampala' struck a sensitive nerve. A disorganized planning committee, an un-gowned choir, a security official's accusations of terrorism, and rejection by an Acholi woman so consumed by her new cosmopolitan and English-speaking existence in Kampala that she treated her own people with condescension, resonated with historical inter-group resentments, and threatened to shame entire groups of people: the eastern Acholi from Kitgum in the eyes of the western Acholi from the Diocese of Gulu, and all of the Acholi in the eyes of the rest of Uganda. Museveni's speech about insufficient *lotuko* in the region seemed merely to articulate an accusation implicit in the event in its entirety.

Few of the people I met had developed a distanced, analytical edge to this theme of humiliation, although the few who had, did so in the culture-enhancing manner identified in earlier research (Robbins and Wardlow 2005). That is, they saw humiliation as a social fact, rather than just an emotion (see Robbins 2005), that desperately required addressing, whether through the revival of clan structures, collective economic empowerment initiatives, or traditional dances and other cultural events.[2] What was more common, however, was for a resistance to shaming to be expressed more inchoately, yet allowed to seep through: in the sarcasm of David's comments about the ability of his choristers to sing even in the language of birds, and in the defiant faith in God's justness expressed by some of the Town Parish singers.

One of these was Sofia, who, with a baby to care for, did not sit with the choir in the sun and was also among those who seemed the least vexed by the events. When I asked her what she thought of it all, she simply stated that God would bring them down, 'the woman from Kampala, and her kind'. Sofia, in the manner of most active Anglicans I knew, often made biblical references in her speech, and likely drew on Luke 1:46–55, where Jesus's mother Mary praises God by saying, 'He has scattered those who are proud in their inmost thoughts. He has brought down rulers from their thrones but has lifted up the humble. He has filled the hungry with good things but has sent the rich away empty.' In this vein, Sofia believed that in the end the powerful and the mighty, those who looked down upon others and treated them disrespectfully, would topple. Porter notes similar attitudes among many Acholi survivors of rape, whom churches have coached to believe in 'God's monopoly on vengeance' (2016, 149). Choir leader David's report also ends in the solid faith that after some rectifications, the Janani Luwum memorials 'are going to be amazing'. It was this conviction, and an orientation towards the future, that helped David, Sofia, and the rest of the choir to overcome their disappointment and persevere in their mission to serve the church with their song: the same conviction that had motivated the choir members to begin practicing together again in the shade of the Town Parish during my 2012–13 fieldwork after years of intra-church conflict that had shaken the whole diocese, as detailed below.

Peacemakers and troublemakers

The moment at which the choir seemed at their most jubilant in Mucwini was when the Archbishop of the Church of Uganda, Stanley Ntagali, was introduced as the caretaker of Kitgum Diocese. This confirmed the good news received a few days previously, when the archbishop had arrived in Kitgum with an entourage of archdiocesan administrators to settle – once and for all it was said – the dispute between the bishop of Kitgum Diocese and the so-called Concerned Christians. The bishop, Rt. Rev. Benjamin Ojwang, had been consecrated in 2001 following the retirement of Rt. Rev. Macleod Baker Ochola. Ochola had been the first bishop of the Diocese, which was divided from the Gulu-based Diocese of northern Uganda only in 1995. He had gained both local and international recognition for his role as one of the founders of the ARLPI, through which he had also forged a close friendship with Catholic Archbishop Odama. Ochola's home village was within Kitgum district, albeit he spent much of his time in a second home within the town. Even after his retirement he has remained a charismatic speaker and engaged commentator, who is widely respected in Kitgum and beyond.

In 2004 a group of members of the synod of the Church of Uganda Diocese of Kitgum presented a memorandum for discussion at the meeting of the Diocesan synod, which levelled a number of accusations at Bishop Ojwang: first, unconstitutional administration, namely a lack of transparency in the use of funds and unfair recruitment policies; and second, the abuse of ecclesiastical office, referencing the bishop's claimed 'non-Anglican' activities.[3] Complaints regarding his administration had simmered since his consecration in 2001, but it was the second batch of accusations that finally provoked members of Kitgum Diocese to take action. These were sparked by events that took place a few months prior to the writing of the memorandum, events which many of my Anglican informants still recounted with much animation almost ten years later.

In May 2004, Ojwang and members of his household were abducted by Lord's Resistance Army rebels, but escaped through the intervention of government soldiers after only four hours of captivity. Sometime after their release, pastors from a local Pentecostal church approached Ojwang and told him there were bad spirits in All Saints Church, the church at the diocesan headquarters, and that Ojwang would die if the church were not cleansed. A prayer session was held, during which the bishop followed the Pentecostal pastors in walking around the church seven times.

At the synod meeting in December of that same year, Ojwang explained that he had been confused following the abduction, and asked the synod for forgiveness for what had transpired at All Saints Church, and also for having appointed a young Catholic woman – a close family friend since becoming saved during secondary school – to a delegation from Kitgum that toured England as guests of the Church of England (see Taylor 2005). The bishop denied, however, all accusations of financial and administrative mismanagement. After many hours of debate during the synod, the house of the clergy recommended that the bishop be forgiven, while the house of the laity, unsatisfied with the bishop's explanations, demanded further action. The synod eventually resolved to invite Archbishop Orombi to come to Kitgum to pray for Ojwang and to 'radiate All Saints Church to God'.

In a letter dated 7 October 2005, almost ten months after the synod meeting at which the invitation had been mooted, Archbishop Orombi responded to the request by acknowledging the concern of Christians in Kitgum, admitting that the prayer in question had indeed been un-Anglican. However, Orombi emphasized that Bishop Ojwang was ordained by God, and that Christians must submit to his authority. He therefore recommended that a 'prayer of support for the bishop and the Diocese' be arranged, culminating in Ojwang's leading Christians around the cathedral singing 'Onward Christian Soldiers'. The archbishop argued that such an action would be 'a challenge against Satan who is trying to tear the church of Christ in the Diocese'.

The Church was, however, already torn. By May 2006, a group calling themselves the Concerned Christians (hereafter CC) had been formalized by those dissatisfied with Ojwang. A stand-off ensued when the CC refused the invitation by the diocesan secretary to a 'reconciliation and thanksgiving prayer'. In place of a *reconciliation* prayer, the CC demanded that a *cleansing* prayer be held, claiming that it could only be arranged should the bishop 'denounce his divisive and dictatorial administration' of the diocese. In letters written by the CC to various Church of Uganda authorities over the following years, as well as in interviews I conducted both with former members of the CC and other Anglicans – many of whom agreed with the CC's arguments by the time of my fieldwork in 2012–13 and even more so by 2015 – concerns about the bishop's conduct as a Christian and an Anglican converge with concerns over his capabilities as an institutional administrator. At the core of the latter was disquiet over Ojwang's preferential treatment of one half of the diocese (Pader) at the expense of the other (Kitgum) and his failure to follow good administrative procedure.

According to the CC, the bishop completely ignored all CoU regulations regarding personnel management, demoting pastors from Kitgum and appointing unqualified pastors from Pader to high positions, allocating study scholarships only to students from Pader, and bullying diocesan staff from Kitgum to resign so as to replace them with staff from Pader. A particularly weighty accusation concerned the bishop's dealings with international faith-based NGOs, which had become numerous in Kitgum at the time, and with the diocese's overseas church partners. The international focus on northern Uganda in the first decade of this century facilitated foreign contact for the bishop and his chosen companions to a far higher degree than during the deepening national and international isolation of Kitgum Diocese during my 2012–13 fieldwork. In the first three years after his ordination in 2001, as the bishop himself told the 2004 synod, Ojwang had travelled to the United States, Malawi, Nigeria, the United Kingdom, Spain and Taiwan. The CC accused the bishop of dealing with the foreign NGOs and churches personally rather than through official channels, and of grabbing benefits for himself and for his home district rather than spreading them equally between parishes in both of the districts belonging to the diocese.[4]

Some parish councils, including that of the Town Parish within Kitgum town, resolved to deny the bishop access to the altar in order to 'safeguard Protestant doctrine'. Over a thousand Christians signed a letter to the leaders of the Church of Uganda, in which they formally denounced Ojwang as bishop, while pledging continued loyalty to the CoU. The CC also advised archdeaconries and parishes to keep their funds in their own accounts and not transfer them to the diocesan account as per CoU regulations. Whether resources, such as money gathered for the construction of the new church at Town Parish, were handled correctly during the years of confusion, and if not, where they went, remains disputed up till this day.

As the years passed, the dispute became increasingly bitter, and advanced to new registers. When the bishop tried to officiate at a service in Town Parish without invitation, he was locked into the vestry. The incident led to the arrest of a number of church members by plainclothes policemen whom the CC later claimed had been planted in the church by the bishop. Despite all manner of mediation attempts by notable politicians, religious leaders, bishops from other districts, and the CoU archbishop, the dispute dragged on, and court cases were instigated both against the bishop and by the bishop. The CC also formally accused the bishop of having consulted witchdoctors, and of having cast a curse on the diocesan accountant resulting in the death of the accountant's son. During my fieldwork, elaborate rumours still circulated of the bishop's housing large snakes that were suspected of being assistants of the Devil, while those loyal to the bishop claimed that the grave illness and eventual death of one of the CC's key leaders was a punishment from God. These threads of the debate relate with Naomi Haynes's observation that among Zambian Pentecostals, 'the English loanword "confusion" connotes the devil's desire to overthrow or undermine the work of the church' (2017, 84). Yet despite occasional references to the role of the Devil in *anyobanyoba* in Kitgum, his role was never at the heart of the debate.

Almost everyone with whom I discussed the topic agreed that part of the intractableness of the dispute related to the bishop's edgy personality and poor social skills, something even his close supporters acknowledged. But what is blatantly clear from all the material I gathered was that for those near the centre of the scuffle, on both sides of the battle line, the wrangle was not only about doctrinal purity or spiritual power, but also money and power. Both Anglicans who were loyal to the bishop and those who thought that the CC and the bishop should drop the nonsense emphasized that the ordination of Ojwang, following Ochola, had been a severe blow to a core group of diocese administrators and clergy close to Ochola. Many also claimed that at stake was a political battle, with Ochola an avowed supporter of the Uganda People's Congress – the traditionally Anglican-aligned party of former president Obote which has been completely marginalized under Museveni's reign – and Ojwang (allegedly) a member of the president's NRM. Rumours were also recounted that the bishop's abduction had been machinated, either by Ojwang himself to garner sympathy from his disloyal flock, or by someone who wanted to get him killed.

Regardless of the truth of these speculations, it is clear that those with most at stake in the dispute – those who held the keys to the diocesan office, managed the diocesan accounts, and set the terms of reference of agreements signed with international partners – were already comparably well-off by local standards: members of the salariat, which Ben Jones (2014, 7), writing of Teso in eastern Uganda, defines as 'those working for the church, the local government or the NGO sector'. This is a point to which no heed is paid in any of the documents drafted by the CC that I have read, or in the majority of the interviews I have held with those who have been close to the race for the bishop's throne.

The issue was certainly not lost on the majority of Anglicans in Kitgum, however, nor on all members of the synod. Minutes from the synod meeting in 2004 read, 'The support given to the Bishop from outside should be spread to benefit the whole Diocese especially to the camps and Night Commuter Centers.' The money used, for instance, to construct a nice guesthouse at the diocese was money directed away from Anglicans living in the frightful, inhumane surroundings of wartime Kitgum. One of the worst of these, and incidentally the first displacement camp I visited while doing master's-level fieldwork in Kitgum in 2006 (an experience that shook me deeply, see Chapter 3), was just a stone's throw away from the diocesan headquarters.

Eventually, in 2014, Ojwang was convinced by the national house of bishops that he should retire and farewell services were arranged, but just months later a group of his supporters convinced him to sue the CoU for unlawful forced retirement. In early 2015 a high court judge advised the parties to sort the issue out among themselves, and finally, late in 2015, a caretaker bishop was appointed to oversee the diocese until a proper election could be arranged. Not long after, a group of notable Anglicans, led by the retired Bishop Ochola, went to the archbishop and to national media with a request that the caretaker be replaced by another. In 2017, Bishop Ojwang left the bishop's house in Kitgum and moved to his home village, but the issues surrounding diocesan leadership in Kitgum took much longer to resolve. There have been demands that the diocese be split between Kitgum and Pader, but sceptics have noted that with church resources extremely limited as they are, duplicating diocesan administration would not serve Christians, but only those lucky few who landed jobs in the new diocese.[5]

How then did all this *anyobanyoba* in the church appear to Anglicans in Kitgum? Opinions differed wildly, based, among other things, on people's proximity to the central parties in the dispute. Many of those who had merely observed the fighting from the side-lines expressed frustration or annoyance towards those who had been at its centre, one of whom was my assistant Monica, who transcribed an interview I conducted with a key figure in the CC (with his consent). Monica attended Town Parish regularly on Sunday mornings, but was not otherwise involved in church activities. During the fight, she had neither joined the CC nor explicitly defended the bishop, yet she was deeply annoyed by the interviewee's long-winded account of the bishop's sins and the CC's virtues. She annotated the transcript with her personal commentary in bold italics, assessing the truthfulness of the elder's claims, imploring me to realize that the man was lying, wishing God would descend to set things straight, and raging at the elder's failure to acknowledge the importance of money to the CC's cause. She writes:

> I think these people they used to enjoy money from the church, and when Ojwang came the money they did not get, and that is why they are bothered! In any case why don't you come and pray just like other people who just come to pray not get anything from the church?

Monica's words are a powerful rebuttal of Gifford's (2015) claim that mainline churches are all about access to money. She acknowledges that money was an issue, but not for everyone – arguably, not for most. All those I interviewed, whether supporters of Ojwang, or of the previous incumbent, Bishop Ochola, or of the CC, readily accepted that the clergy, including the bishop, gained resources from the church with which to send their children to school and live in relative – albeit for most of the Anglican priests, extremely modest – comfort. This is a crucial matter for assessing the ability of churches to affect politics, or to advance peace, as discussed in the previous chapter. As Holly Porter has argued, moral authority in Acholi is deeply embedded in individuals:

> Someone from within the moral community is accountable for his or her leadership. If a particular local leader in a village is seen as unfair they are marginalized or replaced. If they are particularly powerful and people are unable to displace them, they will circumvent and avoid his authority… In the villages where I work, the community's trust in the individuals involved plays a greater role in their effectiveness and credibility than the office they hold.
>
> (Porter 2016, 145)

This is no less the case for the clergy. And in the context of churches, which, after all, are sources of tangible or at least potential material benefits, the fact that authority is embedded in individuals rather than in institutions is also of relevance for understanding church politics, or 'confusion in the church'. For priests and reverends to be regarded as entitled to material benefits, they had to be seen as having sufficient moral authority. In the context of churches, this meant having good relations with church members, a perceived willingness to share the plate, proficiency in spiritual inspiration, consolation, and healing, sufficient doctrinal purity, and divine anointing. Once these were lost – as they were for Bishop Ojwang in the eyes of the CC, and as they were for the clergy collaborating with the CC in the eyes of those supporting Ojwang – the money and power that came with the office was seen as being up for grabs, to be apportioned to a more worthy or properly anointed servant of God, and to the innermost circle of his loyal flock.

As Gifford (2015) argues, and as the case of the Church of Uganda in Kitgum also clearly shows, being active in the church may provide a core group with access to donor resources, and the salaries, houses, land titles or scholarships thus accorded (see also Lauterbach 2017). But for most Anglicans in Kitgum, joining the choir or attending Sunday services offers no promise of access to privilege. Some may be motivated by the slim chance that this could change if they persevere in their commitment to the Church, but for the majority this is not the case.

Whereas Gifford (2015) positions so-called material motivations to participate in church activities in opposition to motivations to access the divine, the two cases presented so far have indicated an intersection of 'the divine' and of 'the mess' engendered by the fact that churches are embedded in the networks which divide and apportion power and resources in society. How 'confusion' is expressed, experienced and addressed relates to the relationships churches have with political parties; to the degree to which their elites correspond to the local salariat; to the strength of their hold on and access to different types of material resources; and to the broader cosmological context in which churches exist, that is, their embeddedness. The third case I present highlights this point even further, and allows me to elaborate on another view of how *anyobanyoba* manifested itself in Kitgum, what the churches had to do with it, and how their members engaged and came to terms with it.

Churches, classes, curses and dealing with confusion

The family of *ladit* Philip Odwong, the retired Catholic teacher whose story I have introduced in earlier chapters, underwent some serious and awe-inspiring experiences during my fieldwork. The family's then twenty-five-year-old daughter, Oyella Irene, had a respected job on the government payroll in another town. *Ladit* Odwong told me that she had been hard-working and diligent, as a result of which she was promoted fairly swiftly, and provided with a new apartment on the premises of the institution where she was employed, one superior to those of many of her former equals. Soon after, she fell critically and mysteriously ill. She was eventually rushed to Mulago, the main government hospital in Kampala, where doctors were unable to discover what was causing her body to malfunction. The doctors warned the family that, since they could find no cause for Irene's suffering, nor discover anything that would improve her condition, she was slowly but surely nearing her death.

A nurse at the Catholic hospital in Kitgum heard of the family's predicament, however, and suggested they contact a Catholic healer she had heard of in Kampala. The family was enormously relieved when the healer visited Irene in Mulago hospital, prayed over her in what *ladit* Odwong described as classic Catholic style, and shortly after, her condition started improving. When I heard the story, the daughter was staying with her parents in Kitgum, still very weak but slowly recuperating from her sickness, for which a medical explanation had still to be discovered. I was told that the Mulago doctors considered her recovery a miracle.

Irene's condition eventually improved enough for her to return to her job but, before she left, a thanksgiving service was arranged at the family's house near Kitgum Mission, presided over by one of the Comboni missionary priests. The healer from Kampala was present, but had requested that he not be publicly pointed out, and had slipped out to catch his bus before the service was over. Irene had asked the man to come and pray in her apartment before she entered it again, but the healer had prayed over some water, advising her to sprinkle it around the home and there would be nothing to fear.

There was much in the account that followed patterns typical to stories of witchcraft and malicious medicines in Acholi (Behrend 1995, 26–8). In this as in many other stories I heard, medicines bringing about otherwise unexplainable sickness were placed in the home of someone of whom the perpetrator was envious, so as to cause their downfall; a fate often referred to as having been 'poisoned' (Victor 2018, 50). In this case, *ladit* Odwong's family believed it was the young woman's rapid rise in the ranks of her job that triggered the envy of her colleagues, and led someone to resort to witchcraft. Accounts where witchcraft is attributed to envy, and the invocation of witchcraft idioms to explain inequalities in social and economic standing and well-being, are commonplace in anthropological literature on the theme (see, e.g., Comaroff and Comaroff 1993; Geschiere and Roitman 1997, 69 & 141–3). As Allen (2015) shows in the Acholi context, this is particularly prevalent in cases where an individual is seen to rise unexpectedly in social standing, like *ladit* Odwong's young and only recently graduated daughter. In my experience, the idiom functions in both directions: those who are seen as unjustifiably successful can be accused by others of using witchcraft, while those who suffer an accident or fall sick can blame identifiable or unidentifiable others for causing their downfall by dubious means.

Irene's case also resonates with trends identified in research on Christian Charismatic healing. The rise of Pentecostal-Charismatic Christianity in Africa is in part credited to the inability of mainline churches to deal with the problem of evil, and to engage meaningfully with the spirit world in which many Africans, regardless of their stated creed, believe (Kalu 2008; Meyer 1994). Like elsewhere (see Behrend 2011; Lindhardt 2012; Omenyo 2003; Wilkens 2011), Kitgum mainline churches were increasingly addressing these issues. At the Anglican Town Parish, Sunday services did not exhibit charismatic features, but faith healing and exorcism were practised at praise meetings and gatherings in parishioners' homes, also drawing on the Balokole heritage of the CoU in Kitgum (see Introduction and Chapter 6). The impact of the charismatic movement, while notable in many Catholic parishes in Acholi, was far less evident at the Kitgum Catholic Mission during my intermittent periods of fieldwork between 2012 and 2016, largely because of the resident Comboni priests' lack of enthusiasm for the revival. Only a handful of charismatics gathered weekly at the mission for praise meetings, and the case of Odwong's daughter stood out as the solitary incident of charismatic healing that I encountered.[6] The Catholic healer's unwillingness to draw attention to himself, and his use of 'by-the-book Catholic', as opposed to notably 'Charismatic' healing practices, are also typical of those Catholic charismatics who wish to remain in the fold of the Church and avoid confrontation with Church leadership.[7]

Where and what was the 'confusion' in this case? At its heart were accusations of jealousy; 'the inversion of a properly functioning relational world, antagonism and scheming where one hopes for cooperation and care' (Haynes 2017, 152); in the form of unclearly defined medicine/poison/witchcraft. Such accusations commonly intersect in Acholi (Allen 2015; p'Bitek 1971a, 137–9), and connect with stories of other things that are hard to pin down – *ajwani* (dirty things) (Victor and Porter 2017); the *lakite* (somehow) of politics (Verma 2013); the family curses that cause strange misfortunes (Meinert 2020). Yet confusion here was also something for which the church – if not the nearby parish, then at least a Catholic healer in Kampala – could provide a solution. Considered in light of Gifford's juxtaposition of churches as either being about accessing the divine or accessing resources, the church here was very much about accessing divine healing. But accessing that healing – the very fact of being able to go to a hospital in Kampala – was enabled by money. As long-term adherents of the Catholic Church, and as trusted confidants of the missionaries for more than a generation, *ladit* Odwong's family had benefitted from direct church support and from the opportunity to settle in the vicinity of the parish, near services, jobs and the church that made them available. The family had also been impacted by a bitter and still unresolved dispute over land surrounding the parish buildings (see Chapter 1 for an outline, and Alava and Shroff 2019 for a closer analysis of the conflict), and had pushed for its peaceful resolution.

The thanksgiving ceremony encapsulates a lot of the complexity I claim for the notions of *anyobanyoba* and embeddedness: presided over by a missionary priest who had been at the heart of the church's attempts to secure its land holdings, the thanksgiving was celebrated in the compound of a family known as one of the mission's closest long-term allies, a compound that is located right along the disputed parish boundary. The purpose of the thanksgiving was to show gratitude for the healing of a daughter whose rise to her position had in part been made possible by the family's faithfulness to the church, and the resources thus secured. The healing was conducted by someone whose style of Charismatic healing was discouraged by the missionaries in their own parish, after the young woman fell sick due to something the missionary priests dealt with only grudgingly: a 'poisoning' that modern medicine failed to diagnose or cure.

The confusion in this story – in any of the stories I have discussed in this chapter – is not an existential confusion of non-understanding or incomprehension. From the horizon of the lives of Catholics and Anglicans in Kitgum, these stories do not leave one confused in the sense of bewildered or confounded. Rather, these are stories that are commonplace and recognizable, that describe the way things are, in all their messiness, that people simply manage with whatever means are available to them.

Mess in the church?

'This is Henni Alava. She's studying all the mess in the church.' I could not help but laugh at the words with which my friend introduced me to his fellow priest, who had just returned to Gulu after studies abroad. Feeling slightly embarrassed, I gently rebuked my friend, 'Come on, that's not what I study!' By the time I had explained that what I was interested in was how churches influenced the way people thought about politics, both priests had ceased listening and were busy getting on with what they had been doing when our paths crossed.

The brief encounter with the two Catholic priests, four months into my fieldwork, opened my eyes to how my research must have appeared to the priests with whom, by then, I had spent a considerable amount of time. The topics that interested me most at the time – the discords, tensions and conflicts of the churches I studied – were perceived as mess: disorderly, unpleasant, even disconcerting. This mess and confusion, whether brought about by politics or witchcraft or a combination of both, appeared incompatible with a vision of the church as a utopic realm of peace. As people often explained to me, before all this had entered the scene, there had been harmonious, respectful co-existence.

The argument emerging from this and previous chapters is that confusion, not only in churches but more broadly in Kitgum, is used as a catch-all concept to allude to misfortunes, injustices and obstacles encountered in the course of life. As such, confusion was attributed to things that happened out of sight, behind the scenes, and resided in darkness: politics, witchcraft and greed, all of which were seen as capable of actively and purposefully creating confusion. In contrast, what in Catholic and Anglican understandings resided in the light – and could bring light, break through, heal, or set right confusion – was God. Such an image of darkness and light, or confusion and clarity, is of course a rough and simplifying schematization, yet it resonates through the cases I have presented. To make this argument more persuasively, let me return to the two aims I set for the chapter: to unpack what confusion is and how it is dealt with in the context of Acholi mainline churches, and to address the claim that mainline churches are primarily about accessing material resources, rather than about accessing the divine.

Churches, I claim, play two parts in relation to 'confusion': they are wrapped into it, but they also provide remedial resources. As institutions, they are deeply implicated in the politics of confusion: the resource and power game, which raised some while lowering others, was played out within local churches as much as in any social location. Confusion was not something external that infiltrated the churches (although that was how it was often perceived), but imbricated in their very structures: national, ethnic, and political contestation and grievance permeated the choir's experience of being sidelined from singing; politics, spirits and dogmatic purity were all brought into play in a complex dispute over resources in the Anglican Church in Kitgum, while envy over inequalities of class and privilege were seen to lead to Irene's inexplicable misfortune. And, like church embroilment in the northern Ugandan war (see Chapters 3 and 6), all these locally experienced events were tied into much broader dynamics, since churches are embedded in contestations over resources and power on a national and sometimes international scale.

Churches are not, however, merely embedded in or permeated by confusion. They also provide their members with resources and tools with which to make sense of, come to terms with, or seek to address confusion. Three stand out in particular: prayer, forgiveness and trust in God's justness. Prayer included both those for healing sickness such as Irene's and the very different kind of 'power prayer' (discussed further in the Conclusion) used by the archbishop of the Church of Uganda to influence Anglicans in Kitgum to bend to his directives. Forgiveness helped individuals to come to terms with pain experienced at the hands of others, and enabled communities to come together despite dispute and conflict, as had happened in Town Parish after the CC dispute, and as embodied in the ARLPI (see Chapter 6, as well as Finnegan 2010; Porter 2016; Whyte, Meinert, and Obika 2015). Finally, trust in a just God allowed those whose wrong-doers showed no remorse to avoid being trapped in anger, and rather to shrug, if not necessarily forgive: there is nothing we can do about it, but God will bring them down. This attitude served whether dealing with an obnoxious woman from Kampala, the abrasive disrespect of a presidential security official, an endlessly misbehaving yet seemingly unconquerable bishop, or a president who seemed to have purposefully punished and humiliated the Acholi for close to three decades.

In the case of a pilgrimage turned sour, *anyobanyoba* appeared as disorganization – information did not reach those who needed it, whether due to administrative incapacity, or to deliberate sidelining; however, it was not just about disorganization but about a play of power that led to some being humiliated, and it was dealt with by trusting that God would settle the score. Yet, rekindled as it had been in the midst of CoU conflict, the choir was itself a means of dealing with confusion. Understanding the choir's importance for its members also addresses Gifford's posited opposition between divinity and funding. Singing in the choir was obviously a chance to engage in networking that might lead to employment. But from what the choir members have told me over the years; and recalling reflections on religious self-creation in anthropologies of ethics and morality (see, e.g., Gusman 2017; Mahmood 2011; Robbins 2004); what was much more important was how the choir enabled them to mould themselves into the godly people they wanted to be. For some, the choir helped guard against behaviour they considered harmful to themselves or their families, such as extramarital affairs or heavy drinking, but for everyone, the choir was a place for friendship, conviviality and the fundamentally good feeling of using one's voice with others to create music: for their own enjoyment during rehearsals, and for the enrichment of the whole church when they performed.

Drawing from my hours and hours of singing with the Janani Luwum choir, I would argue that Acholi churches are neither primarily about accessing divinity, nor solely about accessing resources: judging them on the first scale is overly spiritualizing, while relying on the second is overly materialistic. What the choir, and I believe churches more broadly, were really about, was something simultaneously more and less than either of the above: about being human together, in community with others, sometimes fighting, sometimes forgiving, sometimes arriving, sometimes leaving, sometimes more distant, sometimes close, but still, 'somehow', as the Acholi saying goes, together: indeed, a light but functional version of the Utopia of Peace described in the previous chapter. This may be no miracle cure for the often brutal realities of war's afterlives, but nor is it insignificant, as demonstrated by the case studies presented.

In Acholi, as elsewhere, people who know their churches well are usually aware of their fundamental characters. People understand and know, intuitively, even if they do not explicitly consider the fact, that churches are embedded in their contexts in highly complex ways. Yet, I argue, active members of churches tend to believe, or to at least hope, that churches are somehow more holy, less faulty, more ideal, less messy, than other institutions and communities. Churches, with their utopias of peace, harmony, love, family and forgiveness, obviously feed into these beliefs and hopes in a massive way. I believe it is the contradiction between this cherished belief, and the messy reality of money, power, and the mistakes and conflicts to which they give rise, that people label 'confusion in the church'. The normative and emotive pull of *anyobanyoba i eklisia* comes from the unresolved and, I claim, unresolvable tension between ideal and reality.

The irony is churches provide many of the tools with which this tension may be addressed: the narratives of peace, reconciliation, forgiveness and the religious practices that go with them, are all part of this toolkit. What this chapter has shown is that this whole process – both the appearance of 'confusion' and the attempts to deal with it – is fundamentally affected by, and in turn affects, the broader cosmological, material, social and political contexts in which churches and their members exist. What is more, as I discuss further in the Conclusion, attempts to deal with 'confusion' may well create more of the same. Understanding this – and, I claim, the complex relationship between Christianity and politics anywhere – is significantly aided by an acknowledgement of the complex embeddedness of churches as institutions *and* as communities. In this relationship, material interests are not cordoned off from matters of the 'divine', and nor are institutional and individual concerns and practices clearly distinguishable for the sake of easy analytical clarity; rather, they are considered elements of a complicated yet understandable whole.

Conclusion
The value of embeddedness and confusion

Simplified headlines rarely do justice to complex social realities, yet it is precisely such simplifications that gain traction during war and in reports that percolate out from sites of war. During the northern Ugandan war, local stories concerning this book's topics were simplified into propagandist one-liners: 'This church supports the rebels!' claimed the government; and 'That church collaborates with the government!' claimed the rebels. On the other hand, stories that crossed the international news threshold told of crazy Christian millenarian rebels; of heroic missionaries who risked their lives in the service of Acholi citizens; and, as the ARLPI's activities gained momentum, of churches as the forerunners of peace building. Yet the questions I have posed in attempting to understand Christianity and politics in Acholi all reject brief black-and-white answers: What kind of role did churches play during the war? What type of role do they play now? What makes churches' messages powerful and what makes them fail? What are the relationships between churches and the state, churches and rebels, and churches and political parties?

Answering them led me, in Chapter 1, to trace the contemporary churches' complex historical embeddedness in the missionary-colonial era. Chapter 2 followed the fluctuating relations of churches, states and political parties in the run-up to and following Uganda's independence, and drew on new archival material to illustrate how confusion over the political roles of churches played out during the northern Ugandan war. Chapter 3 described the simultaneous normalcy of life in Kitgum town and the ways in which war's afterlives lingered in the silence surrounding the violent past. In Chapter 4, I analysed churches as arenas for performances of statehood and negotiation over political imaginaries, whereas Chapter 5 traced how rumours, fears and silences limit what people dare envision for themselves and for Uganda. In Chapter 6, I argued that conditions of *anyobanyoba* were the context from which utopian visions of peace, harmony, unity and godly intervention arose, and from which they gained their force.

But as illustrated in Chapter 7, incidents of confusion in the church were also those where the publicly proclaimed Utopia of Peace in mainline Christianity encountered its seemingly unsurpassable boundaries.

Two days prior to the fateful pilgrimage of the Janani Luwum choir to the grave of the martyr after whom they were named (see Chapter 7), I sat with jubilant choir members listening to a spirited speech given by Archbishop Ntagali to an enthusiastic crowd of Christians gathered at the diocesan headquarters in Kitgum. 'Blessed are the peacemakers!' the archbishop declared. After that, in prayer and in the name of the Lord, he bound all those enemies of the church who were bringing confusion and division to Kitgum Diocese, as well as those who were taking it to worldly courts. 'For God is the only judge!' Ntagali shouted, in a scolding manner common in Pentecostal services (Haynes 2017, 85–6). In response, the crowd yelled, 'Amen', and people raised one or both arms high in the air, while Bishop Ojwang, whose legal assistant had recently filed a case against Archbishop Ntagali in the high court in Kitgum, sat with closed eyes and hands held modestly in his lap, and lifted one finger.

Figure 12. The visiting archbishop of the Church of Uganda leads prayers for peace in the diocese of Kitgum. Photo by author.

After many prayers and announcements and praise songs, the master of ceremonies concluded the gathering with a re-capitulation. In case someone had not understood, he explained, the message of the day was that the peacemakers are blessed. He continued:

> Think now of the opposite. If you are not blessed, you are cursed. And if you are not a peacemaker, you are a what? A troublemaker. The troublemakers cannot be children of God. They are then what? Children of the Devil. Let me hear you say it, children of the what?

And the audience shouted in unison: 'THE DEVIL!'

Like so many times before, in the Anglican Church, as in less elaborate and publicized conflicts in the Catholic Church, calls for unity and words of purported peace became weapons to augment increasingly entrenched division and conflict. The Utopia of Peace could not resolve the tensions in society, or provoke into being a whole new world, because it was professed by institutions crosscut by boundaries of ethnicity and class, and beholden to material properties: in short, embedded institutions, steeped in and themselves constantly reconstituting relations of power. This power was one wielded by some over others and had continuously to be renegotiated in order to answer the perennial question, 'Who owns and decides what, and how is the right to own and decide distributed?' Therefore, the Utopia of Peace prompted unity among contestants only when the price of disunity was sufficiently high.

We thus encounter very different uses of utopian narratives of peace and unity in different settings. In the case of conflict over resources and power in the Church of Uganda, narratives of unity and peace were utilized to disparage opponents and to deal with disunity that brought ridicule to the church. In the top echelons of diocesan politics, the narrative of peaceful co-existence was used in an attempt to secure order and rein people in, albeit, as Chapter 7 showed, with very limited success and even divisive impact. In contrast, Chapter 6 illustrated how the ARLPI drew upon resources in religious traditions and in Acholi custom to create an inspirational narrative that brought people together across previously existing boundaries to work for the end of armed violence in the region. Similarly, members of the Town Parish choir saw singing together as a service to a church recovering from bitter divisions within its pews; indeed, their belief in the power of music and making it together was so strong that they came back to sing together even after the conflict had torn the choir apart. These stories show how a utopia may unfold with profound impact when sufficient numbers of people endorse its promise as one worth striving for, despite disabling strictures that render success unlikely.

What these cases highlight is that words in themselves, whether of peace or of war, count only for so much and should never be analysed as separate from their embeddedness in the relationships of those by and amidst whom they are spoken. However inspiring a utopian narrative may be, its impact always unfolds amid the confines and possibilities accorded by the political economy – the division of power and resources – of human relations.

In the remainder of this Conclusion, I consider two questions: what does a focus on embedded political narratives offer to the study of Christianity and politics; and what does the notion of 'confusion' offer to debates over suffering and 'the good' in anthropology, and over ethics and epistemology in research? In sum, my argument is that recognition of both embeddedness and confusion nudges scholars to go beyond simplistic narratives, encourages the transgressing of boundaries of one's own and one's discipline's knowledge, and coaxes acceptance of the fact that even after the greatest effort to craft the most elegant conceptualizations, the complexity of social reality always escapes the desire for complete analytical grasp.

An embedded anthropology of Christianity and politics

This book has proposed the notion of embedded political narratives as a tool for unpacking the 'and' in Christianity and politics. In the following, I re-cap the different aspects of embeddedness, and consider their value for future scholarship.

Social embeddedness highlights that churches are never external entities that preach, serve and interact with communities outside and cut off from them, although this is how they are often conceptualized in analyses of their 'relationship with' other actors. Rather, churches are always bound up in bonds of family, clan and ethnicity in the locations in which they operate; in turn, church personnel's criss-crossing networks of love, respect, loyalty, animosity and resentment influence institutional actions and teachings (Carney 2013). Taking social embeddedness seriously also alerts the scholar to questions of class, and to how social inequalities translate into and are further moulded in the religious realm (B. Jones 2014).

Political embeddedness has been noted in scores of studies on church–state relations in Africa, yet my analysis of churches' utopian visions of peace in Acholi (Chapter 6) draws attention to the need to look beyond institutional relations, to how religion entwines with and impacts on political imaginaries. On the other hand, an emphasis on imagination might lead one to over-interpret the impact of religion, as Maia Green (2006) suggests many studies of religion in Africa do, a caution I believe is particularly relevant for analyses of religion and conflict, and in assessing African political theologies.

A focus on churches' *material embeddedness* tempers these risks by highlighting the rootedness of all discourse, narration and imagination in material realities. The notion thus echoes Ben Jones and Karen Lauterbach's (2005) demand to bring institutions back into the study of Christianity, and the analysis by Catrine Shroff (formerly Christiansen) of how churches' development efforts are entwined with their own institutional development (Christiansen 2010). As Chapter 7 highlighted, besides attention being paid to churches' sometimes considerable overseas funding (Gifford 2015), much more should be said about their internal material resources (Lauterbach 2017). The notion of material embeddedness also draws attention to the land on which church buildings stand. This is a question so far almost completely ignored in research outside of South Africa (Alava and Shroff 2019), yet it is an issue important to anthropological research on churches due to the way in which questions of politics, materiality, belonging and cosmology intertwine in land (Shipton 2009; Wilhelm-Solomon and Jahn 2015).

Cosmological embeddedness refers to the basic premise that Christianity has been shaped by each cultural context, each thought and religious practice it has encountered, and affected them in turn. In Chapter 1, I drew from p'Bitek's (1971a) classic study to trace this colonial-era encounter in Acholi, and in Chapter 6, I considered its manifestation first in Acholi rebel movements, and later in churches' attempts to temper the war. Both Whitmore's anthropological theology (2010b, 2019) and the political theology of Katongole (2011) detail how Christian responses to the war built on theologies of peace and reconciliation. But these responses also resonated with violent legacies of utopian imaginaries in the region – and ultimately, that of missionary expansion.

Considering these entanglements, I find it surprising how little mainline churches have been researched in northern Uganda, where many other topics have received somewhat relentless research attention (Finnström 2019). O'Byrne (2016) and Williams (2019) have highlighted themes central in the anthropology of Christianity by studying Evangelical conversion and Pentecostal healing in Acholi and in adjacent South Sudan's Acholi-speaking Pajok, but recent studies on mainline churches by a philosopher (Hoekema 2019b) and a theologian (Whitmore 2019) have not produced anthropological parallels. Why *do* mainline churches receive so little academic attention, even in so-called research hot-spots where one would think the region's largest religious communities would merit it?

As noted in the Introduction, both theology as a discipline and missionary-established mainline churches continue to be regularly scoffed at by many social scientists, often because they are branded as the morally dubious or somehow inauthentic relics of colonialism. I hope this book has succeeded in showing the importance of attention being paid by researchers in the social sciences – and not only those who specialize in religion – to attempts by religious institutions to effect social change in Uganda and across the African continent. In this context, anthropology's almost-exclusive emphasis on emerging and growing forms of PC Christianity often overlooks the fact that mainline churches remain larger, and still wield crucial influence in social service provision and politics in wide swathes of sub-Saharan Africa. To understand the dynamics of religious change in Africa, it is essential to explore not only that which is new and changing, but to also gain understanding of the religious groups *from which* conversions are taking place.

This is one direction in which the notion of embeddedness might also be applied to well-established discussions in the anthropology of Christianity. As Devaka Premawardhana has recently argued, whereas the idea of modern conversion presupposes 'the privileging of autonomous individuality over embedded sociality' (2020a, 4), change in African Catholicism is more often characterized by ambiguity and nonlinearity. He suggests that exploring situations where 'the religions to (or from) which one is converting are themselves steeped in material, corporeal, and ritual dimensions' (2020a, 4) provides a more 'empirical understanding of religious change in Africa' (ibid., 1). Might foregrounding the complex embeddedness of *all* forms of Christianity – including those that emphasize breaking with the past (Meyer 1998; Robbins 2007) – contribute towards the same goal?

One explanation for the disregard of mainline Christianity in existing research suggests itself in the pews of the churches I studied. There are many moments at the parishes of Saint Mary and Saint Janani Luwum where, discounting Ugandan accents, one can close one's eyes and imagine oneself somewhere totally different. My own mind, for instance, often transported me to Hong Kong where I attended both denominations' services as a child. The same is of course true for charismatic churches, as cultural forms such as Hillsong-style praise can be found the world over. I think there is a difference, however: Pentecostal, Charismatic and Evangelical Christianities – including Charismatic strands of mainline Christianity – retain their place as a 'cultural other' of anthropology

(Harding 2000), despite all the shaking up by anthropologists of Christianity around this point. Not all 'Christians' are equally 'other'; which I think is particularly true for mainline denominations – most particularly Catholicism – which are deeply entwined in the lineages of anthropology (Larsen 2014), even through their rejection (Furani 2019). I feel there is cause to ask, whether research agendas that focus on dramatic and 'exotic' forms of Christianity inadvertently derive from, and perpetuate, the racist and exoticizing legacies of anthropology as a discipline – a point recently also made by Bialecki (2021). After all, it is not only churches that are socially, materially, cosmologically and politically embedded, but academic disciplines too.

Confusion and entangled hopes

In 2015, in the midst of rumours of violence escalating in the shadows at the approach of the 2016 elections, I sighed to my friend Daniel that things did not look good. I heard similar sighs echoing across the ether to me as I finalized this book prior to and following Uganda's 2021 election: tens of opposition protestors were killed by state security forces and teargas filled the streets, including those in Kitgum, to pave way for President Museveni's re-election. In 2015, Daniel cleared his throat, looked me calmly in the eyes and said:

> In life it is so that some people want to create conflict and violence. Some people want everyone to just live in peace. Some people want to create chaos. And it is up to us to decide which path we want to follow.

The words seemed to epitomize what Susan Whyte (2002, 2005) characterizes as the subjunctive mood, which I have argued conditions the pragmatic choices made between the alternative paths that meander through the afterlives of war in northern Uganda. Some of those paths appear ridden with, and productive of, confusion, while others seem embedded in at least the hope of peace. But as I have shown, and as Daniel knew, it really was not this simple. Because it was hard to know what was going on, because there was so much in the shadows that was never spoken about, because *anyobanyoba tye*, one could never be quite sure where the path that one was following would go. Voting for the government might entrench structural inequalities and buffer the power of an unfriendly state, but it might also keep Acholi at peace, however palpably fragile (Alava 2020). Voting for the opposition might bring about change, or war. Supporting one bishop over another might lead to conflict at the church subsiding, or it might entrench disputes that had simmered for years. Yet despite the uncertainties that lingered, the choices had to be made.

At the core of this book's approach to the interrelations of Christianity and politics has been the question of how community is imagined: who is included, who is excluded and how the boundaries between the two are defined – all essential questions for a community ravaged by decades of violence. The ethnographic material has foregrounded that because churches are deeply embedded in their social, political, material and cosmological contexts, the political imaginaries evoked by and in them are likewise embedded – not least in contestations over resources and power.

The task of imagining community is universal as each community, from the smallest village or parish to the largest nation or global church body, must define who is in and who is out. But the manifestations of this task are particular, since political imaginaries both reflect and redefine the cultural, material, religious and cosmological lifeworlds of the communities in which they are woven.

The original *Eutopia*, conjured up in Thomas More's (2001) imagination 500 years ago, was a fully egalitarian society, characterized by religious diversity and tolerance, whose citizens despised war, personal aggrandizement – and atheism. As much as More's vision has instilled awe and inspired entire fields of research (Levitas 2013; Moylan and Baccolini 2007), it is sobering to remember how poorly More himself measured up to his vision. A successful and wealthy lawyer, he despised the first of the Reformation's notable theologians, Martin Luther, and had Protestants tortured and put to death in an attempt to quench anti-Catholic sentiments in England. Eventually More himself was condemned to death by King Henry VIII as a result of his refusal to support Henry's bid for the independence of what was to become the Anglican Church (and its notable coffers) from the authority of the Pope. As one journalist put it, More 'died attempting to defend his sense of community' (Cawthorne 2016), an attempt for which the Catholic Church venerated More as a saint in 1935.

As distant as More's story is in time and space from the Kitgum I have come to know, it strikes me as poignant that the churches I have studied, and the parishes of Saint Mary and Saint Janani Luwum, are descendants of the same 500-year-old schism that led to the demise of Saint Thomas More. Essentially, the story of the man who drew the outlines of *Eutopia*, and the story of how churches have contributed to the crafting of a Utopia of Peace in the aftermath of war in northern Uganda reflect the same dynamics: on the one hand, they exemplify the human proclivity for imagining brighter futures, and on the other, bear witness to how these imaginaries are always embedded in the often violently contested relationships through which power and resources are divided. It is precisely this oscillation between the human desire for the good and the inevitability of violence and suffering in human reality that this book has reflected, meanwhile striving – in response to calls both for anthropologies of suffering (Das 2007; Venkatesan 2015) and of 'the good' (Robbins 2006, 2013) – for complementarity between the two. This stance finds resonance with the view expressed by Taussig:

> [T]hat seems to me what human beings are about – that level of complexity, the ability to hold opposite ideas at once – and I think that is where I would really be most comfortable talking about hope – in a field where hope and lack of hope are organised into a sort of dynamic mix.
>
> (Taussig in Zournazi 2002, 47)

While Kleist and Jansen (2016) have distinguished between 'replicatory' and 'non-replicatory' anthropologies of hope, I have sought to show that this distinction creates an unnecessarily strict opposition between hope as an object of analysis and commitment to a replication of hope as a scholarly disposition. Furthermore, I claim it creates an unnecessary distance between the researcher and the researched, one that arguably adds no credence to the research, and can make the task of addressing research ethical quandaries ever more difficult. Instead, I suggest combining a critical analysis of hope – of its distribution and its transformation through time – with a normative commitment to balancing ontological presuppositions of suffering with those of the good.

'Why is it you go to church?' I asked Sarah, and she responded, 'Aah, it's not something very big. I go there because that's the only place that can give me peace' (see Chapters 4 and 7). Rather than a radical alteration of reality – some kind of massive overhaul of the present political system, or the immediate coming of Christ – what most of the Catholic and Anglican men and women I came to know in Kitgum hoped for was simple everyday peace. A contentment wherein the shadows of violence from the past, or whispers of violence in the present, did not interrupt daily life; a contentment resulting from being able to marry, take their children to school, see adult children thrive, live in peace with their neighbours and find themselves employment. Amid the confusion, fear and silence that I have argued characterize the afterlives of war in Acholi, and more generally the political climate in contemporary Uganda, it was this kind of everyday hope that enabled my fellow choristers to sing with conviction that 'Things are getting better, things are getting better, things are getting better'.

Through the performative, repetitive acts of singing and praise, things already *were* better. This would have been easy to shrug off, but why would I have done so? In a conversation recorded by Zournazi (2002, 44), Michael Taussig expressed the suspicion 'that a lot of intellectual activity, at least in the twentieth-century Western cultural orbit, correlates lack of hope with being smart, or lack of hope with profundity'.

It has been suggested that ethnographic studies of hope beg the question of whether it is the informants' hope, or the ethnographer's hope, that comes to be articulated in the final ethnographic text: 'Though we place them insistently in the individual, neither desire nor hope can be removed from social engagement and implication. We are all, I suppose, caught' (Crapanzano 2004, 123). Certainly, my analysis of how community was imagined by and within the space of mainline Christianity bears the mark of my own scholarly, ethical and political aspirations. I too am caught up in hope: not a fatalist certainty of a better tomorrow, but a subjunctive hope that remains hopeful despite the doubts that linger.

There is an urgent need for scholarship that acknowledges complexity and steps away from uniform conceptualizations of communities influenced by war. Images that romanticize the 'other' – that seek to prove the benign character of religion, or narrate the Acholi as perpetual victims – are just as dangerous as those that demonize by brushing off religion as a malign force in society, or by vilifying one group of people as responsible for all the suffering that has befallen their part of the world. Rather than providing clear-cut answers, the task of anthropology is to ask questions that provoke acknowledgement of complexity and confusion, and in so doing unsettle the certainties of knowledge. In Devaka Premarwardhana's words:

> Given science's hegemonic standing, legitimate academic inquiry across the board is now defined by the imperative to identify hidden forces, explain causal connections, and secure stable knowledge. Amid this all-consuming quest for certainty, what space remains for humility and receptivity, for ambiguity and indeterminacy?
>
> (Premawardhana 2020b, 40)

Recent calls for 'postcritical social science' emphasize that research can only ever provide provisional and uncertain grounds for research engagements and interventions, but that to do even that, it can and must be evacuated of normativity and politics (Jensen 2014, 361). While I am all for arguing that research is always provisional, I also believe that each interpretation of, and vision for, the world is structured by ontological underpinnings (Milbank 1990; Robbins 2006). This book has sought to show that it matters what these underpinnings are: whether they are of violence and suffering, or of goodness and hope, for they influence how the world is seen and reproduced in writing. I have advocated a position that oscillates between social critique and the affirmation of hope, that untangles the suffering induced by the political economy of hope while declining to reject the affect of hopefulness, which, as Zournazi has written, 'sustains life in the face of despair' (2002, 14).

As individuals, we are again and again tasked with the necessity of making what my friend Daniel described as the choice between whether to follow the path of people who want everyone just to live in peace, or of those who want to create chaos. As scholars, our task is to ask questions that expose the complexity of those choices, and the ambiguity of what at first sight may appear clear options between paths of chaos and peace. In a world increasingly driven towards, and compelled by the creation of, oppositional extremes, adoption of such a scholarly disposition appears to me to be as necessary as ever.

Notes

Introduction

1. See Glossary for terminology regarding mainline churches in Uganda.
2. The term 'northern Ugandan war' refers to war waged in Acholi between 1986 and 2006 by rebel groups, ultimately the Lord's Resistance Army, and the Government of Uganda. Besides Acholi, northern Uganda encompasses Karamoja, Lango and the multiethnic West Nile region. Since many of the dynamics I describe affect the region far beyond the boundaries of Acholi alone, I often refer in my analysis to 'northern Uganda' even when speaking of details emerging from within Acholi.
3. The National Resistance Army (NRA) was the military arm of Yoweri Museveni's National Resistance Movement (NRM), a rebel group which took power in Uganda in 1986, and remains, to this day, the ruling political party. The NRA was renamed the Uganda People's Defence Force (UPDF) following a new constitution in 1995. When speaking of the years of war, I refer to the National Resistance Movement/Army exclusively as an army (NRA), since this is how most northern Ugandans experienced it. In discussing the movement as a national party, I refer to it as the NRM.
4. The most important accounts of the history of the war can be found in Atkinson (2010), Behrend (1999), Branch (2003, 2011), Dolan (2009), Finnström (2008), Lamwaka (2016) and Okello (2002). Other central sources include the collection of articles edited by Allen and Vlassenroot (2010), and the invaluable insider perspective to life with the LRA provided by Evelyn Amony (2015) and Ledio Cakaj (2016).
5. The Acholi region, which is administratively known as the Acholi sub-region, is an area inhabited primarily by speakers of the Acholi language, whom I refer to as the Acholi. According to the latest census, there are 1.47 million ethnic Acholi in Uganda, amounting to 4.4 per cent of the total population (UBOS 2016).
6. These themes are the subject of a growing wealth of literature in anthropology and beyond (see, e.g., Harlacher et al. 2006; L. H. Williams 2019; Lagace 2018; Meier 2013; Victor 2018).
7. The Verona missionaries were renamed Comboni missionaries, following their founder Daniel Comboni, in the 1970s. I follow the same practice, referring to the organizations and their staff as Verona missionaries in earlier decades, and as Comboni missionaries after they were renamed.

8   Important examples of scholars in the field speaking to politics (Bialecki 2017; Haynes 2018, 2021; O'Neill 2015) also illustrate how much there is to be gained by such extensions.
9   The numerous schools, government offices, banks and businesses in Kitgum town provide many of its residents with affluence. However, 66 per cent of households in the central municipal zone rely on subsistence farming for their primary income, and 22 per cent of households receive less than two meals a day, which is close to the average level within the district as a whole (UBOS 2014).
10 Christian philosophers have also come to the opposite conclusion. Vattimo (1999), for instance, argues in his interpretation of the nihilism of Heidegger and Nietzsche that Christian transcendentalism is often precisely the tool of violence.

Chapter 1

1   Although Cisternino claims that the mission and the colonial base were shut down simultaneously in 1907 (Cisternino 2004, 374), Wright pinpoints the mission withdrawal to 1909 (Wright 1919, 134).
2   Many of the Payira continue to hold their *rwot* as the paramount chief of all the Acholi, but the issue is contested within the contemporary cultural leaders' group Ker Kwaro Acholi (Paine 2014). Prior to the late nineteenth century, the Payira had been an influential chiefdom, but the office of paramount chief was formally installed only by the British colonialists in their attempt to make the Acholi more easily governable (Atkinson 2010, 266; Finnström 2008, 45; see Mamdani 1996 on 'indirect rule'), and reinstituted with funding from donor agencies during the northern Ugandan war, in 2005.
3   The Verona missionaries comprised priests, nuns and lay monks. As is the practice in Kitgum, I commonly refer to these as Fathers, Sisters and Brothers. In the 1970s the Mission officially adopted the name of its founder Daniel Comboni, since when the missionaries have been referred to as Comboni rather than Verona missionaries. In this book I follow the same practice; referring to Catholic missionaries in the present and in recent decades as Combonis, and as Verona missionaries at earlier phases.
4   The Catholic missionary Crazzolara describes the establishment of Gulu thus: 'On hearing the news, the population is thoroughly shaken. They still have their grains in the fields, but orders are that they must pick up cereals not for themselves but for Gulu town… The government has ordered to burn down any house or village of those who have made remonstrations… I have seen burnt barns everywhere.' (Crazzolara's diary, quoted in Cisternino 2004, 361).
5   *Rwot* is singular for chief, *rwodi* plural.

6   It was during Arab trade, and later through the presence and intermarriage of Nubian soldiers in the greater northern Uganda (i.e., including West Nile), that Islam was introduced to the region (Gingyera-Pinycwa 1976, 16). Proselytism was never on the level of the Christian missions, however, and the number of Muslims in the Acholi region in 1959 was recorded at 1% (ibid.). In the 2002 and 2014 Censuses, religious affiliation was no longer broken down at a district level.
7   According to Russel (1966), Christian churches began to grow considerably only in the 1920s, so that by 1966, he assessed that approximately 30% of the population (then one million people) belonged to either the Catholic or Anglican Church. In the light of the 1959 Census, according to which 36% of the Acholi were Roman Catholic, 22% Anglican, and 1% Muslim (Gingyera-Pinycwa 1976, 20), Russel's estimates are rather low, but perhaps reflect his general sense that at the time of his writing, 'the Christian Faith ha[d] not yet reached the most vital part of the tribal existence' (1966, 7): a sentiment shared by many Anglican and Catholic priests I spoke with in the 2000s, despite the high statistical prevalence of Christianity in the region. According to the 1991 Census, Catholics accounted for as much as 70% of the Acholi population, Anglicans for 25% and Muslims for only 1%. Since the 1991 Census, denominational statistics have not been published at the district level.
8   In the light of the historic relationships between the Acholi and Bunyoro (Atkinson 2010), it can be surmised that the word 'Lubanga' may in fact have been borrowed to Acholi from their Bantu-speaking neighbours (Atkinson, personal communication).
9   Crazzolara (1940) attributes the differentiation of *Rubanga* and *Lubanga* to the borrowing of similar concepts from neighbouring languages, since in Acholi, there is no R/L slippage. Kihangire's (1957, 29–31) account for neighbouring Lango is almost identical. He also observed with appreciation that at the time of his writing, many Langi Christians had adopted the word '*Jok*' to refer to the Supreme God.
10 Cisternino was also an ordained Verona priest.
11 While missionaries and colonialists did have separate institutional structures, they were also not always self-evidently distinguishable from one another. For instance, in years prior to the arrival of missionaries in Acholi, and during the years running up to the Uganda protectorate, both the Catholic White Fathers (which arrived in Uganda in 1879) and the Church Mission Society (CMS) (which arrived in Uganda in 1877) were akin to mini-states; they eventually had their own weapons and armed forces, and in the case of the Anglican CMS, even an adjunct trade company, the Uganda Company (Karugire 1980, 129).
12 The CMS and the Verona missionaries were institutionally each other's competitors but the worst rivalries occurred between individuals, just as continues to be the case between Anglicans and Catholics in contemporary Kitgum (see Chapter Seven). Describing a particularly fierce feud between a Catholic and Anglican missionary, Cisternino writes aptly: '[the CMS Reverend] Fisher and [the Verona

Father] Beduschi were undoubtedly two steel blades, two pieces of flint; and the more sparks they produced the happier they were… The two Missionaries [sic] produced sparks and would set that whole savannah on fire even up to our time, founding a Church and a population which remained divided and always in competition, as had previously happened in Kampala and Hoima' (2004, 392).

13 By 1959 the population had grown exponentially from the early twentieth century, when the population consisted of small scattered settlements, to 3,454 inhabitants. At this point the town only covered approximately 7.8 square kilometres (Ocitti 1966), as compared to the present Town Council area of approximately 30 square kilometres, in which a population of almost 45,000 was recorded in the latest (2014) Census.

14 The catechists are estimated to have been 16–18 and 12–14 respectively at the time of their death (Gulu Archdiocese 2012).

15 A similar ambivalence regarding views on Baker is evident in Girling's ethnography, where he both describes Baker as a man who loved meting out physical punishments to what he saw as the inferior Africans, yet notes how broadly he was revered in Acholi as the man who put an end to slave trade in the region (Girling 1960, 135–41).

Chapter 2

1 Churches were still largely in foreign hands in much of northern Uganda at the time of the country's independence: in Acholi, for instance, there were only ten local diocesan priests working alongside eighty-two Verona missionaries (AMECEA 1965). In an appendix Girling was required by the colonial office to cut from his thesis, Girling notes that about half of the expatriate population in Acholi during the time of his fieldwork in the 1950s were Verona missionaries, the majority of whom were Italian (Girling [1960] 2018, 362, 364).

2 *Dini*, 'religion', originates from Swahili.

3 Muslims, a minority in Uganda, were even fewer in number in Acholi than in the country as a whole (p'Bitek 1971a). For more detail on Islam in Ugandan national politics, see Mazrui (1977) and Soi (2016).

4 Howell (2017) argues that during the late colonial era, highly religious and highly political Anglicans were rarely one and the same, particularly since the Balokole movement in Uganda took to emphasize a rather soft political stance. A different perspective is provided in Earle and Carney's (2021) account of Benedicto Kiwanuka, which highlights the way in which competing Catholic visions impacted and were negotiated in the highest ranks of Ugandan politics at the eve of independence.

5   There is a wealth of recent literature on this theme in Uganda, much more so than on the majority mainline churches that born-again churches are challenging (see, e.g., Bompani 2016, 2018; Boyd 2014; Basoga 2012; Bremner 2013; Gusman 2009; Isiko 2019; B. Jones 2009; Lauterbach 2014; Musana, Crichton, and Howell 2017; Tankink 2007).

6   This pattern has been quite typical for church–state relations in Eastern Africa. In Tanzania Nyerere encouraged religious leaders to wield influence in certain sectors of society, while insisting in others that religion be kept away from politics (Westerlund 1980). In Rwanda, religious leaders have been selectively invited to influence debates over ethnicity whenever their views – or their ethnicity – have suited the political elite of the time (Carney 2013; Longman 2001).

7   For a fascinating account of the history of vehicles in Uganda, of their status value in Acholi, and of their weight as political currency, see Lagace (2018).

8   The FC newsletters were and continue to be compiled monthly in Italy and the author or authors of individual country sections are usually not identified. The sections from Uganda appear to be selectively compiled from letters and reports from individual mission stations and missionaries across the country, primarily in the core area of Comboni work: that is, Acholi, Lango and the West Nile in northern Uganda. The newsletters offer glimpses into enormously diverse topics, indicating a wealth of archival material – the original letters and reports from which the newsletters have been collated, and which likely remain in the organizations' archives – which has to date been unutilized, but would be well worth exploring. In this chapter, all newsletter excerpts are either in the original English, or translated from the original Italian with help from Alessandro Gusman.

9   The Uganda Martyrs were Christian converts within the court of the Kabaka (king) of Buganda kingdom, who were executed upon orders of Kabaka Mwanga II between 1885 and 1887. While the reasons for their killing are debated in contemporary scholarship (see, e.g., Kassimir 1991; Rao 2015), both the Catholic and the Anglican Churches in Uganda commemorate the martyrs as examples of Christian commitment at huge annual pilgrimages to their shrine in Namugongo (Gulu Archdiocese 2012; Office of the Prime Minister 2015).

10 As Catholic missionary numbers declined, those of local diocesan staff grew: In 1965 there were 10 Acholi diocesan priests to 85 Comboni priests, and 56 (Ugandan) Little Sisters of Mary Immaculate to 81 Comboni sisters, whereas by 1981 priests numbered 11 diocesan to 42 Comboni priests, and sisters 162 local to 57 Comboni. Numerical missionary dominance broke during the tumultuous 1980s: in 1991, 42 local priests outnumbered 26 Comboni priests, while the number of local sisters had grown to 252 as opposed to only 36 Comboni sisters. By 2009 the number of diocesan priests had stabilized at 50, with Comboni priests down to 21; and besides 27 ageing Comboni sisters, the number of local sisters

working in Gulu diocese had dropped to 176 from the 2003 war-time peak of 370. Many of the Little Sisters of Mary Immaculate are Ugandans from other parts of the country, whereas diocesan priests are almost exclusively Acholi. Besides Combonis, there have been some other missionary orders working in Gulu diocese, but in very low numbers (AMECEA 1965, 1971, 1976, 1979, 1983, 1993; Uganda Episcopal Conference 2003, 2009).

11 See particularly Allen (1991) and Behrend's (1999) work on the HSMF, and that of Allen and Vlassenroot (2010), Finnström (2008) and Titeca (2010) on the LRA.

12 In this sense certain aspects of the rebellions resonate with other anti-missionary movements in Africa: the Antonian movement's war against Catholic Capuchin missionaries in early-eighteenth-century Congo (Thornton 1998); the distinctly anti-missionary Lumpa church's war against Kaunda's government in 1950s Zambia (Hinfelaar 1991, 102, 105); the Nyabingi rebellion in Uganda's Kigezi (Rutanga 1991); and the Mahdist war which struck down missionaries in later-nineteenth-century Sudan, among them Verona missionaries who then relocated to Acholi (Whitmore 2013). During the colonial era, of course, much of the resistance to missionaries was intertwined with anti-colonial struggle (Wipper 1977).

13 Church statistics for baptisms and marriages in my two case study parishes in Kitgum town did not show great changes during the years of war, but they are also not comparable across time because of fluctuations in the urban population following insecurity-related internal displacement to towns.

14 I have copies of the documents Father Donohue refers to, but have not been able to verify their authenticity, thus base this account on his interpretation of their meaning.

15 According to a report on the 1991–93 peace process, the Catholic Church refused to send representatives to the LRA and government talks, which may have been due to the church's fear, both of government accusations that it was involved with the rebels, and of the rebels, who had targeted the church heavily in preceding years (O'Kadameri 2002).

Chapter 3

1 Furthermore, as the work of Ratele (2016) and Gqola (2016) on rape culture in South Africa shows, even those whose bodies are not directly touched cannot but be profoundly affected when violence cuts across society.

2 An abundance of literature related to trauma, violence and healing was available in the Catholic parishes where I had the opportunity to explore the parish bookshelves. This literature had been published, for instance, by the Uganda Episcopal Conference, the Archdiocese of Gulu, the Comboni Missionaries and

the Italian Catholic NGO AVSI, which had already had a significant presence in northern Uganda before the beginning of the war. Here there was a notable difference to the Church of Uganda, where I did not see similar materials either in the vestry of the Town Parish, in reverends' homes, or at the Diocese office. Nor had the Church of Uganda, as far as I could find, published material on such topics – they simply did not have the resources.

3   Something of this order is suggested by Marsha Henry in a blog that lists reasons 'not to write your master's thesis on sexual violence in situations of war' (Henry 2013). While intended as a thought-provoker for those who do write such theses, that they might then do so in a more ethical way, I think the question of whether we actually should refrain from selecting certain research topics in some locations is one which should be taken seriously in its own right.

4   See Maček (2014b) and Thomson et al. (2013) for researchers' personal reflections on research in such contexts.

5   Maček reflects, on the other hand, on how research on such heavy topics often exhausts and even traumatizes scholars themselves, which does not bear favourably on career development. As she notes, scholars of violence know full well that researching violence is not 'cool', but rather emotionally and ethically exhausting. Yet the respectful awe I have sometimes encountered when telling colleagues about my research in a post-conflict community does speak of a particular and disturbing appeal of research into 'murky' topics such as war, trauma and violence (see also Häkkinen and Salasuo 2015).

Chapter 4

1   The so-called nodding syndrome, which causes epilepsy-type seizures that put patients at risk of falling in water or fires, and makes it difficult for them to eat, was first documented in northern Uganda in the 1990s. The syndrome, which almost exclusively affects children, appeared to be spreading, and was gaining more attention in rural Acholi in the years prior to my 2012–13 fieldwork. The cause of the disease is unclear, which, as Karin van Bemmel has shown, has created fruitful grounds for rumours about its possible relation to the war. The issue has become highly politicized, with many Acholi blaming the government for its inadequate response – instead, local religious leaders, *ajwaki,* and NGOs have sought to intervene through various forms of healing and material assistance (van Bemmel, Derluyn, and Stroeken 2014; van Bemmel 2016).

2   Acholi delicacies, of which *malakwang,* a slightly bitter green vegetable served with a sauce of groundnut paste, is particularly used in Ugandan newspaper cartoons to refer to Acholi people.

3   Daudi and Jildo were the now beatified Catholic catechists who died in 1915 in eastern Kitgum, Janani Luwum the Anglican archbishop murdered by Idi Amin, Matthew Lukwiya the supervisor of the Catholic Lacor Hospital who died of Ebola while leading the hospital's Ebola-care team during the Ebola outbreak in Acholi in 2000, and Okot p'Bitek, Uganda's most famous poet and internationally acknowledged anthropologist.

4   A group of investors which, with the backing of the Ugandan government, has been involved in an enormous and widely disputed acquisition of what is arguably customary communal Acholi land in the western part of the sub-region (see, for instance, Martiniello 2015; Sjögren 2014).

5   During the war between the LRA and the UPDF, Otunnu served as an Under Secretary General of the United Nations, and used his position to draw attention to the ongoing war. At various international venues, Otunnu claimed that the Ugandan government was undertaking deliberate and well-orchestrated genocide of the Acholi people (see, e.g., O. A. Otunnu 2006).

6   In 1986, seventy-one people were killed in Namokora sub-county by NRA soldiers. On the initiative of a Comboni priest of the local parish, Tarcisio Pazzaglia, who lived and worked at Kitgum Mission during my fieldwork, most of the largely decomposed bodies were collected and buried in a mass grave two months after the massacre (Akullo and Ogora 2014).

7   Museveni's mentioning Obote's son Jimmy Akena is an interesting move, since Akena, the MP of Lira, is a representative of the UPC, not of the NRM. It seems Museveni is implying that even getting into the parliament on an opposition ticket is ultimately the president's doing.

8   The Gulu-Kitgum road was completed around the time of the 2016 elections. Its completion has been greatly appreciated, and was cited by many people I spoke with in 2016 as the reason they would vote for Museveni. On the other hand, many people who had homes and business near the road were severely impacted by the building process.

9   Since then, Anywar has truly embraced the role of Museveni's faithful daughter: she broke away from FDC and ran as independent in 2016; voted in favour of legislation to withdraw presidential age limits in 2017; was appointed state minister for the environment in the NRM government in 2019; but lost in the NRM primaries in Kitgum in 2020 (Ocungi 2020).

10 I have heard of a few major church events where strong-willed religious leaders have been able to push politics off the agenda. The overwhelming pattern was for politicians to use their position in planning committees to ensure that they gained their place in the limelight.

11 For more on education, see Higgins (2007), on media freedom, Tripp (2010), on government healthcare, Womakuyu (2012), and on land, e.g. Hopwood & Atkinson (2013), Martiniello (2015) and Sjögren (2014).

Chapter 5

1. For an analysis of the extensive corruption of so-called recovery initiatives in the region, see Atkinson (2018) and Golooba-Mutebi and Hickey (2010). For an analysis of the broader dynamics of civil-military relations in Uganda, of which Operation Wealth Creation is a small but telling reflection, see Khisa (2020).

Chapter 6

1. The mantle of peacemaker was willingly adopted by religious leaders beyond Odama, at times by leaders who are less known for their peace activities, and more for their incisive hate speech against sexual minorities (see Alava 2017a). One such was the archbishop of the Church of Uganda, Henry Luke Orombi, who in his farewell speech to Kitgum Diocese upon his retirement declared: 'For me I am a peace maker. God has given me the work to reconcile people... Acholi we need peace makers! In Kitgum there are many fighters, we need peace makers! Somebody who can reconcile. Somebody who can talk peace so that anger can go. What are we going to earn by being angry with one another?... Be reconciled to God. And when you are reconciled to God, be reconciled with one another' (20 October 2012).
2. Ubuntu theology builds on the Xhosa notion of 'Ubuntu' (and parallel concepts in other Bantu languages), translated as 'personhood' or 'humanity', to reflect on human interdependence, often in connection with racial justice and reconciliation. Its most prominent spokesperson has been Archbishop Desmond Tutu, and it continues to be a debated and influential school of theological thought both in Southern Africa, and among scholars of Black, post- and decolonial theologies around the world (see, e.g., Banda 2019; Battle 2009; Bongmba 2019; Lewis 2010).
3. Like Lakwena's group before his, Lukwoya's much smaller group drew its strongest support base from Kitgum, which was also the target of many of its most deadly attacks (see also Allen 1991). By the time of my fieldwork, Lukwoya had denounced violence but, as it transpired, shortly before my departure from Uganda, he was trying to gain a following for his new church near Kitgum, in Mucwini village (the home village of Janani Luwum; see previous chapter). Since then, local authorities have unsuccessfully attempted to ban his church from operating in the Acholi sub-region, apparently unsuccessfully (Komakech 2015).
4. Meinert and Williams (2019a) have made a similar argument about how the repetition inherent to Pentecostal prayer and healing rituals in Acholi allows adherents to address the 'time disturbance' characteristic of post-traumatic stress disorder, which forces people, through flashbacks for instance, back into the past.

Chapter 7

1. Videos of the choir's performances, recorded by Scandal Studios, can also be found online (Ugandan Recordings 2014).
2. See Komujuni (2019) for a fascinating account of attempts to (re)vitalize traditional authority and 'custom' in Acholi.
3. My account of the dispute in Kitgum Diocese draws on minutes, letters, petitions and reports written by various parties to the dispute, of which I have copies. The documents cover the period from 2004 to 2008, whereas events after 2008 have been reconstructed on the basis of interviews and informal discussions with people on all sides of the debate. Unless otherwise indicated, all direct quotations in this section are from these documents.
4. Since then, the districts have been split even further (see Atkinson 2018; E. Green 2010).
5. Demands for new dioceses in many parts of the Church of Uganda parallel the creation of small and economically unviable districts, which many scholars have argued has multiplied opportunities for patronage, and allowed the state to assert its presence at a local level while whittling down the possibilities of anti-NRM political mobilization (E. Green 2010; Nsamba 2013; Sjögren 2013).
6. After the parish was handed over to the local diocese, this began to change, and by the time I visited in 2019 there was an intense and expanding Catholic charismatic group gathering weekly at the parish hall for exorcism and healing sessions. The group was not under any real guidance from the church hierarchy and hence was becoming a source of concern for the clergy.
7. For an example of a Catholic movement in Uganda that has pushed against these boundaries see Behrend (2011), and for one that radically broke them, Vokes (2013).

References

Abonga, Francis, Raphael Kerali, Holly Porter, and Rebecca Tapscott. 2019. 'Naked Bodies and Collective Action: Repertoires of Protest in Uganda's Militarised, Authoritarian Regime.' *Civil Wars* 22 (2-3): 198–223. doi:10.1080/13698249.2020.1680018.

Abrahamsen, Rita. 2000. *Disciplining Democracy : Development Discourse and Good Governance in Africa*. London: Zed Books.

Acellam, David. 2015. *Choir's Report on St. Janani Luwum Memorial Celebration 2015*. Unpublished report.

Adimola, A. D. 1954. 'The Lamogi Rebellion of 1911–1912.' *The Uganda Journal* 18 (2): 166–7.

Ahmed, Sara. 2000. *Strange Encounters: Embodied Others in Post-Coloniality*. 1st edition. London and New York: Routledge.

Akullo, Evelyn, and Lino Owor Ogora. 2014. *Occupation and Carnage. Recounting Atrocities Committed by the NRA's 35th Battalion in Namokora Sub-County in August 1986*. JRP Field Note XIX, March 2014. Gulu: Justice and Reconciliation Project.

Alava, Henni. 2008. 'Interactions of Conflict and Development Intervention in Northern Uganda.' Master's thesis, Helsinki: University of Helsinki.

Alava, Henni. 2016a. 'Hiljaisuuden Ja Hämmennyksen Etnografiaa Pohjois-Ugandassa.' In *Peilin Edessä. Refleksiivisyys Ja Etnografinen Tieto*, edited by Katja Uusihakala and Jeremy Gould, 113–43. Helsinki: Gaudeamus.

Alava, Henni. 2016b. 'Embeddedness. The Paradox of Development through the Grassroots of Churches.' In *For Better for Worse. The Role of Religion in Development Cooperation*, edited by Robert Odén, 177–87. Uppsala: Swedish Mission Council.

Alava, Henni. 2017a. 'Homosexuality, the Holy Family and a Failed Mass Wedding in Catholic Northern Uganda.' *Critical African Studies* 9 (1): 32–51. doi:10.1080/21681392.2016.1245104.

Alava, Henni. 2017b. 'There Is Confusion. The Politics of Silence, Fear and Hope in Catholic and Anglican Northern Uganda.' PhD thesis, Finland: University of Helsinki.

Alava, Henni. 2017c. '"Acholi Youth Are Lost"? Young, Christian and (a)Political in Uganda.' In *What Politics? Youth and Political Engagement in Africa*, edited by Elina Oinas, Henri Onodera, and Leena Suurpää, 158–76. Leiden: Brill.

Alava, Henni. 2019. 'The Lord's Resistance Army and the Arms That Brought the Lord: Amplifying Polyphonic Silences in Northern Uganda.' *Suomen Antropologi: Journal of the Finnish Anthropological Society* 44 (1): 9–29. doi:10.30676/jfas.v44i1.75028.

Alava, Henni. 2020. 'The Everyday and Spectacle of Subdued Citizenship in Northern Uganda.' In *Practices of Citizenship in East Africa. Perspectives from Philosophical Pragmatism*, edited by Katariina Holma and Tiina Kontinen, 90–104. London: Routledge.

Alava, Henni, and Catrine Shroff. 2019. 'Unravelling Church Land: Transformation in the Relations between Church, State and Community in Uganda.' *Development and Change* 50 (5): 1288–309.

Alava, Henni, and Jimmy Spire Ssentongo. 2016. 'Religious (de)Politicization in Uganda's 2016 Elections.' *Journal of Eastern African Studies* 10 (4): 677–92. doi:10.10 80/17531055.2016.1270043.

Alava, Henni, Twine H. Bananuka, Karembe F. Ahimbisibwe, and Tiina Kontinen. 2020. 'Contextualizing Citizenship in Uganda.' In *Practices of Citizenship in East Africa. Perspectives from Philosophical Pragmatism*, edited by Katariina Holma and Tiina Kontinen, 57–72. London: Routledge.

Allen, Tim. 1991. 'Understanding Alice: Uganda's Holy Spirit Movement in Context.' *Africa* 61 (3): 370–99.

Allen, Tim. 2006. *Trial Justice: The International Criminal Court and the Lord's Resistance Army*. London: Zed Books, in association with International African Institute.

Allen, Tim. 2010. 'Bitter Roots: The "invention" of Acholi Traditional Justice.' In *The Lord's Resistance Army. Myth and Reality*, edited by Tim Allen and Koen Vlassenroot, 242–61. London and New York: Zed Books.

Allen, Tim. 2015. 'Vigilantes, Witches and Vampires: How Moral Populism Shapes Social Accountability in Northern Uganda.' *International Journal on Minority and Group Rights* 22 (3): 360–86. doi:10.1163/15718115-02203004.

Allen, Tim. 2018. 'Introduction. Colonial Encounters in Acholiland and Oxford: The Anthropology of Frank Girling and Okot p'Bitek.' In *Lawino's People: The Acholi of Uganda*, edited by Tim Allen, 7–46. Zürich: LIT Verlag Münster.

Allen, Tim, and Koen Vlassenroot, eds. 2013. *The Lord's Resistance Army. Myth and Reality*. London and New York: Zed Books.

Amanela, Suleiman, et al. 2020. *The Mental Landscape of Post-Conflict Life in Northern Uganda*. Working paper 92. Researching Livelihoods and Services Affected by Conflict. London: Overseas Development Institute. https://www.odi.org/publications/17249-mental-landscape-post-conflict-life-northern-uganda.

AMECEA. 1965. *Catholic Directory of Eastern Africa 1965*. Tabora, Tanzania: Association of Member Episcopal Conferences in Eastern Africa.

AMECEA. 1971. *Catholic Directory of Eastern Africa 1971*. Tabora, Tanzania: Association of Member Episcopal Conferences in Eastern Africa.

AMECEA. 1975. *Catholic Directory of Eastern Africa 1974–1976*. Tabora, Tanzania: Association of Member Episcopal Conferences in Eastern Africa.

AMECEA. 1979. *Catholic Directory of Eastern Africa 1977–1979*. Tabora, Tanzania: Association of Member Episcopal Conferences in Eastern Africa.

AMECEA. 1983. *Catholic Directory of Eastern Africa 1981–1983*. Tabora, Tanzania: Association of Member Episcopal Conferences in Eastern Africa.

AMECEA. 1993. *AMECEA Catholic Directory 1991–1993*. Nairobi: Association of Member Episcopal Conferences in Eastern Africa.

Amnesty International. 1991. *Uganda: Human Rights Violations by the National Resistance Army*. http://www.amnestyusa.org/node/60583.

Amony, Evelyn. 2015. *I Am Evelyn Amony: Reclaiming My Life from the Lord's Resistance Army*, edited by Erin Baines. Women in Africa and the Diaspora. Madison, WI: University of Wisconsin Press.

Andrews, Molly. 2014. *Narrative Imagination and Everyday Life*. Explorations in Narrative Psychology. Oxford and New York: Oxford University Press.

Apuuli, Kasaija Phillip. 2011. 'Peace over Justice: The Acholi Religious Leaders Peace Initiative (ARLPI) vs. the International Criminal Court (ICC) in Northern Uganda.' *Studies in Ethnicity and Nationalism* 11 (1): 116–29. doi:10.1111/j.1754-9469.2011.01101.x.

ARLPI. 2009. *Acholi Religious Leaders Peace Initiative*. Vol. 2012. May/5§.

Atkinson, Ronald R. 2010. *The Roots of Ethnicity: The Origins of the Acholi of Uganda before 1800*. 2nd ed. Fountain Studies in East African History. Kampala: Fountain Publishers.

Atkinson, Ronald R. 2018. 'Our Friends at the Bank? The Adverse Effects of Neoliberalism in Acholi.' In *Uganda: The Dynamics of Neoliberal Transformation*, edited by Jörg Wiegratz, Giuliano Martiniello, and Elisa Greco, 60–77. New York: Zed Books.

Atkinson, Ronald R., and James O. Latigo. 2020. *Protecting Rights to Customary Land in Acholi, Northern Uganda: Second Update*. Paper prepared for presentation at the '2020 World Bank Conference on Land and Poverty' The World Bank – Washington DC, 16–20 March 2020.

Austin, John L. 1975. *How to Do Things with Words*. Cambridge, MA: Harvard University Press.

Baines, Erin. 2010. 'Spirits and Social Reconstruction after Mass Violence: Rethinking Transitional Justice.' *African Affairs* 109 (436): 409.

Baines, Erin. 2007. 'The Haunting of Alice: Local Approaches to Justice and Reconciliation in Northern Uganda.' *The Internaitonal Journal of Transitional Justice* 1: 91–114.

Baines, Erin. 2009. 'Complex Political Perpetrators: Reflections on Dominic Ongwen*.' *The Journal of Modern African Studies* 47 (2): 163–91. doi:10.1017/S0022278X09003796.

Banda, Collium. 2019. 'The Privatised Self? A Theological Critique of the Commodification of Human Identity in Modern Technological Age in an African Context Professing Ubuntu.' *HTS: Theological Studies* 75 (1): 1–10.

Baroin, Catherine. 1996. 'Religious Conflict in 1990–1993 among the Rwa: Secession in a Lutheran Diocese in Northern Tanzania.' *African Affairs* 95 (381): 529–54.

Basoga, David. 2012. 'Pentecostal Gospel Music in Kampala, Uganda: Between the Sacred and the Secular.' In *Ethnomusicology in East Africa: Perspectives from Uganda and beyond*, edited by Sylvia A. Nannyonga-Tamusuza and Thomas Solomon, 141–52. Oxford: African Books Collective.

Battle, Michael. 2009. *Ubuntu. I in You and You in Me*. New York: Seabury Books.

Bayart, Jean-François. 2000. 'Africa in the World: A History of Extraversion.' *African Affairs* 99 (395): 217.

Beckmann, Nadine, Alessandro Gusman, and Catrine Shroff, eds. 2014. *Strings Attached: AIDS and the Rise of Transnational Connections in Africa*. Oxford: Oxford University Press/British Academy.

Beekers, Daan, and Bas van Gool. 2012. 'From Patronage to Neopatrimonialism.' ASC Working Paper 101 African Studies Centre.

Behrend, Heike. 1995. 'The Holy Spirit Movement and the Forces of Nature in the North of Uganda 1985–1987.' In *Religion & Politics in East Africa: The Period since Independence*, edited by Holger B. Hansen and Michael Twaddle, 59–71. London: James Curry.

Behrend, Heike. 1999. *Alice Lakwena & the Holy Spirits. War in Northern Uganda 1985–97*. Oxford, Kampala, Nairobi and Athens: James Currey/Fountain Publishers/EAEP/Ohio University Press.

Behrend, Heike. 2011. *Resurrecting Cannibals: The Catholic Church, Witch-Hunts, and the Production of Pagans in Western Uganda*. Eastern African Studies (London, England). New York: James Currey.

Bialecki, Jon. 2017. 'Eschatology, Ethics, and Ēthnos: Ressentiment and Christian Nationalism in the Anthropology of Christianity.' *Religion and Society* 8 (1): 43–61.

Bialecki, Jon. 2021. 'Coda: An Origin Story (An essay in the Self-Positionality in the Anthropology of Christianity Series).' *New Directions in the Anthropology of Christianity*. 17 May 2021. https://www.new-directions.sps.ed.ac.uk/coda-an-origin-story-an-essay-in-the-self-positionality-in-the-anthropology-of-christianity-series/. Accessed 26 June 2021.

Blaufuss, Kathrin. 2007. 'De-Linking Text from Fieldwork: Exploring Power Imbalances in the Narrative.' *Narrative Inquiry* 17 (1): 13–26.

Bloch, Ernst. 1986. *The Principle of Hope*, translated by Paul Knight, Neville Plaice, and Stephen Plaice. Studies in Contemporary German Social Thought. Cambridge, MA: MIT Press.

Boccassino, Renato. 1939. 'The Nature and Characteristics of the Supreme Being Worshipped among the Acholi of Uganda.' *Uganda Journal* 6 (4): 195–201.

Bompani, Barbara. 2016. '"For God and For My Country": Pentecostal-Charismatic Churches and the Framing of a New Political Discourse in Uganda.' In *Public Religion and the Politics of Homosexuality in Africa*, edited by Adriaan van Klinken and Ezra Chitando, 19–34. Burlington: Routledge.

Bompani, Barbara. 2017. '"Good Christians, Good Citizens". Pentecostal-Charismatic Narratives of Citizenship, Public Action and National Belonging in Contemporary Uganda.' In *Christian Citizens and the Moral Regeneration of the African State*, edited by Barbara Bompani and Caroline Valois, 21–34. Milton, UK: Routledge.

Bompani, Barbara. 2018. 'Religious Economies: Pentecostal-CharismaticChurches and the Framing of a New Moral Order in Neoliberal Uganda.' In *Uganda: The Dynamics of Neoliberal Transformation*, edited by Jörg Wiegratz, Giuliano Martiniello, and Elisa Greco, 303–17. New York: Zed Books.

Bompani, Barbara, and S. Brown. 2014. 'A "Religious Revolution"? Print Media, Sexuality, and Religious Discourse in Uganda.' *Journal of Eastern African Studies* 9 (1): 110–26.

Bompani, Barbara, and Maria Frahm-Arp, eds. 2010. *Development and Politics from Below: Exploring Religious Spaces in the African State*. Houndmills, Basingstoke, England and New York: Palgrave Schol, Print UK.

Bongmba, Elias Kifon. 2016a. 'Church and State in Cameroon: The Political Theology of Christian Cardinal Tumi.' *Journal of Asian and African Studies* 51 (3): 283–304. doi:10.1177/0021909615612110.

Bongmba, Elias Kifon. 2016b. 'Homosexuality, *Ubuntu*, and Otherness in the African Church.' *Religion and Violence in Africa* 4 (1): 15–37.

Bongmba, Elias Kifon. 2019. 'What Has Kinshasa to Do with Athens? Methodological Perspectives on Theology and Social Science in Search for a Political Theology.' In *Faith in African Lived Christianity*, edited by Karen Lauterbach & Mika Vähäkangas, 195–223. Leiden: Brill.

Boyd, Lydia. 2014. 'Ugandan Born-Again Christians and the Moral Politics of Gender Equality.' *Journal of Religion in Africa* 44 (3/4): 333–54. doi:10.1163/15700666-12340025.

Branch, Adam. 2003. 'Neither Peace nor Justice: Political Violence and the Peasantry in Northern Uganda, 1986–1998.' *African Studies Quarterly* 8 (2): 1–31.

Branch, Adam. 2011. *Displacing Human Rights. War and Intervention in Northern Uganda*. New York: Oxford University Press.

Branch, Adam, and Adrian Yen. 2018. 'Neoliberal Discipline and Violence in Northern Uganda.' In *Uganda: The Dynamics of Neoliberal Transformation*, edited by Jörg Wiegratz, Giuliano Martiniello, and Elisa Greco, 78–94. New York: Zed Books.

Bremner, Sophie Elizabeth. 2013. 'Transforming Futures? Being Pentecostal in Kampala, Uganda.' University of East Anglia. https://ueaeprints.uea.ac.uk/42348/1/2013BremnerSEPhD.pdf.

Browne, Craig. 2005. 'Hope, Critique, and Utopia.' *Critical Horizons* 6 (1): 63–86. doi:10.1163/156851605775009483.

Bruner, Jerome S. 1986. *Actual Minds, Possible Worlds*. Cambridge, MA: Harvard University Press.

Burnet, Jennie E. 2012. *Genocide Lives in Us: Women, Memory, and Silence in Rwanda*. Women in Africa and the Diaspora. Madison: The University of Wisconsin Press.

Butler, Judith. 1993. *Bodies That Matter: On the Discursive Limits of 'Sex.'* New York: Routledge.

Butler, Judith. 1997. *Excitable Speech: A Politics of the Performative.* East Sussex: Psychology Press.

Cakaj, Ledio. 2016. *When The Walking Defeats You: One Man's Journey as Joseph Kony's Bodyguard.* London: Zed Books.

Cannell, Fenella. 2006. *The Anthropology of Christianity.* Durham: Duke University Press.

Carbaugh, Donal, Michael Berry, and Marjatta Nurmikari-Berry. 2006. 'Coding Personhood through Cultural Terms and Practices Silence and Quietude as a Finnish "Natural Way of Being."' *Journal of Language and Social Psychology* 25 (3): 203–20. doi:10.1177/0261927X06289422.

Carbone, Giovanni. 2008. *No-Party Democracy?: Ugandan Politics in Comparative Perspective.* Boulder: Lynne Rienner Publishers Inc.

Carney, J. J. 2013. *Rwanda Before the Genocide: Catholic Politics and Ethnic Discourse in the Late Colonial Era.* Oxford: Oxford University Press.

Carney, J. J. 2017. 'The Politics of Ecumenism in Uganda, 1962–1986.' *Church History* 86 (3): 765–95. doi:10.1017/S0009640717001287.

Caruth, Cathy. 1995. *Trauma: Explorations in Memory.* Baltimore and London: Johns Hopkins University Press.

Cawthorne, Ellie. 2016. 'Thomas More: Saint or Sinner?' *BBC History Magazine.* http://www.historyextra.com/article/bbc-history-magazine/thomas-more-saint-or-sinner-tudor-court-Henry-VIII.

Chitando, Ezra, and Adriaan Van Klinken, eds. 2016. *Christianity and Controversies over Homosexuality in Contemporary Africa.* Abingdon, Oxon and New York: Routledge.

Christiansen, Catrine. 2010. 'Development by Churches, Development of Churches. Institutional Trajectories in Rural Uganda.' PhD thesis, Denmark: University of Copenhagen.

Cisternino, Mario. 2004. *Passion for Africa. Missionary and Imperial Papers on the Evangelisation of Uganda and Sudan, 1848–1923.* Kampala: Fountain Publishers.

Coleman, Simon. 2017. *The Anthropology of Catholicism: A Reader*, edited by Kristin Norget, Valentina Napolitano, and Maya Mayblin. Oakland: University of California Press.

Comaroff, Jean, and John L. Comaroff. 1991. *Of Revelation and Revolution. Volume 1, Christianity, Colonialism, and Consciousness in South Africa.* Chicago: University of Chicago Press.

Comaroff, Jean, and John L. Comaroff. 1993. *Modernity and Its Malcontents: Ritual and Power in Postcolonial Africa.* Chicago: University of Chicago Press.

Comboni Missionaries. 2019. *Supreme Witness. Comboni Missionaries Killed in the Line of Duty in Africa and Latin America.* Dublin: Comboni Missionary Publications United Kingdom and Ireland.

Comboni Missionaries Uganda. n.d. *Daniel Comboni: A Prophet for Africa. Based on 'A Heart for Africa, the Life of Bishop Daniel Comboni' by Bernard Ward, MCCJ*. Kampala: Author.

Cook, Dr. A. R. 1904. 'II. Letter from Dr. A. R. Cook to the C.M.S. after a Journey to Inspect the Location of a Site at Which to Open a Permanent Mission in Acholiland, Published as Part of a Collection of Letters under the Title The Commencement of Work in the Nile Province.' *CMS Intelligencer*, November.

Cooke, Bill, and Uma Kothari. 2001. *Participation: The New Tyranny?* London: Zed Books.

Cooper, Elizabeth, and David Pratten. 2015. 'Ethnographies of Uncertainty in Africa: An Introduction.' In *Ethnographies of Uncertainty in Africa*, edited by Cooper, Elizabeth, and David Pratten, 1–16. Houndmills, Basingstoke, Hampshire: Palgrave Macmillan.

Crapanzano, Vincent. 2003. 'Reflections on Hope as a Category of Social and Psychological Analysis.' *Cultural Anthropology* 18 (1): 3–32.

Crapanzano, Vincent. 2004. *Imaginative Horizons: An Essay in Literary-Philosophical Anthropology*. Chicago: University of Chicago Press.

Crazzolara, J. P. 1940. 'Renato Boccassino and Lubanga Jok. A Note Published as Supplement to Wright's Article "The Supreme Being among the Acholi of Uganda – Another Viewpoint."' *Uganda Journal* 7 (3): 130–7.

Crazzolara, J. P. 1950. *The Lwoo Part I: Lwoo Migrations*. Collana Di Studi Africani. Verona: Istituto missioni africane.

Crazzolara, J. P. 1955. *A Study of the Acooli Language. Grammar and Vocabulary*. Second impression (revised). London, New York and Toronto: International African Institute, Oxford University Press.

Crichton, Angus. 2017. '"You will just remain pagans, and we will come and devour you": Christian Expansion and Anglo-Ganda Power in Bunyoro and Bukedi.' In *Ugandan Churches and the Political Centre*. Ngoma series, edited by Paddy Musana, Angus Crichton, and Caroline Howell Cambridge: Ngoma Ecumenical Publishing Consortium, Cambridge Centre for Christianity Worldwide.

Csordas, Thomas J. 2017. 'Possession and Psychopathology, Faith and Reason.' In *The Anthropology of Catholicism: A Reader*, edited by Kristin Norget, Valentina Napolitano, and Maya Mayblin, 293–305. Oakland: University of California Press.

Daily Monitor. 2012. 'Cerinah Nebanda's Death: Pathologist Arrested, Dad Breaks Silence.' *Daily Monitor*, 18 December. http://www.monitor.co.ug/News/National/Cerinah-Nebanda-s-death–Pathologist-arrested/-/688334/1646634/-/7etbhxz/-/index.html. Accessed 27 July 2016.

Das, Veena. 2007. *Life and Words. Violence and the Descent into the Ordinary*. Berkeley: University of California Press.

Daswani, Girish 2021. Christianity as Neither Exception Nor Rule (An essay in the Self-Positionality in the Anthropology of Christianity series). *New Directions in the Anthropology of Christianity*. 10 May 2021. https://www.new-directions.sps.ed.ac.uk/christianity-as-neither-exception-nor-rule.

de Castro, Eduardo Viveiros. 2015. 'Who is Afraid of the Ontological Wolf? Some Comments on an Ongoing Anthropological Debate.' *The Cambridge Journal of Anthropology* 33 (1).

DIvon, Shai André, and Arthur Owor. 2021. 'Aguu: From Acholi Post War Street Youth and Children to "Criminal Gangs" in Modern Day Gulu City, Uganda.' *Journal of Human Security* 16 (2): 82–96.

Dolan, Chris. 2000. *What Do You Remember?: A Rough Guide to the War in Northern Uganda 1986–2000*. Vol. COPE Working paper no. 33. London: Acord. http://www.acord.org.uk/r-pubs-Cope%20Working%20Paper%2033.PDF.

Dolan, Chris. 2009. *Social Torture: The Case of Northern Uganda, 1986–2006*. New York: Berghahn Books.

Donohue, Fr. Paul. 1991. Kitgum Dossier, a report compiled on the basis of copies of official documents, also attached to the report, concerning the dispute over Kitgum High School. Uganda.

Dowd, Robert A. 2015. *Christianity, Islam, and Liberal Democracy: Lessons from Sub-Saharan Africa*. Oxford: Oxford University Press.

Droogers, André. 2012. 'The Power Dimensions of the Christian Community: An Anthropological Model.' *Religion* 33 (3): 263–80. doi:10.1016/S0048-721X(03)00059-9.

Dubal, Sam. 2018. *Against Humanity. Lessons from the Lord's Resistance Army*. Berkeley: University of California Press.

Dunovant, Denise. 2016. 'Northern Uganda: Protection in Displacement, Protection on Return.' *Forced Migration Review* 53: 28–30.

Dwyer, John Orr. 1972. 'The Acholi of Uganda: Adjustment to Imperialism.' PhD thesis, Faculty of Political Science. New York: Columbia University.

Earle, Jonathan & Jay J. Carney (2021). *Contesting Catholics: Benedicto Kiwanuka and the Birth of Postcolonial Uganda*. Woodbridge: Boydell & Brewer

Eastmond, Marita, and Johanna Mannergren Selimovic. 2012. 'Silence as Possibility in Postwar Everyday Life.' *International Journal of Transitional Justice* 6 (3): 502–24.

Edkins, Jenny. 2003. *Trauma and the Memory of Politics*. Cambridge: Cambridge University Press.

Ekitibwa Kya Buganda. 2010. 'Observer Report Concocted Museveni Comments to Incite Tribal Divisions.' *Ekitibwa Kya Buganda*. https://ekitibwakyabuganda.wordpress.com/2010/06/15/observer-report-concocted-museveni-comments-to-incite-tribal-divisions/. Accessed 22 January 2016.

Ellis, Stephen, and Gerrie ter Haar. 2004. *Worlds of Power: Religious Thought and Political Practice in Africa*. Oxford: Oxford University Press.

Engelke, Matthew. 2010. 'Past Pentecostalism: Notes on Rupture, Realignment, and Everyday Life in Pentecostal and African Independent Churches.' *Africa: The Journal of the International African Institute* 80 (2). 177–99.

Englund, Harri. 2011. 'Introduction. Rethinking African Christianities. Beyond the Religion-Politics Conundrum.' In *Christianity and Public Culture in Africa*, edited by Harri Englund, 1–24. Athens: Ohio University Press.

Epstein, Helen. 2014. 'Murder in Uganda.' *The New York Review of Books.* http://www.nybooks.com/articles/2014/04/03/murder-uganda/.

Escobar, Arturo. 1995. *Encountering Development: The Making and Unmaking of the Third World.* Princeton Studies in Culture/Power/History. Princeton: Princeton University Press.

Eskelinen, Teppo, ed. 2020. *The Revival of Political Imagination: Utopias as Methodology.* London: Zed Books Ltd.

Eskelinen, Teppo, Keijo Lakkala, and Maria Laakso. 2020. 'Introduction: Utopias and the Revival of Imagination.' In *The Revival of Political Imagination: Utopias as Methodology*, edited by Teppo Eskelinen, 20–36. London: Zed Books Ltd.

Ezzy, Douglas. 2004. 'Religious Ethnography: Practicing the Witch's Craft.' In *Researching Paganisms*, edited by Douglas Ezzy, Graham Harvey, and Jenny Blain, 113–28. The Pagan Studies Series. Walnut Creek, CA: AltaMira.

Fanon, Frantz. 1967. *The Wretched of the Earth.* London: Penguin Books.

Fassin, Didier, and Richard Rechtman. 2009. *The Empire of Trauma: An Inquiry into the Condition of Victimhood*, translated by Rachel Gomme. Empire Du Traumatisme, Princeton, NJ: Princeton University Press.

Ferguson, James. 1994. *The Anti-Politics Machine: "Development," Depoliticization, and Bureaucratic Power in Lesotho.* Minneapolis: University of Minnesota Press.

Ferguson, James. 2006. *Global Shadows: Africa in the Neoliberal World Order.* Durham: Duke University Press Books.

Finnegan, Amy C. 2010. 'Forging Forgiveness: Collective Efforts amidst War in Northern Uganda.' *Sociological Inquiry* 80 (3): 424–47. doi:10.1111/j.1475-682X.2010.00341.x.

Finnström, Sverker. 2008. *Living with Bad Surroundings: War, History, and Everyday Moments in Northern Uganda.* Durham: Duke University Press.

Finnström, Sverker. 2009. 'Fear of the Midnight Knock. State Sovereignty and Internal Enemies in Uganda.' In *Crisis of the State: War and Social Upheaval*, edited by Bruce Kapferer and Bjorn E. Bertelsen, 124–42. Oxford and New York: Berghahn Books.

Finnström, Sverker. 2012. '"KONY 2012", Military Humanitarianism, and the Magic of Occult Economies.' *Africa Spectrum* 47 (2/3): 127–35.

Finnström, Sverker. 2015. 'War Stories and Troubled Peace.' *Current Anthropology* 56 (S12): S222–S230. doi:10.1086/683270.

Finnström, Sverker. 2019. 'Review of Holly Porter's after Rape: Violence, Justice and Social Harmony in Uganda.' *African Studies Quarterly: The Online Journal of African Studies* 17 (4): 138–9.

Foucault, Michel. 2012. *Mal Faire, Dire Vrai. Fonction de l'aveu En Justice*, edited by Fabienne Brion and Bernard E. Harcourt. Louvain: Presses universitaires de Louvain, University of Chicago Press.

Freston, Paul. 2004. *Evangelicals and Politics in Asia, Africa, and Latin America.* Repr. Cambridge: Cambridge University Press.

Furani, Khaled. 2019. *Redeeming Anthropology: A Theological Critique of a Modern Science.* Oxford and New York: Oxford University Press.

Gardiner, Michael. 1992. 'Bakhtin's Carnival: Utopia as Critique.' *Utopian Studies* 3 (2): 21–49.

Gehlin, Sara. 2015. 'Prospects for Theology in Peacebuilding. A Theological Analysis of the Just Peace Concept in the Textual Process towards an International Ecumenical Peace Declaration, World Council of Churches 2008–2011.' DPhil thesis. Lund: Lund University.

Geschiere, Peter, and Janet Roitman. 1997. *The Modernity of Witchcraft: Politics and the Occult in Postcolonial Africa*. Charlottesville: University of Virginia Press.

Gifford, Paul, ed. 1995. *The Christian Churches and the Democratization of Africa*. Leiden and New York: Brill.

Gifford, Paul. 1998. *African Christianity: Its Public Role*. Bloomington: Indiana University Press.

Gifford, Paul. 2008. 'Trajectories in African Christianity.' *International Journal for the Study of the Christian Church* 8 (4): 275–89. doi:10.1080/14742250802347935.

Gifford, Paul. 2015. *Christianity, Development and Modernity in Africa*. London: Hurst & Company.

Gingyera-Pinycwa, A. G. G. 1976. *Issues in Pre-Independence Politics in Uganda. A Case-Study on the Contribution of Religion to Political Debate in Uganda in the Decade 1952–1962*. Kampala: East African Literature Bureau.

Girling, Frank Knowles. 1960. *The Acholi of Uganda*. London: H.M. Stationery Office.

Girling, Frank Knowles. [1960] 2018. 'The Acholi of Uganda: Cuts Required by the Colonial Office.' In *Lawino's People: The Acholi of Uganda*, edited by Tim Allen, 359–79. Münster: LIT Verlag Münster.

Gollin, Douglas. 2010. *Agriculture, Roads, and Economic Development in Uganda*, edited by Richard Rogerson. NBER Working Paper Series, 15863. Cambridge, MA: National Bureau of Economic Research.

Golooba-Mutebi, Frederick, and Sam Hickey. 2010. 'Governing Chronic Poverty under Inclusive Liberalism: The Case of the Northern Uganda Social Action Fund.' *Journal of Development Studies* 46 (7): 1216–39.

Goodfellow, Tom. 2014. 'Legal Manoeuvres and Violence: Law Making, Protest and Semi-Authoritarianism in Uganda.' *Development and Change* 45 (4): 753–76. doi:10.1111/dech.12097.

Gqola, Pumla Dineo. 2016. *Rape: A South African Nightmare*. Johannesburg, South Africa: Jacana Media.

Graeber, David. 2013. 'It Is Value That Brings Universes into Being.' *HAU: Journal of Ethnographic Theory* 3 (2): 219–43. doi:10.14318/hau3.2.012.

Graeber, David. 2015. 'Radical Alterity Is Just Another Way of Saying "Reality": A Reply to Eduardo Viveiros de Castro.' *HAU: Journal of Ethnographic Theory* 5 (2): 1–41. doi:10.14318/hau5.2.003.

Gray, John. 2008. *Black Mass: Apocalyptic Religion and the Death of Utopia*. New York: Farrar, Straus and Giroux.

Green, Elliott. 2010. 'Patronage, District Creation, and Reform in Uganda.' *Studies in Comparative International Development* 45 (1): 83–103. doi:10.1007/s12116-009-9058-8.

Green, Maia. 2006. 'Confronting Categorical Assumptions about the Power of Religion in Africa.' *Review of African Political Economy* 33 (110): 635–50. doi:10.1080/03056240601119018.

Gubrium, Jaber F., and James A. Holstein. 2008. 'Narrative Ethnography.' In *Handbook of Emergent Methods*, edited by Sharlene Nagy Hesse-Biber and Patricia Leavy, 241–64. New York: Guilford Press.

Gulu Archdiocese. 2002. 'Jildo Irwa and Daudi Okelo. Martyred Catechists.' Gulu Archdiocese.

Gulu Archdiocese. 2012. 'Renewed Hope of Christianity in Uganda. From Namugongo to Paimol Two More Martyrs. Daudi Okelo and Jildo Irwa. Martyrs of Evangelization.' Gulu Archdiocese.

Gupta, Akhil, and Aradhana Sharma. 2006. 'Introduction: Rethinking Theories of the State in an Age of Globalization.' In *The Anthropology of the State: A Reader*, edited by Aradhana Sharma and Akhil Gupta, 1–42. Malden: Blackwell.

Gusman, Alessandro. 2009. 'HIV/AIDS, Pentecostal Churches, and the "Joseph Generation" in Uganda.' *Africa Today* 56 (1): 67–86.

Gusman, Alessandro. 2017. 'Moral Models, Self-Control and the Production of the Moral Citizen in the Ugandan Pentecostal Movement.' In *Christian Citizens and the Moral Regeneration of the African State*, edited by Barbara Bompani & Christine Valois, 177–90. New York: Routledge.

Hage, Ghassan. 2003. *Against Paranoid Nationalism: Searching for Hope in a Shrinking Society*. New South Wales: Pluto Press Australia.

Hage, Ghassan. 2009. 'Waiting Out the Crisis: On Stuckedness and Governmentality.' In *Waiting*, edited by Ghassan Hage, 97–106. Carlton, Victoria: Melbourne University Press.

Häkkinen, Antti, and Mikko Salasuo. 2015. *Salattu, Hävetty, Vaiettu: Miten Tutkia Piilossa Olevia Ilmiöitä*. Julkaisuja/Nuorisotutkimusverkosto & Nuorisotutkimusseura. Tampere: Vastapaino.

Hamber, Brandon, and Richard A. Wilson. 2002. 'Symbolic Closure through Memory, Reparation and Revenge in Post-Conflict Societies.' *Journal of Human Rights* 1 (1): 35–53.

Hankela, Elina. 2013. 'Challenging Ubuntu: Open Doors and Exclusionary Boundaries at the Central Methodist Mission in Johannesburg.' PhD thesis, Helsinki: University of Helsinki.

Hankela, Elina. 2014. *Ubuntu, Migration and Ministry: Being Human in a Johannesburg Church*. Leiden: Brill.

Hansen, Holger Bernt. 1984. *Mission, Church and State in a Colonial Setting: Uganda 1890–1925*. London: Heinemann.

Harding, Susan Friend. 2000. *The Book of Jerry Falwell: Fundamentalist Language and Politics*. Princeton: Princeton University Press.

Harlacher, Thomas, Francis Xavier Okot, Caroline Aloyo Obonyo, Mychelle Balthazard, and Ronald R. Atkinson. 2006. *Traditional Ways of Coping in Acholi*. Gulu, Uganda: Caritas Gulu Archdiocese.

Harnisch, Helle. 2016. 'The First Time You Kill Someone Your Mind Will Not Be Settled: Forced Resilience, Experiences of War and Difficult Demobilizations in Acholiland.' PhD thesis, Denmark: University of Copenhagen.

Harris, Colette. 2017. 'Some Gender Implications of the "Civilising Mission" of the Anglican Church for the Acholi Peoples of Northern Uganda.' *Religions* 8 (11): 245. doi:10.3390/rel8110245.

Harrison, Professor Graham. 2010. *Neoliberal Africa: The Impact of Global Social Engineering*. London and New York: Zed Books.

Hauser, Ellen. 1999. 'Ugandan Relations with Western Donors in the 1990s: What Impact on Democratisation?' *Journal of Modern African Studies* 37 (4): 621.

Haws, Charles G. 2009. 'Suffering, Hope and Forgiveness: The Ubuntu Theology of Desmond Tutu.' *Scottish Journal of Theology* 62 (04): 477–89. doi:10.1017/S0036930609990123.

Hayden, Robert M. 2007. 'Moral Vision and Impaired Insight: The Imagining of Other Peoples' Communities in Bosnia.' *Current Anthropology* 48 (1): 105–31.

Haynes, Naomi. 2017. *Moving by the Spirit: Pentecostal Social Life on the Zambian Copperbelt*. The Anthropology of Christianity. Oakland: California University Press.

Haynes, Naomi. 2018. 'Why Can't a Pastor be President of a "Christian Nation"? Pentecostal Politics as Religious Mediation.' *PoLAR: Political and Legal Anthropology Review*. 41 (1): 50–74.

Haynes, Naomi. 2021. 'Concretizing the Christian Nation: Negotiation Zambia's National House of Prayer.' *Comparative Studies of South Asia, Africa and the Middle East* 41 (2): 166–74.

Henare, Amiria J. M, Martin Holbraad, and Sari Wastell. 2006. *Thinking through Things: Theorising Artefacts Ethnographically*. London: Routledge.

Henry, Marsha. 2013. 'Ten Reasons Not to Write Your Master's Dissertation on Sexual Violence in War.' *Disorder of Things*, 4 June 2013. https://thedisorderofthings.com/2013/06/04/ten-reasons-not-to-write-your-masters-dissertation-on-sexual-violence-in-war/.

Higgins, Kate. 2007. *Regional Inequality and Primary Education in Northern Uganda*. Policy Brief No. 2. Prepared for the World Development Report 2009. United Kingdom: Overseas Development Institute.

Hinfelaar, Hugo. 1991. 'Women's Revolt: The Lumpa Church of Lenshina Mulenga in the 1950s.' *Journal of Religion in Africa* 21 (2): 99–129.

Hodgson, Dorothy L. 2005. *The Church of Women: Gendered Encounters between Maasai and Missionaries*. Bloomington: Indiana University Press.

Hoekema, David A. 2019a. 'Risking Peace. How Religious Leaders Ended Uganda's Civil War.' *Commonweal Magazine*.

Hoekema, David A. 2019b. *We Are the Voice of the Grass: Interfaith Peace Activism in Northern Uganda*. Oxford and New York: Oxford University Press.

Hoel, Nina. 2013. 'Embodying the Field: A Researcher's Reflections on Power Dynamics, Positionality and the Nature of Research Relationships.' *Fieldwork in Religion* 8 (1): 27–49.

The Holy See. 2002. 'Biography: Daudi Okelo and Jildo Irwa (ca. 1902–1918).' *Daily Bulletin of the Holy See Press Office*. http://www.vatican.va/news_services/liturgy/saints/ns_lit_doc_20021020_okelo-irwa_en.html. Accessed 13 September 2018.

Hopwood, Julian. 2021. 'An Inherited Animus to Communal Land: The Mechanisms of Coloniality in Land Reform Agendas in Acholiland, Northern Uganda.' *Critical African Studies*: 1–17. (Published online pre-print)

Hopwood, Julian, and Ronald R. Atkinson. 2013. *Land Conflict Monitoring and Mapping Tool for the Acholi Sub-Region. Final Report – March 2014*. United Nations Peacebuilding Programme in Uganda and Human Rights Focus. http://www.lcmt.org/pdf/final_report.pdf.

Howell, Caroline. 2017. '"In this time of ferment what is the function of the Church?" The Anglican Church and the national politics in late colonial Uganda.' In *Ugandan Churches and the Political Centre*. Vol. 1. Ngoma Series, edited by Paddy Musana, Angus Crichton, and Caroline Howell, 57–75. Cambridge: Ngoma Ecumenical Publishing Consortium, Cambridge Centre for Christianity Worldwide.

Imbo, Samuel O. 2008. 'Okot p'Bitek's Critique of Western Scholarship on African Religion.' In *A Companion to African Philosophy*, edited by Kwasi Wiredu, 364–73. Hoboken: John Wiley & Sons.

Insole, Christopher J. 2004. 'Against Radical Orthodoxy: The Dangers of Overcoming Political Liberalism.' *Modern Theology* 20 (2): 213–41.

Isiko, Alexander Paul. 2019. 'State Regulation of Religion in Uganda: Fears and Dilemmas of Born-Again Churches.' *Journal of African Studies and Development* 11 (6): 99–117. doi:10.5897/JASD2019.0551.

Jackson, Michael. 2013. *Lifeworlds: Essays in Existential Anthropology*. Chicago: University of Chicago Press.

Jansen, Stef. 2016. 'For a Relational, Historical Ethnography of Hope: Indeterminacy and Determination in the Bosnian and Herzegovinian Meantime.' *History and Anthropology* 27 (4): 447–64. doi:10.1080/02757206.2016.1201481.

Jauhola, Marjaana. 2016. '"Conversations in Silence": Ceramic Installations Shaping the Visual and Political Imagination of Gendered Tsunami and Conflict Reconstruction Landscapes in Aceh.' In *Gendered Wars, Gendered Memories: Feminist Conversations on War, Genocide and Political Violence*, edited by Ayşe Gül Altınay & Andrea Pető 229–50. Milton Park: Routledge.

Jauhola, Marjaana. 2018. 'Visual Ethnographic Encounters and Silence in Post-Conflict City of Banda Aceh, Indonesia.' In *Experiences with Violent Research and Researching Violence*, edited by Althea-Maria Rivas and Brendan Browne, 179–84. Cambridge: Polity Press.

Jensen, Casper Bruun. 2014. 'Experiments in Good Faith and Hopefulness. Toward a Postcritical Social Science.' *Common Knowledge* 20 (2): 337–62. doi:10.1215/0961754X-2422980.

Jones, Ben. 2009. *Beyond the State in Rural Uganda*. Edinburgh: Edinburgh University Press for the International African Institute.

Jones, Ben. 2013. 'The Making of Meaning: Churches, Development Projects and Violence in Eastern Uganda.' *Journal of Religion in Africa* 43 (1): 74–95. doi:10.1163/15700666-12341245.

Jones, Ben. 2014. 'A Critical Disposition: Making Sense of Developments in Eastern Uganda.' Unpublished manuscript.
Jones, Ben, and Karen Lauterbach. 2005. 'Bringing Religion Back in: Religious Institutions and Politics in Africa.' *Journal of Religion in Africa* 35 (2): 239–43. doi:10.1163/1570066054024640.
Jones, Herbert Gresford. 1926. *Uganda in Transformation, 1876–1926*. London: Church Missionary Society.
Jordhus-Lier, David and Einar Braathen. 2013. 'Churches and Peace-Building in Eastern DR Congo and Northern Uganda.' *Forum for Development Studies* 40 (1): 111–27. doi:10.1080/08039410.2012.732109.
Kabwegyere, Tarsis B. 2000. *People's Choice, People's Power: Challenges and Prospects of Democracy in Uganda*. Kampala: Fountain Publishers.
Kallinen, Timo. 2014. 'Christianity, Fetishism, and the Development of Secular Politics in Ghana: A Dumontian Approach.' *Anthropological Theory* 14 (2): 153–68. doi:10.1177/1463499614534112.
Kalu, Ogbu. 2008. *African Pentecostalism: An Introduction*. New York: Oxford University Press.
Kanyike, Fr Lawrence. 2003. 'Uganda: Church and State Have Same Lubimbi.' *AllAfrica. Com*. http://allafrica.com/stories/200306160330.html. Accessed 22 January 2016.
Kapferer, Bruce. 2004. 'Ritual Dynamics and Virtual Practice.' *Social Analysis* 48 (2): 35–54.
Kapoor, Ilan. 2004. 'Hyper-Self-Reflexive Development? Spivak on Representing the Third World "Other."' *Third World Quarterly* 25 (4): 627–47.
Karlström, Mikael. 2003. 'On the Aesthetics and Dialogics of Power in the Postcolony.' *Africa* 73 (1): 57–76.
Karugire, Samwiri Rubaraza. 1980. *A Political History of Uganda*. Nairobi and Exeter, NH: Heinemann.
Karugire, Samwiri Rubaraza. 1996. *Roots of Instability in Uganda*. 2nd edition. Kampala: Fountain Publishers.
Kasfir, Nelson. 1998. '"No-Party Democracy" in Uganda.' *Journal of Democracy* 9 (2): 49–63. doi:10.1353/jod.1998.0029.
Kasozi, Abdu B. K. 1974. 'The Spread of Islam in Uganda, 1844–1945.' PhD thesis, Santa Cruz: University of California Santa Cruz.
Kassimir, Ronald. 1991. 'Complex Martyrs: Symbols of Catholic Church Formation and Political Differentiation in Uganda.' *African Affairs* 90 (360): 357–82.
Kassimir, Ronald. 1998. 'The Social Power of Religious Organisation and Civil Society: The Catholic Church in Uganda.' In *Civil Society and Democracy in Africa: Critical Perspectives*, edited by Nelson Kasfir, 54–83. Oxfordshire, England: Routledge.
Kastfelt, Niels, ed. 2004. *Scriptural Politics: The Bible and the Koran as Political Models in the Middle East and Africa*. Trenton: Hurst & Company.
Katongole, Emmanuel. 2011. *The Sacrifice of Africa: A Political Theology for Africa*. Grand Rapids, MI: William. B. Eerdmans Pub.
Katongole, Emmanuel. 2017. *Born from Lament: The Theology and Politics of Hope in Africa*. Michigan: Eerdmans Publishing.

Katongole, Emmanuel, and Chris Rice. 2008. *Reconciling All Things: A Christian Vision for Justice, Peace and Healing*. Resources for Reconciliation. Westmont: InterVarsity Press.

Kaufman, Michael T. 1977. 'Uganda Says Autopsy Confirms Reports on Archbishop's Death in Auto.' *New York Times*, 3, Manhattan, New York.

Keen, David J. 2008. *Complex Emergencies*. 1st edition. Cambridge and Malden: Polity.

Kellner, Douglas. n.d. 'Ernst Bloch, Utopia and Ideology Critique.' Unpublished manuscript, available at: http://www.gseis.ucla.edu/faculty/kellner/kellner.html.

Kemppainen, Lauri. 2016. 'Väkivallan ja rauhan ontologiat.' PhD thesis, Helsinki: University of Helsinki.

Khisa, Moses. 2020. 'Politicisation and Professionalisation: The Progress and Perils of Civil-Military Transformation in Museveni's Uganda.' *Civil Wars* 22 (2–3): 289–312.

Kidron, Carol A. 2009. 'Toward an Ethnography of Silence.' *Current Anthropology* 50 (1): 5–27.

Kihangire, Rev. D. Cyprianus 1957. 'The Marriage Customs of Lango. A Dissertation in Canon Law. Pdf.' Rome: Pont. Universitas De Propaganda Fide.

Kitching, Rev. A. L 1904. 'III. Letter from Rev. A. L. Kitching to the C.M.S. in 1904, Published as Part of a Collection of Letters under the Title The Commencement of Work in the Nile Province.' *CMS Intelligencer*, November.

Kizza, Dorothy, Birthe Loa Knizek, Eugene Kinyanda, and Heidi Hjelmeland. 2012. 'Men in Despair: A Qualitative Psychological Autopsy Study of Suicide in Northern Uganda.' *Transcultural Psychiatry* 49 (5): 696–717. doi:10.1177/1363461512459490.

Kleist, Nauja, and Stef Jansen. 2016. 'Introduction: Hope Over Time – Crisis, Immobility and Future-Making.' *History and Anthropology* 27 (4): 373–92. doi:10.1080/02757206.2016.1207636.

Kollman, Paul. 2010. 'Classifying African Christianities, Part Two: The Anthropology of Christianity and Generations of African Christians.' *Journal of Religion in Africa* 40 (2): 118–48. doi:10.1163/157006610X498724.

Komakech, Dan Michael. 2015. 'Lukoya Severino Conducts Crusade in Kitgum without Hindrance.' *Acholi Times*, June 29 edition. http://acholitimes.com/2015/06/29/lukoya-severino-conducts-crusade-in-kitgum-without-hindrance/.

Komujuni, Sophie. 2019. 'To Be a Chief and to Remain a Chief: The Production of Customary Authority in Post-Post Conflict Northern Uganda.' PhD thesis, Ghent: Ghent University.

Koselleck, Reinhart. 1989. 'Linguistic Change and the History of Events.' *The Journal of Modern History* 61 (4): 649–66.

Kulick, Don. 2020. 'Engaging Anthropology.' *HAU: Journal of Ethnographic Theory* 10 (2): 630–2. doi:10.1086/709581.

Lagace, Martha. 2018. *Farming the Tarmac: Rootedness and Longing for the World in Post-War Northern Uganda*. Boston, MA: Boston University.

Lambek, Michael. 2010. *Ordinary Ethics: Anthropology, Language, and Action*. New York: Fordham University Press.

Lamwaka, Caroline. 2016. *The Raging Storm. A Reporter's Inside Account of the Northern Uganda War 1986-2005*, edited by Ronald R. Atkinson. Kampala: Fountain Publishers.

Landry, Jean-Michel. 2009. 'Confession, Obedience, and Subjectivity: Michel Foucault's Unpublished Lectures on the Government of the Living.' *Telos* 2009 (146): 111–23. doi:10.3817/0309146111.

Larsen, Timothy. 2014. *The Slain God: Anthropologists and the Christian Faith*. New York: Oxford University Press.

Laruni, Elizabeth. 2015. 'Regional and Ethnic Identities: The Acholi of Northern Uganda, 1950-1968.' *Journal of Eastern African Studies* 9 (2): 212–30. doi:10.1080/17 531055.2015.1031859.

Latour, Bruno. 2005. *Reassembling the Social: An Introduction to Actor-Network-Theory*. Clarendon Lectures in Management Studies. Oxford: Oxford University Press.

Lauterbach, Karen. 2013. 'Making Sense of Religious Experience and the "Problem of Belief" When Doing Fieldwork.' *Swedish Missiological Themes* 101 (3–4): 267–80.

Lauterbach, Karen. 2014. 'Religion and Displacement in Africa: Compassion and Sacrifice in Congolese Churches in Kampala, Uganda.' *Religion and Theology* 21 (3–4): 290–308. doi:10.1163/15743012-02103004.

Lauterbach, Karen. 2017. *Christianity, Wealth, and Spiritual Power in Ghana*. London: Palgrave Macmillan.

Lauterbach, Karen, and Mika Vähäkangas, eds. 2019. *Faith in African Lived Christianity: Bridging Anthropological and Theological Perspectives. Faith in African Lived Christianity*. Leiden: Brill.

Lemons, J. Derrick. 2018. *Theologically Engaged Anthropology*. Oxford: Oxford University Press.

Lemons, J. Derrick. 2019. 'An Introduction to Theologically Engaged Anthropology.' *Ethnos* 86 (3) 1–7. doi:10.1080/00141844.2019.1640760.

Levitas, Ruth. 2013. *Utopia as Method: The Imaginary Reconstitution of Society*. Houndmills and New York: Palgrave Macmillan.

Lewis, Berrisford. 2010. 'Forging an Understanding of Black Humanity through Relationship An *Ubuntu* Perspective.' *Black Theology*. 8 (1): 69–85.

Leys, Colin. 1967. *Politicians and Policies: An Essay on Politics in Acholi, Uganda, 1962-65*. Nairobi, Kenya: East African Publishing House.

Lindhardt, Martin. 2012. 'Who Bewitched the Pastor and Why Did He Survive the Witchcraft Attack? Micro-Politics and the Creativity of Indeterminacy in Tanzanian Discourses on Witchcraft.' *Canadian Journal of African Studies/Revue Canadienne Des Études Africaines* 46 (2): 215–32. doi:10.1080/00083968.2012.702085.

Lloyd, A. B. 1904. 'I. Letter from Mr. Lloyd to the C.M.S. after His First Visit to Acholiland in August 1903, Published under the Title The Commencement of Work in the Nile Province.' *CMS Intelligencer*, November.

Lofchie, Michael F. 1972. 'The Uganda Coup-Class Action by the Military.' *The Journal of Modern African Studies* 10 (1): 19–35.

Longman, Timothy. 2001. 'Church Politics and the Genocide in Rwanda.' *Journal of Religion in Africa* 31 (2): 163–86. doi:10.1163/157006601X00112.

Longman, Timothy. 2009. *Christianity and Genocide in Rwanda*. African Studies. Cambridge: Cambridge University Press. doi:10.1017/CBO9780511642043.

Luhrmann, T. M. 2018. 'The Real Ontological Challenge.' *HAU: Journal of Ethnographic Theory* 8 (1–2): 79–82. doi:10.1086/698408.

Lumumba, Patrick. 2014. 'Leadership and Advocacy in Peace Building: A Case Study of the Acholi Religious Leaders Peace Initiative in Northern Uganda.' Master's thesis, Gulu: University of Gulu.

Lundy, Patricia and Mark McGovern. 2006. The ethics of silence: Action research, community 'truth-telling' and post-conflict transition in the North of Ireland. *Action Research* 4 (1), 49–64.

Macdonald, Anna, and Holly Porter. 2016. 'The Trial of Thomas Kwoyelo: Opportunity or Spectre? Reflections from the Ground on the First LRA Prosecution.' *Africa* 86 (4): 698–722. doi:10.1017/S000197201600053X.

Maček, Ivana. 2014a. 'Introduction. Engaging Violence. Trauma, Self-Reflection and Knowledge.' In *Engaging Violence: Trauma, Memory and Representation*, edited by Ivana Maček, 1–24. Cultural Dynamics of Social Representation. London and New York: Routledge.

Maček, Ivana, ed. 2014b. 'Engaging Violence: Trauma, Memory and Representation.' London and New York: Routledge.

Madison, D. Soyini, and Judith Hamera. 2006. 'Performance Studies at the Intersections.' In *The SAGE Handbook of Performance Studies*, edited by D. Soyini Madison, and Judith Hamera, xi–xxv. Thousand Oaks, CA: SAGE Publications.

Magesa, Laurenti. 2002. *African Religion: The Moral Traditions of Abundant Life*. Nairobi, Kenya: Paulines Publications Africa.

Mahmood, Saba. 2011. *Politics of Piety: The Islamic Revival and the Feminist Subject*. Princeton, NJ: Princeton University Press.

Malkki, Liisa H. 2007. 'Tradition and Improvisation in Ethnographic Field Research.' In *Improvising Theory: Process and Temporality in Ethnographic Fieldwork*, edited by Allaine Cerwonka and Liisa H. Malkki, 162–88. Chicago: University of Chicago Press.

Mamdani, Mahmood. 1996. *Citizen and Subject: Contemporary Africa and the Legacy of Late Colonialism*. Fountain Edition 2004. Kampala: Fountain Publishers.

Manglos, Nicolette D., and Alexander A. Weinreb. 2013. 'Religion and Interest in Politics in Sub-Saharan Africa.' *Social Forces* 92 (1): 195–219.

Marriage, Zoe. 2006. *Not Breaking the Rules, Not Playing the Game: International Assistance to Countries at War*. London: Hurst.

Marshall, Ruth. 2009. *Political Spiritualities: The Pentecostal Revolution in Nigeria*. Chicago: University of Chicago Press.

Marshall, Ruth. 2014. 'Christianity, Anthropology, Politics.' *Current Anthropology* 55 (S10): S344–S356.

Martiniello, Giuliano. 2015. 'Social Struggles in Uganda's Acholiland: Understanding Responses and Resistance to Amuru Sugar Works.' *The Journal of Peasant Studies* 42 (3–4): 653–69. doi:10.1080/03066150.2015.1032269.

Martiniello, Giuliano. 2019. 'Social Conflict and Agrarian Change in Uganda's Countryside.' *Journal of Agrarian Change* 9 (3): 550–68.

Mattingly, Cheryl. 2010. *The Paradox of Hope: Journeys through a Clinical Borderland*. Berkeley: University of California Press.

Maxwell, David. 2000. '"Catch the Cockerel before Dawn": Pentecostalism and Politics in Post-Colonial Zimbabwe.' *Africa* 70 (2): 249.

Mazrui, Ali A. 1977. 'Religious Strangers in Uganda: From Emin Pasha to Amin Dada.' *African Affairs* 76 (302): 21–38.

Mbembe, Achille. 1992. 'The Banality of Power and the Aesthetics of Vulgarity in the Postcolony.' *Public Culture* 4 (2): 1.

Mbembe, Achille. 2006. 'On the Postcolony: A Brief Response to Critics.' *African Identities* 4 (2): 143–78. doi:10.1080/14725840600761096.

Mbiti, John S. 1990. *African Religions & Philosophy*. Oxford: Heinemann.

McClendon, Gwyneth H., and Rachel Beatty Riedl 2019. *From Pews to Politics: Religious Sermons and Political Participation in Africa*, 39–59. Cambridge Studies in Comparative Politics. Cambridge: Cambridge University Press. doi:10.1017/9781108761208.003.

Médecins Sans Frontières. 2004. *Immense Suffering in Northern Uganda: Urgent Action Needed*. 8 November 2008. https://www.doctorswithoutborders.org/what-we-do/news-stories/news/immense-sufferingnorthern-uganda-urgent-action-needed. Accessed 16 September 2019.

Meier, Barbara. 2013. '"Death Does Not Rot": Transitional Justice and Local "Truths" in the Aftermath of the War in Northern Uganda.' *Africa Spectrum* 48 (2): 25–50.

Meinert, Lotte. 2009. *Hopes in Friction: Schooling, Health and Everyday Life in Uganda*. Charlotte: Information Age Publishing.

Meinert, Lotte. 2015. 'Tricky Trust: Distrust as a Starting Point and Trust as a Social Achievement in Uganda.' In *Anthropology and Philosophy: Dialogues on Trust and Hope*, edited by Anne Line Dalsgård, Sune Liisberg, and Esther Oluffa Pedersen, 113–36. New York: Berghahn Books.

Meinert, Lotte. 2020. 'Haunted Families after the War in Uganda: Doubt as Polyvalent Critique.' *Ethnos* 85 (4): 595–611. doi:10.1080/00141844.2019.1629981.

Meinert, Lotte, and Susan Reynolds Whyte. 2017. '"These Things Continue": Violence as Contamination in Everyday Life after War in Northern Uganda.' *Ethos* 45 (2): 271–86. doi:10.1111/etho.12161.

Meretoja, Hanna. 2014. *The Narrative Turn in Fiction and Theory: The Crisis and Return of Storytelling from Robbe-Grillet to Tournier*. Houndmills, Basingstoke: Palgrave Macmillan.

Mergelsberg, Ben. 2012. 'The Displaced Family: Moral Imaginations and Social Control in Pabbo, Northern Uganda.' *Journal of Eastern African Studies* 6 (1): 64–80. doi:10.1 080/17531055.2012.664704.

Merz, Johannes, and Sharon Merz. 2017. 'Occupying the Ontological Penumbra: Towards a Postsecular and Theologically Minded Anthropology.' *Religions* 8 (5): 80. doi:10.3390/rel8050080.

Meyer, Birgit. 1994. 'Beyond Syncretism: Translation and Diabolization in the Appropriation of Protestantism in Africa.' In *Syncretism/Anti-Syncretism: The Politics of Religious Synthesis*, edited by Charles Stewart and Rosalind Shaw, 43–64. London: Routledge.

Meyer, Birgit. 1998. '"Make a Complete Break with the Past." Memory and Post-Colonial Modernity in Ghanaian Pentecostalist Discourse.' *Journal of Religion in Africa* 28 (3): 316–49. doi:10.2307/1581573.

Meyer, Birgit. 2011. 'Going and Making Public. Some Reflections on Pentecostalism as Public Religion in Ghana.' In *Christianity and Public Culture in Africa*, edited by Harri Englund, 149–66. Athens: Ohio University Press.

Milbank, John. 1990. *Theology and Social Theory: Beyond Secular Reason*. 2nd edition 2006. Oxford: Blackwell.

Miyazaki, Hirokazu. 2006. *The Method of Hope: Anthropology, Philosophy, and Fijian Knowledge*. 1st edition. Stanford: Stanford University Press.

Moltmann, Jürgen. 2002. *Theology of Hope: On the Ground and the Implications for a Christian Eschatology*. SCM Classics. London: SCM.

Moore, Henrietta L. 2004. 'Global Anxieties: Concept-Metaphors and Pre-Theoretical Commitments in Anthropology.' *Anthropological Theory* 4 (1): 71–88.

More, Thomas. [1516] 2001. *Utopia*. Raleigh: Alex Catalogue.

Moylan, Tom. 2014. *Demand the Impossible: Science Fiction and the Utopian Imagination*. 1st edition. Oxford and New York: Peter Lang AG, Internationaler Verlag der Wissenschaften.

Moylan, Tom, and Raffaella Baccolini. 2007. *Utopia Method Vision: The Use Value of Social Dreaming*. Pieterlen and Bern, Switzerland: Peter Lang.

Mugarura, Augustine, Jino Mwaka, and Celestine Lanek. 1998. *A History of Priestly Training in Northern Uganda*. Gulu, Uganda: Alokolum National Major Seminary.

Musana, Paddy, Angus Crichton, and Caroline Howell, eds. 2017. *Ugandan Churches and the Political Centre*. Vol. 1. Ngoma Series. Cambridge: Ngoma Ecumenical Publishing Consortium, Cambridge Centre for Christianity Worldwide.

Museveni, Yoweni Kaguta. 1997. *Sowing the Mustard Seed*. 1st edition. London: Macmillan Education.

Musisi, Nakanyike. 2002. 'The Politics of Perception or Perception as Politics? Colonial and Missionary Representations of Baganda Women, 1900–1945.' In *Women in African Colonial Histories: An Introduction*, edited by Jean Allman, Susan Geiger, and Nakanyike Musisi, 95–115. Bloomington: Indiana University Press.

Mutibwa, Phares. 1996. *Uganda since Independence. A Story of Unfulfilled Hopes*. London: Hurst Publishers. https://www.hurstpublishers.com/book/uganda-since-independence/.

Mwambari, David. 2019. 'Local Positionality in the Production of Knowledge in Northern Uganda.' *International Journal of Qualitative Methods* 18 (January): 160940691986484. doi:10.1177/1609406919864845.

Mwenda, Andrew M., and Roger Tangri. 2005. 'Patronage Politics, Donor Reforms, and Regime Consolidation in Uganda.' *African Affairs* 104 (416): 449–67. doi:10.1093/afraf/adi030.

Mwenda, Andrew M., and Roger Tangri. 2013. *The Politics of Elite Corruption in Africa: Uganda in Comparative African Perspective*. Routledge Studies on African Politics and International Relations. New York: Routledge.

Nibbe, Ayesha. 2010. *The Effects of a Narrative: Humanitarian Aid and Action in the Northern Uganda Conflict*. PhD dissertation. University of California, Davis.

Nigusie, Alemu Asfaw, and Mohammed Seid Ali. 2020. 'Africa in the Global Economy: Between Integration and Marginalization?' *Bandung* 7 (1): 24–51. doi:10.1163/21983534-00701003.

Niringiye, David Zac. 2016. *The Church in the World: A Historical-Ecclesiological Study of the Church of Uganda with Particular Reference to Post-Independence Uganda, 1962–1992*. Cumbria: Langham Monographs.

Niringiye, David Zac. 2017. 'Being Church in Turbulent Uganda 1980–92: National Identity and the Confluence of Religion and Politics.' In *Ugandan Churches and the Political Centre*, edited by Paddy Musana, Angus Crichton, and Caroline Howell, 119–37. Ngoma Series. Cambridge: Ngoma Ecumenical Publishing Consortium, Cambridge Centre for Christianity Worldwide.

Nkabala, Helen Nambalirwa. 2021. *Kony as Moses. Old Testament Texts and Motifs in the Early Years of the Lord's Resistance Army, Uganda*. Bible and Theology in Africa. Lausanne: Peter Lang Inc., International Academic Publishers.

Nsamba, Morris Adam. 2013. 'Decentralization and Territorial Politics: The Dilemma of Constructing and Managing Identities in Uganda.' *Critical African Studies* 5 (1): 48–60. doi:10.1080/21681392.2013.774835.

Obol, Robert. 2012. *The Life and Lessons from a Warzone. A Memoir of Dr. Robert Nyeko Obol*. Milton Keynes, UK: Lulu self-publishing.

O'Byrne, Ryan. 2015. *Deities, Demons, and Outsiders: The Cosmological Dimensions of (In)Security and (In)Justice in Pajok, South Sudan*. JSRP Paper 21. London: Justice and Security Research Programme, London School of Economics.

O'Byrne, Ryan. 2016. 'Becoming Christian: Personhood and Moral Cosmology in Acholi South Sudan.' PhD thesis, Anthropology, London: University College London.

O'Neill, Kevin Lewis. 2015. *City of God: Christian Citizenship in Postwar Guatemala*. Berkeley: University of California Press.

The *Observer*. 2010. 'What Museveni Said in Bunyoro,' 21 June. http://www.observer.ug/component/content/article?id=8948:what-museveni-said-in-bunyoro. Accessed 22 January 2016.

Ochola, Robert Lukwiya. 2008. 'The Acholi Religious Leaders' Peace Initiative in the Battlefield of Northern Uganda. An Example of an Integral, Inculturated and

Ecumenical Approach to Pastoral Work in a War Situation.' Master's thesis, Leopold-Franzens-Universität Innsbruck.

Ocitti, J. P. 1966. 'Kitgum: An Urban Study.' *East African Geographical Review* 4: 37–48.

Ocungi, Julius. 2020. 'Serving in the Opposition Affected My Service Delivery – Anywar:' *Uganda Radionetwork*. https://ugandaradionetwork.net/story/-serving-in-the-opposition-affected-my-service-delivery-betty-anywar. Accessed 21 September 2020.

Odoi-Tanga, Fredrick. 2009. 'Politics, Ethnicity and Conflict in Post Independent Acholiland, Uganda 1962–2006.' PhD thesis, Pretoria: University of Pretoria.

Odonga, Alexander. 2005. *Lwo-English Dictionary*. Kampala: Fountain Publishers.

Odwong, Philip. 2019. *Wang Loyo Ajwaka. Kwo Pa Ladit Odwong Philip. Kwo i Lobo Acoli 1941–2019*. [The life of sir Philip Odwong. Life in Acholi land 1941–2019]. Unpublished autobiography. Kitgum, Uganda.

Office of the Prime Minister. 2015. 'President Museveni Contributes Another 400 Million to Renovate Namugongo Martyr's Shrine.' *News Archive*, 20 August 2015. http://opm.go.ug/news-archive/president-museveni-contributes-another-400-million-to-renovate-namugongo-martyrs-shrine.html.

Ogora, Lino Owor. 2013. 'The Contested Fruits of Research in War-Torn Countries: My Insider Experience in Northern Uganda.' In *Emotional and Ethical Challenges for Field Research in Africa: The Story behind the Findings*, edited by Susan Thomson, An Ansoms, and Jude Murison, 27–41. New York: Palgrave Macmillan.

Oinas, Elina. 2001. *Making Sense of the Teenage Body. Sociological Perspectives on Girls, Changing Bodies and Knowledge*. Akademisk Avhandling. Turku: Åbo Akademi University Press.

O'Kadameri, Billie. 2002. 'LRA and Government Negotiations 1993–1994.' In *Protracted Conflict, Elusive Peace: Initiatives to End the Violence in Northern Uganda*, edited by Lucima Okello, 34–41. London: Conciliation Resources and Kacoke Madit.

Okello, Lucima. 2002. *Protracted Conflict, Elusive Peace. Initiatives to end the Violence in Northern Uganda*. Conciliation Resources and Kacoke Madit, London.

Okuku, Juma Anthony. 2003. 'Civil Society and the Democratisation Processes in Kenya and Uganda: A Comparative Analysis of the Contribution of the Church and NGOs.' *Politikon: South African Journal of Political Studies* 30 (1): 51.

Olsson, Hans. 2016. 'Jesus for Zanzibar. Narratives of Pentecostal Belongin, Islam, and Nation.' PhD thesis, Lund: Lund University.

Omara-Otunnu, A. 1987. *Politics and the Military in Uganda, 1890–1985*. New York: St Martin's Press.

Omenyo, Cephas N. 2003. 'Charismatization of the Mainline Churches in Ghana.' In *Charismatic Renewal in Africa. A Challenge for African Christianity*, edited by Mika Vähäkangas and Andrew A. Kyomo, 5–26. Nairobi: Acton Publishers.

Onono-Ongweng, Nelson, Peter Holmes, and Patrick Lumumba. 2004. *Celebrating 100 Years of Christianity in Acoli Land*. Gulu: Church of Uganda.

Ortner, Sherry. 2016. 'Dark Anthropology and Its Others. Theory since the Eighties.' *Hau: Journal of Ethnographic Theory* 6 (1): 47–73.

Otunnu, Ogenga. 2002. 'Causes and Consequences of the War in Acholiland.' In *Protracted Conflict, Elusive Peace: Initiatives to End the Violence in Northern Uganda*, edited by O. Lucima. London: Conciliation Resources and Kacoke Madit.

Otunnu, Ogenga. 2016. *Crisis of Legitimacy and Political Violence in Uganda, 1890–1979*. New York: Palgrave Macmillan.

Otunnu, Olara. 2020. *Archbishop Janani Luwum. The Life and Witness of a 20th Century Martyr*. Kampala: Fountain Publishers.

Otunnu, Olara A. 2006. *Northern Uganda: Profile of a Genocide*. Available at: https://nointervention.com/archive/Africa/Uganda/000290.html. Accessed 1 September 2021.

Oxford Dictionary of English 2020. *Confusion*. Oxford: Oxford University Press. Available at: https://www-sanakirja-fi.ezproxy.jyu.fi/ Accessed 10 June 2021

p'Bitek, Okot. 1971a. *Religion of the Central Luo*. Nairobi: East African Literature Bureau.

p'Bitek, Okot. 1971b. *African Religions in Western Scholarship*. Kampala: East African Literature Bureau.

p'Bitek, Okot. 1972. *Song of Lawino and Song of Ocol*. Nairobi: East African Publishing House.

Page, Tiffany. 2017. 'Vulnerable Writing as a Feminist Methodological Practice.' *Feminist Review* 115 (1): 13–29. doi:10.1057/s41305-017-0028-0.

Paine, Clare. 2014 'Ker Kwaro Acholi: A Re-invention of Traditional Authority in Northern.' MPhil thesis, Aberystwyth: Aberystwyth University.

Peel, J. D. Y. 1977. 'Conversion and Tradition in Two African Societies: Ijebu and Buganda.' *Past and Present* 77 (1): 108–141.

Pellegrini, Vincent. 1949. *Lok Pa Acoli Macon*, translated by Ketty Anyeko. 2006th edition. Gulu, Uganda: Gulu Catholic Church.

Perrot, Sandrine, Sabiti Makara, and Jérôme Lafargue, eds. 2014. *Elections in a Hybrid Regime. Revisiting the 2011 Ugandan Polls*. Kampala: Fountain Publishers.

Phiri, Isaac. 2001. *Proclaiming Political Pluralism: Churches and Political Transitions in Africa*. Westport: Greenwood Publishing Group.

Pirouet, M. Louise. 1978. *Black Evangelists: Spread of Christianity in Uganda, 1891–1914*. London: Rex Collings.

Pirouet, M. Louise. 1980. 'Religion in Uganda under Amin.' *Journal of Religion in Africa* 11 (1): 13–29. doi:10.2307/1580791.

Porter, Holly. 2013. 'After Rape. Justice and Social Harmony in Northern Uganda.' PhD thesis, London: London School of Economics and Political Science.

Porter, Holly. 2016. *After Rape: Violence, Justice and Social Harmony in Uganda*. Cambridge: Cambridge University Press.

Postlethwaite, John Rutherfoord Parkin. 1947. *I Look Back*. Welwyn: T. V. Boardman and Company Limited.

Premawardhana, Devaka. 2020a. 'Reconversion and Retrieval: Nonlinear Change in African Catholic Practice.' *Religions* 11 (353).

Premawardhana, Devaka. 2020b. 'In Praise of Ambiguity: Everyday Christianity through the Lens of Existential Anthropology.' *Journal of World Christianity* 10 (1): 39–43.

Prevost, Elizabeth E. 2010. *The Communion of Women: Missions and Gender in Colonial Africa and the British Metropole*. Oxford and New York: Oxford University Press.

Prunier, Gérard. 1996. *The Rwanda Crisis: History of a Genocide*. New York: Columbia University Press.

Prunier, Gérard. 2004. 'Rebel Movements and Proxy Warfare: Uganda, Sudan and the Congo (1986–99).' *African Affairs* 103 (412): 359–83.

Prunier, Gérard. 2008. *Africa's World War: Congo, the Rwandan Genocide, and the Making of a Continental Catastrophe*. Oxford, England: Oxford University Press.

Rao, Rahul. 2015. 'Re-Membering Mwanga: Same-Sex Intimacy, Memory and Belonging in Postcolonial Uganda.' *Journal of Eastern African Studies* 9 (1): 1–19. doi:10.1080/17531055.2014.970600.

Ratele, Kopano. 2016. *Liberating Masculinities*. Cape Town: HSRC press.

Reuss, Anna, and Kristof Titeca. 2017. 'When Revolutionaries Grow Old: The Museveni Babies and the Slow Death of the Liberation.' *Third World Quarterly* 38 (10): 2347–66. doi:10.1080/01436597.2017.1350101.

Rice, Xan. 2011. 'Pakalast: It Means Yoweri Museveni Wants to Be Uganda's President for Life.' *The Guardian*, 16 February. http://www.theguardian.com/world/2011/feb/16/uganda-election-yoweri-museveni-kizza-besigye. Accessed 2 June 2014.

Robbins, Joel. 2003. 'What Is a Christian? Notes toward an Anthropology of Christianity.' *Religion* 33 (3): 191–9. doi:10.1016/S0048-721X(03)00060-5.

Robbins, Joel. 2004. *Becoming Sinners. Christianity and Moral Torment in a Papua New Guinea Society*. Berkeley: University of California Press.

Robbins, Joel. 2005. 'Introduction: Humiliation and Transformation: Marshall Sahlins and the Study of Cultural Change in Melanesia.' In *The Making of Global and Local Modernities in Melanesia: Humiliation, Transformation and the Nature of Cultural Change*, edited by Joel Robbins & Holly Wardlow, 3–22. Aldershot: Ashgate Publishing Ltd.

Robbins, Joel. 2006. 'Anthropology and Theology: An Awkward Relationship?' *Anthropological Quarterly* 79 (2): 285–94.

Robbins, Joel. 2007. 'Continuity Thinking and the Problem of Christian Culture: Belief, Time, and the Anthropology of Christianity.' *Current Anthropology* 48 (1): 5–38. doi:10.1086/508690.

Robbins, Joel. 2013. 'Beyond the Suffering Subject: Toward an Anthropology of the Good.' *Journal of the Royal Anthropological Institute* 19 (3): 447–62. doi:10.1111/1467-9655.12044.

Robbins, Joel, and Holly Wardlow. 2005. *The Making of Global and Local Modernities in Melanesia: Humiliation, Transformation and the Nature of Cultural Change*. Aldershot: Ashgate Publishing Ltd.

Rodríguez, Carlos. 2002. 'The Role of the Religious Leaders.' In *Protracted Conflict, Elusive Peace. Initiatives to End the Violence in Northern Uganda*, edited by Lucima Okello, 34–41. London: Conciliation Resources and Kacoke Madit. https://rc-services-assets.s3.eu-west-1.amazonaws.com/s3fs-public/Protracted_conflict_elusive_peace_Initiatives_to_end_the_violence_in_northern_Uganda_Accord_Issue_11.pdf.

Ruether, Rosemary Radford, and Marion Grau. 2006. *Interpreting the Postmodern: Responses to 'Radical Orthodoxy.'* New York: A&C Black.

Rutanga, Murindwa. 1991. 'Nyabingi Movement: People's Anti-Colonial Struggles in Kigezi 1910–1930.' *CBR Working Paper*, no. 18: 166.

Sabar, Galia. 2001. *Church, State and Society in Kenya: From Mediation to Opposition*. 1st edition. London: Routledge.

Scharen, Christian, and Aana Marie Vigen, eds. 2011. *Ethnography as Christian Theology and Ethics*. New York: Continuum.

Schomerus, Mareike. 2012a. '"They Forget What They Came for": Uganda's Army in Sudan.' *Journal of Eastern African Studies* 6 (1): 124–53. doi:10.1080/17531055.2012.664707.

Schomerus, Mareike. 2012b. 'Even Eating You Can Bite Your Tongue: Dynamics and Challenges of the Juba Peace Talks with the Lord's Resistance Army.' PhD thesis, The London School of Economics and Political Science (LSE). http://etheses.lse.ac.uk/734/.

Schomerus, Mareike. 2021. *The Lord's Resistance Army. Violence and Peace-Making in Africa*. Cambridge: Cambridge University Press.

Schwartz, Nancy. 2005. 'Dreaming in Color: Anti-Essentialism in Legio Maria Dream Narratives.' *Journal of Religion in Africa*. 35 (2): 159–96. doi:10.1163/1570066054024631.

Schulz, Philipp. 2018. 'The "Ethical Loneliness" of Male Sexual Violence Survivors in Northern Uganda: Gendered Reflections on Silencing.' *International Feminist Journal of Politics* 20 (4): 583–601. doi:10.1080/14616742.2018.1489732.

Schulz, Philipp. 2020. *Male Survivors of Wartime Sexual Violence. Perspectives from Northern Uganda*. Oakland: University of California Press

Shaw, Timothy M., and Pamela K. Mbabazi. 2007. 'Two Ugandas and a "Liberal Peace"? Lessons from Uganda about Conflict and Development at the Start of a New Century.' *Global Society* 21 (4): 567–78. doi:10.1080/13600820701562801.

Shepherd, Arthur P. 1929. *Tucker of Uganda, by Arthur P. Shepherd (1929)*. London, England: London Student Christian Movement.

Sheriff, Robin E. 1999. 'The Theft of Carnaval: National Spectacle and Racial Politics in Rio de Janeiro.' *Cultural Anthropology* 14 (1): 3–28. doi:10.1525/can.1999.14.1.3.

Shipton, Parker. 2009. *Mortgaging the Ancestors: Ideologies of Attachment in Africa*. New Haven: Yale University Press.

Sjögren, Anders. 2013. *Between Militarism and Technocratic Governance. State Formation in Contemporary Uganda*. Kampala: Fountain Publishers.

Sjögren, Anders. 2014. 'Scrambling for the Promised Land: Land Acquisitions and the Politics of Representation in Post-War Acholi, Northern Uganda.' *African Identities* 12 (1): 62–75. doi:10.1080/14725843.2013.868671.

Smith, James Howard., Rosalind I. J. Hackett, and R. Scott Appleby. 2012. *Displacing the State: Religion and Conflict in Neoliberal Africa*. Kroc Institute Series on Religion, Conflict, and Peace Building. Notre Dame: University of Notre Dame Press.

Soi, Isabella. 2016. 'The Muslim Minority in Uganda: The Historical Quest for Unity and Inclusion.' *Africana: Rivista di Studi Extraeuropei 2016*, 167–80.

Soto, Carlos Rodríguez. 2009. *Tall Grass. Stories of Suffering and Peace in Northern Uganda*. Kampala: Fountain Publishers.

Ssekika, Edward. 2010. 'Museveni to Mengo: I'll Cut Your Head Off.' *The Observer*, 14 June. http://www.observer.ug/component/content/article?id=8856:museveni-to-mengo-ill-cut-off-your-head. Accessed 22 January 2016.

Sykes, Peter, and John Krish. 1979. *The Jesus Film (1979) – IMDb*. Burbank: Inspiration Films, Warner Bros.

Takyi, Baffour K., Chris Opoku-Agyeman, and Agnes Kutin-Mensah. 2010. 'Religion and the Public Sphere: Religious Involvement and Voting Patterns in Ghana's 2004 Elections.' *Africa Today* 56 (4): 62–86.

Tamale, Sylvia. 1999. *When Hens Begin to Crow: Gender and Parliamentary Politics in Uganda*. Boulder: Westview.

Tankink, Marian. 2007. '"The Moment I Became Born-Again the Pain Disappeared": The Healing of Devastating War Memories in Born-Again Churches in Mbarara District, Southwest Uganda.' *Transcultural Psychiatry* 44 (2): 203–31.

Tapscott, Rebecca. 2017. 'The Government Has Long Hands. Institutionalized Arbitrariness and Local Security Initiatives in Gulu, Northern Uganda.' *Development & Change* 48 (2): 263–85.

Tapscott, Rebecca. 2021. *Arbitrary States. Social Control and Modern Authoritarianism in Museveni's Uganda*. Oxford and New York: Oxford University Press.

Taub, Amanda, ed. 2012. *Beyond Kony2012: Atrocity, Awareness, & Activism in the Internet Age*. Victoria, Canada: Leanpub. https://leanpub.com/beyondkony2012. Accessed 6 September 2014.

Taussig, Michael T. 2011. *I Swear I Saw This: Drawings in Fieldwork Notebooks, Namely My Own*. Chicago: University of Chicago Press.

Taylor, Jenny. 2005. 'Taking Spirituality Seriously: Northern Uganda and Britain's "Break the Silence" Campaign.' *Round Table* 94 (382): 559–74.

Thomson, Susan, An Ansoms, and Jude Murison. 2013. *Emotional and Ethical Challenges for Field Research in Africa: The Story behind the Findings*. New York: Palgrave Macmillan.

Thornton, John K. 1998. *The Kongolese Saint Anthony*. Cambridge, UK and New York: Cambridge University Press.

Tiberondwa, Ado K. 1977. *Missionary Teachers as Agents of Colonialism in Uganda. A Study of Their Cativities in Uganda, 1877–1925*. Kampala: Fountain Publishers.

Titeca, Kristof. 2010. 'The Spiritual Order of the LRA.' In *The Lord's Resistance Army. Myth and Reality*, edited by Tim Allen and Koen Vlassenroot, 59–73. London and New York: Zed Books.

Titeca, Kristof. 2013. 'The (LRA) Conflict: Beyond the LRA Lobby & the Hunt for Kony… and towards Civilian Protection.' *African Arguments*. 17 May 2013. https://africanarguments.org/2013/05/17/the-lra-conflict-beyond-the-lra-lobby-the-hunt-for-kony-and-towards-civilian-protection-by-kristof-titeca/. Accessed 11 March 2020.

Titeca, Kristof. 2019. 'Analysis | I Testified at the Trial of One of Joseph Kony's Commanders. Here's What the Court Didn't Understand.' *Washington Post*, January 17 edition, The Monkey Cage. https://www.washingtonpost.com/news/monkey-cage/wp/2019/01/17/i-testified-at-the-icc-trial-of-one-of-joseph-konys-commanders-heres-what-the-law-doesnt-seem-to-understand/.

Titeca, Kristof, and Théophile Costeur. 2015. 'An LRA for Everyone: How Different Actors Frame the Lord's Resistance Army.' *African Affairs* 114 (454): 92–114. doi:10.1093/afraf/adu081.

Titeca, Kristof, and Paul Onyango. 2012. 'The Carrot and the Stick: The Unlevel Playing Field in Uganda's 2011 Elections.' In *L'Afrique Des Grands Lacs: Annuaire 2010–2011*, edited by F. Reyntjens, S. Vandeginste, and M. Verpoorten, 111–30. Paris: Harmattan.

Tripp, Aili Mari. 2000. *Women & Politics in Uganda*. Madison: University of Wisconsin Press.

Tripp, Aili Mari. 2010. *Museveni's Uganda: Paradoxes of Power in a Hybrid Regime*. Boulder: Lynne Rienner Publishers.

Trouillot, Michel-Rolph. 2003. 'Anthropology and the Savage Slot: The Poetics and Politics of Otherness.' In *Global Transformations: Anthropology and the Modern World*, 7–28. New York: Palgrave Macmillan.

Turner, Simon. 2015. '"We Wait for Miracles": Ideas of Hope and Future among Clandestine Burundian Refugees in Nairobi.' In *Ethnographies of Uncertainty in Africa*, edited by Elizabeth Cooper and David Pratten, 173–92. Houndmills, Basingstoke and Hampshire: Palgrave Macmillan.

Twesigye, Emmanuel K. 2010. *Religion, Politics and Cults in East Africa: God's Warriors and Mary's Saints*. Pieterlen and Bern: Peter Lang.

UBOS. 2010. *Uganda Census of Agriculture 2008/2009. Volume 1 – Summary Report*. Uganda Bureau of Statistics. http://www.ubos.org/onlinefiles/uploads/ubos/pdf%20documents/UCASummary.pdf. Accessed 18 April 2016.

UBOS. 2016a. *Census 2014 Report Northern Region*. National Population and Housing Census 2014 Subcounty Report. Kampala: Uganda Bureau of Statistics. http://www.ubos.org/onlinefiles/uploads/ubos/census_2014_regional_reports/Census_2014_Report_Northern_Region.pdf. Accessed 13 June 2016.

UBOS. 2016b. *National Population and Housing Census 2014 – Main Report*. Kampala: Uganda Bureau of Statistics. http://www.ubos.org/onlinefiles/uploads/ubos/

NPHC/2014%20National%20Census%20Main%20Report.pdf. Accessed 8 August 2016.

Uganda Episcopal Conference. 1999. *True Peace Comes from Respect for Human Rights. A Pastoral Letter of the Catholic Bishop of Uganda to All Catholics and People of Goodwill in Uganda*. January 1999. Kampala.

Uganda Episcopal Conference. 2003. *Uganda Catholic Directory 2003*. Kampala.

Uganda Episcopal Conference. 2004. *A Concern for Peace. Easter Pastoral Letter of the Catholic Bishops of Uganda*. Kampala.

Uganda Episcopal Conference. 2009. *Uganda Catholic Directory 2009*. Uganda Episcopal Conference, Kampala.

Ugandan Recordings. 2014. *St. Janani Luwum Choir – Come Together to the Lord* Kitgum, Uganda: Scandal Studios. http://www.ugandanrecordings.com/st-janani-luwum-choir-come-together-to-the-lord/.

UNDP. 2015. *Uganda Human Development Report 2015. Unlocking the Development Potential of Northern Uganda*. Kampala, Uganda: United Nations Development Programme.

University of the Sacred Heart Gulu. 2020. 'University of the Sacred Heart Gulu – Health of Mind, Heart and Body for Integral Development.' https://ush.ac.ug/.

Vähäkangas, Mika. 2008. *Between Ghambageu and Jesus. The Encounter between the Sonjo Traditional Leaders and Missionary Christianity*. Studia Missiologica et Oecumenica Fennica 61. Jyväskylä: Luther-Agricola-Society.

Vähäkangas, Mika, and Karen Lauterbach, eds. 2019. 'Faith in African Lived Christianity – Bridging Anthropological and Theological Perspectives: Introduction.' In *Faith in African Lived Christianity: Bridging Anthropological and Theological Perspectives*, 1–15. Leiden: Brill.

Valois, Catherine. 2014. *Public Rebirth. Pentecostal-charismatic Christianity, Sexuality and Nation Building in the Ugandan Public Sphere*. Phd Dissertation, University of Edinburgh.

van Bemmel, Karin. 2016. 'The Quest for Treatment. The Violated Body of Nodding Syndrome in Northern Uganda.' *Journal of Peace and Security Studies* 2 (2): 63–78.

van Bemmel, Karin, Ilse Derluyn, and Koen Stroeken. 2014. 'Nodding Syndrome or Disease? On the Conceptualization of an Illness-in-the-Making.' *Ethnicity & Health* 19 (1): 100–18. doi:10.1080/13557858.2013.780233.

Van Klinken, Adriaan. 2019. *Kenyan, Christian, Queer: Religion, LGBT Activism, and Arts of Resistance in Africa*. Africana Religions. University Park: Penn State University Press.

Vattimo, Gianni. 1999. *Belief*, translated by Luca D'Isanto and David Webb. Cambridge: Polity Press.

Venkatesan, Soumhya. 2015. 'There Is No Such Thing as the Good: The 2013 Meeting of the Group for Debates in Anthropological Theory.' *Critique of Anthropology* 35 (4): 430–80. doi:10.1177/0308275X15598384.

Verma, Cecilie Lanken. 2013. 'Guns and Tricks. State Becoming and Political Subjectivity in War-Torn Northern Uganda.' PhD thesis, Denmark: University of Copenhagen.

Victor, Letha. 2018. 'Ghostly Vengeance: Spiritual Pollution, Time, and Other Uncertainties in Acholi.' PhD thesis, Toronto: University of Toronto.

Victor, Letha, and Holly Porter. 2017. 'Dirty Things: Spiritual Pollution and Life after the Lord's Resistance Army.' *Journal of Eastern African Studies* 11 (4): 590–608.

Vokes, Richard. 2013. *Ghosts of Kanungu*. Reprint edition. Melton, England: James Currey.

Vokes, Richard, and Sam Wilkins. 2016. 'Party, Patronage and Coercion in the NRM'S 2016 Re-Election in Uganda: Imposed or Embedded?' *Journal of Eastern African Studies* 10 (4): 581–600. doi:10.1080/17531055.2016.1279853.

Vorhölter, Julia. 2014. *Youth at the crossroads. Discourses on socio-cultural change in post-war Northern Uganda*. Göttingen Series in Social and Cultural Anthropology. Göttingen: Göttingen University Press.

Vuola, Elina. 2006. 'Radical Eurocentrism. The Crisis and Death of Latin American Liberation Theology and Recipes for Its Improvement.' In *Interpreting the Postmodern: Responses to 'Radical Orthodoxy,'* edited by Rosemary Radford Ruether and Marion Grau, 57–75. London: A&C Black.

Waliggo, John Mary, Emmanuel Katongole, and Benedict Jr. Ssettuuma. 2013. 'The Social Teaching of the Uganda Catholic Bishops: 1962–2012.' *The Waliggo: A Philosophical and Theological Journal* 4 (2): 7–50.

Wamala, Emmanuel. 1991. *Statement to the Press by the Chairman of the Uganda Episcopal Conference – 15 June 1991*. Kampala: Uganda Episcopal Conference.

Ward, Kevin. 1991. 'A History of Christianity in Uganda.' In *From Mission to Church: A Handbook of Christianity in East Africa*, edited by Zablon Nthamburi. Nairobi: Uzima Press. Available at https://dacb.org/histories/uganda-history-christianity/. Accessed 10 October 2021.

Ward, Kevin. 2001. '"The Armies of the Lord": Christianity, Rebels and the State in Northern Uganda, 1986–1999.' *Journal of Religion in Africa* XXXI (2): 187–221.

Ward, Kevin. 2005. 'Eating and Sharing: Church and State in Uganda.' *Journal of Anglican Studies* 3 (1§): 99–120.

Ward, Kevin, and Emma Wild-Wood, eds. 2012. *The East African Revival: History and Legacies*. New edition. Farnham, Surrey and Burlington: Routledge.

Warner, Michael. 2002. 'Publics and Counterpublics.' *Public Culture* 14 (1): 49–90.

Webster, J. B. 1969. *Acholi Historical Text Nr 15*. The 'History of Uganda' Project under the Direction of the Department of History, Makerere University College. Unpublished manuscript.

Welbourn, Frederick Burkewood. 1965. *Religion and Politics in Uganda, 1952–1962*. Nairobi, Kenya: East African Pub. House.

Werbner, Richard P. 2002. 'Postcolonial Subjectivities: The Personal, the Political and the Moral.' In *Postcolonial Subjectivities in Africa*, edited by Richard P. Werbner, 1–22. London and New York: Zed Books.

Westerlund, David. 1980. *Ujamaa Na Dini: A Study of Some Aspects of Society and Religion in Tanzania, 1961–1977*. Stockholm Studies in Comparative Religion, ISSN 0562-1070; 18. Stockholm: Almqvist & Wiksell.

Whitaker, Beth Elise. 2007. 'Exporting the Patriot Act? Democracy and the "War on Terror" in the Third World.' *Third World Quarterly* 28 (5): 1017–32. doi:10.1080/01436590701371751.

Whitmore, Todd D. 2010a. '"If They Kill Us at Least the Others Will Have More Time to Get Away": The Ethics of Risk in Ethnographic Practice.' *Practical Matters* 3 (23 May 2012): 1–28.

Whitmore, Todd D. 2010b. 'My Tribe Is Humanity. An Interview with Archbishop John Baptist Odama.' *Journal for Peace and Justice Studies* 20 (2): 61–75.

Whitmore, Todd D. 2011. 'Whiteness Made Visible: A Theo-Critical Ethnography in Acoliland.' In *Ethnography as Christian Theology and Ethics*, edited by Christian Scharen and Aana M. Vigen, 207–24. New York: Continuum.

Whitmore, Todd D. 2013. 'Sequela Comboni: Writing Theological Ethnography in the Context of Empire.' *Practical Matters*, no. 6: 1–39.

Whitmore, Todd D. 2019. *Imitating Christ in Magwi: An Anthropological Theology*. London, England: T&T Clark.

Whyte, Susan Reynolds. 2002. 'Subjectivity and Subjunctivity: Hoping for Health in Eastern Uganda.' In *Postcolonial Subjectivities in Africa*, edited by Richard P. Werbner, 171–90. London and New York: Zed Books.

Whyte, Susan Reynolds. 2005. 'Uncertain Undertakings: Practicing Healthcare in the Subjunctive Mood.' In *Managing Uncertainty: Ethnographic Studies of Illness, Risk and the Struggle for Control*, edited by Richard Jenkins, Hanne Jessen, and Vibeke Steffen, 245–64. Copenhagen: Museum Tusculanum Press.

Whyte, Susan Reynolds, Lotte Meinert, and Julaina Obika. 2015. 'Untying Wrongs in Northern Uganda.' In *Evil in Africa. Encounters with the Everyday*, edited by William C. Olsen and Walter E.A. Van Beek, 43–60. Bloomington: Indiana University Press.

Wiegratz, Jörg, Giuliano Martiniello, and Elisa Greco. 2018. 'Introduction: Interpreting Change in Neoliberal Uganda.' In *Uganda: The Dynamics of Neoliberal Transformation*, edited by Jörg Wiegratz, Giuliano Martiniello, and Elisa Greco, 1–42. New York: Zed Books.

Wilhelm-Solomon, Matthew, and Ina Rehema Jahn. 2015. '"Bones in the Wrong Soil": Reburial, Belonging, and Disinterred Cosmologies in Post-Conflict Northern Uganda.' *Critical African Studies* 7 (2): 182–201.

Wilkens, Katharina. 2011. *Holy Water and Evil Spirits: Religious Healing in East Africa*. Berlin: LIT Verlag.

Williams, Beth Ann. 2018. 'Mainline Churches: Networks of Belonging in Postindependence Kenya and Tanzania.' *Journal of Religion in Africa* 48 (3): 255–85. doi:10.1163/15700666-12340140.

Williams, Lars Hedegaard. 2019. 'In Search of a Stable World: Contamination of Spirits and Mental Disorder in Post-Conflict Northern Uganda.' PhD thesis, Aarhus: Aarhus University.

Williams, Lars Hedegaard, and Lotte Meinert. 2020. 'Repetition Work: Healing Spirits and Trauma in the Churches of Northern Uganda.' In *Time Work. Studies of Temporal Agency*, edited by Michael G. Flaherty, Lotte Meinert, and Anne Line Dalsgård, 31–49. New York and Oxford: Berghahn Books.

Willis, Right Rev. John Jamieson. 1914. *The Church in Uganda. A Charge to Missionaries of the Uganda Mission 1913*. London: Longmans Green and Co.

Wipper, Audrey. 1977. *Rural Rebels: A Study of Two Protest Movements in Kenya*. 1st edition. Nairobi: Oxford University Press.

Womakuyu, Frederick. 2012. 'Kitgum Hospital: A Facility Falling Apart.' *New Vision*, 24 January.

Wright, Rev. H. T. 1919. 'A Harvest from a Hard Ground.' *The C.M.S. Gleaner*, 1 October.

Zeller, Wolfgang. 2013. 'Get It While You Can: Governance between Wars in the Uganda-South Sudan Borderland.' In *Violence on the Margins: States, Conflict, and Borderlands*, edited by Benedikt Korf and Timothy Raeymaekers, 193–217. Palgrave Series in African Borderlands Studies. New York: Palgrave Macmillan. doi:10.1057/9781137333995_8.

Zlomislic, Marko. 2012. *The Poverty of Radical Orthodoxy*, edited by Lisa Isherwood. Eugene: Pickwick Publications.

Zournazi, Mary. 2002. *Hope: New Philosophies for Change*. Annandale: Pluto Press Australia.

Index

Acholi cosmology 37–43, 77, 172
Acholi language 8–10, 20, 33, 56, 63, 136, 139–42, 146, 150
  anyobanyoba (*see* confusion)
  condescension of 188–9, 193
  notions of politics 117–18, 141, 202
  translation by missionaries 37–43
Acholi people
  clan structures 37, 174, 193
  collective identity 159–60, 168–9
  conceptualizations of authority 199
  divisions between 62–3, 66–7, 196–8
  gender dynamics (*see* gender, marriage *and* patriarchy)
  missionary perceptions of 37–41
Acholi region *map xviii* 218 n.5
  colonization of (*see* colonialism)
  marginalization of 8, 63–4, 74, 154–5, 192–3
Acholi Religious Leader's Peace Initiative (ARLPI) 16–17, 83, 159–63, 172
  activities by 166–7
  peace advocacy 182–4
  resonance with rebel millenarianism 171
  significance of 162–3, 170–1, 183–4
Acoli Macon 45, 53–4
Akena, Jimmy 129, 225
anyobanyoba (*see* confusion)
All Africa Council of Churches 64
Allen, Tim 29, 79, 171–3, 201–2
Amin, Idi 4, 16, 187, 191
Andrews, Molly 12–13, 25, 137, 161
Anglican church (*see* Church Missionary Society *and* Church of Uganda)
Anglican-Catholic relations 5, 17, 41
  changes under NRM 68–71
  collaboration in ARLPI 83, 89, 194, 205
  in contemporary Acholi 67–8, 90–1
  denominational identity 18, 47–9
  during colonialism 45–6, 61–3
  during the Reformation 214
  stereotypes 67–9
  tensions during the northern Ugandan war 5, 84–9
anthropology
  of Christianity 1–2, 11–12, 16, 210–13
  of hope 26–9, 162, 164–5, 215–16
  and politics 11–12
  racism of 212–13
  of suffering and the good 26–8, 214–15
  and theology 20, 24–5
anyobanyoba (*see* confusion)
Anywar, Beatrice 124–4, 127
apology 129, 131–2 (*see also* forgiveness)
Atkinson, Ronald R. 35, 62–3, 70
Atwoma, Tiberio Okeny 87, 120–31, 140, 147

Balokole (*see* East African Revival)
Bible, references to 37, 78, 159, 174, 193
  Ten Commandments 41–2
  translation of 37–43
Bigombe, Betty 84–5
Bloch, Ernst 27, 164
Bongmba, Elias 12
Branch, Adam 76–7, 151
Brussels Act 44
Buganda 35–6, 133–41
  colonial emphasis 62–3, 129
  martyrs 222
  religious wars in 45
Burnet, Jennie 97–9, 105, 110
Bush War 65, 75–7, 135, 171–2
Butler, Judith 119, 135

Carney, Jay J. 63–6, 210, 221
catechists 55–6 (*see also* Paimol martyrs)
  during the colonial era 18, 40, 44, 47–8
  during the northern Ugandan war 77–9, 82, 173

Catholic Church (*see also* Comboni
    missionaries)
  accusations of rebel collaboration 76,
    84–7
  Charismatic movement 200–3
  divisions in Acholi 66–7
  pastoral letters 66, 72
  political alliances (*see* Democratic
    Party)
  Uganda martyrs 222 (*see also* Paimol
    martyrs)
cattle, theft during war 76–7, 150–1, 154
cen 77, 172
Charismatic revival (*see also* Pentecostal-
    Charismatic)
  in Anglican Church 15–16, 68, 152,
    173, 202, 208–9
  in Catholic Church 200–3, 227
chiefs 34–6, 160
  deposal of 51, 54, 67–8
  relationship with missionaries 43–6,
    50–2
choir (*see* Janani Luwum Choir)
Chosen Evangelical Revival 15
Christ 25, 161, 166, 174, 180
church events 117–18, 139–42
  as lenses on church-state relations
    131–4
  as sites for public debate 117–20,
    137–8
  curtailing of speech at 149–55
Church Mission(ary) Society (CMS) 34,
    37–41, 45–6
  competition with Comboni
    missionaries 45–6, 82, 220–1
  connections to colonial government
    34–6, 43–6
Church of Uganda 4, 18–19, 67, 168–9
    (*see also* church-state relations)
  Anglican theology 185, 191
  charismatic prayer in 15
  conflict in Kitgum Diocese 194–200
  donor funding 196
  music (*see* Janani Luwum Choir)
  opposition to Idi Amin 191–2
  political affiliations (*see* Uganda
    People's Congress)
  proper conduct of bishops 194–6
  purity of doctrine and tradition 192–6
  resource constraints 82
  statements on northern Ugandan war
    73
church politics 1, 6, 10, 22, 64–7, 84–5,
    185–7, 194–200
church schools 2–4, 17, 59
  dispute over 59, 61, 67, 85, 88, 90–1
  missionary focus on 44–5, 51–2
  nationalization of 64
  Phelps-Stokes Commission 44
  as sites of political mobilization 61–2
church-state relations 152–3 (*see also*
    church events)
  church advocacy 63–6
  competing models 43
  during Bush War 65–6
  national-local linkages 88–9
  negotiating at public events 133–4
  patronage 70, 133–4, 190
  political parties (*see under individual
    parties*)
  pre-independence debates 61 (*see also*
    church schools)
  under NRM 69–73
churches as embedded institutions and
    communities 10, 12, 209
churches (mainline) (*see also* Catholic
    Church *and* Church of Uganda)
  contrasting ideals and realities 205–6
  disciplining at 174–5
  disregard for in research 11, 211–13
  division during Bush War 65
  financial resources of 70, 133–4, 185–6,
    190, 196
  institutional tensions 66–7, 196–8
  local-national-global 59, 82, 204
  mismanagement of funds 194–200
  offering hope and peace 29, 175–9
  political patronage 70, 133–4, 190
  providing access to power or benefits
    48, 62, 185–6, 198–200, 202–3
  reasons for attending 200, 205–6
  service provision 212 (*see also*
    churches during war)
  surveillance of 143
churches during the northern Ugandan
    war
  attacks on 75–6, 78–80
  attendance 81, 223 n.13
  human rights work 83
  national churches' response 72–3

peace advocacy 1, 66, 89, 90, 180–1
positioning vis-à-vis armed groups 59, 73–9, 83, 89–91
providing shelter 31, 82, 100–1
service provision 75–6, 82–3, 86–7
spiritual responses 81, 177
state limitations on 75–6, 84–9
citizenship 140–1, 149, 157
clergy (*see also* churches during the northern Ugandan war)
   abductions of 78, 194–5
   loss of authority 199–200
   political connections 83, 118
   shunning by non-Acholi colleagues 72–3
   views on inculturation 53
colonialism
   church-state relations under 43–6, 61–6
   contemporary silencing by churches 50–6
   missionary critique of 46, 54
   missionary support for 34, 36, 43, 220 n.11
   opposition to in Acholi 34–6, 44–5, 50
   violence of 34–6, 43, 51–4, 117–18
Comboni, Daniel 35, 45, 53, 218
Comboni (Verona) missionaries 35, 40, 66, 76, 84, 150, 218 n.7, 219 n.3
   competition with CMS 45–6, 220–1 n.12 (*see also* church schools)
   development work 48–9
   Familia Comboniana newsletters 74–83, 87, 222 n.8
   numbers of 222–3
   relationship with rebels 79–80, 83, 88
   responses to northern Ugandan war 75–84
   rumours about 67–8
   state restrictions during war 75–6, 84–9
   theology 60, 81–2, 177
Concerned Christians 186–7, 191, 194–5
confusion 3, 8–10, 145, 204
   as ambiguity and messiness 145, 185–7
   amid the afterlives of war 9, 73–4, 142, 159–62, 180–1
   Christianity as the answer to 55, 173–5, 202–3

   as church politics 1, 8, 84–5, 185–7, 194–200
   Churches' responses to 159–62, 180–1, 204
   as contrast between ideal and reality 206
   and the Devil 197, 209
   and inequalities 145–6, 197–204
   as research ethical stance 3, 30, 111–12, 213–17
   ways of dealing with 149, 155–8, 204–5
conversion
   in Acholi 37, 56, 48–9
   material benefits of 48–9
   to Pentecostal-Charismatic churches 9, 49, 70, 211–12
corruption 55, 151, 226 (*see also* patronage)
Crazzolara, J.P. 9, 37, 40, 219–20
cung i wibye (standing on anthills) 122–31, 154, 161, 189–90
   churches as sites of 118, 127, 133–4
   competing narratives at 119, 121–2, 136–8, 180
   definition 117–18
   as performance 119
   as state-making 131–8
   underlying violence 139–42

Das, Veena 26, 97–9, 156, 215
Democratic Party (DP) 4–6, 61–9, 122–3, 126–7, 135
   relationship to Catholic Church 4–5, 61–3, 68–9
development aid (*see* humanitarian aid *and* faith-based development)
dini (religion) 39
displacement camps (*see* internal displacement)
divinity (*see also* God *and* spirits)
   intersections with materiality 185–7
Donohue, Father Paul 84–9
DP (*see* Democratic Party)

Earle, Jonathan 63, 221
East African Revival 15, 68, 152, 173, 202, 221 n.4
ecumenism 64, 190–2 (*see also* Acholi Religious Leaders Peace Initiative)

Edkins, Jenny 119, 156
education (*see* church schools)
elections 65, 70, 118
  effect on political space 136, 139, 143, 147–8, 155
  under NRM 68, 127, 213, 225
embeddedness
  analytical value 59, 203–6, 210–11
  compounding complexity 185
  as constraint 90, 135, 162, 174, 179
  cosmological 37–43, 211–12
  definition of 2, 12, 29–30, 200
  enabling peace work 83
  material 47–50, 185–6, 196–200
  political 43–6, 210–11
  social 47–50, 210
embodiment
  in research ethics 106–8, 107
  of rituals of peace 176–8
emotion (*see also* love *and* humiliation)
  overwhelming experiences in fieldwork 101–11, 224 n.5
  sudden expression of 99–101
  and trauma 95–101, 108
empathy 96, 100, 104–8
Englund, Harri 11, 39
ethics (*see* research ethics)
ethnicity
  anti-Acholi sentiments 72, 153, 168, 192
  bridging of 172, 179
  colonial stereotyping 62
  contemporary tensions 135–6
  divisions in churches 64–5
  intersecting with religion 61–3
  national divisions 63, 74, 150, 166, 170, 193, 204
  politicized 8, 69, 131
  pride in 168–70, 192
  in tension with unity 63–4, 167–70

faith-based development 17, 162–3, 186, 196
Familia Comboniana newsletters (FC) 74–83, 87, 222 n.8
fieldwork with family 108–11, 182–3
Finnegan, Amy 168–9
Finnström Sverker 7–8, 28, 78, 104, 145, 153–4, 211
forgiveness 122, 138, 157
  absence in Ugandan politics 180
  apology by Museveni 129
  in ARLPI theology 157–8, 161, 171–3
  in the Bible 127
  and healing 156–7, 204–5
  as response to confusion 204–6

gender 174–5 (*see also* marriage *and* patriarchy)
  and expression of emotion 106–10
  gender-based violence 175
  heteronormativity 175
  intervention by missionaries 48–9
  in Ugandan politics 131–2, 136
  united under humanity 162
gerontocracy 174–5, 179–81, 182–3
Gifford, Paul 70, 185–6, 199, 205–6
God
  Acholi concepts of 40–1, 220
  as guarantor of justice 193, 205, 208–9
  as solution to confusion 204

healing 15–16, 199, 202–3, 205, 211, 226 n.4, 227 n.6
  and trauma 94–5, 97–8, 101, 106–7, 112, 156
Holy Spirit Mobile Forces (HSMF) 77–9
  utopian visions of 171–3
hope
  affirmation through research 27, 29, 179–80, 216–17
  anthropology of 26–8, 215–17
  and disappointment 26, 34
  in the everyday 3, 6, 155–8, 175–9, 184
  for peace 161–2, 213–4
  political economy of 27, 217
  search for 22, 56, 114–15
  subjunctivity of 26, 216
  theology of 27, 81, 165–6, 177–9
  transitive and intransitive 165, 180–1
  and utopia 163–6, 179–80
human rights 72, 122, 152, 164
  abuses during war 83, 152
  and the trauma paradigm 113
humanitarian aid (*see also* churches during war)
  by churches 75–6, 82, 86–7
  dominant trauma paradigm in 96
  during war 7, 22

scaling out 93
   theft of 86-7, 151
humanity 162
   brokenness of 167
   in relation to ethnicity 166-9
   and Ubuntu theology 168, 226
humiliation 76, 153-5, 159, 192-3
   responses to 204-5
   as social fact 193

imaginaries (*see* political narratives)
inclusion and exclusion 162, 168-70, 173-5, 180
inculturation 37-43
   clergy's views 53
interdisciplinarity 12, 20-1
internal displacement 7, 31, 82, 93, 110-11, 126, 166, 182, 198, 223 n.13
   as cause for 'confusion' 8-9, 159-60
Islam
   in Acholi 7, 16-17, 83, 89, 182, 220
   insinuation of role in colonial violence 54-5
   in Ugandan politics 64, 221

Jansen, Stef 27, 164-5, 180, 215
Janani Luwum Choir 5, 13-16, 178-9, 187-93
   as a response to confusion 179, 205
Jauhola, Marjaana 97, 99
jok 39-41, 220
Jones, Ben 20, 197, 201-11

Kapferer, Bruce 119, 137
Karugire, Samwiri Rubaraza 35, 43, 45, 62
Katongole, Emmanuel 23-5, 165-70, 180, 211
Ker Kwaro Acholi 172, 174, 219 n.2
King's African Rifles 63
Kitgum mission 3-6, 16-18, 78, 84-9
   founding of 47-9
   handover to diocese 118, 133, 139, 149-54
Kiwanuka, Benedicto 63, 67-8, 221
Kleist, Nauja 27, 163, 165, 180, 215
Kony, Joseph 7-8, 57, 72, 77-8, 171-3

Lakwena, Alice (*see* Holy Spirit Mobile Forces)
lamentation 143, 160, 167

Lamogi rebellion 36, 50, 52
Lamwaka, Caroline 77, 79, 87
land 5, 31, 135, 150
   church holdings 5, 9, 17-18
   and churches' embeddedness 47-8, 211
   disputes over church land 5-6, 31, 45, 47-8, 90, 185-6, 203
   grabbing in Acholi 125-6, 136, 151
   Temporary Occupation Licences 48
   under colonialism 35, 48
Larsen, Timothy 22, 213
laughter 101, 123-7, 130, 132, 203
   impossibility under violence 154-5
Lauterbach, Karen 11, 16, 20, 24, 126, 200, 211
Legio Maria 15
Levitas, Ruth 163-5, 179-80
Little Sisters of Mary Immaculate 17, 81, 222-3 n.10
liturgy 176-8 (*see also* rituals *and* music)
Lord's Resistance Army 7, 57
   attacks on churches 80
   Christianity in 57, 77-8
   political agenda 80
   utopian visions of 171-3
love 107, 138
   of God 122, 162
Lukwoya, Severino 77-9, 173
Lutheran identity and theology 19-21
Luwum, Archbishop Janani 16, 64, 131, 150-3
   contemporary significance of 191-2
   national commemoration of 118, 139, 149-54, 157, 187-94
Luwum, Phoebe 152-3

mainline churches (*see* churches; Church of Uganda *and* Catholic Church)
Mao, Norbert 122-3, 126-30, 135
marriage 21, 48-9, 56, 81, 151
Mbembe, Achille 141, 153-5
Meinert, Lotte 97, 107, 149, 156, 226 n.4
memories
   constraining imagination 142
   silenced 60, 103-4, 107, 139-40, 178-9
   triggering of 139-40, 144-7
   of war 94, 97-101, 103-8
Meretoja, Hanna 12-13, 23

Index

millenarian movements (*see* Holy Spirit Mobile Forces *and* Lord's Resistance Army)
missionaries 16 (*see also* Church Mission Society *and* Comboni missionaries)
   competition between 45–6, 220–1 (*see also* church schools)
   contemporary critique in Acholi 53–6
   development work by 44, 47–9, 186
   during the World Wars 44
   education (*see* church schools)
   funding for 186
   impact on Acholi cosmology 37–43
   landholdings 45, 47–8, 90
   negative attitudes in academia 20–1
   opposition to 77–80, 223
   relationship with chiefs 43–6, 50–2
   relationship with colonialism 33–6, 43–6, 52, 220
   and translation 37–43
Miyazaki, Hirokazu 27, 161, 165, 179–80
money (*see* material embeddedness)
morality 35, 61, 70, 78, 95–6, 134, 159–60, 172, 174–6
More, Thomas 163, 214
Museveni, Yoweri 15, 139, 149–55
   centrality for political system 131–4
   at commemoration of Luwum 189
   public criticism of 123–8, 142, 135–6
   public praise for 123, 127–8
   speeches in Kitgum 129–30, 149–51
music 121 (*see also* Janani Luwum Choir)
   Anglican hymns 13–14, 187–8
   anthems 122–3, 143, 187–8
   Catholic hymns 122, 176–7, 191
   classical opera 189
   impact of 13–14, 21, 56, 178
   jeering songs 3, 6
   praise music 178, 189
   in rebel movements 77
   significance in Anglican tradition 190
Mwambari, David 28, 102

narrative imagination (*see* political narratives)
nation-building 6, 138, 165
   churches' role in 64, 137–8
   national unity 69, 161–2
   rhetoric and reality of 134–8

National Resistance Army (NRA) 5, 7, 65, 218
   arrest of Acholi leaders 5, 86–7, 120
   atrocities in Acholi 75–7, 124, 139–40
   cattle raids 76
   deportation of missionaries 84–9
   Museveni's apology for violence 129, 131–2
   relationship with churches 76, 78–80, 87, 89–90
   violence against churches 75–7
National Resistance Movement NRM 141–2, 188, 218, 227
   co-option of opposition politicians 225
   patronage by 123–4, 133–4, 129, 152–3, 190
   relationship with churches 68–73, 83–4, 133–4
   surveillance 147–9
   (*see also under* Museveni, Yoweri *and* state)
Nebanda, Cerinah 141–3
neopatrimonialism (*see* patronage)
Niringiye, Zac 63, 73
Nkabala, Helen Nambalirwa 78
nodding disease 124, 224 n.1
normative underpinnings of research 22, 29–30, 103, 112–13, 215
northern Ugandan war 73–89 (*see also under names of armed groups*)
   abductions 4–5, 78, 100, 111, 166, 182, 194–5
   cattle theft 76–7, 150–1, 154
   churches' role (*see* churches during the northern Ugandan war)
   Comboni archival sources on 73–89, 222 n.8
   ethics of researching 101–5
   humanitarian crisis (*see* humanitarian aid *and* internal displacement)
   new archival sources 59, 222 n.8
   regional connections 8, 74, 88
   religious aspects of 2–3, 77–9, 171–3, 207
   simplified media accounts of 1, 7–8, 207
nuns 49, 79, 81, 177, 219 n.3 (*see also* Comboni missionaries)
   Little Sisters of Mary Immaculate 17, 81, 222–3 n.10
Ntagali, Archbishop Stanley 194, 208

O'Byrne, Ryan 39–40, 211
Obote, Milton 4, 63–5, 67–9, 76, 83, 128, 197
   son, Jimmy Akena 129, 225
Ochola, Bishop Macleod Baker 16, 83, 169, 194, 197–9
Odama, Archbishop John Baptist 122, 159, 194
   theology of 166–7
Odwong, Philip 3–6, 31, 84, 86, 87–8
Ogora, Lino Owor 101–2
Oinas, Elina 99
Ojwang, Rt Rev Benjamin 194–9, 208
ontology 23–8
   critique of ontological turn 25
   and theology 23–6
   as underpinning research 23–4, 112–13, 215–17
opposition parties (*see also* Democratic Party *and* Uganda People's Congress)
   public debates 122–38
   risk of supporting 124–5, 144, 154–5, 213
   silencing of 152–3
orientation towards the future 161, 175–9, 193–4
Orombi, Bishop Henry Luke 168, 195, 226
Oryem, Henry Okello 128–9, 153
Otunnu, Ogenga 117–18
Otunnu, Olara 125–6, 128–9, 135, 152, 225
Oulanyah, Jacob 128–9

P'Bitek, Okot 37–41, 53, 78
Paimol martyrs 50–7, 192
patriarchy 174, 179–81
   in politics 132
   promotion by churches 174–5, 180, 184
patronage 131–4
   in church-state relations 70, 133–4, 190
   public negotiation of 123–4, 129, 152–3, 190
peace (*see also* Acholi Religious Leaders' Peace Initiative)
   as an experience 177–9
   narratives of 1, 157–8
   as pacification 34–7, 208–9
   prayers for 83, 122, 159, 176–7, 182–4, 208
   as stasis and as struggle 170
   violence of 173–5, 181
Pentecostal-Charismatic churches 17, 21, 49, 90–1, 182, 190, 208
   in Acholi 16
   conversion to 9, 49, 70, 212
   dealing with evil 202
   growth of 11, 70
   healing in 226
   over-emphasis in research 11, 211–13
   political positioning 68–70
   role in Anglican church conflict 194–5
performance 117–20, 131–5
performativity 119, 135
political narratives 1, 25, 60, 137–8
   as analytical tool 12, 20–6, 210–14
   at church events 119, 121–2, 136–8, 180
   constrained by violence 142
   contestation between 131, 160–2, 208
   embeddedness of 210–14
   embeddedness of churches in 157
   and hope 163–5, 171, 179–80
   and theology 23–4, 165–6
   underpinning the state 23–4, 70, 165–6
   utopian (*see* utopia)
political theology 12, 161, 211
   limitations of 170
   of peace and unity 165–71
   Radical Orthodoxy 23–4
politicians
   donations to churches 71, 133, 190
   involvement in church disputes 197–8
   and lying 15, 117, 130
   relations to churches 83, 118, 152–3
politics
   Acholi conceptualizations of 117–18
   gendered nature of 132
   of representation 112–14
   violence belying 139–42
Pope John Paul II 5, 72
Porter, Holly 39, 113–14, 174–5, 199
positionality
   and hope 27–8, 215–16
   and religion 19–22
   and silence 101–4, 104–8
post-secular anthropology 21–2

post-coloniality
  critique of mission 50–6
  theory 141, 149, 153–5
Postlethwaite, J.R.P. 54, 117–18
poverty 151, 178–9
  the poor as church priority 55–6, 191–2
prayer (*see also* healing)
  for peace 83, 122, 159, 176–7, 182–4, 208
Premawardhana, Devaka 11, 212, 216

racism 153, 212–15
rape 100, 113, 174, 193, 223
re-orientation of temporality 161, 178–81
reconciliation 12 (*see also* forgiveness)
  as alternative to criminal justice 16, 175, 205
  calls for 95, 122, 127, 172, 183
  for church disputes 195, 206
  and healing 97
  in HSMF 171–2
  public apology 129, 131–2
  theology of 168, 179–83, 211, 226
relationality 103–7, 111–14
religion
  in Acholi 3–9, 15–17
  assessing societal impact 22, 216
  religious leaders (*see* Acholi Religious Leaders Peace Initiative *and* clergy)
research ethics
  collective research fatigue 101–2
  confusion as approach to 3, 30, 111–12, 213–17
  embodied limits to 104–8
  everyday, ordinary 103–4, 114–15
  objectification of 103–4, 114–15
  and the politics of representation 112–14, 213
  post-conflict hotspots 101–4
  relationality 104–8
rituals
  church cleansing 195
  cleansing and reintegration 172–3
  healing 201
  of peace 177
  producing citizens 134–6
  of state-making 117–20, 131–4, 136–8, 153

Robbins, Joel 20, 23–6, 193, 212, 215, 217
rumours 67–8, 140–1, 153, 157
  about clergy 197
  of political murder 142–3
  of spies 143–4
Rwanda, Ugandan involvement in 88

Saint Janani Luwum parish (*see* Town Parish)
Saint Mary's parish (*see* Kitgum Mission)
Sheriff, Robin 138
Shroff, Catrine 9, 11, 18, 47–8, 186, 203, 211
sickness
  Charismatic healing of 15, 200–3
  missionary hospitals 17, 42, 75–6, 78, 80–3, 150, 225 n.3
silence
  about war 93–4
  beyond the trauma paradigm 97–101, 108
  choosing to shield 101–6
  churches' on colonial violence 64–6
  as coping 97
  cultural appropriateness 108–11
  embodied expressions 99–101
  ethics of studying 93–116
  healing through 98–101
  and listening 99–108
  and mourning 113
  polyphonic 95
  and tension 143–7
  under fear of repercussions 157
  and unspeakability 101
slave trade in Acholi 16, 35, 54
smallpox 51
social fabric 97–8
  Christianity as repair for 172
social imaginary (*see* political imaginary)
speech acts 119, 135
spirits 15, 195, 204
  contention over during war 77–9
spirituality 8, 37–9, 197–9, 205–6
Ssentamu, Archbishop John 149, 187, 189
standing on anthills (*see cung i wibye*)
state (*see also* National Resistance Movement)
  and the church (*see* church–state relations)

colonial 34–6, 43–7 (*see also* colonialism)
  as performance 23–4, 116–20, 131–4
  political theology of 23–4, 170
  violence of 139–44, 147–9 (*see also under* National Resistance Army)
  subdued citizenship 140–2, 153–4
subjunctivity 26, 142
  of hope 216
  subjunctive mood 156–7, 213
suffering 95–6, 99–101
  anthropology of 26–8, 210–11, 214–17
  in research on Acholi 28–9
syncretism (*see* tic Acholi)

Tapscott, Rebecca 120, 144
Temporary Occupation Licence 48
Ten Commandments 1, 41–2
theology
  Anglican 185, 191
  and anthropology 10–12, 20, 24–5, 170, 211
  centering trauma 95, 223–4 n.2
  Combonian 60, 81–2, 177
  of peace and unity 134–5, 162, 166–70
  political 12, 165–70
  Radical orthodoxy 23–4
  of submitting to authority 157
tic Acholi 39
torture 5, 87, 95
Town Parish 18–19, 175–9 (*see also* Janani Luwum Choir)
trauma
  alternative perspectives on 94–101
  church concern for 60, 95–6, 223 n.2
  collective 96, 168–9
  dominant paradigm 95–101, 112–14
  and healing 94–5, 97–8, 101, 106–7, 112, 156
  normalization of 100–1
  researching 23, 28–30, 224
  and silence 95–104
  and strength 105, 156
  triggering of 98–100
trust (*see also* authority)
  in Acholi after war 145, 149
  in fieldwork relationships 99, 105–7
  in a just God 193, 205, 208–9

Ubuntu theology 168, 226
Uganda *map xvii*
  British colonialism in (*see* colonialism)
  ethnic divides (*see* ethnicity)
  limitations on media 124–5
  North-South division 63–4, 74, 150–1
  political system
  religious dynamics in 11, 64, 70 (*see also* church-state relations)
Uganda Joint Christian Council (UJCC) 64
Uganda National Liberation Army (UNLA) 65, 76–7
Uganda People's Congress (UPC) 4, 61, 128–9, 135, 152, 167, 225 n.7
  Connection to Church of Uganda 61–3, 68–9, 152
Uganda People's Defence Army 76–7, 79
Uganda People's Defence Force (UPDF) 8, 147, 184, 218
  takeover of rural development 155
  (*see also* National Resistance Army)
unity
  of humanity 166–9
  national 69, 161–2
  religious 79, 122, 171 (*see also* Acholi Religious Leaders Peace Initiative)
  rhetoric of 69, 134–6
  utopia of 166–71
  violence of 173–5, 208–10
utopia 134–5, 137, 163–5, 179–81
  anti-utopians 163–4
  critical utopia 165, 179–81
  critiques of 163–4
  material boundedness 208–9
  relation to hope 163–6
  as response to confusion 159–63
  Thomas More's *Eutopia* 163, 214
Utopia of Peace 30–1, 169–70, 206, 208–9, 214
  conflicting uses 209
  definition of 160–2
  as embodied practice 175–9
  limits of 185
  promotion of patriarchy 173–5, 184
  as public narrative 166–71, 179
  resonance with rebel millenarianisms 171–3

Vähäkangas, Mika 11, 16, 24, 39, 42
Van Klinken, Adriaan 24–5
Verma, Cecilie 120, 141, 144, 202
Verona missionaries (*see* Comboni missionaries)
Victor, Letha 39, 201
violence 105 (*see also* northern Ugandan war)
   at the core of politics 136–8 (*see also* cung i wibye)
   during elections 213
   memories of 99, 104–8, 106
   by the police 127, 130
   as a selling point for publications 105
vulnerable research 3, 10, 21, 106, 111–12

wang oo 160
Ward, Kevin 61, 64–6, 70, 72–3, 82–3
Warner, Michael 24, 175
Whitmore, Todd 46, 53–5, 81, 177, 211
Whyte, Susan 26, 28, 98, 142, 156, 213
witchcraft 49, 171 (*see also* tic acholi)
   accusations 187, 197, 201–2, 204
   negative connotations 39

www.ingramcontent.com/pod-product-compliance
Lightning Source LLC
Chambersburg PA
CBHW052216300426
44115CB00011B/1715